Lecture Notes in Computer Science 13783

More information about this series at https://link.springer.com/bookseries/558

Lejla Batina · Stjepan Picek ·
Mainack Mondal (Eds.)

Security, Privacy, and Applied Cryptography Engineering

12th International Conference, SPACE 2022
Jaipur, India, December 9–12, 2022
Proceedings

 Springer

Editors
Lejla Batina ⓘ
Radboud University
Nijmegen, The Netherlands

Stjepan Picek ⓘ
Radboud University
Nijmegen, The Netherlands

Mainack Mondal ⓘ
Indian Institute of Technology Kharagpur
Kharagpur, India

ISSN 0302-9743   ISSN 1611-3349 (electronic)
Lecture Notes in Computer Science
ISBN 978-3-031-22828-5   ISBN 978-3-031-22829-2 (eBook)
https://doi.org/10.1007/978-3-031-22829-2

This Springer imprint is published by the registered company Springer Nature Switzerland AG
The registered company address is: Gewerbestrasse 11, 6330 Cham, Switzerland

Preface

The 12th International Conference on Security, Privacy, and Applied Cryptography Engineering 2022 (SPACE 2022), was held during December 9–12, 2022. This annual event is devoted to various aspects of security, privacy, applied cryptography, and cryptographic engineering. This is a challenging field, requiring expertise from diverse domains, ranging from mathematics and computer science to circuit design. The event was hosted by the Center for Cryptography, Cyber Security and Digital Forensics (C3-SDF) at The LNM Institute of Information Technology, Jaipur, India.

This year we received 61 submissions from authors in many different countries, mainly from Asia and Europe. The submissions were evaluated based on their significance, novelty, technical quality, and relevance to the SPACE conference. The submissions were reviewed in a double-blind mode by at least two members of the Program Committee, which consisted of 47 members from all over the world. After an extensive review process, 18 papers were accepted for presentation at the conference, leading to an acceptance rate of 29.5%.

The program also included five keynotes and four tutorials on various aspects of applied cryptology, security, and privacy delivered by world-renowned researchers: Ingrid Verbauwhede, Nele Mentens, Jeyavijayan "JV" Rajendran, Chester Rebeiro, Sanjay K. Jha, Łukasz Chmielewski, Sikhar Patranabis, Nitin Singh, and Matthias Kannwischer. We sincerely thank the invited speakers for accepting our invitations in spite of their busy schedules. As in previous editions, SPACE 2022 was organized in cooperation with the International Association for Cryptologic Research (IACR). We are grateful to general chairs Jayaprakash Kar and Debdeep Mukhopadhyay for their willingness to host it physically at LMNIT Jaipur.

There is a long list of volunteers who invested their time and energy to put together the conference. We are grateful to all the members of the Program Committee and their sub-reviewers for all their hard work in the evaluation of the submitted papers. We thank our publisher Springer for agreeing to continue to publish the SPACE proceedings as a volume in the Lecture Notes in Computer Science (LNCS) series. We are grateful to the local Organizing Committee who invested a lot of time and effort in order for the conference to run smoothly.

Last, but not least, our sincere thanks go to all the authors who submitted papers to SPACE 2022 and everyone who participated (either in person or virtually).

December 2022

Lejla Batina
Stjepan Picek
Mainack Mondal

Organization

General Chairs

Jayaprakash Kar   The LNM Institute of Information Technology,
                               India
Debdeep Mukhopadhyay   Indian Institute of Technology, Kharagpur, India

Program Committee Chairs

Lejla Batina   Radboud University, The Netherlands
Mainack Mondal   Indian Institute of Technology, Kharagpur, India
Stjepan Picek   Radboud University, The Netherlands

Program Committee

Amr Youssef   Concordia University, Canada
Anupam Chattopadhyay   Nanyang Technological University, Singapore
Bodhisatwa Mazumdar   Indian Institute of Technology, Indore, India
Bohan Yang   Tsinghua University, China
Chester Rebeiro   Indian Institute of Technology, Madras, India
Chitchanok Chuengsatiansup   University of Adelaide, Australia
Claude Carlet   University of Bergen, Norway and University of
                               Paris 8, France
Dirmanto Jap   Nanyang Technological University, Singapore
Domenic Forte   University of Florida, USA
Eran Toch   Tel Aviv University, Israel
Fan Zhang   Zhejiang University, China
Guilherme Perin   Radboud University, The Netherlands
Ileana Buhan   Radboud University, The Netherlands
Jakub Breier   Silicon Austria Labs, Austria
Jayaprakash Kar   The LNM Institute of Information Technology,
                               India
Jean-Luc Danger   Télécom Paris, France
Kazuo Sakiyama   University of Electro-Communications, Japan
Kerstin Lemke-Rust   Bonn-Rhein-Sieg University of Applied Sciences,
                               Germany
Kostas Papagiannopoulos   University of Amsterdam, The Netherlands
Luca Mariot   Radboud University, The Netherlands
Lukasz Chmielewski   Radboud University, The Netherlands

Maël Gay	University of Stuttgart, Germany
Marc Stoettinger	RheinMain University of Applied Science, Germany
Marc Manzano	Sandbox@Alphabet, Spain
Marine Minier	Université de Lorraine and Loria, France
Martin Henze	Fraunhofer FKIE, Germany
Md Masoom Rabbani	KU Leuven, Belgium
Nadia El Mrabet	EMSE, France
Nalla Anandakumar Nachimuthu	University of Florida, USA
Naofumi Homma	Tohoku University, Japan
Nele Mentens	Leiden University, The Netherlands
Olga Gadyatskaya	Leiden University, The Netherlands
Peter Schwabe	MPI-SP, Germany, and Radboud University, The Netherlands
Rahul Chatterjee	University of Wisconsin-Madison, USA
Rajat Subhra Chakraborty	Indian Institute of Technology, Kharagpur, India
Rajesh Pillai	DRDO, India
Ruben Niederhagen	University of Southern Denmark, Denmark
Sébastien Canard	Orange Labs, France
Shivam Bhasin	Nanyang Technological University, Singapore
Sikhar Patranabis	IBM Research, India
Silvia Mella	Radboud University, The Netherlands
Sk Subidh Ali	Indian Institute of Technology, Bhilai, India
Somitra Sanadhya	Indian Institute of Technology, Jodhpur, India
Soumyajit Dey	Indian Institute of Technology, Kharagpur, India
Sujoy Sinha Roy	TU Graz, Germany
Urbi Chatterjee	Indian Institute of Technology, Kanpur, India
Vishal Saraswat	Bosch Engineering and Business Solutions, Bengaluru, India

Additional Reviewers

Martin Serror	Fraunhofer FKIE, Germany
Wenping Zhu	Tsinghua University, China
Soumyadyuti Ghosh	Indian Institute of Technology, Kharagpur, India
Rajat Sadhukhan	Indian Institute of Technology, Kharagpur, India
Durba Chatterjee	Indian Institute of Technology, Kharagpur, India

Contents

Hardware Security and AI

Network Security, Authentication, and Privacy

Symmetric Cryptography

Modeling Large S-box in MILP and a (Related-Key) Differential Attack on Full Round PIPO-64/128

Tarun Yadav$^{(\boxtimes)}$ and Manoj Kumar

Scientific Analysis Group, DRDO, Metcalfe House Complex, Delhi 110 054, India
{tarunyadav.sag,manojkumar.sag}@gov.in

Abstract. The differential characteristic search problem is converted into mixed integer linear programming (MILP) model to get the bound against differential attack. The difference distribution table is used to write the linear inequalities for MILP modeling of S-box. To construct a reduced set of such inequalities, we present the approaches based on Quine-McCluskey(QM) and Espresso algorithms that are used for active S-box minimization and probability optimization respectively. These approaches are used to search the differential characteristics for lightweight block cipher PIPO-64/128. There are 20621 inequalities in 23 variables corresponding to possible difference transitions in the DDT and these are minimized to 6035 inequalities. MILP model based on these inequalities is used to optimize the probability of differential and impossible differential characteristics for PIPO-64/128 reduced to 9 and 4 rounds respectively. We construct an iterative 2-round related-key differential characteristic with the probability of 2^{-4} and that is used to present a full round related-key differential distinguisher with the probability of 2^{-24}. We develop a key recovery attack using related keys on full round PIPO-64/128 with the data complexity of 2^{32}. We present a major collision in PIPO-64/128 which produces the same ciphertext (C) by encrypting the plaintext (P) under two different keys.

Keywords: Block cipher · Differential cryptanalysis · Lightweight cryptography · MILP · S-box

1 Introduction

Differential attack is one of the most powerful techniques for the cryptanalysis of block ciphers [4]. For new block ciphers, it is a mandatory design criterion to provide proof of resistance against the differential attack [6]. The high probability relations between the input and output differences of a block cipher are utilized to distinguish it from the uniform distribution [5]. We need a differential characteristic with the probability of 2^{-p}, where $p \lll n$, to mount the attack on n-bit block cipher [16]. To estimate the strength of a block cipher against differential attack, we calculate a lower bound on the number of active

© The Author(s), under exclusive license to Springer Nature Switzerland AG 2022
L. Batina et al. (Eds.): SPACE 2022, LNCS 13783, pp. 3–27, 2022.
https://doi.org/10.1007/978-3-031-22829-2_1

S-boxes in a differential characteristic. Then, an upper bound on the probability is estimated using this lower bound and maximum differential probability of the S-box [18]. Initially, branch-and-bound based techniques were used to search the high probability differential characteristics [19,23]. Nowadays, automated solvers based on mixed integer linear programming (MILP) [24], satisfiability modulo theory (SAT/SMT) [10], constraint programming (CP) problems [13,33], and machine learning based techniques [14,34] are used to test the differential attack resistance. In 2012, MILP-aided differential cryptanalysis for block ciphers was proposed by Mouha *et al.* This technique proved to be very successful to mount the differential attack on block ciphers.

Mixed integer linear programming is used frequently to solve optimization problems. MILP deals with optimizing the objective function $f(x_1, x_2, \cdots, x_n)$ subject to a set of linear inequalities $Ax \leq b$ which involves decision variables $x_i, 1 \leq i \leq n$ with restrictions on certain variables to take integer values. We can convert the differential characteristic search problem into a MILP model [24]. Then, optimization problem solvers (viz. Gurobi [15] and CIPLEX [11]) are used to solve the MILP model to get a lower bound on the number of active S-boxes and search for high probability differential characteristics. The linear layers (viz. key addition and permutation layer) of a block cipher are easily converted into linear inequalities. The S-box is a non-linear component of the block cipher and DDT of the S-box is used to write the linear inequalities satisfying each possible propagation. This set contains a large number of inequalities and it becomes hard to solve the MILP model based on this set. Therefore it is required to minimize the number of inequalities to obtain the solution efficiently. Various methods have been proposed in the literature to optimize the number of inequalities in this set.

Mouha *et al.* showed the use of MILP in differential cryptanalysis of block ciphers and used optimization solvers to get the security bounds [24]. They presented a framework to get the least number of active S-boxes in a differential characteristic of word oriented ciphers. This technique was illustrated on Advanced Encryption Standard (AES) and least number of active S-boxes in 4-round differential characteristic of AES were obtained by solving the MILP model.

Sun *et al.* extended the use of MILP for bit oriented ciphers and two methods based on logical condition modeling and convex hull computation were proposed to get the MILP model of S-box [27,28]. The DDT of S-box was used to write the linear inequalities for possible propagations using the SageMath tool [29]. Then greedy search algorithm was used to reduce the number of inequalities in this model. For a 4-bit S-box, the reduced set contains about 30 inequalities. Due to the limitation of SageMath, this method is not practical for the S-box of size greater than 6-bit. Sasaki and Todo proposed another method for MILP modeling of S-box to reduce the number of inequalities [30–32]. They proposed a MILP based method to reduce the inequalities using impossible propagations in the DDT. For a 4-bit S-box, this method provides around 20 linear inequalities that are used to minimize the number of active S-boxes. This method was also used to model the MILP problem for lightweight block cipher WARP [20]. This method uses SageMath to write the inequalities, therefore it also does not work for S-boxes of size more than 6-bit.

For 8-bit S-box, 16 variables are needed to write the linear inequalities for possible and impossible difference transitions in the DDT. For large S-boxes, Abdelkhalek et al. generated the linear inequalities using Logic Friday [22] (based on Espresso algorithm). The pb-DDT approach was proposed to optimize the probability of a differential characteristic by separating the DDT into multiple tables according to the probabilities. Boura and Coggia [8] proposed another approach to generate and minimize the number of linear inequalities for 8-bit S-boxes based on the impossible transitions in the DDT. This method was used to minimize the number of linear inequalities for AES S-box in [8]. The time complexity to get the 2882 linear inequalities for AES S-box was 22 d. They did not mention about the number of linear inequalities for partial or full DDT that will be required to optimize the probability of differential characteristics.

Our Contribution: The existing works focused on minimizing the number of linear inequalities to represent the DDT of large S-boxes. Whereas, the time complexity to minimize the number of inequalities for large S-boxes was several days [8]. Our aim is to generate a minimized set of linear inequalities within the practical time limit (≤ 5 h). We present a new method to generate the additional set of linear inequalities using intermediate output of the QM algorithm and get the minimized set of linear inequalities in practical time. We also solve the MILP model to optimize the number of active S-boxes in PIPO using two different set of linear inequalities. These experiments show that there is no significant difference in the time complexity to solve the MILP problem using large or small set of linear inequalities. For probability optimization part, we generate the linear inequalities for full DDT using our tool MILES (based on Espresso). We show the application of MILES to search the differential, impossible differential and related-key differential characteristics of lightweight block cipher PIPO-64/128 [17]. We achieve the designer's bound for differential and impossible differential characteristics. We present the full round related-key differential distinguishers and mount a key recovery attack on full round PIPO-64/128. Using MILES and MILP modeling of related-key differential search, we show the collisions in PIPO-64/128.

Organisation: The paper is organised as follows. In Sect. 2, we discuss MILP modeling of block ciphers with 8-bit S-boxes. We present approaches based on QM and Espresso algorithms to minimize the number of linear inequalities and compare the results for AES, SKINNY and PIPO S-boxes. In Sect. 3, we show the application of MILES to model the MILP problem to optimize the probability of differential characteristics in lightweight block cipher PIPO-64/128. The impossible differential characteristics search procedure is discussed and a full round related-key differential attack is presented. The paper is summarised with conclusion in Sect. 4.

2 MILP Based Differential Characteristic Search

To search the differential characteristics of a block cipher, the problem of optimizing the probability of differential characteristics is converted into the MILP problem. The objective function is the optimization of probabilities subject to the constraints based on linear inequalities. SPN and Feistel based block ciphers mainly consist of round key addition, substitution and permutation layers. The key addition layer does not contribute in the MILP model to search the differential characteristics. The input and output variables corresponding to the permutation layer are easily represented by linear inequalities. The substitution layer uses a non-linear S-box which cannot be easily represented by linear inequalities. SageMath is a popular tool that is used to obtain the linear inequalities using possible difference transitions in the DDT. In [31,32], Sasaki and Todo proposed the impossible transitions based approach to design a MILP problem to minimize the number of linear inequalities. This approach was later used by many researchers to design the MILP models of various 4-bit S-boxes [35]. The linear inequalities of permutation and substitution layers are used to model the MILP problem, that is solved by MILP solver GUROBI [15] or CPLEX [11].

In general, MILP based differential characteristics search is two stage process. Firstly, number of active S-boxes is minimized and then probability of differential characteristic is optimized using these active S-boxes. The outer and inner modules of MILP are designed corresponding to these stages. The outer module minimizes the number of active S-boxes while inner module optimizes the probabilities of differential characteristics.

2.1 Modeling Large S-box

An S-box is a non-linear component and its DDT is converted into linear inequalities to model the MILP problem. SageMath is used to generate the linear inequalities for DDT of the S-box. For m-bit S-box, the size of DDT is $2^m \times 2^m$ and it represents the number of occurrences of possible output differences corresponding to each input difference. SageMath uses the H-representation of convex hull to generate linear inequalities for the S-box. SageMath has practical-time limitation on the dimension of such convex hulls, so this method can be used to generate the linear inequalities for small S-boxes only. Therefore, this method cannot be used to model the outer module of MILP problem for S-boxes of size greater than 6 bits.

For large (8-bit) S-boxes, Abdelkhalek *et al.* [1] addressed this problem using the Espresso based tool Logic Friday [22] that reduces the inequalities by minimizing the product of sum of boolean functions. Boura and Coggia [8] proposed another method, inspired from QM algorithm, to reduce the number of linear inequalities of AES [26] and SKINNY [9] S-boxes. The proposed methods minimize the number of inequalities significantly in comparison to the existing approaches but at the cost of time and resources. The minimization process may take several days to get the reduced set of linear inequalities. The techniques presented in [1] and [8], were used to minimize the number of active S-boxes for 8-bit S-box based ciphers.

To optimize the probability of differential characteristic, Abdelkhalek *et al.* used *pb*-DDT based approach by separating the DDT for each probability [1]. These DDTs are represented by 8-bit input difference and 8-bit output difference. The method was proposed due to limitation of logic friday to process the input with dimension more than 16. Although, this method is used to optimize the probability of differential characteristic, it may not be efficient due to the of use of *pb*-DDT instead of full DDT. Based on the full DDT of 4-bit S-box, Sun *et al.* [28] suggested the method of using extra variable for each unique probability. Using this method, linear inequalities will be generated in more than 16 input variable for 8-bit S-box. As Logic Friday is unable to handle more than 16 input variable, we use a Espresso based tool namely MILES[1] (Appendix B and C) that handles more than 16 variables to minimize the set of linear inequalities. Linear inequalities generated from MILES are used to design the outer and inner modules of MILP model which optimizes the probability of differential characteristic.

2.2   Linear Inequalities for Minimization of Active S-boxes

Constructing linear inequalities for S-box is the first step towards the MILP modeling of differential attack. To minimize the number of active S-boxes, the MILP model requires linear inequalities corresponding to all possible transitions in DDT. Some of the existing approaches e.g. H-representation of convex hull and QM algorithm are not time efficient for large ($n \geq$ 8-bit) S-boxes due to large dimension ($2n$). Espresso algorithm works efficiently for large S-boxes but provides a large set of minimized inequalities. To minimize the set of inequalities, Boura and Coggia [8] used prime implicants of QM algorithm to get an initial set of inequalities and proposed an algorithm to introduce a new set of inequalities. The combined set of linear inequalities is minimized by removing the impossible transitions [8,28]. The proposed method reduces the number of inequalities significantly but the time complexity to achieve this reduction is very high. Although, smaller MILP model with lesser inequalities does not guarantee a faster solution, yet MILP model having less number of inequalities is a preferred choice.

We present a new method[2] to minimize the number of linear inequalities for large S-box within the practical time limit. This method uses the output of QM algorithm partially and introduce a novel approach to add a better set of linear inequalities. The QM algorithm can be divided into three parts. In first part (QM_1), it constructs prime implicants from impossible transitions of the DDT. In second part (QM_2), prime implicants are reduced to get the essential prime implicants. These essential prime implicants are further reduced using the

---

[1] https://github.com/tarunyadav/MILES.

[2] https://github.com/tarunyadav/PIPO-MILP/tree/main/PIPO-MILP-Ineq-Reduction.

coverage approach in third part (QM_3). In our method, we use the output of QM_2 and introduce an inequality corresponding to each essential prime implicant $a = (a_0, a_1, \cdots, a_{n-1})$ (Eq. 1). Our method is applied in four phases as described in Algorithm 1. The set of initial inequalities (L) is constructed in phase 1 and a new set of linear inequalities is introduced using L in phase 2. For each impossible transition in DDT, we add the inequalities which remove that impossible transition. We introduce an additional inequality corresponding to all possible transitions in DDT. This inequality is constructed by adding all the inequalities in the set L. This inequality with new linear inequalities (L_{new}) are combined with initial set (L) to get a larger set of inequalities. In phase 3, we construct the MILP model to minimize the number of linear inequalities using the approach proposed in [28]. For each impossible transition, we add a constraint such that at least one inequality removing this transition remains in the minimized set. Using such constraints, we want to ensure that all impossible transitions are removed using the minimum number of linear inequalities. The objective of this MILP problem is minimization of the set of linear inequalities (L). In phase 4, we solve the MILP model using GUROBI solver to get the minimized set of linear inequalities (L_{min}).

$$\sum_{i=0}^{n-1}(1 - a_i)x_i + a_i(1 - x_i) \geq 1 \qquad (1)$$

We compare the number of linear inequalities and time complexity of our algorithm with existing results for 8-bit S-boxes of AES, SKINNY-128 and PIPO-64/128 in Table 1. It is evident that our algorithm optimizes the trade-off between number of inequalities and time efficiency. For PIPO-64/128, we have solved the MILP model for active S-box minimization with 4476 inequalities constructed by MILES and 3276 inequalities constructed using Algorithm 1. The comparison of time to reach the lower bound is presented in Table 2. T_{OB} and T_{OS} represent the time to reach the optimal bound(OB) and time to conclude that the given optimal bound is the optimal solution respectively. It can be observed from Table 2 that the T_{OS} is always lesser for the larger set of inequalities(Model 1) which suggests that more constraints speeds up the process to eliminate impossible space. There is no such relation in T_{OB} that means smaller set of inequalities may not reach the optimal bound faster. The comparison concludes that lesser inequalities construct smaller model but may not always yield a faster solution.

2.3   Linear Inequalities for Optimization of Probability

Once active S-boxes are minimized, the next step is to optimize the probability corresponding to these active S-boxes. To optimize the probability, construction of linear inequalities corresponding to each possible probabilistic transition in DDT is required. To construct such linear inequalities, Abdelkhalek *et al.* [1] used the approach to construct separate DDT for each probability. These *pb*-DDTs are used to construct linear inequalities in the same manner as described in Sect. 2.2. Linear inequalities for each *pb*-DDT can be generated either using Espresso or

---

Algorithm 1. Linear Inequalities Minimization for 8-bit S-boxes

---

Input: 8-bit Sbox

Output: L_{min} = Set of minimized linear inequalities

1: $DDT \leftarrow$ Difference Distribution Table of S-box

Phase 1 - Initial Set of Linear Inequalities

2: Prime Implicants $\leftarrow QM_1$(Impossible Transitions of DDT)

3: Essential Prime Implicants $\leftarrow QM_2$(Prime Implicants)

4: $L \leftarrow$ Linear inequalities corresponding to each essential prime implicant (Eqn 1)

Phase 2 - Adding New Inequalities

5: $L_{new} \leftarrow \phi$

6: **for all** Impossible Transitions $(X \rightarrow Y)$ in DDT **do**

7:     $S_{ineq} \leftarrow \{l_i, \forall l_i \in L \text{ and } l_i(X,Y) < 0\}$

8:     $L_{new} \leftarrow L_{new} \cup \{\sum S_i \; \forall S_i \in S_{ineq}\}$ ▷ Addition of coefficients

9: **end for**

10: $L \leftarrow L \cup L_{new} \cup \{\sum l_i \; \forall l_i \in L\}$

Phase 3 - MILP Modeling M (Objective and Constraints in Binary Variables)

11: $M.constraints \leftarrow \phi$

12: **for all** Impossible Transitions $(X \rightarrow Y)$ in DDT **do**

13:     $Z \leftarrow \{Z_i, \forall l_i \in L \text{ and } l_i(X,Y) < 0\}$ ▷ Z_i is a binary variable

14:     $M.constraints \leftarrow M.constraints \cup \{\sum Z \geq 1 \}$

15: **end for**

16: $M.objective \leftarrow Min(\sum\{Z_i, \forall l_i \in L\})$

Phase 4 - Minimization using GUROBI Solver

17: $L_{min} \leftarrow M.optimize()$

Table 1. Comparison of time required to minimize linear inequalities of S-box

Algorithm	Output	S-box		
		AES	SKINNY	PIPO
QM	L_{min}	–	392	–
	Time	5 h	7707 s	5 h
Espresso	L_{min}	8389	377	4474
	Time	100 s	2 s	41 s
Algo 1 in [8]	L_{min}	7461	372	–
	Time	20d	120 m	–
Algo 3 in [8]	L_{min}	2882	302	–
	Time	Several days	120 m	–
Algorithm 1	L_{min}	5461	315	3276
	Time	5 h	900 s	5 h

Table 2. Comparison of time required (in seconds) to attain optimal bound/solution for PIPO-64/128 osing different sets of linear inequalities

Round	OB	Model 1			Model 2		
		Inequalities of S-box = 4474			Inequalities of S-box = 3276		
		Size (KB)	T_{OB}	T_{OS}	Size (KB)	T_{OB}	T_{OS}
1	1	4462	0.47	0.47	3902	0.81	0.81
2	2	8923	5.19	5.19	7802	2.00	9.32
3	4	13384	7.00	50.51	11704	4.00	745.23
4	6	17845	22.00	550.11	15602	28.00	8597.95
5	9	22305	208.00	–	19502	1546.00	–
6	11	26766	2290.00	–	23403	112.00	–

QM algorithm. QM based reduction depends on the characteristics of impossible transitions of the S-box and it needs to run for several days to provide a result. The algorithm proposed in [8] also suffers from similar drawback due to large number of impossible transitions in pb-DDTs. Due to the use of essential prime implicants in Algorithm 1, we get faster results than the existing approaches but still lack the time efficiency. There are some cases (Table 3) where the Algorithm 1 is not able to produce the result due to lesser number of possible transitions in DDT. The time complexity to produce the sets of minimized linear inequalities for each pb-DDT using MILES is less but each set contains the large number of inequalities. We compare the number of inequalities and execution time for pb-DDTs of AES, SKINNY and PIPO in Table 3.

The pb-DDT approach was proposed to overcome the limitation of Logic Friday since it becomes computationally infeasible to reduce the higher dimension inequalities of full DDT using Logic Friday. MILES uses the Espresso in its original form for reduction in higher dimension inequalities. Therefore, we can use the full DDT of S-box instead of pb-DDT. We use the approach proposed in [28] to construct the probability based possible transitions and introduce additional variable for each probability. We use MILES to construct the linear inequalities for these transitions and show that reduction using Espresso in higher dimension is faster than pb-DDT approach. Although, the use of full DDT may produce larger set of linear inequalities but it simplifies the MILP model as there is no need to choose different pb-DDT each time for an active S-box. We have already discussed (Table 2) that smaller set of linear inequalities doesn't guarantee the faster solution for optimal bound but may take more time to conclude the optimal solution. For PIPO-64/128, we use the approach of additional variables to utilize full DDT and apply the Espresso to construct a minimized set of inequalities. These inequalities will be used to optimize the probability of differential characteristics in the next section.

Table 3. Comparison of time required (in seconds) to get minimized set of linear inequalities to represent pb-DDT, p-TT and f-TT

Structure (S-box)	Probability	QM ([1]) (pb-DDT)	MILES (p-TT)		Algo 1 (p-TT)		MILES (f-TT)	
		L_{min}	L_{min}	Time	L_{min}	Time	L_{min}	Time
AES	2^{-7}	-	8312	84	5542	14963	8720	220
	2^{-6}	-	349	1	327	12478		
	Total	-	*8661*	*85*	*5869*	*27441*	*8720*	*220*
SKINNY	2^{-7}	206	208	1	187	8928	799	305
	2^{-6}	275	281	0.5	192	3903		
	$2^{-5.415037}$	33	34	0.3	-	-		
	2^{-5}	234	240	1.2	167	15903		
	$2^{-4.415037}$	42	47	0.2	-	-		
	2^{-4}	147	155	1.2	-	-		
	$2^{-3.678071}$	15	15	0.2	-	-		
	$2^{-3.415037}$	24	26	0.2	-	-		
	$2^{-3.192645}$	15	15	0.1	-	-		
	2^{-3}	62	69	0.3	-	-		
	$2^{-2.678071}$	16	16	0.1	-	-		
	$2^{-2.415037}$	17	17	0.1	-	-		
	2^{-2}	37	38	0.1	-	-		
	Total	*1123*	*1161*	*5.5*	-	-	*799*	*305*
PIPO	2^{-7}	-	3410	23	2464	14382	6035	2220
	2^{-6}	-	2211	24	1993	6446		
	$2^{-5.415037}$	-	519	5	479	7046		
	2^{-5}	-	355	7	294	10442		
	$2^{-4.678072}$	-	26	0.2	24	1566		
	$2^{-4.415037}$	-	20	0.1	20	1907		
	2^{-4}	-	93	0.5	57	10115		
	Total	-	*6634*	*59.8*	*5331*	*51904*	*6035*	*2220*

3 Application to Lightweight Block Cipher PIPO-64/128

Lightweight cryptography has become an important topic in cryptology [7] and NIST has also called for a competition to design the lightweight cryptographic primitives [25]. PIPO-64/128 is a lightweight block cipher which was recently proposed by Kim *et al.* at ICISC 2020 [17]. The design highlights are its security for side-channel protected and unprotected environments. Its diffusion layer is designed to optimize the efficiency in hardware as well as software applications. Its diffusion layer can be implemented in software using the cyclic shift rotations.

For hardware applications, its diffusion layer can be visualised as bit permutation on 64 bits and can be implemented using wiring only. The 8-bit S-box is specifically designed for PIPO-64/128 so that it can be represented using the minimum number of non-linear equations. This also ensures the protection of the design against side channel attacks.

3.1   Specification of PIPO-64/128

PIPO-64/128 is a 64-bit lightweight block cipher with 128 and 256 bits key sizes [17]. It consists of 13/17 rounds for 128/256 bits key variants respectively. It is based on substitution permutation network (SPN) structure. The lightweight 8-bit S-box, having differential branch number 3, is specifically designed to use in the confusion layer of PIPO-64/128. For each 8-bit word, diffusion layer uses a cyclic rotation with different shift values for each word. The round function of PIPO-64/128 is explained by dividing it into an 8×8 matrix. It applies the diffusion layer row-wise and 8-bit S-box is applied column-wise. For each variant, a simple key selection algorithm is used. For 128-bit key $K = (K_1 \parallel K_0)$, the rounds keys are selected as $RK_i = K_{i(mod2)}, 0 \leq i \leq 13$. For 256-bit key $K = (K_3 \parallel K_2 \parallel K_1 \parallel K_0)$, the rounds keys are selected as $RK_i = K_{i(mod4)}$, $0 \leq i \leq 17$.

Algorithm 2. Encryption Algorithm of PIPO-64/128

Input: P and $RK_i, 0 \leq i \leq 13$
Output: $C = (c_{63}, c_{62}, \cdots, c_0)$
1: $U_0 \leftarrow P \oplus RK_0$
2: $U_0 = (u_{63}, u_{62}, \cdots, u_0)$
3: **for** i=1 to 13 **do**
4:     **for** j=0 to 7 **do**
5:         $(v_{56+j} \parallel v_{48+j} \parallel v_{40+j} \parallel v_{32+j} \parallel v_{24+j} \parallel v_{16+j} \parallel v_{8+j} \parallel v_j)$
6:         $\leftarrow S_8(u_{56+i} \parallel u_{48+i} \parallel u_{40+j} \parallel u_{32+j} \parallel u_{24+j} \parallel u_{16+j} \parallel u_{8+j} \parallel u_j)$
7:     **end for**
8: **end for**
9: $V_i = (v_{63}, v_{62}, \cdots, v_0)$
10: $U_i \leftarrow B_P(V_i) \oplus RK_i \oplus i$
11: $U_i = (u_{63}, u_{62}, \cdots, u_0)$

For MILP modeling, we describe the encryption algorithm of PIPO-64/128 in a different way (Algorithm 2). Round function is described using substitution layer, permutation layer and add round key operations. Substitution layer applies 8-bit S-box (S) (Table 4) on 8 bits extracted from eight different positions of input and output bits from S-box are sent back to the same positions.

Permutation layer uses a 64-bit permutation (B_P) (Table 5) on the output from S-box layer. The round keys (RK_i) and constants ($i = round\,number$) are simply XOR-ed with the output of diffusion layer.

Table 4. 8-bit S-box of PIPO-64/128

S_8	0	1	2	3	4	5	6	7	8	9	A	B	C	D	E	F
0	5E	F9	FC	00	3F	85	BA	5B	18	37	B2	C6	71	C3	74	9D
1	A7	94	0D	E1	CA	68	53	2E	49	62	EB	97	A4	0E	2D	D0
2	16	25	AC	48	63	D1	EA	8F	F7	40	45	B1	9E	34	1B	F2
3	B9	86	03	7F	D8	7A	DD	3C	E0	CB	52	26	15	AF	8C	69
4	C2	75	70	1C	33	99	B6	C7	04	3B	BE	5A	FD	5F	F8	81
5	93	A0	29	4D	66	D4	EF	0A	E5	CE	57	A3	90	2A	09	6C
6	22	11	88	E4	CF	6D	56	AB	7B	DC	D9	BD	82	38	07	7E
7	B5	9A	1F	F3	44	F6	41	30	4C	67	EE	12	21	8B	A8	D5
8	55	6E	E7	0B	28	92	A1	CC	2B	08	91	ED	D6	64	4F	A2
9	BC	83	06	FA	5D	FF	58	39	72	C5	C0	B4	9B	31	1E	77
A	01	3E	BB	DF	78	DA	7D	84	50	6B	E2	8E	AD	17	24	C9
B	AE	8D	14	E8	D3	61	4A	27	47	F0	F5	19	36	9C	B3	42
C	1D	32	B7	43	F4	46	F1	98	EC	D7	4E	AA	89	23	10	65
D	8A	A9	20	54	6F	CD	E6	13	DB	7C	79	05	3A	80	BF	DE
E	E9	D2	4B	2F	0C	A6	95	60	0F	2C	A5	51	6A	C8	E3	96
F	B0	9F	1A	76	C1	73	C4	35	FE	59	5C	B8	87	3D	02	FB

Table 5. Bit permutation in PIPO-64/128

i	0	1	2	3	4	5	6	7	8	9	10	11	12	13	14	15
$B_P(i)$	0	1	2	3	4	5	6	7	15	8	9	10	11	12	13	14
i	16	17	18	19	20	21	22	23	24	25	26	27	28	29	30	31
$B_P(i)$	20	21	22	23	16	17	18	19	27	28	29	30	31	24	25	26
i	32	33	34	35	36	37	38	39	40	41	42	43	44	45	46	47
$B_P(i)$	38	39	32	33	34	35	36	37	45	46	47	40	41	42	43	44
i	48	49	50	51	52	53	54	55	56	57	58	59	60	61	62	63
$B_P(i)$	49	50	51	52	53	54	55	48	58	59	60	61	62	63	56	57

Table 6. Difference distribution table of PIPO-64/128

$\Delta_j \rightarrow$ $\Delta_i \downarrow$	0	1	2	3	4	5	6	7	8	9	A	B	C	D	...	FF
0	256	0	0	0	0	0	0	0	0	0	0	0	0	0	...	0
1	0	0	0	0	0	0	0	0	0	0	0	0	0	0	...	0
2	0	0	0	0	0	16	0	0	0	0	0	0	0	0	...	0
3	0	0	0	0	0	16	0	0	0	0	0	0	0	0	...	0
4	0	0	0	0	0	0	0	0	0	0	0	0	0	0	...	0
5	0	0	0	0	0	0	0	0	0	0	0	0	0	0	...	0
6	0	0	0	0	0	16	0	0	0	0	0	0	0	0	...	0
7	0	0	0	0	0	16	0	0	0	0	0	0	0	0	...	0
...															...	
8F	0	0	0	0	0	8	0	0	0	8	0	0	0	0	...	0
9F	0	0	16	0	0	0	0	4	2	0	0	0	0	0	...	0
AF	0	2	16	0	0	0	0	0	0	0	0	2	0	0	...	0
BF	0	2	0	0	0	0	0	4	0	0	0	2	0	0	...	0
CF	0	2	0	0	0	0	0	0	2	0	0	0	0	4	...	2
DF	0	2	16	0	0	0	0	4	0	0	4	0	0	4	...	2
EF	0	0	16	0	0	0	0	0	2	0	0	0	2	0	...	0
FF	0	0	0	0	0	0	0	4	0	0	2	0	0	0	...	2

3.2   MILP Modeling for PIPO-64/128

The model for valid differential propagations of PIPO-64/128 is constructed bit-wise. In each round, subkey addition, S-box, and bit permutation operations are used. Block size in PIPO-64/128 is 64-bit and it consists of 13 rounds. For 64-bit plaintext difference, binary variables $u_{63}, u_{62}, \cdots u_0$ represent active or inactive bits for first round. The variables to represent active or inactive bits in the difference after first round are updated to $u_{127}, u_{126}, \cdots u_{64}$ and so on. The variables $u_{832}, u_{831}, \cdots u_{768}$ represent the active or inactive bits in the ciphertext difference after 13 rounds. In first round, the variables representing the bits of input and output differences to S-box layer are represented as follows:

$$
\begin{bmatrix}
u_7 & u_6 & u_5 & u_4 & u_3 & u_2 & u_1 & u_0 \\
u_{15} & u_{14} & u_{13} & u_{12} & u_{11} & u_{10} & u_9 & u_8 \\
u_{23} & u_{22} & u_{21} & u_{20} & u_{19} & u_{18} & u_{17} & u_{16} \\
u_{31} & u_{30} & u_{29} & u_{28} & u_{27} & u_{26} & u_{25} & u_{24} \\
u_{39} & u_{38} & u_{37} & u_{36} & u_{35} & u_{34} & u_{33} & u_{32} \\
u_{47} & u_{46} & u_{45} & u_{44} & u_{43} & u_{42} & u_{41} & u_{40} \\
u_{55} & u_{54} & u_{53} & u_{52} & u_{51} & u_{50} & u_{49} & u_{48} \\
u_{63} & u_{62} & u_{61} & u_{60} & u_{59} & u_{58} & u_{57} & u_{56}
\end{bmatrix}
\rightarrow
\begin{bmatrix}
u_{71} & u_{70} & u_{69} & u_{68} & u_{67} & u_{66} & u_{65} & u_{64} \\
u_{78} & u_{77} & u_{76} & u_{75} & u_{74} & u_{73} & u_{72} & u_{79} \\
u_{83} & u_{82} & u_{81} & u_{80} & u_{87} & u_{86} & u_{85} & u_{84} \\
u_{90} & u_{89} & u_{88} & u_{95} & u_{94} & u_{93} & u_{92} & u_{91} \\
u_{101} & u_{100} & u_{99} & u_{98} & u_{97} & u_{96} & u_{103} & u_{102} \\
u_{108} & u_{107} & u_{106} & u_{105} & u_{104} & u_{111} & u_{110} & u_{109} \\
u_{112} & u_{119} & u_{118} & u_{117} & u_{116} & u_{115} & u_{114} & u_{113} \\
u_{121} & u_{120} & u_{127} & u_{126} & u_{125} & u_{124} & u_{123} & u_{122}
\end{bmatrix}
$$

The permutation layer is applied on the output from S-box layer and output of the permutation layer which acts as an input to the second round is represented as follows:

$$\begin{bmatrix} u_{71} & u_{70} & u_{69} & u_{68} & u_{67} & u_{66} & u_{65} & u_{64} \\ u_{79} & u_{78} & u_{77} & u_{76} & u_{75} & u_{74} & u_{73} & u_{72} \\ u_{87} & u_{86} & u_{85} & u_{84} & u_{83} & u_{82} & u_{81} & u_{80} \\ u_{95} & u_{94} & u_{93} & u_{92} & u_{91} & u_{90} & u_{89} & u_{88} \\ u_{103} & u_{102} & u_{101} & u_{100} & u_{99} & u_{98} & u_{97} & u_{96} \\ u_{111} & u_{110} & u_{109} & u_{108} & u_{107} & u_{106} & u_{105} & u_{104} \\ u_{119} & u_{118} & u_{117} & u_{116} & u_{115} & u_{114} & u_{113} & u_{112} \\ u_{127} & u_{126} & u_{125} & u_{124} & u_{123} & u_{122} & u_{121} & u_{120} \end{bmatrix}$$

We describe all possible propagation patterns for S-box with a system of linear inequalities.

$$e.g. (u_7, u_6, u_5, u_4, u_3, u_2, u_1, u_0 \rightarrow u_{71}, u_{70}, u_{69}, u_{68}, u_{67}, u_{66}, u_{65}, u_{64})$$

The variables corresponding to bits having the difference takes '1' and it takes '0' otherwise. A constraint $u_0 + u_1 + \cdots + u_{63} \geq 1$ is added to ensure that plaintext difference has at least one active bit.

Modeling 8-bit S-box. To model the 8-bit S-box of PIPO-64/128, we generate the DDT (Table 6) for each possible input and output difference (Δ_i, Δ_j) using MILES. The entries (i, j) in the Table 6 corresponds to the number of occurrences for output differences Δ_j when the input differences were set as Δ_i. We get a 256×256 DDT for an 8-bit S-box. The non-zero values in the DDT corresponds to a possible difference propagation and zero values indicates an impossible propagation.

Linear Inequalities for Outer Module of MILP Model. The DDT generated in previous step is used in MILES to derive the truth table ($\star$-TT). The $\star$-TT of PIPO-64/128 contains 20621 entries which are further minimized by our tool. MILES minimizes the $\star$-TT to $\star$-TT$_{min}$ with 4474 entries. We convert each entry of $\star$-TT$_{min}$ into a linear inequality. We represent each entry of $\star$-TT$_{min}$ using 16 binary variables $(x_0, x_1, x_2, x_3, x_4, x_5, x_6, x_7, y_0, y_1, y_2, y_3, y_4, y_5, y_6, y_7)$, where first eight variables $(x_0, x_1, x_2, x_3, x_4, x_5, x_6, x_7)$ represent the input difference and remaining variables $(y_0, y_1, y_2, y_3, y_4, y_5, y_6, y_7)$ represent the output difference. These linear inequalities are used as constraints in the outer module and minimization of number of active S-boxes is used as objective function.

Linear Inequalities for Inner Module of MILP Model. Differential probability of S-box was used to design MILP model by Sun et al. in [27] and this technique was also used by Zhu et al. to present the MILP based differential attack on round-reduced GIFT in [35]. We optimize the probability of differential characteristics in the inner module of MILP model. For this purpose, we need the linear inequalities for all non-zero entries in the DDT which corresponds to the possible difference propagation and their probabilities. In the DDT of PIPO-64/128 S-box, there are seven different values for the probability of possible difference propagations i.e. 2^{-0}, $2^{-4.00}$, $2^{-4.41}$, $2^{-4.67}$, $2^{-5.00}$, $2^{-5.41}$, $2^{-6.00}$, $2^{-7.00}$ (Table 7). This requires seven extra binary variables to represent the probability of each possible propagation. MILES uses DDT to generate truth table (f-TT) with 20621 entries. Each entry of the f-TT is represented by 23 binary variables where 16 input variables $(x_0, x_1, x_2, x_3, x_4, x_5, x_6, x_7, y_0, y_1, y_2, y_3, y_4, y_5, y_6, y_7)$ represents the input and output differences. The remaining seven input variables $(p_0, p_1, p_2, p_3, p_4, p_5, p_6)$ represent the probabilities of corresponding difference propagations. MILES minimizes the f-TT to f-TT$_{min}$ which results in 6035 entries in f-TT$_{min}$. Each entry of f-TT$_{min}$ is converted into the linear inequality using Eq. 1. This set of linear inequalities is used to optimize the probability of differential characteristics in the block cipher PIPO-64/128.

Table 7. Binary variables to encode the probabilities in DDT of PIPO-64/128

$Pr[(x_0, x_1, \cdots, x_7) \rightarrow (x_8, x_9, \cdots, x_{15})]$	$(p_0, p_1, \cdots, p_6)$
$1 = 2^{-0}$	(0,0,0,0,0,0,0)
$2/256 = 2^{-7.00}(Pr_6)$	(0,0,0,0,0,0,1)
$4/256 = 2^{-6.00}(Pr_5)$	(0,0,0,0,0,1,0)
$6/256 = 2^{-5.41}(Pr_4)$	(0,0,0,0,1,0,0)
$8/256 = 2^{-5.00}(Pr_3)$	(0,0,0,1,0,0,0)
$10/256 = 2^{-4.67}(Pr_2)$	(0,0,1,0,0,0,0)
$12/256 = 2^{-4.41}(Pr_1)$	(0,1,0,0,0,0,0)
$16/256 = 2^{-4.00}(Pr_0)$	(1,0,0,0,0,0,0)

3.3   Differential Cryptanalysis of PIPO-64/128

We solve the MILP model using Gurobi solver [15] to optimize the probability of differential characteristics for PIPO-64/128. In the outer-MILP module, the objective function is to minimize the number of active S-boxes in the differential characteristics. We get 13 active S-boxes for 7 rounds differential characteristics in PIPO-64/128. The objective function for the inner-MILP module is to maximize the probability of differential characteristics using the positions of active S-boxes obtained in the outer module. The objective function is defined as minimization of Eq. 2 over active S-boxes (AS).

$$\sum_{\forall AS} \sum_{i=0}^{6} -\log_2(Pr_i) \times (p_0 + p_1 + p_2 + p_3 + p_4 + p_5 + p_6) \tag{2}$$

We constructed[3] many differential characteristics for PIPO-64/128 reduced to 6/7 rounds. There does not exist any 6-round differential characteristic with the probability better than $2^{-54.4}$ and best differential characteristics for 7-round PIPO-64/128 exists with the probability of 2^{-65}. We constructed the 7-round differential characteristics for PIPO-64/128 using the inequalities generated with MILES which is shown in Table 8.

Table 8. 7-round differential characteristics for PIPO-64/128

Round (r)	Input difference (Δ_r)	Probability
0	0x0101000101000001	1
1	0x0000000000008000	2^{-4}
2	0x0000000000080080	2^{-4}
3	0x2011112000800080	2^{-11}
4	0x404100408101c080	2^{-19}
5	0x0000101000100000	2^{-16}
6	0x0000000080000000	2^{-7}
7	0x0001000004084000	2^{-4}

3.4 Impossible Differential Cryptanalysis of PIPO-64/128

Impossible differential attack is opposite to differential attack. The basic idea is to use zero probability differential characteristics in place of a high probability characteristic to filter out the wrong keys [3]. For this purpose, the zero probability characteristics are constructed by proving a contradiction between the two differential characteristics of probability one each. This approach is known as miss-in-the-middle technique to search an impossible differential characteristic. Nowadays, the MILP based technique is used to search these zero probability differential characteristics. The MILP model to search the high probability differential characteristics with some added constraint is used to search the impossible differential characteristic.

To search the impossible differential, we iterate all (Δ_i, Δ_o) pairs with one active bit in the input and output. For this purpose, additional constraints to fix the input and output differences are added in the MILP model. The gurobi solver is used to solve the outer module of MILP model as discussed in Sect. 3.2. The input and output differences corresponding to infeasible solution are considered as impossible differential characteristic. Using this method[4], we obtain the

---

[3] https://github.com/tarunyadav/PIPO-MILP.

[4] https://github.com/tarunyadav/PIPO-MILP/tree/main/PIPO-MILP-Impossible-Differential.

following 4-round impossible differential characteristics (Δ_0, Δ_4). However, our bound for impossible differential attack is similar to that of the designers claim.

0000000000000000000000000000000000000000000000000000000000000001→
0000000000000000000000000000000000000000000000000000000000010000

3.5   Related-Key Differential Distinguisher for PIPO-64/128

Resistance to related-key attacks was not considered by the designers of PIPO-64/128 and any security claim in the related-key setting is not provided. In differential attack, the adversary is allowed to choose a difference in the plaintexts and observe the differences in ciphertexts. In related-key differential attack, the adversary is allowed to choose a relation (difference) in the key together a relation (difference) in the plaintexts [2,21]. The adversary is allowed to get the encryption of first plaintext using the secret key and a key related to this key is used to encrypt the another plaintext. We model an MILP problem to search the related-key differential characteristic in PIPO-64/128.

3.5.1   MILP Model for Related-Key Differential Characteristic. The secret key K is divided into the two 64-bit keys K_0 and K_1 which are used as round subkeys in PIPO-64/128. We model the similar MILP problem to search the related-key differential characteristic as described in Sect. 3.2. Additionally, we need to model the key addition layer and solve the MILP model in order to get the optimal related-key characteristics in PIPO-64/128 [27].

Modeling Key Addition Layer. We need to introduce the additional constraints in the MILP model corresponding to the round keys. The 128 new variables are introduced corresponding to the 128-bit secret key. The 64 key variables are added in one round and the other 64 key variables are added in the subsequent round. To add the constraints for key addition layer, for each bit of input x_i and key k, we follow the conditions on bit variables to exclude the impossible patterns (Eq. 3). Here, x_i and k refer to the input bit and corresponding key bit. The bit variable x_{i+1} is an output of the XOR operation i.e. $x_{i+1} = k \oplus x_i$.

$$
\begin{aligned}
x_i + k - x_{i+1} &\geq 0 \\
x_i - k + x_{i+1} &\geq 0 \\
-x_i + k + x_{i+1} &\geq 0 \\
x_i + k + x_{i+1} &\leq 2
\end{aligned}
\tag{3}
$$

3.5.2   Full-Round Related-Key Differential Distinguisher. We solve[5] the MILP model to search the related-key differential characteristics using gurobi solver. We get a 2-round iterative related-key characteristic with the probability

---

[5] https://github.com/tarunyadav/PIPO-MILP/tree/main/PIPO-MILP-Related-Key-Differential.

of 2^{-4}. The optimal related-key differential characteristic for full round PIPO-64/128 is obtained with a probability of 2^{-24} using 2-round iterative characteristic (Table 9). We also get full-round characteristics with probability of 2^{-28} under zero difference in the plaintext as well as in the ciphertext (Table 10).

3.5.3 Collisions in PIPO-64/128. The zero difference related-key characteristics will lead to a collision in the hash function designed using PIPO-64/128. We searched for the existence of input and output pairs under different keys following zero difference characteristic (collision). We encrypt the 2^{28} random samples under related keys and one such pair is expected in each experiment. Therefore, we can construct as many samples providing us the collision in the input and output under the different keys. We have verified these plaintext and ciphertext samples by using the designers program. One such collision in PIPO-64/128 is presented in the Table 10. We have also provided other samples showing a collision in the Appendix A.

Table 9. 13-round (related-key) differential characteristic for PIPO-64/128 with probability 2^{-24}

Round (r)	Difference (Δ_r) $\Delta K = $ 0x00200000200000000040000801001000	Probability
0	0x0040000801001000	1
1	0x0020000020000000	1
2	0x0000000000000000	2^{-4}
3	0x0020000020000000	1
4	0x0000000000000000	2^{-4}
5	0x0020000020000000	1
6	0x0000000000000000	2^{-4}
7	0x0020000020000000	1
8	0x0000000000000000	2^{-4}
9	0x0020000020000000	1
10	0x0000000000000000	2^{-4}
11	0x0020000020000000	1
12	0x0000000000000000	2^{-4}
13	0x0020000020000000	1

Table 10. Zero difference characteristics with an example of collision

Round	$E_K(P_r)$, $K = (K_1 \| K_0)$	$E_{K'}(P_r')$, $K' = (K_1' \| K_0')$	Difference	Probability
(r)	$K_1 = $ 0x6DC416DD779428D2	$K_1' = K_1 \oplus$ 0x0040000801001000	($\Delta_r = P_r \oplus P_r'$)	
	$K_0 = $ 0x7E1D20AD2E152297	$K_0' = K_0 \oplus$ 0x0020000020000000		
0	0xFFEAF697D7FCE742	0xFFEAF697D7FCE742	0x0000000000000000	1
1	0xD76EFD65756940C0	0xD76EFD65756940C0	0x0000000000000000	2^{-4}
2	0x4FA59C5858EDC4FF	0x4F859C5878EDC4FF	0x0020000020000000	1
3	0x8F6ACEC7A220C121	0x8F6ACEC7A220C121	0x0000000000000000	2^{-4}
4	0x406AD151D57A997B	0x404AD151F57A997B	0x0020000020000000	1
5	0xC5F53C44C408AC2D	0xC5F53C44C408AC2D	0x0000000000000000	2^{-4}
6	0xCFD8867C58BFCFD9	0xCFF8867C78BFCFD9	0x0020000020000000	1
7	0xC99B445F8E203697	0xC99B445F8E203697	0x0000000000000000	2^{-4}
8	0xD12CCC87E5585504	0xD10CCC87C5585504	0x0020000020000000	1
9	0x01D75CDC373A6F41	0x01D75CDC373A6F41	0x0000000000000000	2^{-4}
10	0x41C1CE1756D7C045	0x41E1CE1776D7C045	0x0020000020000000	1
11	0x388794675E6B5EDE	0x388794675E6B5EDE	0x0000000000000000	2^{-4}
12	0x1FDB4194BF26AC3B	0x1FFB41949F26AC3B	0x0020000020000000	1
13	0xCDE57DF09ECF4F7D	0xCDE57DF09ECF4F7D	0x0000000000000000	2^{-4}

3.6   Related-Key Differential Attack on Full-round PIPO-64/128

We use the related-key differential characteristic described in the Table 10 to present a full-round differential attack on PIPO-64/128. We used 11-round differential characteristics ($\Delta_1 \rightarrow \Delta_{12}$) with the probability of 2^{-20} and added one round at the beginning as well as at the end of the characteristic (Table 11). Using the 11-round differential characteristic, we can launch a key recovery attack on the 13-round PIPO-64/128. The 11-round characteristic is chosen in particular to maximize the number of recovered key bits. In each round, 64-bit round key is required and it is extracted directly from the 128-bit key $K = (K_1, K_0)$. The key K_0 is used for whitening and for even numbered rounds while the odd numbered rounds use the key K_1. We need to guess the round keys which correspond to the actives S-boxes.

Table 11. Related-key differential attack on 13-round PIPO-64/128

$\Delta K_1 \rightarrow$	0000 0000 0100 0000 0000 0000 0000 1000 0000 0001 0000 0000 0001 0000 0000 0000
$\Delta K_0 \rightarrow$	0000 0000 0010 0000 0000 0000 0000 0000 0010 0000 0000 0000 0000 0000 0000 0000
Δ_0	00?0 0000 00?0 0000 00?0 0000 00?0 0000 00?0 0000 00?0 0000 00?0 0000 00?0 0000
$\oplus \Delta K_0$	00?0 0000 00?0 0000 00?0 0000 00?0 0000 00?0 0000 00?0 0000 00?0 0000 00?0 0000
S-Box	0000 0000 0010 0000 0000 0000 0010 0000 0010 0000 0000 0000 0010 0000 0000 0000
Permutation	0000 0000 0100 0000 0000 0000 0000 1000 0000 0001 0000 0000 0001 0000 0000 0000
Δ_1	0000 0000 0000 0000 0000 0000 0000 0000 0000 0000 0000 0000 0000 0000 0000 0000
.	
.	
.	
Δ_{12}	0000 0000 0010 0000 0000 0000 0000 0010 0000 0000 0000 0000 0000 0000 0000 0000
S-Box	00?0 0000 00?0 0000 00?0 0000 00?0 0000 00?0 0000 00?0 0000 00?0 0000 00?0 0000
Permutation	?000 0000 0?00 0000 0000 0?00 0000 ?000 0000 000? 0000 00?0 000? 0000 00?0 0000
Δ_{13}	?000 0000 0?00 0000 0000 0?00 0000 ?000 0000 000? 0000 00?0 000? 0000 00?0 0000

$\Delta_1 = Permutation \oplus K_1$; $\Delta_{13} = Permutation \oplus K_1$

3.6.1   Data Collection

We can build $2^n (n \leq 56)$ structures corresponding to the fixed bits in the input difference (Δ_0). The objective is to minimize the value of n such that sufficient number of right pairs are left for key guessing phase. Each structure traverses the 8 undetermined (?) bits in Δ_0 (Table 11). Thus, each structure generates $2^{8*2-1}(= 2^{15})$ pairs[6] satisfying the differential. Therefore, the total number of pairs generated by the 2^n structures are 2^{n+15}. In Table 11, such a pair will meet the second round differential with an average probability of 2^{-8}. The probability of obeying the differential after 12th round for the pair encrypted with the right key is 2^{-20}. Therefore, the number of pairs satisfying the differential after 12th round for a right key guess will be $2^{n+15} \times 2^{-8} \times 2^{-20} (= 2^{n-13})$. Hence, we choose $n = 17$ so that we could get at least $2^4 (= 16)$ right pairs under the correct key guessing.

3.6.2   Key Recovery

In this phase, we guess the key bits corresponding to the undetermined bits(?) in Δ_0 and Δ_{13} and nonzero fix difference. This guess includes $K_0^5, K_0^{13}, K_0^{21}, K_0^{29}, K_0^{37}, K_0^{45}, K_0^{53}, K_0^{61}, K_1^{12}, K_1^{24}, K_1^{35}, K_1^{54}$ in 1st round and $K_1^5, K_1^{12}, K_1^{17}, K_1^{24}, K_1^{35}, K_1^{42}, K_1^{54}, K_1^{63}$ in 13th round. Since $K_1^{12}, K_1^{24}, K_1^{35}, K_1^{54}$ are involved in 1st and 13th round, total 16 unique key bits are involved in the key recovery phase. Hence, we construct 2^{16} counters corresponding to the possible values of 16 bits of the key.

With $n = 17$, we repeat the key guessing procedure for each of the $2^{17+15}(= 2^{32})$ pairs. We experimented with 2^{32} pairs and find that there are at least 2^4 pairs remaining after filtered by zero difference in Δ_{13}. Therefore, the expected counter value for a wrong key guess will be $2^{4-8-8}(= 2^{-12})$ after filtered by the undetermined bits in Δ_0 and Δ_{13}. As discussed in Sect. 3.6.1, there are at least 16 right pairs remaining after 12th round. These right pairs will be used for key guessing and a key with the highest counter value will be the correct key.

3.6.3   Complexity

There are 2^n structures and 2^8 pairs(fixing the undetermined bits in Δ_0) can be generated for each structure. As discussed in Sect. 3.6.2, we need 2^{32} pairs to get 2^4 right pairs. Therefore, we choose n(=24) structure and the data complexity of the 13-round related-key differential attack on PIPO-64/128 becomes $2^{24+8}(= 2^{32})$. We need to store the counters corresponding to 16 bits of the key, so the memory complexity of the attack becomes 2^{16}. In the first round, for each of the 2^4 pairs, we need to guess the 12 bits of the key corresponding to the active S-box. Therefore, time complexity of the first round becomes $2^{4+12}(= 2^{16})$. Similarly time complexity of the 13th round is $2^{4+4}(= 2^8)$ because four bits of the key are already guessed in the first round. Hence, the time complexity of the whole attack is bounded by the 2^{32} chosen plaintexts.

---

[6] In this calculation, we consider a pair (a, b) same as (b, a).

4   Conclusion

In this paper, we have presented the approaches to construct the linear inequalities corresponding to the DDT of 8-bit S-boxes. These inequalities are used to minimize the number of active S-boxes in PIPO-64/128. The experimental results indicate that there is no significant difference in the time complexity to solve the MILP models with a smaller set of linear inequalities. Therefore, we have used full DDT to construct a simplified MILP model for probability optimization instead of using the existing pb-DDT approach. The linear inequalities corresponding to the full DDT of PIPO-64/128 are constructed using the MILES tool. These linear inequalities are used to model the MILP problem for searching the differential, impossible differential and related-key differential characteristics. We have presented the full-round related-key differential distinguisher and a key recovery attack on full-round PIPO-64/128 with 2^{32} data complexity. We have also presented several collisions in the plaintext and ciphertext using different keys.

Appendix

A $C = E(P, K) = E(P, K')$ where $K' = K \oplus \Delta K$
$K = $ 0x6DC416DD779428D27E1D20AD2E152297
$\Delta K = $ 0x0040000801001000002000002000000

No.	Plaintext (P)	Ciphertext (C)
1	0xFFEAF697D7FCE742	0xCDE57DF09ECF4F7D
2	0xFCFFE1E57B3EE1B0	0x964DFE673B256413
3	0xFE9DAF4B7CDF3C62	0x5A204F91F5B3BEE2
4	0xBFE622F4EDF3FF2A	0x2C41558C8D728AD0
5	0xE7FFA8E4E8F95AF5	0xEB10BDFF059CF6A0
6	0xBDFDE7BAFFF6E73E	0x009AEE178347B174
7	0x7FFB2EFE657B19E7	0xD387F51CC4D0755A
8	0x2FF9393C75FB73F1	0x46B43D51ABE5146D
9	0x6EFE60A8EFFF5F2F	0x4F687CEC564569ED
10	0xF8EFFEB4EFFC9A70	0x923B7FDBAE0812CC
11	0xFD976646A1A3B40C	0xC433269EE6751443
12	0x6FF431B77B748CB5	0x5041B64C120B2673
13	0xE3EBED217F6FEB3F	0x56072F13AA0DB152
14	0xE35BF593EB9D32F0	0x1046EFDED93A860F
15	0xFFF76DCC8F77FA1B	0x73D7C7FFE4A78EF6
16	0x77FF282B3F7F8121	0xAD7D75F547410892
17	0x3E6FAB372BFB5F23	0x17C097CDE69D86BA
18	0xEFFABDB4F6F7032E	0x98731593F9EFC0D7
19	0x75926BBA4F77726F	0xDF4974E78B9FEC13
20	0xEBE465797D6BAD63	0x7432FC827038315B

B   MILES: MInimized Linear inEqualities for Large S-Boxes

We present expresso based tool MILES to generate the linear inequalities for larges S-boxes and this tool is based on the Espresso algorithm [12]. The S-box is given as an input to the tool and it outputs a minimized set of linear inequalities that is required to model the MILP problem. MILES is the first tool that uses the full DDT of 8-bit S-box to generate the linear inequalities. In MILES, there are four processes which are applied sequentially to generate the minimized linear inequalities. These process are described as follows:

1. **DDT generation.** In this process, MILES takes m-bit S-box ($m{\geq}3$) as input and generates a DDT of the S-box. The DDT ($2^m \times 2^m$) is 2-Dimensional array where row indices (y-axis) define input difference while column indices (x-axis) define the output difference. We define a function $f_{i,j}$ to represent the DDT of S-box which provides the number of occurrences of output difference Δ_j corresponding to input difference Δ_i (Eq. 1).

$$f_{i,j} = Frequency_{\Delta_i \to \Delta_j} \text{where } 0 \leq i,j \leq m \qquad (4)$$

   This DDT is used as an input in the next process.

2. **DDT to truth table conversion.** In this process, the input DDT is converted into a truth table. This truth table specifies the input and output points of the DDT as input variables. To simplify it, we specify only non-zero entries of the DDT and corresponding output variable as 1. MILES can generate three kinds of truth tables ($\star$-TT,p-TT,f-TT) from the DDT. The $\star$-TT table corresponds to the non-zero entries in the DDT and p-TT corresponds to the non-zero entries in DDT for a specific probability (p). The f-TT table corresponds to the non-zero entries with extra input variable for each probability.

3. **Truth table minimization.** MILES interfaces with Espresso to perform minimization of the truth table. The output of minimization is TT_{min} which is used to generate the minimized linear inequalities. The TT_{min} is similar to the truth table and it contains an additional symbol ('−'). The output variable in TT_{min} is independent of input variable corresponding to this additional symbol. The minimization process can be performed with various modes available in Espresso algorithm. These options are chosen in MILES as minimization strategy. These strategies are problem specific and a particular strategy may not provide best solution for all problems. The minimized truth tables corresponding to $\star$-TT, p-TT, and f-TT are represented as $\star$-TT_{min}, p-TT_{min}, and f-TT_{min} respectively.

4. **Linear inequalities generation.** After minimization process, MILES generate the linear inequalities. Each linear inequality corresponds to one entry in TT_{min}. If a value in the entry is 0 then it is expressed as variable x and if it is 1 then it is expressed as $1 - x$. The value '−' in the TT_{min} does not contribute in the inequality generation process.

C   Example: Linear Inequalities Generation using MILES

We describe the process to generate the linear inequalities for a 3-bit S-box (Table 12). The DDT (Table 13), f-TT (Table 14), and f-TT$_{min}$ (Table 15) are generated using MILES. The set of minimized linear inequalities for this S-box is given in Table 16.

Table 12. 3-bit S-box

x	0	1	2	3	4	5	6	7
S(x)	3	6	5	7	0	2	4	1

Table 13. DDT of S-box

	0	1	2	3	4	5	6	7
0	8	0	0	0	0	0	0	0
1	0	0	4	0	0	4	0	0
2	0	2	0	2	2	0	2	0
3	0	2	0	2	2	0	2	0
4	0	2	0	2	2	0	2	0
5	0	2	0	2	2	0	2	0
6	0	0	0	0	0	4	0	4
7	0	0	4	0	0	0	0	4

Table 14. f-TT of DDT

x_1	x_2	x_3	y_1	y_2	y_3	p_1	p_2	f
0	0	0	0	0	0	0	0	1
0	0	1	0	1	0	1	0	1
0	0	1	1	0	1	1	0	1
0	1	0	0	0	1	0	1	1
0	1	0	0	1	1	0	1	1
0	1	0	1	0	0	0	1	1
0	1	0	1	1	0	0	1	1
0	1	1	0	0	1	0	1	1
0	1	1	0	1	1	0	1	1
0	1	1	1	0	0	0	1	1
0	1	1	1	1	0	0	1	1
1	0	0	0	0	1	0	1	1
1	0	0	0	1	1	0	1	1
1	0	0	1	0	0	0	1	1
1	0	0	1	1	0	0	1	1
1	0	1	0	0	1	0	1	1
1	0	1	0	1	1	0	1	1
1	0	1	1	0	0	0	1	1
1	0	1	1	1	0	0	1	1
1	1	0	1	0	1	1	0	1
1	1	0	1	1	1	1	0	1
1	1	1	0	1	0	1	0	1
1	1	1	1	1	1	1	0	1

Table 15. f-TT$_{min}$ for f-TT

x_1	x_2	x_3	y_1	y_2	y_3	p_1	p_2	f
0	0	1	0	1	0	1	0	1
0	0	1	1	0	1	1	0	1
1	1	1	0	1	0	1	0	1
1	1	0	1	-	1	1	0	1
1	1	-	1	1	1	1	0	1
0	0	0	0	0	0	0	0	1
1	0	-	1	-	0	0	1	1
0	1	-	1	-	0	0	1	1
1	0	-	0	-	1	0	1	1
0	1	-	0	-	1	0	1	1

Table 16. Linear inequalities generated from f-TT_{min}

1	$x_1 + x_2 - x_3 + y_1 - y_2 + y_3 - p_1 + p_2 + 2 \geq 0$
2	$x_1 + x_2 - x_3 - y_1 + y_2 - y_3 - p_1 + p_2 + 3 \geq 0$
3	$-x_1 - x_2 - x_3 + y_1 - y_2 + y_3 - p_1 + p_2 + 4 \geq 0$
4	$-x_1 - x_2 + x_3 - y_1 - y_3 - p_1 + p_2 + 4 \geq 0$
5	$-x_1 - x_2 - y_1 - y_2 - y_3 - p_1 + p_2 + 5 \geq 0$
6	$x_1 + x_2 + x_3 + y_1 + y_2 + y_3 + p_1 + p_2 - 1 \geq 0$
7	$-x_1 + x_2 - y_1 + y_3 + p_1 - p_2 + 2 \geq 0$
8	$x_1 - x_2 - y_1 + y_3 + p_1 - p_2 + 2 \geq 0$
9	$-x_1 + x_2 + y_1 - y_3 + p_1 - p_2 + 2 \geq 0$
10	$x_1 - x_2 + y_1 - y_3 + p_1 - p_2 + 2 \geq 0$

References

1. Abdelkhalek, A., Sasaki, Y., Todo, Y., Tolba, M., Youssef, A.M.: MILP modeling for (large) S-boxes to optimize probability of differential characteristics. IACR Trans. Symmetric Cryptol. **2017**(4), 99–129 (2017). ISSN 2519-173X, https://doi.org/10.13154/tosc.v2017.i4.99-129

2. Biham, E.: New types of cryptanalytic attacks using related keys. J. Cryptol. **7**(4), 229–246 (1994). https://doi.org/10.1007/BF00203965

3. Biham, E., Biryukov, A., Shamir, A.: Cryptanalysis of skipjack reduced to 31 rounds using impossible differentials. In: Stern, J. (ed.) EUROCRYPT 1999. LNCS, vol. 1592, pp. 12–23. Springer, Heidelberg (1999). https://doi.org/10.1007/3-540-48910-X_2

4. Biham, E., Shamir, A.: Differential cryptanalysis of DES-like Cryptosystems. J. Cryptol. **4**, 3–72 (1991). Springer

5. Biham, E., Shamir, A.: Differential cryptanalysis of the full 16-round DES. In: Brickell, E.F. (ed.) CRYPTO 1992. LNCS, vol. 740, pp. 487–496. Springer, Heidelberg (1993). https://doi.org/10.1007/3-540-48071-4_34

6. Bogdanov, A.: Analysis and design of block cipher constructions. Ph.D. thesis (2009)

7. Bogdanov, A., et al.: PRESENT: an ultra-lightweight block cipher. In: Paillier, P., Verbauwhede, I. (eds.) CHES 2007. LNCS, vol. 4727, pp. 450–466. Springer, Heidelberg (2007). https://doi.org/10.1007/978-3-540-74735-2_31

8. Boura, C., Coggia, D.: Efficient MILP modelings for S-boxes and linear layers of SPN ciphers. IACR Trans. Symmetric Cryptol. **3**, 327–361 (2020)

9. Beierle, C., et al.: The SKINNY family of block ciphers and its low-latency variant MANTIS. In: Robshaw, M., Katz, J. (eds.) CRYPTO 2016. LNCS, vol. 9815, pp. 123–153. Springer, Heidelberg (2016). https://doi.org/10.1007/978-3-662-53008-5_5

10. 'CryptoMiniSat5'. https://www.msoos.org/cryptominisat5

11. IBM ILOG: IBM ILOG CPLEX Optimization Studio V12.7.0 documentation (2016). Official webpage https://www-01.ibm.com/software/websphere/products/optimization/cplex-studio-community-edition/

12. Espresso Logic Minimizer. https://ptolemy.berkeley.edu/projects/embedded/pubs/downloads/espresso/

13. Gerault, D., Lafourcade, P., Minier, M., Solnon, C.: Revisiting AES related-key differential attacks with constraint programming. Cryptology ePrint Archive (2017)
14. Gohr, A.: Improving attacks on round-reduced Speck32/64 using deep learning. In: Boldyreva, A., Micciancio, D. (eds.) CRYPTO 2019. LNCS, vol. 11693, pp. 150–179. Springer, Cham (2019). https://doi.org/10.1007/978-3-030-26951-7_6
15. Gurobi Optimizer 7.5.2. https://www.gurobi.com
16. Hays, H.M.: A Tutorial on linear and differential cryptanalysis. Cryptologia **26**(3), 188–221 (2002)
17. Kim, H., Jeon, Y., Kim, G., Kim, J., Sim, B.-Y., Han, D.-G., Seo, H., Kim, S., Hong, S., Sung, J., Hong, D.: PIPO: a lightweight block cipher with efficient higher-order masking software implementations. In: Hong, D. (ed.) ICISC 2020. LNCS, vol. 12593, pp. 99–122. Springer, Cham (2021). https://doi.org/10.1007/978-3-030-68890-5_6
18. Knudsen, L., Robshaw, M.J.B.: Block Cipher Companion. Springer, Heidelberg (2011). ISBN 978-3-642-17341-7. https://doi.org/10.1007/978-3-642-17342-4
19. Kumar, M., Suresh, T.S., Pal, S.K., Panigrahi, A.: Optimal differential trails in lightweight block ciphers ANU and PICO. Cryptologia **44**(1), 68–78 (2020)
20. Kumar, M., Yadav, T.: MILP based differential attack on round reduced WARP. In: Batina, L., Picek, S., Mondal, M. (eds.) SPACE 2021. LNCS, vol. 13162, pp. 42–59. Springer, Cham (2022). https://doi.org/10.1007/978-3-030-95085-9_3
21. Kelsey, J., Schneier, B., Wagner, D.: Related-key cryptanalysis of 3-WAY, Biham-DES,CAST, DES-X, NewDES, RC2, and TEA. In: Han, Y., Okamoto, T., Qing, S. (eds.) ICICS 1997. LNCS, vol. 1334, pp. 233–246. Springer, Heidelberg (1997). https://doi.org/10.1007/BFb0028479
22. Logic Friday. https://sontrak.com/
23. Matsui, M.: On correlation between the order of S-boxes and the strength of DES. In: De Santis, A. (ed.) EUROCRYPT 1994. LNCS, vol. 950, pp. 366–375. Springer, Heidelberg (1995). https://doi.org/10.1007/BFb0053451
24. Mouha, N., Wang, Q., Gu, D., Preneel, B.: Differential and linear cryptanalysis using mixed-integer linear programming. In: Wu, C.-K., Yung, M., Lin, D. (eds.) Inscrypt 2011. LNCS, vol. 7537, pp. 57–76. Springer, Heidelberg (2012). https://doi.org/10.1007/978-3-642-34704-7_5
25. National Institute of Standards and Technology: Lightweight Cryptography, Finalists. NIST (2021). https://csrc.nist.gov/projects/lightweight-cryptography/finalists
26. National Institute of Standards and Technology: Federal Information Processing Standards Publication 197: Advanced Encryption Standard (AES). NIST (2001)
27. Sun, S., Hu, L., Wang, P., Qiao, K., Ma, X., Song, L.: Automatic security evaluation and (related-key) differential characteristic search: application to SIMON, PRESENT, LBlock, DES(L) and other bit-oriented block ciphers. In: Sarkar, P., Iwata, T. (eds.) ASIACRYPT 2014. LNCS, vol. 8873, pp. 158–178. Springer, Heidelberg (2014). https://doi.org/10.1007/978-3-662-45611-8_9
28. Sun, S., Hu, L., et al.: Towards finding the best characteristics of some bit-oriented block ciphers and automatic enumeration of (related-key) differential and linear characteristics with predefined properties. Cryptology ePrint Archive, Report 2014/747 (2014)
29. SAGE. https://www.sagemath.org/index.html
30. Sasaki, Yu., Todo, Y.: New differential bounds and division property of LILLIPUT: block cipher with extended generalized feistel network. In: Avanzi, R., Heys, H. (eds.) SAC 2016. LNCS, vol. 10532, pp. 264–283. Springer, Cham (2017). https://doi.org/10.1007/978-3-319-69453-5_15

31. Sasaki, Yu., Todo, Y.: New impossible differential search tool from design and cryptanalysis aspects. In: Coron, J.-S., Nielsen, J.B. (eds.) EUROCRYPT 2017. LNCS, vol. 10212, pp. 185–215. Springer, Cham (2017). https://doi.org/10.1007/978-3-319-56617-7_7

32. Sasaki, Yu., Todo, Y.: New algorithm for modeling S-box in MILP based differential and division trail search. In: Farshim, P., Simion, E. (eds.) SecITC 2017. LNCS, vol. 10543, pp. 150–165. Springer, Cham (2017). https://doi.org/10.1007/978-3-319-69284-5_11

33. Sun, S., et al.: Analysis of AES, SKINNY, and others with constraint programming. IACR Trans. Symmetric Cryptol. 1, 281–306 (2017)

34. Yadav, T., Kumar, M.: Differential-ML distinguisher: machine learning based generic extension for differential cryptanalysis. In: Longa, P., Ràfols, C. (eds.) LAT-INCRYPT 2021. LNCS, vol. 12912, pp. 191–212. Springer, Cham (2021). https://doi.org/10.1007/978-3-030-88238-9_10

35. Zhu, B., Dong, X., Yu, H.: MILP-based differential attack on round-reduced GIFT. In: Matsui, M. (ed.) CT-RSA 2019. LNCS, vol. 11405, pp. 372–390. Springer, Cham (2019). https://doi.org/10.1007/978-3-030-12612-4_19

Light but Tight: Lightweight Composition of Serialized S-Boxes with Diffusion Layers for Strong Ciphers

Rajat Sadhukhan[1]([✉]), Anirban Chakraborty[1], Nilanjan Datta[2],
Sikhar Patranabis[3], and Debdeep Mukhopadhyay[1]

[1] Indian Institute of Technology Kharagpur, Kharagpur, India
rajatssr835@gmail.com
[2] IAI, TCG Crest, Kolkata, India
[3] IBM Research India, Bengaluru, India

Abstract. The widespread advent of the Internet-of-Things has motivated new design strategies for lightweight block ciphers. In particular, security against traditional cryptanalysis should ideally be complemented by resistance to side-channel attacks, while adhering to low area and power requirements. In FSE 2018, Ghoshal et al. proposed a dedicated design strategy based upon Cellular Automata (CA) for S-Boxes that are amenable to side-channel secure threshold implementations. However, CA-based S-Boxes have some limitations concerning the absence of BOGI properties and low branch numbers making them vulnerable to classical cryptanalysis attacks. In this paper, we address the vulnerabilities of these weak S-Boxes by complementing them with an ultra-lightweight linear layer and subsequently building (Light but Tight) LbT - the *area-efficient* and *side-channel resilient* family of block ciphers. This *super-optimal* cellular automata (CA)-rule-based S-Box layer is appropriately complemented with a linear layer consisting of shuffle cells and matrix multiplication with an *ultra-lightweight almost-MDS matrix with only 6-XOR gates*. This ensures high diffusion at the cost of a minimal area overhead. Hence, we show that these vulnerable S-Boxes are not weak but when complemented appropriately with proper linear layer can lead to cryptographically strong as well as lightweight cipher design. *Overall, the TI-protected circuit of LbT requires an area footprint of only 3063 GE, which is 12% lower than any first-order side-channel protected implementation among all of the existing lightweight block ciphers. Finally, we illustrate that LbT-64-128 obtains a reasonable throughput when compared to other lightweight block ciphers.*

Keywords: Block cipher · Lightweight · Side channel resistance · Cellular automata · Threshold implementation

1 Introduction

The advent of ubiquitous computing and the Internet of Things (IoT) has resulted in billions of interconnected devices exchanging (potentially sensitive)

L. Batina et al. (Eds.): SPACE 2022, LNCS 13783, pp. 28–49, 2022.
https://doi.org/10.1007/978-3-031-22829-2_2

messages over the network. This presents security researchers with the unique challenge of enabling data protection and secure communication in devices that are extremely resource-constrained. These devices are practically incapable of supporting heavy cryptographic machinery, including even widely used symmetric-key algorithms such as AES-128 [1] and the SHA family of hash functions [29].

Lightweight Cryptography. The need for secure yet low area and power overhead computing has motivated *lightweight cryptography* - a branch of cryptography that is specially dedicated to designing cryptographic algorithms with extremely efficient implementations, yet with the same level of security as traditional cryptographic algorithms. This presents significant theoretical and engineering challenges, since the designer is significantly more constrained as compared to the attacker, who continues to be all-powerful (albeit within the realm of probabilistic polynomial-time computation).

The efficiency of a cryptographic implementation is typically measured in terms of parameters such as area footprint, power, energy requirements, and throughput. An "ideal" lightweight cryptographic algorithm should allow for an implementation that is resource-efficient, concerning all these parameters, but this is usually non-trivial to achieve. In most cases, depending on the target application, a reasonable trade-off between the various parameters is aimed for; often with special emphasis on ensuring low area and low energy requirements [3].

The study of lightweight cryptography has received a significant impetus with the announcement of a lightweight cryptography project by NIST [24]. In recent years, a number of lightweight symmetric-key cryptographic algorithms have been proposed, and analyzed including (but not limited to) block ciphers [5,8, 13], hash functions [12,26], and specialized modes for lightweight authenticated encryption [36].

Implementation-Level Attacks and Countermeasures. Implementation-level attacks on crypto primitives, such as side-channel analysis attacks [31] and fault injection analysis attacks [38], constitute a major threat to the security of real-world systems. The threat is observed even when the underlying cryptographic algorithms are (provably or heuristically) secure against known cryptanalytic techniques. This threat is further amplified with the increased deployment of lightweight cryptography to protect ubiquitous computing, since a multitude of physically accessible inter-connected devices in the wild offer numerous implementation-level attack avenues.

There are many possible strategies to protect cryptographic implementations against side-channel and fault injection attacks. The most popularly deployed one today is an "after-thought"-style strategy, where the initial focus is purely on designing a cryptographic algorithm, ensuring security against "black-box" cryptographic analysis. In this approach, protection against side-channel and fault analysis is only achieved via additional implementation-level reinforcements/countermeasures, which are incorporated on top of the original algorithm, e.g., constant-time implementations, masked/threshold implementations [10,33, 37], and redundancy/error-correcting code-based implementations [40,41]).

However, this approach has its drawbacks. In particular, the ad-hoc incorporation of countermeasures into existing cryptographic implementations often leads to designs that are highly area and/or power-consuming. For example, initial studies on masked/threshold implementations of block cipher components, such as S-Boxes, reveal a significant blow-up in area footprint and power/energy consumption [27]. The same holds for generic implementations with redundancy and error-correcting codes [30].

As a concrete example, consider the lightweight block cipher GIFT-128-128 (with 128-bit block size and 128-bit key size) proposed in [5]. In its vanilla form, GIFT is significantly more lightweight as compared to AES-128. However, a naïvely engineered end-to-end threshold implementation of GIFT has a greater area footprint in hardware ((16170 GE as per [27]) as compared to AES ((14872 GE as per [19]). This clearly illustrates the fact that ad-hoc imposition of generic countermeasures on top of cryptographic algorithms can be counterproductive in lightweight applications.

1.1 Related Work

Over the past few years, since the announcement of the NIST competition, "specialized design"-based strategy for achieving cryptographic implementations that are protected against side-channel and fault attacks have gained a lot of impetus. For instance, in [42], the authors have proposed an Authenticated Encryption called FRIET with integrated fault detection scheme. A collection of lightweight S-Boxes having low AND-depth and AND-gate count, that are easier to mask, have been proposed in [11]. The authors in [2,9,17,20] proposed cipher implementations with built-in low-cost side channel attack countermeasures. In [22], Ghoshal et al. demonstrated a dedicated design strategy based upon Cellular Automata (CA) for S-Boxes, that are amenable to side-channel secure threshold implementations. They proposed highly optimized TI circuits for such S-Boxes, that consume nearly 40% less area and power as compared to popular S-Boxes such as PRESENT and GIFT. However, a major issue with all of the CA-derived S-Boxes is that they have fixed-points and do not exhibit BOGI (Bad Output must go to Good Input) [5] property; hence prone to various types of classical cryptanalytic attacks. A prominent example of such a case is observed in the case of NIST LWC candidate, TRIFLE[1]. Even though the structure of TRIFLE AEAD scheme resisted standard cryptanalytic attacks, certain inherent weaknesses in the CA-derived S-Boxes made the structure prone to classical cryptanalytic attacks [28]. Hence, in this work our main focus is to make CA-based S-Boxes resistive against classical cryptanalysis attacks by complementing it with appropriate diffusion layer and constitute an alternative to these approaches.

1.2 Our Contributions

In this work, we first propose a lightweight diffusion layer having a high branch number that strengthens the weakness of CA-based S-Boxes and resists classical

---

[1] https://csrc.nist.gov/CSRC/media/Projects/Lightweight-Cryptography/document s/round-1/spec-doc/trifle-spec.pdf.

cryptanalytic attacks. Then we propose a complete *area-efficient* and *side-channel resilient* family of block ciphers, called LbT. These block ciphers protected with *composite-TI* [22] employ substitution-permutation networks (SPN) with cellular automata (CA)-rule-based substitution boxes (S-Boxes), that is combined with the specially crafted *ultra-lightweight* almost-MDS matrix.

Area-Efficient CA-derived S-Boxes. It is typical of lightweight block ciphers to have 4×4 S-Boxes to minimize area footprint. Hence, for our LbT-64-128 cipher family, we build on an approach introduced by Ghoshal *et al.* in [22] that proposes lightweight S-Boxes from cellular automata (CA) rules. Our key contribution lies in identifying how such S-Boxes can be efficiently yet securely combined with a similarly lightweight and side-channel linear layer to achieve adequate resistance against popular cryptanalytic attacks. To see why this is a challenge, consider the space of all cryptographically optimal 4×4 S-Boxes that can be derived using CA rules. As reported in [22], all CA-derived S-Boxes have a branch number as small as 2. In addition, they do not exhibit highly specialized properties such as BOGI (Bad Output must go to Good Input) that S-Boxes in other block ciphers such as GIFT imply [5]. This leads us to the following question, which we investigate in this paper: *How do we combine CA-derived S-Boxes with a lightweight linear layer to achieve high linear and differential characteristics in reasonably many rounds?* This question has not been studied in the lightweight cryptography literature to the best of our knowledge (even without focus on side-channel resistance).

Super-Optimal S-Boxes and Almost-MDS Linear Layers. To address this question, we start with *super-optimal* class of S-Boxes proposed in TRIFLE. Intuitively, a super-optimal S-Box allows $1 - 1$ differential and linear transitions, while *simultaneously* ensuring that the probabilities for these $1 - 1$ transitions are *significantly lower* than the differential (respectively, linear) characteristic of the S-Box. An example of such S-Box having *difference distribution table* (DDT) is shown in Fig. 1(a), where Δ_{in} and Δ_{out} is the input and output difference respectively. The numbers marked in red are the number of $1 - 1$ transitions. A quick check on the DDT table shows that there exists 4 Hamming weight 1 differential transitions, namely $1 \to 2$, $2 \to 4$, $4 \to 8$, $8 \to 1$. In other words, regardless of the position of the single active bit input, there always exists a single active bit output. Now, since these super optimal S-Boxes exhibit $1-1$ differential and linear transitions, it can lead to long $1 - 1$ differential and linear trails as shown in Fig. 1(b). Moreover, there exists a possibility of keyless decryption, as shown in Fig. 1(c), where 2 of the 4 S-Boxes (red and blue) in the previous round of cipher is not masked by any key material. *We can readily combine such S-Boxes with a carefully chosen lightweight almost-MDS linear layer to achieve the desired linear and differential characteristic within a reasonable number of rounds along with mitigating keyless decryption. The linear layer in the case of our construction only takes 6-XOR gates.*

Optimal State-Permutation and Round Constant. Next, we propose the state-permutation and set of round constants for our LbT-64-128 cipher family. We choose a state-permutation and a minimal set of round constants such that

$\Delta_{in} \rightarrow$ / $\Delta_{out} \downarrow$	0	1	2	3	4	5	6	7	8	9	A	B	C	D	E	F
0	16	0	0	0	0	0	0	0	0	0	0	0	0	0	0	0
1	0	0	2	2	0	0	2	2	0	2	2	0	0	2	2	0
2	0	0	0	2	2	2	2	0	0	0	0	2	2	2	2	0
3	0	0	0	0	2	0	2	0	4	0	2	2	0	2	2	0
4	0	0	0	0	0	0	2	2	2	2	2	2	2	2	0	0
5	0	0	0	2	0	4	0	2	0	0	2	0	2	2	0	2
6	0	4	0	0	0	2	0	2	2	0	0	2	2	2	0	0
7	0	4	2	2	0	0	4	0	0	0	0	0	0	0	2	2
8	0	2	0	2	0	2	0	2	0	2	0	2	2	0	2	0
9	0	0	2	2	4	2	0	2	0	0	0	0	0	2	2	0
A	0	0	0	0	0	2	2	0	0	2	4	2	0	0	2	2
B	0	2	0	4	0	0	0	2	4	2	0	0	0	0	0	2
C	0	2	4	0	0	0	0	2	0	2	2	2	2	0	0	2
D	0	0	0	0	4	0	0	0	2	4	0	2	2	0	0	2
E	0	0	4	0	2	0	2	0	0	0	0	0	4	2	0	2
F	0	2	2	0	2	2	0	0	2	0	2	0	0	0	0	4

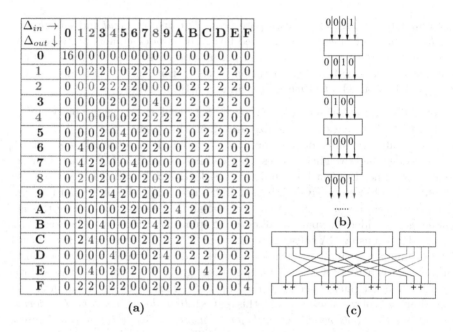

(a)   (b)   (c)

Fig. 1. (a) S-Box DDT (b) long $1-1$ differential characteristic (c) key-less decryption ('+' denotes key XOR in that branch)

optimal diffusion can be achieved in four rounds, together with a good margin of security against a special class of attacks called *invariant subspace attacks* [32]. This class of attack mainly arises due to presence of fixed points in an S-Box. In our work we show that proper choice of round constants ensures that *presence of fixed points is not a serious cryptanalytic issue*.

Side-Channel Resistance via *composite-TI*. Finally, we demonstrate that our LbT-64-128 cipher family is highly amenable to side-channel secure implementations. More specifically, we show that any LbT-64-128 block cipher instance can be protected against side-channel attacks using a highly area-efficient *composite-TI* implementation. We use *composite-TI* implementation technique proposed in [22], that allows for highly optimized TI designs of CA rules, in comparison to direct sharing techniques. We establish the side-channel resistance of this implementation via test vector leakage assessment (TVLA) over 100K leakage samples.

2   *Ultra-lightweight* Almost-MDS Matrix

In this section, we construct an ultra-lightweight diffusion layer to complement a CA-based S-Box, in order to make it robust against classical cryptanalytic attacks. A 4×4 CA-based S-Box consist of a demux, cyclic shifter and a CA-rule implementation [22]. At every clock cycle, the input bits are cyclically rotated and CA-rule is iterated to generate 1-bit of S-Box output. Hence, in four clock cycles, 4-bits of S-Box output is produced. Let $[X_0 X_1 X_2 X_3]^T$ represent 4-nibble state matrix where $X_i \in \mathbb{F}_2^4$ ($0 \leq i \leq 3$) and each X_i consist of 4-bits $[x_{i3}, x_{i2}, x_{i1}, x_{i0}]$ where x_{i0} and x_{i3} represents LSB and MSB respectively. Let S_i ($0 \leq i \leq 3$) define 4×4 S-Boxes defined by CA-rule f_i ($0 \leq i \leq 3$) such that

$$S_i(X_i) = S_i([x_{i3}, x_{i2}, x_{i1}, x_{i0}]) = Y_i = [y_{i3}, y_{i2}, y_{i1}, y_{i0}]$$

where Y_i is formed as

$$[y_{i3}, y_{i2}, y_{i1}, y_{i0}]$$
$$= [f_i(x_{i3}, x_{i2}, x_{i1}, x_{i0}), f_i(x_{i0}, x_{i3}, x_{i2}, x_{i1}), f_i(x_{i1}, x_{i0}, x_{i3}, x_{i2}), f_i(x_{i2}, x_{i1}, x_{i0}, x_{i3})]$$

Similarly, $[Y_0 Y_1 Y_2 Y_3]^T$ represents a 4-nibble state matrix where $Y_i \in \mathbb{F}_2^4$ ($0 \leq i \leq 3$) and each Y_i consist of 4-bits $(y_{i3}, y_{i2}, y_{i1}, y_{i0})$ where y_{i0} and y_{i3} represents LSB and MSB respectively. The product of circulant matrix $circ(0, 1, 1, 1)$ (represented as M), defined over $\mathbb{F}_2^4$, with state matrix $[Y_0 Y_1 Y_2 Y_3]^T$ can be expressed as follows where $+$ denotes $\mathbb{F}_2^4$ addition:

$$M([Y_0 Y_1 Y_2 Y_3]^T) = \begin{bmatrix} 0 & 1 & 1 & 1 \\ 1 & 0 & 1 & 1 \\ 1 & 1 & 0 & 1 \\ 1 & 1 & 1 & 0 \end{bmatrix} \begin{bmatrix} Y_0 \\ Y_1 \\ Y_2 \\ Y_3 \end{bmatrix} = \begin{bmatrix} Y_1 + Y_2 + Y_3 \\ Y_0 + Y_2 + Y_3 \\ Y_0 + Y_1 + Y_3 \\ Y_0 + Y_1 + Y_2 \end{bmatrix} = \begin{bmatrix} Y_0 + Y_1 + Y_2 + Y_3 + Y_0 \\ Y_0 + Y_1 + Y_2 + Y_3 + Y_1 \\ Y_0 + Y_1 + Y_2 + Y_3 + Y_2 \\ Y_0 + Y_1 + Y_2 + Y_3 + Y_3 \end{bmatrix}$$

$$= \begin{bmatrix} (s_3 + y_{03}, s_2 + y_{02}, s_1 + y_{01}, s_0 + y_{00}) \\ (s_3 + y_{13}, s_2 + y_{12}, s_1 + y_{11}, s_0 + y_{10}) \\ (s_3 + y_{23}, s_2 + y_{22}, s_1 + y_{21}, s_0 + y_{20}) \\ (s_3 + y_{33}, s_2 + y_{32}, s_1 + y_{31}, s_0 + y_{30}) \end{bmatrix}$$

where $s_0 = y_{00} + y_{10} + y_{20} + y_{30}$, $s_1 = y_{01} + y_{11} + y_{21} + y_{31}$, $s_2 = y_{02} + y_{12} + y_{22} + y_{32}$ and $s_3 = y_{03} + y_{13} + y_{23} + y_{33}$. This M layer has branch number 4 and is also used as a diffusion layer in MIDORI [4]. As the CA-rule is iterated while input bits are cyclically shifted to generate the S-Box outputs, this M layer multiplication can also be achieved simultaneously, as shown in Fig. 2, with only 6 XOR-gates. The bits generated at cycle 1, cycle 2, cycle 3, and cycle 4 are denoted by red, blue, green, and brown colored fonts respectively. In our circuit, we prefer to use one 3 input XOR-gate and one 2 input XOR-gate to generate s_i bit, rather than three 2 input XOR-gates. This preference is based on the recommendation in [4] that points out that in most of the standard cell libraries, the area footprint of two 2 input XOR-gate is greater than one 3 input XOR-gate. Hence a combined usage of 2 and 3 input XOR-gates during synthesis gives the most optimized area footprint. The comparison of hardware overhead of our linear layer construction with other lightweight linear layers is shown in Table 1. The critical path length and the overall area of the circuit, shown in Fig. 2, are compared with the setup where four LUT-based implementations of LbT S-Boxes are instantiated with the linear layer of MIDORI [4] and is given in Table 2. From the table, it can be seen that there is a saving of 10% area in the proposed setup when compared to LUT-based implementation. Another interesting point to be noted here is

Table 1. Hardware overhead comparison with other lightweight linear layers

Matrix	# 3-input xor Gate	# 2-input xor Gate
Ours	1	5
MIDORI [4]	16	4
PRINCE [4]	16	4
QARMA [4]	16	4
SKINNY [4]	12	0
Serial Matrix [39]	0	16

Table 2. Area, critical path length and clock-cycle requirement comparison for CA-based and LUT-based implementation (S-box + linear layer)

Implementation	Critical path length (ns)	Area (GE)	Clock cycle requirement
CA-Based	0.35	111.75	4
LUT-Based	1.28	124	1

that our proposed CA-based S-Box combined with the M layer takes lesser time to execute i.e. 0.35 ns, while for naive implementation it is 1.24 ns. Then the overall latency of our design is $0.35 \times 4 = 1.4$ ns (4 bits generated in 4 clock cycles) while that of naive implementation is 1.24 ns, thereby capping the overall increase in latency to just 9% but with 10% area saving. If a designer wants to develop an application that requires a very low area footprint and low latency at the same time, then our proposal with double clock architecture [39] is best suitable. We would like to point out that the lightweight bit-wise rotation trick is not applicable directly for the block cipher decryption. Note that the ordering of operations in case of decryption is $S(M(x))$, as compared to $M(S(x))$ in case of encryption. Since bits are generated serially, we might need an extra register for storing the bits which would make the circuit a bit costly in terms of hardware. In this regard, we would like to emphasise that our proposed design primarily targets inverse-free authenticated cipher modes. Note that an authenticated encryption is called inverse-free if both the encryption and the verified decryption algorithm do not invoke block-cipher inverse. This property is particularly useful for area-efficient lightweight AE designs, especially when both encryption and verified decryption are implemented in the same device. Note that most of block cipher based AEAD constructions targeting area-efficiency, proposed in the CAESAR or ongoing NIST LwC competition, such as SAEB [35], OTR [34], Sundae [6], COFB [15], HyENA [14], are inverse-free. Our proposed block cipher would be ideal for these authenticated cipher modes. In the next section, we discuss how to combine our proposed *lightweight* almost-MDS layer along with *super-optimal* S-Boxes to construct a cipher.

3   LbT-n-κ: Specification and Design Rationale

In this section, we propose LbT-n-κ, a family of n bit (where we assume $n = 64$) CA-based side-channel resistant block cipher with κ bit (we typically use $\kappa = 128$) key. It receives an n bit plaintext which can be viewed as $n/4$ many 4-bit nibbles, represented as $W = W_{n/4-1}\|W_{n/4-2}\|\cdots\|W_0$. Along with the plaintext, the cipher also receives a 128-bit key $K = K_7\|K_6\|\cdots\|K_0$ as the key state, where each K_i is a 16-bit word.

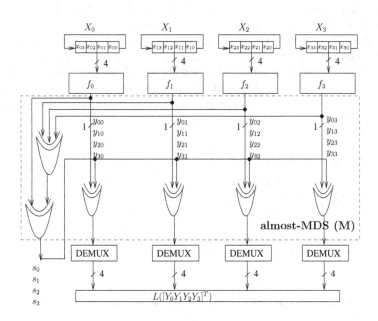

Fig. 2. Linear layer M augmented with CA-based S-Box layer.

3.1   Formal Specification of LbT-64-128

LbT-64-128 is composed of 18 rounds and each round is composed of the following operations:

SubCells. All the CA-based S-Boxes has branch number 2 and do not exhibit special properties such as BOGI. LbT uses an invertible CA-based super-optimal 4-bit S-Box from $(3, 2, 2)$ class as proposed in [22] and applies it to every nibble of the cipher state. Description of the S-Box is given in Table 3.

Table 3. The LbT S-Box [22].

x	0	1	2	3	4	5	6	7	8	9	A	B	C	D	E	F
$S(x)$	0	C	9	7	3	5	E	4	6	B	A	2	D	1	8	F

Table 4. The LbT-64 ShuffleCell P_{16}.

i	0	1	2	3	4	5	6	7	8	9	10	11	12	13	14	15
$P(i)$	5	10	15	0	9	14	3	4	13	2	7	8	1	6	11	12

MixColumn. A circulant matrix $circ(0,1,1,1)$ denoted as M defined over $\mathbb{F}_2^4$ is applied to each column of the state matrix for LbT-64-128 as:

$$[W_{i+3}W_{i+2}W_{i+1}W_{i+0}] = M \times [W_{i+3}W_{i+2}W_{i+1}W_{i+0}]^T \ and \ i = 0,4,8,12$$

Note that M, shown in Fig. 3b, is an almost-MDS matrix, and hence has the differential branch number 4.

ShuffleCell. LbT uses an optimal state permutation to create maximal diffusion and resistance against invariant subspace attack [32] with lesser number of round constants. This state mapping is presented in Table 4. Note that this permutation maps state position i of the cipher to state position $P(i)$.

AddRoundKey. In this step a 32 bit round key is extracted from the key state, and the round key is xored with $\{X_{4i}, X_{4i+1}\}_{i=0,\dots,15}$ of the cipher state. The round-keys are generated using a key scheduling algorithm which updates the key state at each round using some simple word-wise rotations and bit-wise rotations within a word. This key generation algorithm is similar to the one used in GIFT-64 [5].

Rounds	1	2	3	4	5	6	7	8	9
C_1	0	b	2	5	6	2	e	f	7
C_2	f	6	b	c	9	6	e	9	1
C_3	5	f	5	b	1	d	4	9	b
C_4	7	6	5	1	2	9	e	6	e
C_5	0	6	0	2	0	3	9	a	7

(a)

$$M = \begin{bmatrix} 0 & 1 & 1 & 1 \\ 1 & 0 & 1 & 1 \\ 1 & 1 & 0 & 1 \\ 1 & 1 & 1 & 0 \end{bmatrix}$$

(b)

Fig. 3. (a) LbT round constants (b) almost MDS matrix M

AddRoundConst. In this step a 5 many 4-bit round constants are generated as shown in Fig. 3a. The round constant C_5 is constructed from C_1, C_2, C_3 and C_4 and is given as:

$$C_5 = (C_1[0]\&C_2[0])\|(C_1[2]\&C_3[2])\|C_3[0]|C_4[0].$$

Recall that $C_i[0]$ and $C_i[3]$ denote the least significant bit and most significant bit of the nibble C_i respectively. The round constants are xored with the following 5 cipher state nibbles: $W_{11}, W_{12}, W_{13}, W_{14}, W_{15}$. The round constants for first 9 rounds are given. The round constants for round i is same as the round constants for round $(i-9)$ for any $i > 9$. Complete specification of LbT is presented in Algorithm 1.

3.2   Choice of the Linear Layer

As mentioned in previous sections that CA-based S-Boxes have branch number 2 and do not possess BOGI property, due to which there always exists a single long differential trail and at most one active S-Box per round of the cipher. The attacker can choose a high probability differential trail in the first round that propagates to a single active output bit with probability 2^{-2}. From the second round, having r such rounds the single bit differential trail holds with probability 2^{-3r}. Therefore, for $r + 1$-rounds, differential characteristic has a maximum differential probability of 2^{-2-3r} [28]. Therefore, with just a bit of state permutation, a designer cannot remove such trails or increase the number of active S-Boxes per round.

Use of Almost-MDS Matrix. To address the above-mentioned issue, there is a need to augment a linear layer with a branch number of at least ≥ 2. In our proposal, we express a circulant matrix $circ(0, 1, 1, 1)$ defined over $\mathbb{F}_2^4$ using a lightweight hardware trick as described in Sect. 2 such that the hardware equivalent of the expression when augmented to CA-rule blows up the overall branch number preserving the low area footprint of CA-based S-Box.

Choice of the Cell Permutation. The Cell-Permutation Layer is chosen accordingly to the Optimal Diffusion and Invariant Subspace Attack Resistance. We performed an exhaustive search to find an optimal cell permutation such that it satisfies the following two conditions:

1. A full diffusion is reached in 4 rounds.

Algorithm 1. LbT Block cipher Algorithm.

```
 1: function LbT-64(K, X)
 2:     for i = 1 to 18 do
 3:         X ← SubCells(X)
 4:         X ← MixColumn(X)
 5:         X ← ShuffleCell(X)
 6:         (K, X) ← AddRoundKey(K, X)
 7:         X ← AddRoundConst(C, i, X)
 8:     return X

 9: function SubCells(X)
10:     (X₁₅, ..., X₀) ←⁴ X
11:     for i = 0 to 15 do
12:         Xᵢ ← S-box(Xᵢ)
13:     return X

14: function MixColumn(X)
15:     (X₃, ..., X₀) ←¹⁶ X
16:     for i = 0 to 3 do
17:         Xᵢ ← M × (Xᵢ)
18:     return X

19: function ShuffleCell(X)
20:     (X₁₅, ..., X₀) ←⁴ X
21:     for i = 0 to 15 do
22:         X_P(i) ← Xᵢ
23:     return X
```

```
 1: function AddRoundKey(K, X)
 2:     (K₇, ..., K₀) ←¹⁶ K
 3:     (X₆₃, ..., X₀) ←¹ X
 4:     (U, V) ← (K₁, K₀)
 5:     (U₁₅, ..., U₀) ←¹ U
 6:     (V₁₅, ..., V₀) ←¹ V
 7:     for i = 0 to 15 do
 8:         j ← 4i
 9:         X_{j+1} ← X_{j+1} ⊕ Uᵢ
10:         Xⱼ ← Xⱼ ⊕ Vᵢ
11:     K₇‖···‖K₀ ← K₁^{≫2}‖K₀^{≫12}‖K₇‖···‖K₂
12:     return (K, X)

13: function AddRoundConstant(C, i, X)
14:     (C₅, ..., C₁) ←⁴ RoundConstant(C, i)
15:     (X₁₅, ..., X₀) ←⁴ X
16:     for i = 1 to 5 do
17:         X_{10+i} ← X_{10+i} ⊕ Cᵢ
18:     return X
```

2. Minimize the number of round constants required to resist the cipher against invariant subspace attack.

We undertake the row-based followed by column-based cell permutation search option and found the following state permutation is optimum and satisfies the above two conditions.

$$(s_0, s_1, \ldots, s_{15}) \leftarrow (s_5, s_{10}, s_{15}, s_0, s_9, s_{14}, s_3, s_4, s_{13}, s_2, s_7, s_8, s_1, s_6, s_{11}, s_{12}).$$

3.3 Choice of the Key Scheduling and Add Round Key Operations

The primary goal while designing the key schedule is to minimize the hardware area, and hence we chose bit permutation which essentially is the shuffling of wires and requires no hardware area at all. To make it software friendly, the entire key state rotation is done in blocks of 16-bits, and bit rotations within some 16-bit blocks. The key state blocks are updated only after it has been extracted as a round key, as otherwise, it becomes redundant. To have the effect of the entire key into the cipher state as fast as possible, the key state blocks that are extracted as the round key are chosen such that all the key materials are introduced into the cipher state in the least possible number of rounds.

We xor the round key to only half of the cipher state to optimize the hardware performance. This saves a significant amount of hardware area in a round-based implementation. To make it software friendly, we xor the round key at the same i-th bit positions of each nibble. This makes the bit-slice implementation more efficient. In addition, since all nibbles contain some key material, the entire state will be dependent on the key after a SubCells operation.

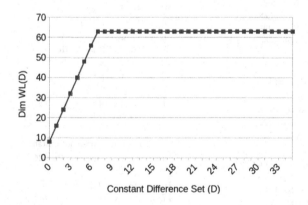

Fig. 4. Variation of Dim $W_L(D)$ with D for our cell permutation

3.4 Choice of the Round-Constants

Here we justify our choice for the round constants. Let $D = \{c_1, c_2, \ldots c_n\} \in \mathbb{F}_2^4$ be the set of xor differences between all possible round constants over the rounds under the same round key and $W_{DL}(D)$ denotes the smallest L-invariant subspace of $\mathbb{F}_2^4$ that contains all elements of D, where DL is the linear layer in matrix form. Then $W_{DL}(D)$ is given as:

$$W_{DL}(D) = \text{Dim}(\{DL^i * c \mid i \in \{0, 1, \ldots, M_o\} \text{ and } c \in \{c_1, c_2, \ldots, c_n\}\})$$

where M_o is the multiplicative order of DL. In case of our design, DL layer is state permutation layer combined with $circ(0, 1, 1, 1)$ matrix. Using the theory proposed by Beierle et al. [7], a design can guarantee resistance against invariant subspace attack if $W_{DL}(D) = n - 1$, unless S-Box has component of degree 1. For LbT-64-128, a random set of round constants are generated and using the above cell permutation, the cardinality of set D is found to be 8 for $W_{DL}(D)$ to reach $n - 1$ i.e. 63, which is the minimum we could get as shown in Fig. 4.

4   Security Evaluation

Differential Cryptanalysis. The minimum number of active S-Boxes for the differential trails is shown below in Table 5. It is easy to see that, 18 rounds of the cipher would contain at least 68 active S-Boxes, and hence even with very naïve calculation the differential probability of the full cipher is at most $(2^{-2})^{68} = 2^{-136}$. Therefore, to mount differential cryptanalysis on the cipher, an attacker would require the order of 2^{136} known plaintexts/ciphertexts, which exceed the available data limit. This ensures that the full round cipher should resist differential attacks.

Table 5. Differential/linear characteristic of LbT-64-128.

Round number	2	3	4	5	6	7	8	16
# Active S-Boxes	4	7	16	17	20	23	32	64

Linear Cryptanalysis. The minimum number of active S-Boxes for the linear trails are also shown in Table 5. It is easy to see that, 18 rounds of the cipher would contain at least 68 active S-Boxes, and we can use it directly to bound the maximal bias of a 18-round linear approximation by $2^{67}(2^{-2})^{68} = 2^{-69}$. Therefore, linear cryptanalysis of the cipher would require of the order of 2^{136} known plaintext/ciphertexts, which exceed the available text, and hence we can conclude that the cipher would not be secure from linear attacks.

Invariant Subspace Cryptanalysis. Let there be a cipher defined by round function $F_{K_i}(P) = C$, where P, C and K_i are plaintext, ciphertext and round key respectively. Assume there exist two constants $u, v \in F_2^n$ and subspaces $A_1, A_2 \subseteq F_2^n$ such that $S(u \oplus A_1) = v \oplus A_2$, where $S(.)$ is S-Box. If all subkeys $K_i \in u \oplus v \oplus (A_1 \cap A_2)$, then following holds irrespective of number of rounds:

$$F_{K_i}(v \oplus A_2) = S(v \oplus A_2 \oplus K_i) = v \oplus A_2$$

Hence, if $P \in v \oplus A_2$, then $C \in v \oplus A_2$ irrespective of number of rounds. The S-Box of LbT-64-128 has 4 fixed points and some subspace transitions of the S-Box are listed in Table 6. But, we guarantee resistance against invariant subspace attack by carefully designing the round constants such that it satisfies the condition as in [7], where $W_{DL}(D)$ should cover the whole input space as shown in Fig. 4.

Table 6. Some subspace transitions of LbT-64-128

A_1	u	v	A_2
{1,c,0,d}	0	1	{1,c,0,d}
{0,2,9,b}	9	2	{0,2,9,b}
{0,3,4,7}	4	7	{0,3,4,7}
{0,5,a,f}	5	0	{0,5,a,f}
{0,6,8,e}	0	0	{0,6,8,e}
{0,5}	a	f	{0,5}
{0,f}	5	5	{0,f}
{0,a}	0	0	{0,a}
{0,6}	8	8	{0,e}

Impossible Differential Cryptanalysis. Impossible differential cryptanalysis for r rounds exploits a pair of difference Δ_1 and Δ_2 such that the state difference Δ_1 never reaches the state difference Δ_2 after r rounds. We have implemented impossible differential search tool based on MILP [16], considering the differential distribution through the S-Box. We have exhaustively tested input and output differences satisfying the following conditions:

- The input difference activates exactly one of the 16 S-Boxes for LbT.
- The output difference also activates exactly one of the 16 S-Boxes LbT.

In case of LbT-64-128, we have performed the experiment with 16 many input differences as well as 16 many output differences. Together, we have tested $16 \times 16 = 256$ pairs of input and output differences and the search results show that 192 pairs are actually impossible for 2 rounds and 112 pairs are impossible for 3 rounds. We extend the search for 4 rounds and have not found any impossible differentials. Thus, our choice of optimal state-permutation ensures that impossible differentials are present for only a few number of rounds. Hence, we believe that full round cipher should be secure against these attacks.

Integral Cryptanalysis. Integral cryptanalysis, a higher-order differential cryptanalysis, is a more generalized form of square attack [18]. The goal of integral cryptanalysis is to find a set of input and output bits, such that setting those input bits to all possible values will result in balanced property in the set of output bits. We have followed the MILP approach mentioned in [43], to find the distinguisher present in our design. LbT S-Box can be described via 10 inequalities given below to model its bit-based division property:

$$a_3 + a_2 + a_1 + a_0 - b_3 - b_2 - b_1 - b_0 \geq 0$$
$$-b_3 - b_2 + 2b_1 - b_0 + 1 \geq 0$$
$$-b_3 - b_2 - b_1 + 2b_0 + 1 \geq 0$$
$$-a_3 - a_2 - a_1 - a_0 + 3b_3 + 3b_2 + 3b_1 + 3b_0 \geq 0$$
$$-b_3 + 2b_2 - b_1 - b_0 + 1 \geq 0$$
$$2b_3 - b_2 - b_1 - b_0 + 1 \geq 0$$
$$-a_3 - a_1 - a_0 + 2b_3 + 3b_2 + 3b_1 + 3b_0 \geq 0$$
$$-a_2 - a_1 - a_0 + 3b_3 + 3b_2 + 3b_1 + 2b_0 \geq 0$$
$$-a_3 - a_2 - a_1 + 3b_3 + 3b_2 + 2b_1 + 3b_0 \geq 0$$
$$-a_3 - a_2 - a_0 + 3b_3 + 2b_2 + 3b_1 + 3b_0 \geq 0$$

The feasible solutions to these inequalities are exactly the 54 division trails of LbT S-Box described in Table 7. We evaluated LbT-64-128 to find distinguishers using the tool proposed in [21]. By varying 1-bits, 2-bits, 3-bits, 4-bits, 8-bits and fixing 63-bits, 62-bits, 61-bits, 60-bits, 56-bits respectively, no integral distinguishers were found till 6-rounds.

5   Threshold Implementation in Hardware

In this section, we present an overview of the TI circuit for the LbT S-Box. In particular, we first illustrate how the CA rule describing the S-Box can be expressed as a composition of two CA rules of lower algebraic degrees. We then present the overall hardware architecture, where the TI circuits corresponding to these rules are cascaded in series to preserve functionality while ensuring side-channel resistance.

5.1   CA Rule Decomposition

We define class (a, b, c) of CA-rule as a tuple of three elements, where a, b, and c denote number of degree 3, degree 2, and degree 1 terms respectively in the CA-rule. The CA-rule that describes our S-Box has an algebraic degree of 3 and we express a degree 3 function into a combination of degree 2 functions to construct *composite TI* targeting low area footprint and power consumption. We then identify uniform and non-complete sharing for each of these sub-functions and finally cascade them to obtain the final output. We decompose the function from degree 3 to degree 2 as shown below:

Table 7. Division trail of LbT S-Box.

Input division property	Output division property
(0,0,0,0)	(0,0,0,0)
(0,0,0,1)	(0,0,0,1),(0,0,1,0),(0,1,0,0),(1,0,0,0)
(0,0,1,0)	(0,0,0,1),(0,0,1,0),(0,1,0,0),(1,0,0,0)
(0,0,1,1)	(0,0,0,1),(0,0,1,0),(0,1,0,0),(1,0,0,0)
(0,1,0,0)	(0,0,0,1),(0,0,1,0),(0,1,0,0),(1,0,0,0)
(0,1,0,1)	(0,0,1,0),(0,1,0,0),(1,0,0,0)
(0,1,1,0)	(0,0,0,1),(0,0,1,0),(0,1,0,0),(1,0,0,0)
(0,1,1,1)	(0,0,1,0),(0,1,0,0),(1,0,0,0)
(1,0,0,0)	(0,0,0,1),(0,0,1,0),(0,1,0,0),(1,0,0,0)
(1,0,0,1)	(0,0,0,1),(0,0,1,0),(0,1,0,0),(1,0,0,0)
(1,0,1,0)	(0,0,0,1),(0,0,1,0),(0,1,0,0),(1,0,0,0)
(1,0,1,1)	(0,0,0,1),(0,0,1,0),(0,1,0,0)
(1,1,0,0)	(0,0,0,1),(0,0,1,0),(0,1,0,0),(1,0,0,0)
(1,1,0,1)	(0,0,1,0),(0,1,0,0),(1,0,0,0)
(1,1,1,0)	(0,0,0,1),(0,0,1,0),(1,0,0,0)
(1,1,1,1)	(0,0,1,0),(1,1,0,0)

$$f(x_0, x_1, x_2, x_3) = x_0 \cdot x_1 \cdot x_2 \oplus x_0 \cdot x_2 \cdot x_3 \oplus x_1 \cdot x_2 \cdot x_3 \oplus x_0 \cdot x_2 \oplus x_2 \cdot x_3 \oplus x_0 \oplus x_1$$

$$f = f_3(x_2, f_1, f_2) = x_2 \cdot f_1 \oplus f_2$$

$$f_1(x_0, x_1, x_3) = x_0 \cdot x_1 \oplus x_0 \cdot x_3 \oplus x_1 \cdot x_3 \oplus x_0 \oplus 1$$

$$f_2(x_0, x_1, x_2, x_3) = x_2 \cdot x_3 \oplus x_0 \oplus x_1 \oplus x_2$$

5.2   TI Decomposition

In this section, we illustrate the uniform three-share decomposition of every function obtained in Sect. 5.1. Let s_i denotes the ith share. Then we follow the below nomenclature to denote the shares:

$$x_0 = x_0^1 \oplus x_0^2 \oplus x_0^3, \quad x_1 = x_1^1 \oplus x_1^2 \oplus x_1^3, \quad x_2 = x_2^1 \oplus x_2^2 \oplus x_2^3, \quad x_3 = x_3^1 \oplus x_3^2 \oplus x_3^3,$$

$$f_1 = f_1^1 \oplus f_1^2 \oplus f_1^3, \quad f_2 = f_2^1 \oplus f_2^2 \oplus f_2^3, \quad f_3 = f_3^1 \oplus f_3^2 \oplus f_3^3$$

Therefore, the decomposition of f_1, f_2 and f_3 are

$$f_1^1 = 1 \oplus x_0^3 \oplus x_0^2 \cdot x_1^3 \oplus x_0^2 \cdot x_1^2 \oplus x_0^3 \cdot x_1^2 \oplus x_0^2 \cdot x_3^3 \oplus x_0^2 \cdot x_3^2 \oplus x_0^3 \cdot x_3^2 \oplus x_1^2 \cdot x_3^3 \oplus x_1^2 \cdot x_3^2 \oplus x_1^3 \cdot x_3^2$$

$$f_1^2 = x_0^1 \oplus x_0^3 \cdot x_1^1 \oplus x_0^1 \cdot x_1^3 \oplus x_0^1 \cdot x_1^1 \oplus x_0^3 \cdot x_3^1 \oplus x_0^1 \cdot x_3^3 \oplus x_0^1 \cdot x_3^1 \oplus x_1^3 \cdot x_3^1 \oplus x_1^1 \cdot x_3^3 \oplus x_1^1 \cdot x_3^3$$

$$f_1^3 = x_0^2 \oplus x_0^1 \cdot x_1^2 \oplus x_0^1 \cdot x_1^1 \oplus x_0^2 \cdot x_1^1 \oplus x_0^1 \cdot x_3^2 \oplus x_0^1 \cdot x_3^1 \oplus x_0^2 \cdot x_3^1 \oplus x_1^1 \cdot x_3^2 \oplus x_1^1 \cdot x_3^1 \oplus x_1^2 \cdot x_3^1$$

$$f_2^1 = x_2^2 \cdot x_3^2 \oplus x_2^2 \cdot x_3^3 \oplus x_2^3 \cdot x_3^2 \oplus x_0^2 \oplus x_1^2 \oplus x_2^2$$

$$f_2^2 = x_2^3 \cdot x_3^3 \oplus x_2^1 \cdot x_3^3 \oplus x_2^3 \cdot x_3^1 \oplus x_0^3 \oplus x_1^3 \oplus x_2^3$$

$$f_2^3 = x_2^1 \cdot x_3^1 \oplus x_2^1 \cdot x_3^2 \oplus x_2^2 \cdot x_3^1 \oplus x_0^1 \oplus x_1^1 \oplus x_2^1$$

$$f_3^1 = x_2^2 \cdot f_1^2 \oplus x_2^2 \cdot f_1^3 \oplus x_2^3 \cdot f_1^2 \oplus f_2^2$$

$$f_3^2 = x_2^3 \cdot f_1^3 \oplus x_2^3 \cdot f_1^1 \oplus x_2^1 \cdot f_1^3 \oplus f_2^3$$

$$f_3^3 = x_2^1 \cdot f_1^1 \oplus x_2^1 \cdot f_1^2 \oplus x_2^2 \cdot f_1^1 \oplus f_2^1$$

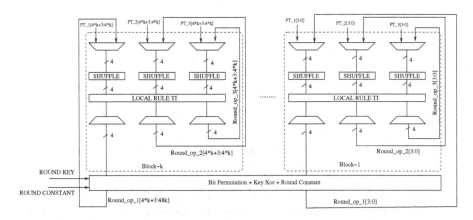

Fig. 5. Basic hardware architecture for LbT-n-128.

5.3 Implementation Results of the Full Cipher

Our main aim is to implement a full cipher that is area efficient with reasonable throughput. Hence, we choose to implement round-based approach where we integrate first-order protected CA-based S-Box with our lightweight linear layer. The hardware architecture of the round-based implementation of LbT-64-128 is shown in Fig. 5. It uses k ($k = 16$) blocks where each block processes PT_i and $Round\_op\_i$ ($1 \leq i \leq 3$) denotes i-th share of plaintext and round output respectively. The cipher takes 8 clock cycles to complete each round, hence $18 \times 8 + 2 = 146$ cycles for an encryption (2 extra cycles for loading plaintext and final cipher text). The synthesis is done by setting 10 ns as clock period and under this setting throughput is found to be 87.67 Mbps. We used Cadence Genus version I-2013.12-SP5-4 for synthesis and for simulation we used Cadence Ncverilog version I-2014.03-SP1-1. The standard cell library TSL18FS120 at 180 nm from Tower Semiconductor Ltd. is used during physical design synthesis. The area overhead for all implemented circuits are measured in terms of gate equivalents (GE), where a GE in our case is equal to the lowest area occupied by a 2-input NAND gate of 1x drive of 180 nm technology. The area overhead for LbT-64-128 occupies 11639.8 GE.

5.4 Resilience Against Probing Attacks

The single core block implementing the TI circuit for the CA rule as described in [22] draws input shares by cyclically rotating the shift register. When the register rotates, the input to the core TI block instantly changes which will result in side channel leakage if the number of input shares is two. As an example, consider $X_1 Z_1 W_2$ as one of the terms of output share f in the CA rule of an S-Box and assume two shares per input variable are used to evaluate the function. Let $\{X_j, Z_j, W_j\}_{j \in [1,2]}$ denote the shares for the input bits X, Z and W, respectively. A tracepoint during trace collection reflects the power consumption of a circuit

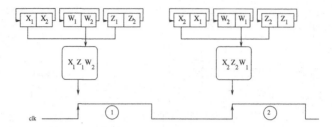

Fig. 6. Two shares are vulnerable to leakages

between two rising or falling edges of a clock. As shown in Fig. 6, during the rising edge of the first clock cycle, the circuit evaluates $X_1 Z_1 W_2$ and during the rising edge of the second clock cycle, the same circuit evaluates $X_2 Z_2 W_1$, which means the attacker can probe the leakage of the circuit which depends on both shares of X, Z and W during the clock transition, thereby violating the non-completeness property. However, as the number of input shares increases from more than two, even if the attacker probes the leakage of the circuit during clock transition only information about two shares is revealed. Since our scheme uses three-share implementation, it is leakage resistant against such probing attacks.

5.5   Test Vector Leakage Analysis (TVLA)

To evaluate the security of LbT-64-128 we have tested it on the SAKURA-G platform with Spartan-6 LX75 logic. We have performed *non-specific* Welch t-test [23] on each of our designs by collecting 100,000 traces, using Tektronix MSO54-C011756 oscilloscope having a sampling frequency of 1.2 Gs/s and the designs running at 45.4 Mhz. We collected power traces for one round cipher operation having around 520 sample points and the t-test plot is shown in Fig. 7. It is evident from the figure that the t-test(t) values for the cipher are within the prescribed range of $-4.5 \leq t \leq 4.5$.

5.6   Comparative Study

In this section, we provide a comparison of the estimated area of the TI circuit of our design with other prominent lightweight SPN-based block ciphers. To have a fair comparison with the existing results, we skip the area required for the key storage and key scheduling part. This is because, for most of these ciphers, existing results on the TI circuit area do not include the key scheduling area. In Table 8, we have compared popular lightweight block ciphers, the sum of the total area footprint (using technology platform at 180 nm) of the 16 4 × 4 S-Boxes along with their corresponding linear layer (typically almost-MDS or bit permutation) and throughput as given in [22] with ours. For each of the ciphers, their corresponding throughout is measured using the borderline clock period at which the circuit passes the setup and hold time constraints. An

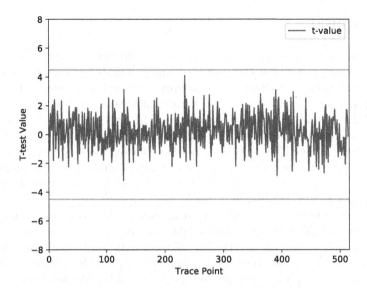

Fig. 7. TVLA of composite TI circuits for LbT-64-128

interesting point to observe here is that due to induction of lightweight almost-MDS layer full diffusion is reached in lesser rounds and hence the number of round requirement is less when compared to GIFT cipher. In addition due to low area footprint of our serialized S-Box, the critical path length of our design is less compared to others. In that way, we get better throughput compared to other lightweight ciphers. Moreover, even though the S-Box used in our cipher construction is serial, the throughput value is reasonably better when compared to other lightweight ciphers. It is worth mentioning here that the throughput value in case of MIDORI is moderately more than LbT, as the number of rounds in case of MIDORI is lesser than LbT-64-128. However, one must note that MIDORI has been cryptanalytically broken using Invariant Subspace Attack by the authors in [25].

Table 8. Area and throughput comparison for TI of 64-bit SPN based block ciphers

Block cipher	# Rounds	Area (GE) (w/o KS)	Throughput (MBps)
LbT-64-128	18	3 133.79 [this paper]	87.67 [this paper]
PRESENT-64-80	31	4 451.15	61.41
GIFT-64-128	28	3 484.27	71.42
Skinny-64-128	32	5 356.46	62.5
Midori-64-128	16	6 093.26	125.0

6   Conclusion

In this paper, we proposed the first *area-efficient* and side-channel resilient family of block ciphers, called LbT. Our proposed family of block ciphers strengthens the use of weak CA-based S-Boxes that is appropriately complemented with a linear layer consisting of shuffle cells and matrix multiplication with an ultralightweight almost-MDS matrix with just 6-XOR gates. This ensures high diffusion at the cost of a minimal area overhead. We demonstrate the significance of the design by providing a complete TI circuit and showing that our proposed cipher achieves 12% lower TI hardware area overhead concerning existing prominent lightweight SPN-based block ciphers. Our proposed cipher brings out reasonable throughput when compared with popular lightweight block ciphers.

An interesting future direction is to investigate whether we can make the linear layer of LbT even more lightweight. As already discussed, one can not achieve the desired security levels with a bit-permutation-based linear layer. An interesting yet challenging question is whether it is possible to have an efficient, secure and cheaper linear layer (say with differential branch number 3).

References

1. Daemen, J., Rijmen, V.: AES proposal: Rijndael. Gaithersburg, MD, USA (1999)
2. Andreeva, E., et al.: Primates v1. Submission to the CAESAR Competition (2014)
3. Banik, S., Bogdanov, A., Regazzoni, F.: Exploring energy efficiency of lightweight block ciphers. In: Dunkelman, O., Keliher, L. (eds.) SAC 2015. LNCS, vol. 9566, pp. 178–194. Springer, Cham (2016). https://doi.org/10.1007/978-3-319-31301-6_10
4. Banik, S., Funabiki, Y., Isobe, T.: More results on shortest linear programs. In: Attrapadung, N., Yagi, T. (eds.) IWSEC 2019. LNCS, vol. 11689, pp. 109–128. Springer, Cham (2019). https://doi.org/10.1007/978-3-030-26834-3_7
5. Banik, S., Pandey, S.K., Peyrin, T., Sasaki, Yu., Sim, S.M., Todo, Y.: GIFT: a small present. Towards reaching the limit of lightweight encryption. In: Fischer, W., Homma, N. (eds.) CHES 2017. LNCS, vol. 10529, pp. 321–345. Springer, Cham (2017). https://doi.org/10.1007/978-3-319-66787-4_16
6. Banik, S., et al.: SUNDAE: small universal deterministic authenticated encryption for the internet of things. IACR Trans. Symmetric Cryptol. **2018**(3), 1–35 (2018). https://doi.org/10.13154/tosc.v2018.i3.1-35, https://tosc.iacr.org/index.php/ToSC/article/view/7296
7. Beierle, C., Canteaut, A., Leander, G., Rotella, Y.: Proving resistance against invariant attacks: how to choose the round constants. In: Katz, J., Shacham, H. (eds.) CRYPTO 2017. LNCS, vol. 10402, pp. 647–678. Springer, Cham (2017). https://doi.org/10.1007/978-3-319-63715-0_22
8. Beierle, C., Leander, G., Moradi, A., Rasoolzadeh, S.: Craft: lightweight tweakable block cipher with efficient protection against dfa attacks. Cryptology ePrint Archive, Report 2019/210 (2019). https://eprint.iacr.org/2019/210
9. Bellizia, D., et al.: Spook: sponge-based leakage-resistant authenticated encryption with a masked tweakable block cipher. IACR Trans. Symmetric Cryptol. **2020**(S1), 295–349 (2020)

10. Bilgin, B.: Threshold implementations: as countermeasure against higher-order differential power analysis (2015)
11. Bilgin, B., et al.: Low and depth and efficient inverses: a guide on s-boxes for low-latency masking. IACR Trans. Symmetric Cryptol. **2020**(1), 144–184 (2020). https://doi.org/10.13154/tosc.v2020.i1.144-184, https://tosc.iacr.org/index.php/ToSC/article/view/8562
12. Bogdanov, A., Knežević, M., Leander, G., Toz, D., Varıcı, K., Verbauwhede, I.: SPONGENT: a lightweight hash function. In: Preneel, B., Takagi, T. (eds.) CHES 2011. LNCS, vol. 6917, pp. 312–325. Springer, Heidelberg (2011). https://doi.org/10.1007/978-3-642-23951-9_21
13. Bogdanov, A., et al.: PRESENT: an ultra-lightweight block cipher. In: Paillier, P., Verbauwhede, I. (eds.) CHES 2007. LNCS, vol. 4727, pp. 450–466. Springer, Heidelberg (2007). https://doi.org/10.1007/978-3-540-74735-2_31
14. Chakraborti, A., Datta, N., Jha, A., Mitragotri, S., Nandi, M.: From combined to hybrid: making feedback-based AE even smaller. IACR Trans. Symmetric Cryptol. **2020**(S1), 417–445 (2020)
15. Chakraborti, A., Iwata, T., Minematsu, K., Nandi, M.: Blockcipher-based authenticated encryption: how small can we go? In: Fischer, W., Homma, N. (eds.) CHES 2017. LNCS, vol. 10529, pp. 277–298. Springer, Cham (2017). https://doi.org/10.1007/978-3-319-66787-4_14
16. Coron, J.-S., Nielsen, J.B. (eds.): EUROCRYPT 2017. LNCS, vol. 10212. Springer, Cham (2017). https://doi.org/10.1007/978-3-319-56617-7
17. Daemen, J., Hoffert, S., Van Assche, G., Van Keer, R.: The design of xoodoo and xoofff. IACR Trans. Symmetric Cryptol. **2018**, 1–38 (2018)
18. Daemen, J., Knudsen, L., Rijmen, V., The block cipher square: The block cipher square. In: Biham, E. (ed.) FSE 1997. LNCS, vol. 1267, pp. 149–165. Springer, Heidelberg (1997). https://doi.org/10.1007/BFb0052343
19. De Cnudde, T., Bilgin, B., Reparaz, O., Nikov, V., Nikova, S.: Higher-order threshold implementation of the AES S-Box. In: Homma, N., Medwed, M. (eds.) CARDIS 2015. LNCS, vol. 9514, pp. 259–272. Springer, Cham (2016). https://doi.org/10.1007/978-3-319-31271-2_16
20. Dobraunig, C., Eichlseder, M., Mendel, F., Schläffer, M.: Ascon v1. 2: lightweight authenticated encryption and hashing. J. Cryptol. **34**(3), 1–42 (2021)
21. Eskandari, Z., Kidmose, A.B., Kölbl, S., Tiessen, T.: Finding integral distinguishers with ease. Cryptology ePrint Archive, Report 2018/688 (2018). https://eprint.iacr.org/2018/688
22. Ghoshal, A., Sadhukhan, R., Patranabis, S., Datta, N., Picek, S., Mukhopadhyay, D.: Lightweight and side-channel secure 4 × 4 s-boxes from cellular automata rules. IACR Trans. Symmetric Cryptol. **2018**(3), 311–334 (2018). https://doi.org/10.13154/tosc.v2018.i3.311-334
23. Goodwill, G., Jun, B., Jaffe, J., Rohatgi, P.: P.: a testing methodology for side-channel resistance validation, NIAT (2011)
24. Gueron, S., Lindell, Y.: Simple, submission to nist lightweight cryptography project 2019 (2019)
25. Guo, J., Jean, J., Nikolic, I., Qiao, K., Sasaki, Y., Sim, S.M.: Invariant subspace attack against midori64 and the resistance criteria for s-box designs. IACR Trans. Symmetric Cryptol. **2016**(1), 33–56 (2016). https://doi.org/10.13154/tosc.v2016.i1.33-56, https://tosc.iacr.org/index.php/ToSC/article/view/534
26. Guo, J., Peyrin, T., Poschmann, A.: The PHOTON family of lightweight hash functions. In: Rogaway, P. (ed.) CRYPTO 2011. LNCS, vol. 6841, pp. 222–239. Springer, Heidelberg (2011). https://doi.org/10.1007/978-3-642-22792-9_13

27. Gupta, N., Jati, A., Chattopadhyay, A., Sanadhya, S.K., Chang, D.: Threshold implementations of gift: a trade-off analysis. Cryptology ePrint Archive, Report 2017/1040 (2017). https://eprint.iacr.org/2017/1040

28. Gutiérrez, A., Sim, S., Peyrin, T., Sarkar, S., Sasaki, Y.: Official comment: trifle. email to LWC-forum (2019). https://csrc.nist.gov/CSRC/media/Projects/Lightweight-Cryptography/documents/round-1/official-comments/TRIFLE-official-comment.pdf

29. Handschuh, H.: SHA family (secure hash algorithm). In: van Tilborg, H.C.A. (eds.) Encyclopedia of Cryptography and Security. Springer, Boston (2005). https://doi.org/10.1007/0-387-23483-7_388

30. Cheng, H., Heys, H.M.: Compact ASIC implementation of the iceberg block cipher with concurrent error detection. In: 2008 IEEE International Symposium on Circuits and Systems, pp. 2921–2924 (2008)

31. Kocher, P., Jaffe, J., Jun, B.: Differential power analysis. In: Wiener, M. (ed.) CRYPTO 1999. LNCS, vol. 1666, pp. 388–397. Springer, Heidelberg (1999). https://doi.org/10.1007/3-540-48405-1_25

32. Leander, G., Abdelraheem, M.A., AlKhzaimi, H., Zenner, E.: A cryptanalysis of PRINTCIPHER: the invariant subspace attack. In: Rogaway, P. (ed.) CRYPTO 2011. LNCS, vol. 6841, pp. 206–221. Springer, Heidelberg (2011). https://doi.org/10.1007/978-3-642-22792-9_12

33. Mangard, S., Pramstaller, N., Oswald, E.: Successfully attacking masked AES hardware implementations. In: Rao, J.R., Sunar, B. (eds.) CHES 2005. LNCS, vol. 3659, pp. 157–171. Springer, Heidelberg (2005). https://doi.org/10.1007/11545262_12

34. Minematsu, K.: AES-OTR v3.1. Submission to CAESAR (2016). https://competitions.cr.yp.to/round3/aesotrv31.pdf

35. Naito, Y., Matsui, M., Sugawara, T., Suzuki, D.: SAEB: a lightweight blockcipher-based AEAD mode of operation. IACR Trans. Cryptogr. Hardw. Embed. Syst. **2018**(2), 192–217 (2018)

36. Naito, Y., Sugawara, T.: Lightweight authenticated encryption mode of operation for tweakable block ciphers. Cryptology ePrint Archive, Report 2019/339 (2019). https://eprint.iacr.org/2019/339

37. Nikova, S., Rechberger, C., Rijmen, V.: Threshold implementations against side-channel attacks and glitches. In: Ning, P., Qing, S., Li, N. (eds.) ICICS 2006. LNCS, vol. 4307, pp. 529–545. Springer, Heidelberg (2006). https://doi.org/10.1007/11935308_38

38. Piret, G., Quisquater, J.-J.: A differential fault attack technique against SPN structures, with application to the AES and KHAZAD. In: Walter, C.D., Koç, Ç.K., Paar, C. (eds.) CHES 2003. LNCS, vol. 2779, pp. 77–88. Springer, Heidelberg (2003). https://doi.org/10.1007/978-3-540-45238-6_7

39. Sarkar, S., Syed, H., Sadhukhan, R., Mukhopadhyay, D.: Lightweight design choices for LED-like block ciphers. In: Patra, A., Smart, N.P. (eds.) INDOCRYPT 2017. LNCS, vol. 10698, pp. 267–281. Springer, Cham (2017). https://doi.org/10.1007/978-3-319-71667-1_14

40. Satoh, A., Sugawara, T., Homma, N., Aoki, T.: High-performance concurrent error detection scheme for AES hardware. In: Oswald, E., Rohatgi, P. (eds.) CHES 2008. LNCS, vol. 5154, pp. 100–112. Springer, Heidelberg (2008). https://doi.org/10.1007/978-3-540-85053-3_7

41. Schneider, T., Moradi, A., Güneysu, T.: ParTI – towards combined hardware countermeasures against side-channel and fault-injection attacks. In: Robshaw, M., Katz, J. (eds.) CRYPTO 2016. LNCS, vol. 9815, pp. 302–332. Springer, Heidelberg (2016). https://doi.org/10.1007/978-3-662-53008-5_11

42. Simon, T., et al.: FRIET: an authenticated encryption scheme with built-in fault detection. In: Canteaut, A., Ishai, Y. (eds.) EUROCRYPT 2020. LNCS, vol. 12105, pp. 581–611. Springer, Cham (2020). https://doi.org/10.1007/978-3-030-45721-1_21

43. Xiang, Z., Zhang, W., Bao, Z., Lin, D.: Applying milp method to searching integral distinguishers based on division property for 6 lightweight block ciphers. Cryptology ePrint Archive, Report 2016/857 (2016). https://eprint.iacr.org/2016/857

Hardware Implementation of Masked SKINNY SBox with Application to AEAD

Mustafa Khairallah[1,2] and Shivam Bhasin[1(✉)]

[1] Nanyang Technological University, Singapore, Singapore
sbhasin@ntu.edu.sg
[2] Seagate Research, Singapore, Singapore
mustafa.khairallah@seagate.com

Abstract. Hardware masking is an important countermeasure for cryptographic schemes. In this paper, we study the hardware implementations of the SKINNY SBox using first-order Boolean masking. We implement the SKINNY 8-bit SBox using a wide range of masking schemes, and show the different security goals achieved by each implementation using formal verification. We develop and adapt a practical unit testing framework based on the Sasebo-GII FPGA board, and identify an issue with all the considered masking schemes. Based on the explanations in literature to similar observations, we propose a new implementation of the SBox that can be verified/validated using TVLA even in high SNR environments. We provide a full implementation of two of the Romulus AEAD modes, which can be configured with any of the SBox implementations proposed. We provide synthesis results using ASIC.

Keywords: Masking · Hardware · TVLA · Lightweight · Authenticated encryption · Romulus

1 Introduction

Boolean masking is one of the oldest, and yet most relevant, countermeasure against statistical Side-Channel Analysis (SCA) of cryptographic implementations. Several efforts over the years have been performed to improve the security and efficiency of masked ciphers. Moreover, the security models of masked ciphers are also improving to better capture the side-channel leakage of real-world implementations. Work on masked ciphers can be classified into 4 main categories:

1. Design and implementation of secure masking schemes, such as Ishai-Sahai-Wagner (ISW) [16], Threshold Implementations (TI) [6], Domain-Oriented Masking (DOM) [15], Hardware Private Circuits (HPC) [9].

This work was done while the first author was working in Nanyang Technological University.

© The Author(s), under exclusive license to Springer Nature Switzerland AG 2022
L. Batina et al. (Eds.): SPACE 2022, LNCS 13783, pp. 50–69, 2022.
https://doi.org/10.1007/978-3-031-22829-2_3

2. Modeling hardware and software implementations in order to have better understanding of their behavior, *e.g.* the probing model, Non-Interference (NI), Strong Non-Interference (SNI) [2], Probe-Isolating Non-Interference (PINI) [10].
3. Attacking masked implementations using SCA techniques, *e.g.* Differential Power Analysis (DPA) [23], Correlation Power Analysis (CPA) [7].
4. Designing evaluation frameworks in order to measure the security order of different circuits and implementations, *e.g.* maskVerif [1] and SILVER [22] for formal verification of circuits and frameworks based on statistical test (TVLA [27], χ^2-test [25]) for assessing practical leakages.

However, one area that remains roughly under-studied is the hardware implementations of masked ciphers. Since the introduction of masking as a counter-measure, researchers have shown shortcomings of the idealized security models. Initially, masking schemes were designed to be secure in the probing model, i.e., a dth-order masked implementation should be secure as long as the adversary can observe at most d internal wires (or probes) of the circuit. It was shown that hardware glitches can lead to problems in this model [6]. By hardware glitches, we refer to imbalances in the physical delay of different paths of the same circuit. Such imbalances can lead to exposing more than d variables by observing only $\leq d$ wires. While some variants of probing model like robust probing models [13] can handle glitches, it fails to address a few advanced attacks like horizontal attacks [4]. In order to overcome such issues, new security models were introduced, including Non-Interference (NI), Strong NI (SNI) and Probe-Isolated NI (PINI). These new security models are based on the notion of composability of smaller masked gadgets [2] which satisfy certain security properties. A gadget is considered NI secure if and only if every set of at most d internal probes can be simulated with at most d shares of each input. This is further extended to SNI, where the attacker is allowed to also observe the outputs. It was shown that NI gadgets do not offer composability and SNI offers composability to single-output gadgets [2]. This issue was solved in PINI which can offer composability for multiple output gadgets [10].

Glitches are not the only physical anomaly that leads to a gap between theoretical models and physical implementations. Two problems that have been observed in several works are transitions and coupling. Transitions refer to shared variables being recombined due to the transition of values inside flip-flops, while coupling refers to dependencies in the electric current of two or more wires that are close to each other and that should carry independent variables. Coupling in particular can be very problematic. The probing security model is built on a fundamental assumption that the leakage observed from different independent wires of the circuit are independent. However, it has been observed time and time again that a correct masked implementation (of any order) experiences first-order leakage [11] when implemented on FPGA. The authors of [11] have analyzed this issue and provide explanations from a VLSI point of view. Besides, the authors of [24] have shown that this issue can lead to attacks on masked implementations. While ASIC implementations are less studied from this point of view, it is more conservative to assume the same issue will arise in an ASIC implementation.

Another issue facing benchmarking of SCA-protected implementation is defining and assigning a security order for a given implementation. A common approach to assess first-order security is using Welch's *fixed vs. random* t-test [14]. The test in its basic form compares two populations of samples; one with a fixed plaintext and the other with randomly sampled plaintexts, against an equality of mean assumption. The test statistic is given by

$$t = \left| \frac{\mu_f - \mu_r}{\sqrt{\frac{s_f^2}{N_f} + \frac{s_r^2}{N_r}}} \right|$$

A widely accepted threshold for the t-value is 4.5, where samples that lead to higher values are said to exhibit observable first-order leakage. In other words, first-order leakage is observable when the mean of observed samples is data-dependent. When it comes to higher-order leakage, the definition becomes more ambiguous. Two versions of the t-test are used to detect higher-order leakage. The univariate higher-order test is performed in two steps. First, preprocessing the samples, where for each sample $L_x(i)$ in the population $x \in \{f, r\}$,

$$L_x'(i) = (L_x(i) - \mu_x)^o$$

where o is the order of the test. Second, the first-order t-test is performed on the preprocessed samples.

$$t = \left| \frac{\mu_f' - \mu_r'}{\sqrt{\frac{(s')_f^2}{N_f} + \frac{(s')_r^2}{N_r}}} \right|$$

The other higher-order t-test is the multivariate t-test. The first step, is performed as follows

$$L_x'(N_x * i + j) = (L_x(i) - \mu_x) \times (L_x(j) - \mu_x) \forall 0 \le i, j \le (N_x - 1)$$

The two versions of the t-test differ in what they measure and also their computational cost. The univariate test captures leakage in higher statistical moments of the samples (assuming parallel computation of shares), while the multivariate test captures leakage that requires combining samples from different timestamps (where share computation can be distributed over time). When it comes to computational complexity, in the worst case, it involves calculating the mean of each sample, exponentiation, and the t-test. If the cost of exponentiation is c_e, the length of each trace is s, and the cost of the first order test is c_1, then the upper bound of the cost of the univariate higher-order test is

$$c_o \le c_1 + s \cdot (N_f + N_r) \cdot c_e + s \cdot (c_{\mu_f} + c_{\mu_r}) \le 2 \cdot c_1 + s \cdot (N_f + N_r) \cdot c_e$$

For small order, o and c_e are small. Hence, the univariate higher-order test is not significantly more complex than the first order variant, *i.e.* $c_o \le a \cdot c_1$, where

a is a small constant. On the other hand, the multivariate test increases the complexity significantly, since the number of samples per trace increases from s to s^o. This exponential growth makes the test very expensive for higher orders.

Besides, the χ^2-test has been proposed [25] to detect higher order univariate leakage, *i.e.* leakage not based on the difference of means. The cost of χ^2-test is higher than, but comparable to, that of the univariate t-test. Hence, implementations that pass higher-order tests do not offer a significant security gains compared to implementations that pass the first-order t-test but fail higher-order tests. The difference between univariate and multivariate t-test is captured by whether the combined information come from leakage at the same point in time or not. In other words, univariate higher-order leakage can usually be observed in implementations that processes the different shares of the masked implementation in parallel.

For a standardization project such the NIST lightweight cryptography project, benchmarking has to be done on a variety of platforms. The main platforms for hardware benchmarking are FPGA and ASIC. Since the manufacturing cost of ASIC is too high and sometimes prohibitive for academic projects, ASIC benchmarking is usually done at a pre-fabrication level. However, when it comes to SCA, we need to question whether this high-level abstraction is sufficient. On the other hand, FPGA are more accessible in a lab settings and FPGA boards optimised for SCA evaluation are easily available. While FPGA do not represent most of the use cases of lightweight cryptography, they can be used as a starting point for evaluation.

Contributions. In this paper, we start from the literature on masked hardware implementations of block ciphers and look at the challenges and inconsistencies of implementing a masked Tweakable Block Cipher (TBC)-based Authenticated Encryption with Associated Data (AEAD) scheme. While some masked implementations of the SKINNY TBC have been proposed [8], mainly using TI, they have not been studied deeply and implementations using other masking schemes, *e.g.* DOM and HPC have not been proposed. Besides, masked implementations of Romulus, a finalist of the NIST lightweight cryptography, have not been properly studied. Our contributions can be listed as follows:

1. We propose implementations of SKINNY using a variety of masking schemes, including the first implementation for some of the masking schemes.
2. We study the security of the SKINNY 8-bit SBox using both formal verification and practical side-channel testing.
3. We propose a new method of implementing the DOM in order to achieve security against coupling.
4. We provide implementations of the Romulus-N and Romulus-M AEAD modes.
5. We discuss some of the issues related to benchmarking such implementations.

Our code is open-source and available at:
https://github.com/mustafa-khairallah/skinny_128_384_plus_sca

2 Background

In this section, we give a brief of introduction to some of the topics helpful for understanding the paper.

2.1 Hardware Masking, Revisited [11]

De Cnudde *et al.* investigated the validity of long standing assumption that power consumption or leakage from independent shares of a masking scheme are also independent. They showed that such assumption is not true in FPGA where activity in one power domain can have influence other power domains as well. This can be further amplified by choosing favorable (for attacker) parameters like higher supply voltage, lower shunt resistor, higher temperature etc. As a result, they demonstrate first-order leakage in otherwise secure masking schemes like TI [12] and DOM [15]. through extensive experimentation. Their findings are further supported by arguments from the VLSI theory. As a potential solution to implement secure masking on FPGA, De Cnudde *et al.* briefly proposed temporal non-completeness i.e. process d-shares in sequence at the cost of performance. No concrete implementation of this solution was provided. We develop on this avenue and explore answers to *"How to design a first order secure masking implementation on FPGA at the register-tranfer level"?*

2.2 SKINNY [5]

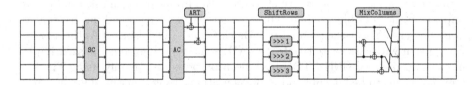

Fig. 1. The SKINNY round function applies five different transformations: SubCells (SC), AddConstants (AC), AddRoundTweakey (ART), ShiftRows (SR) and MixColumns (MC). [18]

SKINNY is a family of TBCs which support block size of 64-bits and 128-bits. It is based on TWEAKEY framework [19]. We focus on the version with block size of $n = 128$-bit block and tweakey size $t = 384$-bits (known as SKINNY-128/384+), it being a building block of Romulus. Each round of SKINNY-128/384+ is composed of five operations in the following order: SubCells, AddConstants, AddRoundTweakey, ShiftRows and MixColumns (see Fig. 1). The 8×8 SBox used in the SubCells library is depicted in Fig. 2. In total, SKINNY-128/384+ has 40 rounds. In [8], Caforio *et al.* studied first-order threshold implementations of SKINNY. We refer to their paper for the details on the implementation. In our study, we use their fastest implementation as a representative of threshold implementations. We refer to it as TI33.

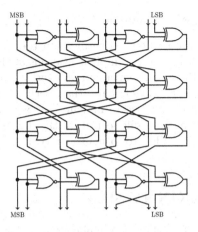

Fig. 2. The SKINNY 8-bit SBox [18]

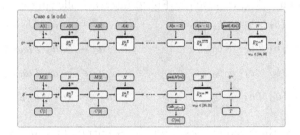

Fig. 3. The Romulus-N AEAD scheme [17].

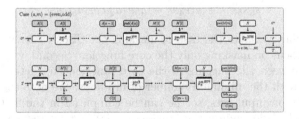

Fig. 4. The Romulus-M AEAD scheme [17].

2.3 Romulus

Romulus [17] is a finalist of the NIST lightweight cryptography standardization project. It involves TBC-based schemes. Originally, it consisted of two variants: Romulus-N and Romulus-M. Romulus-N is a nonce-respecting variant, depicted in Fig. 3, while Romulus-M, depicted in Fig. 4 is a two-pass nonce misuse resistant scheme.

2.4   SILVER Leakage Assessment Tool

SILVER [22] is an open-source formal verification tool proposed by Knichel *et al.* to analyze and verify the masked implementations at the gate-level. It can be applied on gate-level netlist of a given circuit and verify its security against different security models. For each model, it returns whether it is secure with glitches (+), secure only without glitches (y) or insecure (-). Security with glitches refers to practical hardware scenarios while security without glitches refers to software-based solutions. We use SILVER to formally verify a group of implementations of the SKINNY SBox.

3   Masking the SKINNY SBox

The most critical task of masking any cipher is masking its non-linear blocks. In this section we look at masking the SKINNY 8-bit SBox. We can untangle the SKINNY 8-bit SBox, depicted in Fig. 2, into the following iterative process:

$$a_0 \leftarrow \neg(b_7 \vee b_6) \oplus b_4 \qquad\qquad a_4 \leftarrow \neg(a_1 \vee b_3) \oplus b_1$$

$$a_1 \leftarrow \neg(b_3 \vee b_2) \oplus b_0 \qquad\qquad a_5 \leftarrow \neg(a_2 \vee a_3) \oplus b_7$$

$$a_2 \leftarrow \neg(b_2 \vee b_1) \oplus b_6 \qquad\qquad a_6 \leftarrow \neg(a_3 \vee a_0) \oplus b_3$$

$$a_3 \leftarrow \neg(a_0 \vee a_1) \oplus b_5 \qquad\qquad a_7 \leftarrow \neg(a_4 \vee a_5)xx \oplus b_2$$

where $b_7...b_0$ are the 8 input bits, and the 8 output bits are $s_7 s_6 \cdots s_0$, and assigned using the following permutation

$$s_6 s_5 s_2 s_7 s_3 s_1 s_4 s_0 \leftarrow a_0 a_1 a_2 a_3 a_4 a_5 a_6 a_7$$

This modularity makes the task of masking the SBox easier in two regards. First, we can focus on masking only the core function. Second, we can check the dependency between the outputs of the core function and determine the way to implement with the minimum number of flip-flops. We note that a_0, a_1 and a_2 depend only on input bits, so the can be computed in the first iteration in parallel. a_3 and a_4 depend on the previous 3 bits and are independent of each other, so the can be computed in the second iteration. Similarly, a_5 and a_6 are computed in the third iteration, while a_7 is computed in the fourth iteration.

A useful transformation to the core function is to change its representation to

$$a \leftarrow (\neg x \wedge \neg y) \oplus z$$

which computes exactly the same value, but helps visualize the impact of using different masking schemes. Depending on the masking scheme used to mask the core function, one iteration can consist of one or more cycles, leading to SBoxes that require 4 or more cycles, respectively.

We can also speed the latency on the SBox by flattening 3 of the logic functions as follows

$$a_3 \leftarrow ((\neg b_7) \wedge (\neg b_6) \wedge (\neg b_3) \wedge (\neg b_2)) \oplus$$
$$((\neg b_7) \wedge (\neg b_6) \wedge (\neg b_0)) \oplus$$
$$((\neg b_4) \wedge (\neg b_3) \wedge (\neg b_2)) \oplus$$
$$((\neg b_4) \wedge (\neg b_0)) \oplus b_5$$
$$a_4 \leftarrow ((\neg b_3) \wedge (\neg b_2)) \oplus$$
$$((\neg b_0) \wedge (\neg b_3)) \oplus b_1$$
$$a_7 \leftarrow ((\neg a_2) \wedge (\neg a_3) \wedge (\neg a_4)) \oplus$$
$$((\neg b_7) \wedge (\neg a_4)) \oplus b_2$$

which can be implemented using 2-input, 3-input and 4-input AND gates (AND2, AND3 and AND4). Implementing AND2 using any masking scheme is straightforward. We call implementations based on this strategy "Rapid".

4   Formal Verification

We implemented the SKINNY 8-bit SBox using most 2-share masking schemes, with the results shown in Table 1. The schemes considered are Domain-Oriented Masking (DOM) [15], Consolidated Masking Schemes (CMS) [26], ISW [16], Hardware Private Circuits (HPC), PARA [3], and PINI [10]. We have also included the 2-cycle 4-share threshold implementation proposed in [8]. For circuit utilizing AND3 and AND4 gates using DOM and CMS, the computational cost for verifying the whole circuit was too high, so we only verified the individual gates, relying on composability assumptions to argue about the security of the full circuit.

Our results show that DOM as originally defined (DOM1 in Table 1) does not achieve any security with glitches. However, it achieves probing security with glitches when the outputs of all the AND gates are registered (DOM1-Pipelined in Table 1). DOM1-SNI achieves SNI security at the expense of doubling the clock cycle count. CMS1 achieves NI security with glitches, making it one grade better than DOM1-Pipelined. ISW1, HPC, HPC2 and PARA are one grade better than CMS1, achieving SNI security with glitches. ISW1-PINI achieves the highest possible security model, PINI-security with glitches, while HPC2 achieves PINI-security but not SNI-security. However, the authors of [22] showed a similar observation on another implementation of HPC2 and pointed out that PINI security is more general than SNI security. For AND3 and AND4, we observe that ANDx-DOM1 achieves NI security with glitches, while ANDx-CMS1 achieves SNI security with glitches ($x \in \{3, 4\}$). The implementation of DOM1-Rapid and CMS1-Rapid was too complex for SILVER to assess. DOM1-NC is a serialzed version of DOM1-SNI which we describe in details in Sect. 5.3.

Table 1. Formal verification of different SKINNY SBox implementations using SIL-VER [22]. + means secure with glitches, y means secure without glitches and - means not secure. R is the number of fresh random bits needed, while r is the maximum number of random bits needed *in one clock cycle.*

Scheme	Cycles	Shares	R	r	Probing	NI	SNI	PINI
DOM1	4	2	8	3	y	y	y	-
DOM1-Pipelined	4	2	8	3	+	y	y	-
DOM1-SNI	8	2	8	3	+	+	+	-
DOM1-Rapid	2	2	25	19	?	?	?	?
CMS1	4	2	32	12	+	+	y	-
CMS1-Rapid	2	2	76	56	?	?	?	?
ISW1	8	2	8	3	+	+	+	-
ISW1-PINI	12	2	16	6	+	+	+	+
HPC	12	2	8	3	+	+	+	-
HPC2	12	2	16	6	+	+	y	+
PARA1	8	2	16	6	+	+	+	-
PINI1	4	2	8	3	y	y	y	y
TI33	2	4	0	0	+	-	-	-
DOM1-NC	24	2	8	3	+	+	+	-
AND3-DOM1	1	2	3	3	+	+	y	-
AND4-DOM1	1	2	7	7	+	+	y	-
AND3-CMS1	1	2	8	8	+	+	+	-
AND4-CMS1	1	2	16	16	+	+	+	-

5   Unit Testing

Unit-testing is the process of testing the building blocks of a digital circuits at the early stages of design before the circuit is integrated, to make sure each unit is operating correctly on its own. It is relevant to the concept of composability, and should be part of the design flow of masked implementations for two reasons:

1. Unit-testing is part of the design process of digital circuits in general. In side-channel analysis, unit-testing can help catch issues with the implementation at an early stage, and help explain issues with the overall implementation in general.
2. Composability is an important assumption in many masking schemes. The overall circuit is assumed to be secure by virtue of the security of its smaller components, and the assumption on the composability of these circuits.

While a lot of work focuses on these composability assumptions and their shortcomings, which led to models such as glitch-extended probing and SNI, the assumption requires that the building blocks are themselves secure. Hence, unit testing should be used at the early stages of design to validate it. The main challenge to such approach is the test complexity. Consider a scenario where the designer is choosing between 10 different building blocks; they would have to evaluate each of these building blocks, which may require more time than the project allows. Hence, techniques to accelerate the test for similar scenarios are required.

5.1   Accelerated Test Set-Up

We have designed a unit testing framework for high speed testing of SBoxes at the early phases of designing RTL code. The framework is shown in Fig. 5. A Deterministic Random Bit Generator (DRBG) based on a low-latency implementation of the GIFT-128 block cipher in the counter mode is used to generate the masked shares and decide whether the next sample is fixed or random. A gardening period of 200 cycles is applied between generating the shares and updating the SBox, to avoid leakage from DRBG circuit. The oscilloscope sends a START command, which triggers the setup to calculate 15,000 samples. After 15,000 samples, the set-up halts, allowing the oscilloscope to synchronize and store the acquired traces. The samples are calculated in less than a second, and storing them requires about 18 s. Hence, it takes about 1 h to calculates and process 3 million traces.

5.2   Amplification of SNR

On top of the high-speed set-up, in order to reduce the trace acquisition complexity, we need to artificially raise the Signal-to-Noise Ratio (SNR). We propose to do so by replicating the Unit-Under-Test (UUT) multiple times, forcing the FPGA to perform the same logic multiple times simultaneously. This can have an amplifying effect similar to computing the same trace multiple times and averaging out the noise, which was proposed in [28]. However, it achieves the same effect with a lot less traces. This enables very fast early testing of SBoxes, where with 9× replications, a few thousand traces aare enough to highlight flaws in most SBox variants.

5.3   The Practical Issue with Hardware Masking and How to Address It

A common assumption is that the leakage observed by the adversary/evaluator is the sum of independent leakage components. Hence, an adversary observing the combined leakage

$$\mathsf{L} = \mathsf{L}_0 + \mathsf{L}_1 + \cdots + \mathsf{L}_{d-1}$$

cannot detect any first-order leakage, as each of the components is independently distributed. However, it was shown by De Cnudde *et al.* [11], that in FPGA this assumption may not be true, due to what became later known as coupling, where the power consumption and power supply noise from one share,

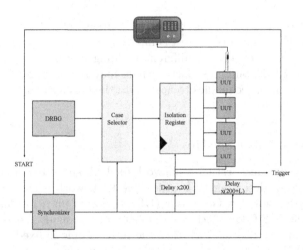

Fig. 5. Amplifying SNR through replication.

e.g. L_0 may impact the power consumption of the other shares. Consequently, they observed first order leakage on FPGA for several circuits, including masked AES MixColumn and SBox. In [24], it was shown that such coupling effects can be exploited in SCA attacks, and is not just an observable leakage. The authors of [11] proposed some suggestions on how to mitigate this issue, which include VLSI-based solutions to isolate the power supplies of different shares and serializing implementations in order to achieve *"hardware non-completeness"*, where at any point in time only a single share is being processed.

While VLSI-based solutions may mitigate the coupling issue for first-order leakage, we argue in this paper that for certifiable implementations, a.k.a implementations that claim a given security order, that hardware non-completeness should be considered a goal.

Serializing masked implementation can lead to transitional leakage. For example: A flip-flop holding the value x^0 may be updated at some point with x^1, which can lead to leakage that depends on both shares. The same thing can happen in logic gates, where unintended values can be processed by the logic gates, leading to unintended share combining.

Power Gating. [20] Power-gating is a technique used for low-power digital design, where a logic circuit that is not frequently used can be turned off by forcing all its inputs and outputs to 0. It is usually combined with clock gating, where the clock is turned off for flip-flops that are not being updated.

Non-Complete DOM (DOM1-NC) Implementation. In order to implement DOM such that only one share of each variable is being processed at a time, we treat each sub-share during the internal computation as a tiny power domain, having its own enable/disable signal. The share computation operation is updated as shown below.

$$s^3 \leftarrow e_0 \wedge ((e_0 \wedge x^1) \wedge (e_0 \wedge y^1) \oplus (e_0 \wedge z^1)$$

$$s^2 \leftarrow e_1 \wedge ((e_1 \wedge x^1) \wedge (e_1 \wedge y^0) \oplus (e_1 \wedge r))$$
$$s^1 \leftarrow e_2 \wedge ((e_2 \wedge x^0) \wedge (e_2 \wedge y^1) \oplus (e_2 \wedge r))$$
$$s^0 \leftarrow e_3 \wedge ((e_3 \wedge x^0) \wedge (e_3 \wedge y^0) \oplus (e_3 \wedge z^0))$$
$$a^0 \leftarrow e_4 \wedge ((e_4 \wedge s^0) \oplus (e_4 \wedge s^1))$$
$$a^1 \leftarrow e_5 \wedge ((e_5 \wedge s^2) \oplus (e_5 \wedge s^3))$$

At any point in time, at most one of the signals e_0, e_1, e_2, e_3, e_4 and e_5 is set to 1. Due to the structure of the circuit, it targets SNI security with glitches and inherets the formal analysis of DOM-SNI. It helps reducing leakage in two ways:

1. Making sure both shares of the same variable are never carried by two adjacent wires or gates and never stored into flip-flops at the same time, the coupling effect is removed to a very large extent.
2. Reducing the power consumption of the SBox as a whole leads to less exploitable leakage.

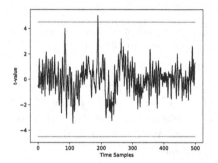

Fig. 6. TVLA output for DOM with 9 replicas after 7,784 traces.

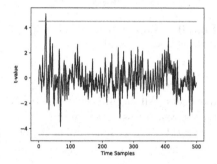

Fig. 7. TVLA output for DOM-SNI with 9 replicas after 2,140 traces.

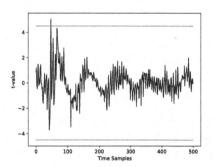

Fig. 8. TVLA output for TI33 with 9 replicas after 1,393 traces.

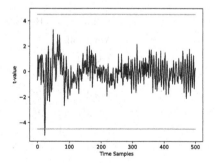

Fig. 9. TVLA output for TI33 with 1 replica after 62,924 traces.

In Table 2, we show the SNR and number of traces required for each method of implementing DOM. The results show that our proposed implementation (DOM1-NC) is several orders of magnitude more secure than other methods. It requires about 1000× more traces for the same number of replications and 10× higher SNR. With low SNR, the implementation did not show leakage even with more than 200 million traces. The t-value outcome for each of the implementations is show in Figs. 6, 7, 8, 9, 10 and 11.

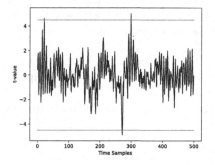 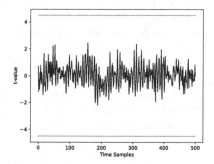

Fig. 10. TVLA output for NC with 9 replicas after 6,190,00 traces.

Fig. 11. TVLA output for NC with only 1 replica after 210,000,000 traces.

In order to verify our findings, we also performed the χ^2 test on the same data sets. All circuits that failed TVLA fail the χ^2 test with less than 30,000 traces, regardless of the number of replicas. On the other hand, the χ^2 test passes for DOM1-NC with 1 replica for 30 million traces. We did not run the test for more traces due to its higher computational complexity.

Table 2. The masking schemes, number of UUT replicas, the SNR ($\frac{\mu}{\sigma}$) and number of traces required to fail the TVLA test.

Scheme	Replicas	SNR	Traces
Mask off			
DOM1-SNI	1	174.3	823
TI33	1	172.3	1,536
Mask on			
DOM	9	174.5	7,784
DOM-SNI	9	173.3	2,140
TI33	9	804.7	1,393
TI33	1	864.19	62,924
DOM1-NC	99	2028.44	5,913,875
DOM1-NC	9	1183.08	6,190,000
DOM1-NC	1	33.57	>200,000,000

6 Implementation of the Full Romulus Modes

The designers of Romulus [17] proposed several design strategies for implementing hardware accelerators for Romulus-N and Romulus-M, where the computation is performed entirely based on the TBC implementation, without any extra storage. These design strategies can be extended to the masked implementations, as well. Figure 12 shows an architecture based on these strategies. The proposed architecture is compliant with the lightweight cryptography hardware API proposed in [21]. This choice is to allow fair comparison to other implementations and to allow a full implementation that does not ignore any hidden costs such as key storage, nonce storage or message padding. The architecture, depicted in Fig. 12, is built based on 4 register files:

1. State Register File (SRF): consists of 8 words, each of 32 bits.
2. Key Register File (KRF): consists of 4 or 8 words, each of 32 bits.
3. Tweak Register File (TRF): consists of 8 words, each of 32 bits. Since the tweak is always public, it does not need to be masked.
4. Counter Register File (CRF): consists of 128 bits.

The SRF is reset to 0 at the beginning a new encryption or decryption instruction. It is loaded in the feedback mode, where the G function is applied to the bottom word in a byte-wise fashion. It transforms each byte as follows:

$$(x_0, x_1, x_2, x_3, x_4, x_5, x_6, x_7) \rightarrow$$

$$(x_1, x_2, x_3, x_4, x_5, x_6, x_7, x_0 \oplus x_7)$$

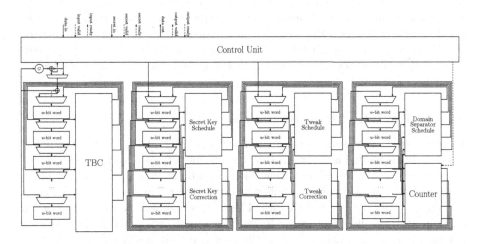

Fig. 12. Architecture of the Romulus accelerator. Solid arrows are w-bit wide, where w is the configurable bus width. The dotted arrows are control signals. Some of the control signals are omitted from the diagram for simplicity including multiplexers' selectors, registers enables and resets. The red arrow is only needed for Romulus-M and can be removed if Romulus-M support is not required. The blue multiplexer is used to switch between encryption and decryption.

The output of this transformation is XORed with the input word (from the control unit) to generate the plaintext during encryption and the ciphertext during decryption. The plaintext is XORed with bottom register to generate the feedback word that get fed from the top, while all the other words are shifted down. In order to support Romulus-M, a bypass connection is needed such that the tag from the top operation in Fig. 4 is fed back into the SRF. This bypass connection is shown in red in Fig. 12. The KRF and TRF are similar, where they are loaded from the top down, with no feedback needed. The CRF is used to hold the block counter and the domain separator; the constant part of the public tweak. It does not need a load operation, as it is reset to the initial value of the counter. Each register file can also be read and written in parallel, where the masked SKINNY round function is represented in Fig. 12 by the combination of TBC, Key Schedule, Tweak Schedule and Domain Separator Schedule.

During execution, the nonce will be stored in the TRF, while the secret key will be stored in the KRF. There values will be changed, and needs to be corrected, which is the purpose of the Secret Key Correction and Tweak Correction circuits. These operations, alongside the Counter, are performed in between the TBC calls, in parallel to loading the SRF.

Since the feedback function is linear and operates on each byte independently, no area overhead is required, as shares are loaded and read serially (word by word), and the feedback function is applied locally on each byte of the shares. The key shares can be processed independently by applying the key schedule and key correction functions on each one of the key shares, independently. Besides, it is easy to choose whether the key is protected or not. On the other hand, the tweak and counter do not need to be protected. This means that only the odd blocks of A need to be shared. For Romulus-M, the situation is slightly different, since some of the blocks M are also processed as tweak, then the designer can decide whether to mask the tweak or not, based on the security assumptions. By the same analysis of whether or not the key-schedule needs to be protected, we can argue about the security of not masking the tweak. We only consider the case where the tweak is not masked.

6.1   Double-Edged Implementations

Usually, hardware masking is considered on the primitive level, where the number of clock cycles needed is determined by the number of flip-slop stages needed for the masked circuit. We observe that these flip-flop stages can be be very short in terms of the critical path of stage, with some stages consisting of 1 AND gate, and the majority have very low depth. This means that the SBox implementation can run at very high frequency. On the other hand, when a full AEAD mode is implemented, the critical path of the overall circuit is slower, dominated by the control FSM, which includes block counters, state registers, control signal logic,... etc.. In order to reduce the impact of the lower frequency imposed by the control circuits, we propose double-edged implementations of the SBox, where odd flip-flop stages are clocked on the negative edge and even stages clocked normally on the positive edge. For example, in case of DOM1, a_0, a_1, a_2, a_5 and

a_6 are clocked using the negative clock edge. This strategy cuts the latency of the TBC by almost half, in the context of the overall scheme.

7 Synthesis Results

We have synthesized our implementations using the different SBox implementations with Synopsys Design Compiler and TSMC general purpose 65nm library. The results are presented in Table 3. Each implementation requires 8 cycles to load one plaintext block and $40 \times (c + 1)$ cycles for each TBC call, where c is the number of cycles needed for the SBox implementation. For DOM1-NC, *i.e.* the power gated implementation, $40 \times (c + 2)$ as it takes 2 cycles to compute the linear layer of the cipher, 1 cycle per share. In Table 4, we show the latency, throughput and area needed to encrypt 1600 bytes of A and M using different masking schemes.

Table 3. Synthesis results of different implementations of the overall design using Synopsys Design Compiler and TSMC 65 nm. The table shows area in GE. All implementations are synthesized for about 2 GHz († means less than 2 GHz).

Implementation	Protected key		Unprotected key	
	SE	DE	SE	DE
DOM1	13395.97	15269.5†	11889.72	13579.51†
DOM1-Pipelined	14619.5	14886.5	13068.47	13276.52
DOM1-Rapid	20634.3	22230.6†	19103.47	20716.25†
DOM1-SNI	15818.3	15977.99	14481.73	14441.25
DOM1-Dep.	15557.2	18265.97†	13945	16670.49†
CMS1	15912.7	16165.97	14372.01	14595.28
CMS1-Rapid	23344	24570.5†	21811.74	22474.72†
HPC	18585	18830.76	17338.75	17234.76
HPC2	19344	19905.48	18397.22	18280.28
ISW	16055.5	16264.72	14667.01	14541.74
ISW-PINI	17626.5	17944.1	16422.01	16266.52
PARA	15048.3	15139.5	13589.2	13577.01
PINI	16286.7	17991.25	14625.97	16321.5
TI33	31137.99	34550.97	29433.27	33131.25
DOM1-NC	16455	17272.5	14825.1	15029.7

Table 4. Comparison of Encrypt 1600 bytes of both A and M using Romulus-N using different implementations. The goals stand for: - for unprotected, P for probing, NI, SNI, and C for coupling resistance

Implementation	Cycles	Critical path (ns)	Throughput (Gbps)	Area (GE)	Goal
Unmasked, 4 rounds/cycle	2318	2	5.52	10124.24	–
Unmasked, 1 round/cycle	6048	1.11	3.81	7348.61	–
Masked, 1 cycle/round	8636	0.65	4.56	33131.25	P
Masked, 2 cycles/round	12088	0.6	2.35	20716.25	P
Masked, 3 cycles/round	18128	0.5	2.82	13276.52	P
Masked, 5 cycles/round	30208	0.5	1.69	14441.25	SNI
Masked, 7 cycles/round	42288	0.5	1.21	16266.52	PINI
Masked, 14 cycles/round	84568	0.5	0.6	15029.7	C

8   Concluding Thoughts

Boolean masking is an important countermeasure for hardware cryptographic permutations. In this paper, we show that the application of such countermeasure to symmetric-key schemes, and specifically TBC-based schemes is tricky. We confirm observations made by other researcher that almost all masking schemes are based on assumptions that are not true for hardware implementations, mainly, the independence of leakage from different shares and composability. The first can be shown to not be true by analyzing the SBoxes using TVLA. The second one is not violated in itself, but relies on sub-blocks, known as gadgets, being secure, which depends on the level and nature of security required. On the other side, since it is not clear if such leakage is exploitable, it is up to the system designers to deploy extra countermeasures or assess the risk involved in using such implementations. We do not claim that these implementations are of no use in practice.

When it comes to Romulus, we showed in this paper that applying masking schemes to it incurs a significant overhead; between 2 times and 4 times the area for first-order masking and a significant increase in latency. However, using double-edged SBoxes we were able to reduce the latency by almost half and using TI33 we were able to get an implementation that requires only 40 cycles per TBC (same as the unprotected round-based implementation). The double-edge clocking strategy is helpful only for implementations that operate on different SBox calls in parallel, as it requires the internal registers of the SBox to be independent of the overall circuit control unit and in case of byte-serial implementations, a lot of cycles are spent just to move bytes around.

TI33 requires 4 shares for the TBC state and does not require any extra random bits to execute. It has almost $4\times$ overhead compared to unprotected implementations. However, since its SBox fails TVLA, we should be careful about the conclusions we make. DOM1-NC, on the other hand, requires at least 14 cycles per round. On the positive side, when area is the most important aspect, the area overhead for DOM1-NC is about 2× only. This is since most of the state of Romulus is either public tweaks or the secret key.

We should note that the overhead due to the high-level mode of Romulus is almost negligible and almost all the cost comes from the underlying TBC. The limitations and speed degradation of the scheme comes primarily from the inefficiency of SKINNY when masked and the inability to use optimizations such as round unrolling for masked implementations. This opens an important research question regarding the design of masking friendly TBCs. While a small number of proposals exist, they either have security weaknesses, not widely studied or are not compatible with Romulus due to supporting only short tweaks.

Finally, in this paper we opted for evaluating the gadgets practically and relying on composability for the security of the overall implementation. Part of the future work is practically performing TVLA on full AEAD scheme.

Acknowledgement. We would like to thank Nele Mentens and the anonymous reviewers for their detailed comments and helpful suggestions. The first author was supported in this work by a joint Wallenberg Artificial Intelligence, Autonomous Systems and Software Program-Nanyang Technological University (WASP-NTU) grant. The second author acknowledges the support from the Singapore National Research Foundation ("SOCure" grant NRF2018NCR-NCR002-0001 – www.green-ic.org/socure).

References

1. Barthe, G., Belaïd, S., Cassiers, G., Fouque, P.-A., Grégoire, B., Standaert, F.-X.: maskVerif: automated verification of higher-order masking in presence of physical Defaults. In: Sako, K., Schneider, S., Ryan, P.Y.A. (eds.) ESORICS 2019. LNCS, vol. 11735, pp. 300–318. Springer, Cham (2019). https://doi.org/10.1007/978-3-030-29959-0_15

2. Barthe, G., Belaïd, S., Dupressoir, F., Fouque, P.A., Grégoire, B., Strub, P.Y., Zucchini, R.: Strong non-interference and type-directed higher-order masking. In: Proceedings of the 2016 ACM SIGSAC Conference on Computer and Communications Security, pp. 116–129 (2016)

3. Barthe, G., Dupressoir, F., Faust, S., Grégoire, B., Standaert, F.-X., Strub, P.-Y.: Parallel implementations of masking schemes and the bounded moment leakage model. In: Coron, J.-S., Nielsen, J.B. (eds.) EUROCRYPT 2017. LNCS, vol. 10210, pp. 535–566. Springer, Cham (2017). https://doi.org/10.1007/978-3-319-56620-7_19

4. Battistello, A., Coron, J.-S., Prouff, E., Zeitoun, R.: Horizontal side-channel attacks and countermeasures on the ISW masking scheme. In: Gierlichs, B., Poschmann, A.Y. (eds.) CHES 2016. LNCS, vol. 9813, pp. 23–39. Springer, Heidelberg (2016). https://doi.org/10.1007/978-3-662-53140-2_2

5. Beierle, C., et al.: The SKINNY family of block ciphers and its low-latency variant MANTIS. In: Robshaw, M., Katz, J. (eds.) CRYPTO 2016. LNCS, vol. 9815, pp. 123–153. Springer, Heidelberg (2016). https://doi.org/10.1007/978-3-662-53008-5_5

6. Bilgin, B., Gierlichs, B., Nikova, S., Nikov, V., Rijmen, V.: A more efficient AES threshold implementation. In: Pointcheval, D., Vergnaud, D. (eds.) AFRICACRYPT 2014. LNCS, vol. 8469, pp. 267–284. Springer, Cham (2014). https://doi.org/10.1007/978-3-319-06734-6_17

7. Brier, E., Clavier, C., Olivier, F.: Correlation power analysis with a leakage model. In: Joye, M., Quisquater, J.-J. (eds.) CHES 2004. LNCS, vol. 3156, pp. 16–29. Springer, Heidelberg (2004). https://doi.org/10.1007/978-3-540-28632-5_2

8. Caforio, A., Collins, D., Glamočanin, O., Banik, S.: Improving first-order threshold implementations of skinny. In: Adhikari, A., Küsters, R., Preneel, B. (eds.) Progress in Cryptology - INDOCRYPT 2021, pp. 246–267. Springer International Publishing, Cham (2021)

9. Cassiers, G., Grégoire, B., Levi, I., Standaert, F.X.: Hardware private circuits: From trivial composition to full verification. IEEE Trans. Comput. **70**(10), 1677–1690 (2020)

10. Cassiers, G., Standaert, F.X.: Trivially and efficiently composing masked gadgets with probe isolating non-interference. IEEE Trans. Inform. Forensics Security **15**, 2542–2555 (2020)

11. De Cnudde, T., Ender, M., Moradi, A.: Hardware masking, revisited. IACR Transactions on Cryptographic Hardware and Embedded Systems, pp. 123–148 (2018)

12. De Cnudde, T., et al.: Masking AES with $d + 1$ shares in hardware. In: Gierlichs, B., Poschmann, A.Y. (eds.) CHES 2016. LNCS, vol. 9813, pp. 194–212. Springer, Heidelberg (2016). https://doi.org/10.1007/978-3-662-53140-2_10

13. Faust, S., Grosso, V., Pozo, S., Paglialonga, C., Standaert, F.X.: Composable masking schemes in the presence of physical defaults & the robust probing model (2018)

14. Gilbert Goodwill, B.J., Jaffe, J., Rohatgi, P., et al.: A testing methodology for side-channel resistance validation. In: NIST non-invasive attack testing workshop, vol. 7, pp. 115–136 (2011)

15. Groß, H., Mangard, S., Korak, T.: Domain-oriented masking: Compact masked hardware implementations with arbitrary protection order. Cryptology ePrint Archive (2016)

16. Ishai, Y., Sahai, A., Wagner, D.: Private circuits: securing hardware against probing attacks. In: Boneh, D. (ed.) CRYPTO 2003. LNCS, vol. 2729, pp. 463–481. Springer, Heidelberg (2003). https://doi.org/10.1007/978-3-540-45146-4_27

17. Iwata, T., Khairallah, M., Minematsu, K., Peyrin, T.: Romulus v1.3. Finalist in the NIST lightweight cryptography project (2019)

18. Jean, J.: TikZ for Cryptographers. https://www.iacr.org/authors/tikz/ (2016)

19. Jean, J., Nikolić, I., Peyrin, T.: Tweaks and keys for block ciphers: the TWEAKEY framework. In: Sarkar, P., Iwata, T. (eds.) ASIACRYPT 2014. LNCS, vol. 8874, pp. 274–288. Springer, Heidelberg (2014). https://doi.org/10.1007/978-3-662-45608-8_15

20. Jiang, H., Marek-Sadowska, M., Nassif, S.R.: Benefits and costs of power-gating technique. In: 2005 International Conference on Computer Design, pp. 559–566. IEEE (2005)

21. Kaps, J.P., Diehl, W., Tempelmeier, M., Homsirikamol, E., Gaj, K.: Hardware api for lightweight cryptography, pp. 1–26 (2019). https://cryptography.gmu.edu/athena/index.php

22. Knichel, D., Sasdrich, P., Moradi, A.: SILVER – statistical independence and leakage verification. In: Moriai, S., Wang, H. (eds.) ASIACRYPT 2020. LNCS, vol. 12491, pp. 787–816. Springer, Cham (2020). https://doi.org/10.1007/978-3-030-64837-4_26

23. Kocher, P., Jaffe, J., Jun, B.: Differential power analysis. In: Wiener, M. (ed.) CRYPTO 1999. LNCS, vol. 1666, pp. 388–397. Springer, Heidelberg (1999). https://doi.org/10.1007/3-540-48405-1_25

24. Levi, I., Bellizia, D., Standaert, F.X.: Reducing a masked implementation's effective security order with setup manipulations: And an explanation based on externally-amplified couplings. IACR Transactions on Cryptographic Hardware and Embedded Systems, pp. 293–317 (2019)

25. Moradi, A., Richter, B., Schneider, T., Standaert, F.X.: Leakage detection with the χ^2-test. In: IACR Transactions on Cryptographic Hardware and Embedded Systems, pp. 209–237 (2018)

26. Reparaz, O., Bilgin, B., Nikova, S., Gierlichs, B., Verbauwhede, I.: Consolidating masking schemes. In: Gennaro, R., Robshaw, M. (eds.) CRYPTO 2015. LNCS, vol. 9215, pp. 764–783. Springer, Heidelberg (2015). https://doi.org/10.1007/978-3-662-47989-6_37

27. Schneider, T., Moradi, A.: Leakage assessment methodology. In: Güneysu, T., Handschuh, H. (eds.) CHES 2015. LNCS, vol. 9293, pp. 495–513. Springer, Heidelberg (2015). https://doi.org/10.1007/978-3-662-48324-4_25

28. Standaert, F.-X.: How (Not) to use Welch's T-test in side-channel security evaluations. In: Bilgin, B., Fischer, J.-B. (eds.) CARDIS 2018. LNCS, vol. 11389, pp. 65–79. Springer, Cham (2019). https://doi.org/10.1007/978-3-030-15462-2_5

Bias Cancellation of MixColumns

Subhadeep Banik[1]([✉]), Andrea Caforio[2], Kostas Papagiannopoulos[3],
and Francesco Regazzoni[1,3]

[1] Universita della Svizzera Italiana, Lugano, Switzerland
subhadeep.banik@usi.ch
[2] LASEC, Ecole Polytechnique Fédérale de Lausanne, Lausanne, Switzerland
andrea.caforio@epfl.ch
[3] University of Amsterdam, Amsterdam, The Netherlands
{k.papagiannopoulos,f.regazzoni}@uva.nl

Abstract. At COSADE'2020, Carré et al. established a novel bias-cancelling property of the AES MixColumns matrix that effectively corrects any skewed output distribution of a state byte due to a faulty substitution box. Consequently, any effected byte is rendered uniform upon passing through the MixColumns layer.

In this work in progress paper, we revisit and generalize this result and in the process identify a large class of matrices that exhibit this bias cancellation phenomenon and conclude with a foray into how this property is advantageous in the design of countermeasures against Persistent Fault Injections.

Keywords: Block cipher · PFA · AES · MixColumns · Countermeasure

1 Introduction

Persistent faults in cryptographic algorithms attempt to bridge the gap between short-lived and permanent faults as they remain intact over multiple encryptions but vanish once the device is rebooted. The study of such faults, termed Persistent Fault Analysis (PFA), gained traction at TCHES'18 in a work by Zhang et al. [8]. Their attack exploits the statistical imbalance in a collected set of ciphertexts, caused by one or more overwritten S-box elements, to recover the last round key of substitution-permutation networks. The idea is based on the fact that in most SPN ciphers, such as AES, a skewed substitution layer distribution translates directly into a skewed ciphertext distribution. To see this, let an S-box operation followed by a key addition during the last round. Suppose the element u does not appear anymore in the S-box output due to the persistent fault injection. As a consequence, $u \oplus k$ is an impossible ciphertext word, where k is a last round key word. Hence, after enough collected ciphertexts from the faulty device, k can be uniquely identified. The authors subsequently show that approximately 1500 ciphertexts are sufficient to recover the last round-key of AES in the presence of a single overwritten S-box element. They further demonstrate how to use the Rowhammer attack [5] in order to provoke persistent fault injections in the S-box of vulnerable AES software implementations.

L. Batina et al. (Eds.): SPACE 2022, LNCS 13783, pp. 70–80, 2022.
https://doi.org/10.1007/978-3-031-22829-2_4

The study of persistent faults was deepened in ensuing works that extended the baseline attack to the setting of multiple persistent faults [3,7] and reverse engineering endeavours [1]. At TCHES'20 Zhang et al. improved the overall complexity of their white paper attack by choosing a different statistical angle [9] concerning the analysis of the set of collected ciphertexts, which was subsequently optimized by Carré et al. [2]. This attack took advantage of the fact that if the statistical distribution of the of the bytes at the input of the faulty S-box was uniform, then one byte at the output of the S-box was likely to occur twice as much as any other byte. The attacker can leverage this fact to mount a more efficient attack. It turns out that the input distribution of bytes at the beginning of the last AES round is uniform due to a special bias-cancelling property of the AES MixColumns matrix. In short, the bias cancellation property may be stated as follows: let the four input bytes to the MixColumns matrix be drawn from a skewed distribution D in which one specific byte y^- occurs with zero probability, and another y^+ occurs with double probability i.e., $\frac{2}{256}$, and all other byte values occur with the same probability $\frac{1}{256}$ (this distribution captures the situation encountered doing PFA in which one S-box table entry is overwritten by y^+). Then the four output bytes of the MixColumns operation are uniformly distributed.

Contributions and Organization. In the paper by Carré et al. [2], it was additionally observed that the inverse MixColumns matrix of AES does not exhibit this bias-cancelling property. In a first step, we revisit this result and ultimately generalize it in a manner that clearly characterizes a set of all possible matrices that possess this trait. The ease of mounting a Persistent Fault attack and ultimately its acute destructiveness are crucial issues that need to be addressed in the form of an effective countermeasure. A preliminary treatment of this subject was commenced in [1] which introduced a probabilistic counter-based hardware structure enhancing an unprotected block cipher circuit. Although this solution provided adequate protection for constructions with many rounds it was severely lacking when it comes to AES. In the second part of this work, we explore the design space of countermeasures that utilize the bias-cancelling property of the class of matrices established in the first part in order to nullify Persistent Fault Analysis where a single fault is affecting the S-box lookup table of an AES implementation without relying on a probabilistic data structure. Ultimately, we conclude this work in progress by mapping out open problems with respect to stronger attack models.

This paper is organized in the following way: In Sect. 2, we prove a theorem that identifies a large class of bias-cancelling matrices. Subsequently, in Sect. 3, we explore PFA countermeasures that are based on this property. Section 4 concludes this work with a list of open problems.

2   Bias Cancellation

For the remainder of the paper, we adhere to the fault model where the attacker can inject a *single* fault in the AES S-box table that alters one entry thus skewing the output distribution. More formally, such a fault overwrites an element y^- with a new value y^+, effectively duplicating it. This results in a bias in the output distribution of the lookup table. Assuming a uniformly distributed input, the value y^- cannot be observed at all as the output, while the value y^+ is observed with an increased probability of $\frac{2}{256}$ and other values are observed with an unchanged probability of $\frac{1}{256}$. More formally, the output probability distribution D is defined as:

$$
D_{y^+,y^-}(y) = \begin{cases} 0, & \text{if } y = y^- \\ \frac{2}{256} & \text{if } y = y^+ \\ \frac{1}{256} & \text{otherwise.} \end{cases} \tag{1}
$$

Proposition 1 (MixColumns Bias Cancellation [2]). *Let us denote by $y^-, y^+ \in \mathbb{F}_{256}$ the overwritten and duplicated element after a persistent fault injection and let the distribution $D(y^+, y^-)$ be defined by Eq. (1). Denote by $B_0, B_1, B_2, B_3 \in \mathbb{F}_{256}$ the four bytes representing an AES state column before a MixColumns operation, independent and identically distributed according to distribution D. Then each byte $Z_0, Z_1, Z_2, Z_3 \in \mathbb{F}_{256}$ representing an AES state column after a MixColumns operation is uniformly distributed.*

The above proposition ensures that any byte output of the MixColumn layer, and thus every byte input to the Substitution layer, is uniformly distributed. Through maximum likelihood arguments, it is then possible to extract the secret key in significantly fewer encryption queries than originally suggested in the PFA white paper. The authors further pointed out that not all matrices exhibit this property. For example, the inverse MixColumns does not posses any bias cancelling powers. In this work, we wanted to find out what the general characteristics of matrices are that have this property, i.e., whether it is immediately identifiable from its algebraic structure.

Theorem 1. *Consider an arbitrary linear layer $L : \mathbb{F}_{256}^4 \to \mathbb{F}_{256}$ defined as*

$$
L(B_0, B_1, B_2, B_3) = \alpha B_0 \oplus \beta B_1 \oplus \gamma B_2 \oplus \delta B_3,
$$

where $\alpha, \beta, \gamma, \delta \in \mathbb{F}_{256} \setminus \{0\}$ are non-zero coefficients of the MixColumns matrix. Let each B_i be distributed according to the density function D_{y^+,y^-} in Eq. (1). Then the byte $Z = L(B_0, B_1, B_2, B_3)$ is distributed uniformly if and only if either one of the four expressions hold:

$$
\begin{aligned}
&1) \ \alpha \oplus \beta \oplus \gamma = 0 \\
&2) \ \alpha \oplus \beta \oplus \delta = 0 \\
&3) \ \alpha \oplus \gamma \oplus \delta = 0 \\
&4) \ \beta \oplus \gamma \oplus \delta = 0
\end{aligned}
$$

Proof. The idea is to show that if B_0, B_1, B_2, B_3 are distributed according to D_{y^+,y^-}, then each value of Z occurs equally frequently. Given two lists L_1, L_2

of n-bit vectors over $\mathbb{F}_2$ such that the vector $u \in \mathbb{F}_2^n$ appears in L_1 a total of a_u times and in L_2 a total of b_u times. If we make a combined list $L_1 \oplus L_2$, of size $|L_1| \cdot |L_2|$ by XORing each element if L_1 with each element of L_2, then the number of times u appears in this combined list is given by $c_u = \sum_{i \in \mathbb{F}_2^n} a_i \cdot b_{i \oplus u}$. This kind of convolution can be calculated quickly using the Fast Walsh-Hadamard Transform (FWHT).

If A, B, C are vectors of length 2^n over the integers $\mathbb{Z}$, containing the a_i, b_i and c_i respectively, then we have $C = \text{FWHT}(\text{FWHT}(A) * \text{FWHT}(B))$, where $*$ represents element-wise integer multiplication. The above result can be also extended to multiple lists, meaning that if A_i denotes the vector of frequencies in the list L_i then the corresponding frequency vector C in $\bigoplus L_i$, is similarly given as $C = \text{FWHT}(\prod \text{FWHT}(A_i))$. Let us now construct the lists L_0, L_1, L_2, L_3 in the following way:

1. $\alpha \cdot B_0 \in L_0$, when B_0 is a list of length 256 which has all other byte values once, y^+ twice but does not have y^-.
2. $\beta \cdot B_1 \in L_1$, when B_1 is same as B_0.
3. $\gamma \cdot B_2 \in L_2$, when B_2 is same as B_0.
4. $\delta \cdot B_3 \in L_3$, when B_3 is same as B_0.

It can be easily seen, for example, that the list L_0 does not contain $\alpha \cdot y^-$ but $\alpha \cdot y^+$ appears twice, and all other vectors appear exactly once. So we can write $A_0 = U + T(\alpha \cdot y^+, \alpha \cdot y^-)$, where U is the all 1 vector and $T(\alpha \cdot y^+, \alpha \cdot y^-)$ is a vector with 1 at location $\alpha \cdot y^+$, -1 at $\alpha \cdot y^-$, and remaining locations 0. Now we have $C = \text{FWHT}(\prod_{i=0}^{3} \text{FWHT}(A_i))$. For C to represent the uniform distribution, then from the properties of FWHT, we know that $\prod_{i=0}^{3} \text{FWHT}(A_i)$ must have only one non-zero element (in the 0-th location). The remaining $2^n - 1$ entries of this array must be 0. This is a characterizing condition: if C does not represent the uniform distribution, then $\prod_{i=0}^{3} \text{FWHT}(A_i)$ must have multiple non-zero entries.

Now $\text{FWHT}(A)$ is essentially a linear transform, and is given by the matrix-vector product $F \cdot A$ over (Z). Here F is a matrix of size $2^n \times 2^n$ over $\mathbb{Z}$, and the (i,j)-th element of F is given by $(-1)^{\langle i,j \rangle}$. The expression $\langle i,j \rangle$ denotes the dot product between i, j over $\mathbb{F}_2$. For example, for $n = 4$, $\langle 0011, 1110 \rangle = 0 \cdot 1 \oplus 0 \cdot 1 \oplus 1 \cdot 1 \oplus 1 \cdot 0 = 1$. Therefore we have,

$$\text{FWHT}(A_0) = F \cdot A_0$$
$$= F \cdot U + F \cdot T(\alpha \cdot y^+, \alpha \cdot y^-)$$
$$= (2^n, 0, 0, \ldots, 0) + V_{\alpha \cdot y^+} - V_{\alpha \cdot y^-}.$$

Here, V_i represents the i-th column of F. Therefore the j-th element of V_i is given as $(-1)^{\langle i,j \rangle}$. Therefore for non-zero j, the j-th element of $\text{FWHT}(A_0)$ is $(-1)^{<\alpha \cdot y^+, j>} - (-1)^{<\alpha \cdot y^-, j>}$. Denote $\Delta = y^+ \oplus y^-$, then we have

$$\text{FWHT}(A_0)[j] = \begin{cases} 0, & \text{if } \langle \alpha \cdot y^+, j \rangle = \langle \alpha \cdot y^-, j \rangle \Rightarrow \langle \alpha \cdot \Delta, j \rangle = 0 \\ \pm 2, & \text{if } \langle \alpha \cdot y^+, j \rangle \neq \langle \alpha \cdot y^-, j \rangle \Rightarrow \langle \alpha \cdot \Delta, j \rangle = 1 \end{cases}$$

We can make similar deductions about all the other $\mathrm{FWHT}(A_i)$. Let us assume that one of the four conditions in the theorem statement holds. Without loss of generality, let us say that $\alpha \oplus \beta \oplus \gamma = 0$ holds. Note that any non-zero j-th element of the product of $\prod_{i=0}^{3} \mathrm{FWHT}(A_i)$ is non-zero if and only if we have a $j \neq 0$ such that

$$\langle \alpha \cdot \Delta, j \rangle = \langle \beta \cdot \Delta, j \rangle = \langle \gamma \cdot \Delta, j \rangle = \langle \delta \cdot \Delta, j \rangle = 1 \qquad (2)$$

We can see that no such j can exist as $\langle \alpha \cdot \Delta, j \rangle = \langle \beta \cdot \Delta, j \rangle = \langle \gamma \cdot \Delta, j \rangle = 1$ implies that $\langle (\alpha \oplus \beta \oplus \gamma) \cdot \Delta, j \rangle = 1 \Rightarrow \langle 0, j \rangle = 1$, which is clearly not possible. So all non-zero locations of $\prod_{i=0}^{3} \mathrm{FWHT}(A_i)$ must have 0, which implies that C represents the uniform distribution.

To prove the *only if* part, let us assume that none of the four theorem statements hold. We show that for such a set of coefficients C can not represent the uniform distribution, in other words $\prod_{i=0}^{3} \mathrm{FWHT}(A_i)$ must have multiple non-zero entries, thus Eq. (2) must have multiple non-zero solutions j. Consider the matrix M of size $4 \times n$ over $\mathbb{F}_2$ whose four rows are given by the vectors $\alpha \cdot \Delta, \beta \cdot \Delta, \gamma \cdot \Delta, \delta \cdot \Delta$. Equation (2) is the same as saying that $M \cdot j = (1, 1, 1, 1)^T$ has a solution, where j over here is seen as a column of n bits. If the rank of M is 4, then the map $j \to M \cdot j$ is obviously subjective over $\mathbb{F}_2^4$ and thus $(1, 1, 1, 1)^T$ is surely in the image of $M \cdot j$. This guarantees that Eq. (2) has a solution. If not, consider the following cases:

- **Case 1.** If the rank of M is 1, which means that $\alpha = \beta = \gamma = \delta$, and the four rows of M are identical. Since $\alpha \cdot \Delta$ is non zero there must be at least one column (say k-th) of M which has all 1. Thus we can then select j to be the column vector which has only one 1 in the k-th location and remaining zeros.

- **Case 2.** If the rank of M is 2, then (up to a permutation of values) we can either have coefficients of the form $\alpha = \beta = x$ and $\gamma = \delta = y$, or $\alpha = \beta = \gamma = x$ and $\delta = y$, with $x \neq y$. Note that coefficients of the form $\alpha = x, \beta = y$ and $\gamma = x \oplus y$ and $\delta = x$ or y or $x \oplus y$ are not permitted since we will then have $\alpha \oplus \beta \oplus \gamma = 0$. For the first sub-case, again since $x \cdot \Delta \neq 0$, there must be one column of M (say k_1-th) with first two entries 1. We then construct $j = j_1$ as in the previous case. If the other 2 entries of the k_1-th column are also 1, then we have $M \cdot j_1 = (1, 1, 1, 1)^T$ and we are done. If not we have $M \cdot j_1 = (1, 1, 0, 0)^T$. Since $y \cdot \Delta \neq 0$, we can similarly construct j_2 such that $M \cdot j_2 = (0, 0, 1, 1)^T$. This implies that $M \cdot (j_1 \oplus j_2) = (1, 1, 1, 1)^T$. The analysis for the second sub-case is exactly similar.

- **Case 3.** If the rank of M is 3, then (up to a permutation of values) we have $\alpha = x, \beta = y, \gamma = z$ and $\delta = x \oplus y \oplus z / x / y / z$. Again note that $\delta = x \oplus y / y \oplus z / x \oplus z$ are not permitted since then we would have one of the 3-wise sums of $\alpha, \beta, \gamma, \delta$ equal to 0. Consider the matrix M' of size $3 \times N$, which is constructed by removing the $\delta \cdot \Delta$ row from M. Clearly M' has rank 3, and so the map $j' \to M' \cdot j'$ is obviously subjective over $\mathbb{F}_2^3$. And so we must have a j' such that $M' \cdot j' = (1, 1, 1)^T$. This means that

$$\langle \alpha \cdot \Delta, j' \rangle = \langle \beta \cdot \Delta, j' \rangle = \langle \gamma \cdot \Delta, j' \rangle = 1.$$

And so $\langle(\alpha\oplus\beta\oplus\gamma)\cdot\Delta, j'\rangle = 1\oplus1\oplus1 = 1$. This implies that $M\cdot j' = (1,1,1,1)^T$ for all the four values of $\delta = x \oplus y \oplus z/x/y/z$ so we are done. The three cases above prove that Eq. (2) must have a solution in all cases, and so C does not represent the uniform distribution.

Corollary 1. It can be seen that for the AES MixColumns matrix $\alpha = 2, \beta = 3, \gamma = 1, \delta = 1$. We have that $\alpha \oplus \beta \oplus \gamma = 0$ and so by the previous theorem, this matrix has bias cancellation property. However, for the inverse MixColumns matrix we have $\alpha = $ 0xe, $\beta = $ 0xb, $\gamma = $ 0xd, $\delta = $ 0x9. None of the 3-wise sums for this set of coefficients result in 0, and hence the inverse AES MixColumns matrix does not have the property of bias-cancellation.

3   Applications

We observe that PFA works because in the last AES round the MixColumns operation is *not* performed. The biased output of the faulty S-box is directly XORed with the last round key to produce the ciphertext bytes. Subsequently the ciphertext can be accessed by the attacker to craft a statistical distinguisher. Whereas the bias cancelling property of the AES MixColumns was actually used by [2] to perform a more efficient PFA on AES, one can see that this same bias cancelling property can completely prevent the attack, if one were to include the MixColumns operation in the 10th and last AES round. With this particular AES modification, any bias in the distribution of the bytes in last the S-box layer would be cancelled by the MixColumns layer, making it hard to craft a statistical distinguisher. To analyze the behavior of this countermeasure we simulated again a single-fault PFA. Testing yields positive results; a modified AES with an extra MixColumns operation before the last AddRoundKey is able to prevent PFA as devised in [2,8].

Naturally the question arises as to whether modifying the 10th AES round to include a MixColumns layer effectively thwarts any PFA. The answer is however negative. An attack exists that targets single bytes at the S-box output of the penultimate round and works by inverting the MixColumns operation during the last round and performing 2^{32} key guesses [4,6]. The attack is explained diagrammatically in Fig. 1. Note all the distribution of bytes in the states in pink/gray background are unbiased/biased respectively. The main idea is that we guess one column of the 10th round key K_{10}, and compute backwards. This enables us to compute the first column of the states marked C, D and the main diagonal of B. For a correct guess of the round-key column we are expected to observe in the bias in the distribution of the bytes in B. We can use this as a distinguisher to find the correct round key column.

To demonstrate this, we performed a single-fault PFA and found the secret key of the modified AES after 10k encryptions. In conclusion, modifying AES with an additional MixColumns prevents only the standard version of PFA and forces the adversary to do additional encryption queries and incurs an increased key guess complexity.

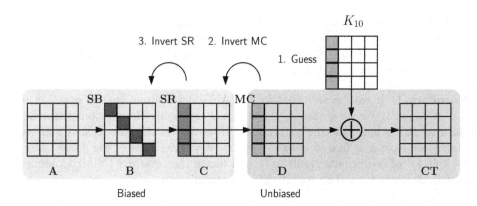

Fig. 1. Persistent Fault Analysis on an AES instance with a modified 10th round.

3.1   Adding an 11th Round

However one may think that adding an additional round after the modified 10th encryption round may remove all bias in the distribution of the ciphertext bytes and at the same time prevent the attack due to [6]. This additional round would omit the substitution layer and consist of only ShiftRows, Forward MixColumns and AddRoundKey operations. Owing to the bias cancellation property of the forward MixColumns matrix, there would not exist any bias to exploit in the distribution of the ciphertext bytes. An exploitable bias in distribution exists only after the 10th round substitution layer. To exploit this bias, the attacker would have to (a) guess the entire 11th round key and invert the key schedule to compute the 10th round key, (b) then use the guessed key values to invert the entire 11th round and part of the 10th round to compute the value of any byte b just after the 10th substitution operation, (c) compute the distribution of b over many collected ciphertexts. If the guessed key values are correct then the attacker will observe bias in b as expected. However this requires guessing the entire 11th round key and thus is not better than exhaustive search. The steps are shown Fig. 2.

This looks promising, because guessing part of the 11th round key would be insufficient to perform the attack. For example, if we guess only the first column of K_{11}, then we will only find the main diagonal of the state marked E in Fig. 2. Now even if we guess the entire of K_{10}, it is insufficient to find an entire column of D, which prevents us from computing the inverse MixColumns operation to find any byte of C.

Nevertheless, we can again demonstrate an attack on this structure with a total complexity of 2^{32} key guesses. This uses the fact that all operations after the 10th round are completely linear. Thus functionally, one may bring forward a linear multiple of the 11th round key and merge with the 10th round key addition operation. The process is explained in Fig. 3. So if we define $\text{Lin} = SR \circ MC$, then we can basically mount the same attack as in Fig. 1, with the only difference that we now guess a column of $K_{10} \oplus \text{Lin}^{-1}(K_{11})$.

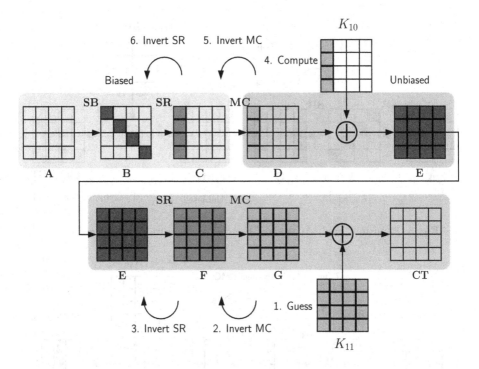

Fig. 2. Modified 10th and 11th round of a PFA-protected AES instance.

3.2 Adding Non-Linearity

The above analysis is instructive in the sense that highlights the fact that even after cancelling distribution bias by adding an additional MixColumns layer, the construction can not prevent PFA without additional non-linearity injected into it. The easiest way to do this on most software platforms is modular addition. One can define a modular addition layer as follows: if c_0 and c_1 are two columns then define $c_0 \boxplus c_1$ as modulo 256 addition between each of the individual bytes of c_0/c_1. After this we can define a Modular Addition (MA) layer as

$$MA : (c_0, c_1, c_2, c_3) \rightarrow (c_0 \boxplus c_1, \ c_1 \boxplus c_2, \ c_2 \boxplus c_3, \ c_0 \boxplus c_1 \boxplus c_2)$$

The operation is invertible as given by

$$MA^{-1} : (c_0, c_1, c_2, c_3) \rightarrow (c_3 \boxminus c_1, \ c_0 \boxplus c_1 \boxminus c_3, \ c_3 \boxminus c_0, \ c_0 \boxplus c_2 \boxminus c_3)$$

We chose this particular structure of MA as this is relatively efficient to implement in software, and is invertible. It is indeed possible to select other invertible layers with similar efficiency in software. This allows us to begin the additional 11th round with a MA layer before the linear layers. The best attack on this construction takes at least 2^{64} key guesses to find one key column. The idea is shown in Fig. 4. We move the 11th AddRoundkey operation before the Mix-Columns layer and guess 2 diagonals of $MC^{-1}(K_{11})$ and one column of K_{10} get

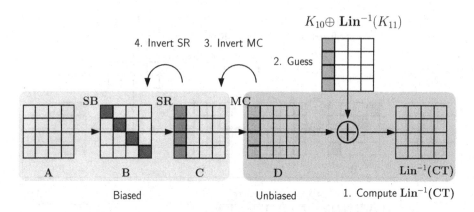

Fig. 3. Persistent Fault Analysis of the countermeasure proposed in Fig. 2.

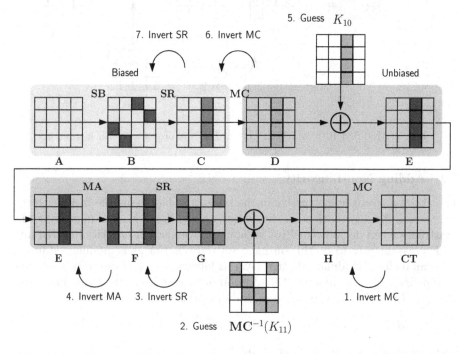

Fig. 4. Attacking an additional round equipped with non-linear modulo addition.

the bytes after the 10th round SubBytes. It may appear that the guess complexity is 2^{96}. However, note that we can get the correct value of the column in the state E, for incorrectly computed columns in F too. This is since, if f_3 and f_0 are the correct values of the columns in F, then $f_3 \boxplus \Delta$ and $f_0 \boxplus \Delta$ also lead to the correct computation of the column in E for any $\Delta \in \{0,1\}^{32}$. Thus around 2^{32} guesses of the diagonals of $MC^{-1}(K_{11})$ lead to a successful attack. If we choose the diagonals randomly, then by birthday assumptions, 2^{32} guesses of the diagonal values are sufficient to mount a successful attack. We further observe that adding a 12th similar round may make the complexity of PFA close to that of exhaustive search.

4   Conclusion and Future Work

In this paper, we investigated the design space of countermeasures based on the bias-cancelling matrices in the setting of a single Persistent Fault injection within the S-box lookup table. However, in practice a fault injection may affect multiple bytes of the S-box which subsequently can be exploited in a similar fashion. It is straightforward to see that the class of matrices identified in Theorem 1 do not cancel any bias occurring in two or more input bytes which subsequently nullifies the countermeasure proposed in Sect. 3. Furthermore, the integration of such a countermeasure requires a thorough study of the induced overhead in both software and hardware environments. In summary, the following salient directions are left as open problems.

- Prove a more general variant of Theorem 1 that allows the characterization of matrices that allow for the cancellation of an arbitrary amount of biased inputs bytes.
- Deepen the study of applications of this new class of matrices in terms of a PFA countermeasure.
- Explore the implementation space of the proposed countermeasure in both software and hardware with regard to efficiency.

References

1. Caforio, A., Banik, S.: A study of persistent fault analysis. In: Bhasin, S., Mendelson, A., Nandi, M. (eds.) SPACE 2019. LNCS, vol. 11947, pp. 13–33. Springer, Cham (2019). https://doi.org/10.1007/978-3-030-35869-3_4
2. Carré, S., Guilley, S., Rioul, O.: Persistent fault analysis with few encryptions. In: Bertoni, G.M., Regazzoni, F. (eds.) COSADE 2020. LNCS, vol. 12244, pp. 3–24. Springer, Cham (2021). https://doi.org/10.1007/978-3-030-68773-1_1
3. Engels, S., Schellenberg, F., Paar, C.: SPFA: SFA on multiple persistent faults. In: 17th Workshop on Fault Detection and Tolerance in Cryptography, FDTC 2020, Milan, Italy, 13 September 2020, pp. 49–56. IEEE (2020). https://doi.org/10.1109/FDTC51366.2020.00014
4. Fuhr, T., Jaulmes, É., Lomné, V., Thillard, A.: Fault attacks on AES with faulty ciphertexts only. In: Fischer, W., Schmidt, J. (eds.) 2013 Workshop on Fault Diagnosis and Tolerance in Cryptography, Los Alamitos, CA, USA, 20 August 2013, pp. 108–118. IEEE Computer Society (2013). https://doi.org/10.1109/FDTC.2013.18
5. Gruss, D., Maurice, C., Mangard, S.: Rowhammer.js: a remote software-induced fault attack in JavaScript. In: Caballero, J., Zurutuza, U., Rodríguez, R.J. (eds.) DIMVA 2016. LNCS, vol. 9721, pp. 300–321. Springer, Cham (2016). https://doi.org/10.1007/978-3-319-40667-1_15

6. Li, W., et al.: Ciphertext-only fault analysis on the led lightweight cryptosystem in the internet of things. IEEE Trans. Dependable Secur. Comput. **16**(3), 454–461 (2019). https://doi.org/10.1109/TDSC.2018.2857770
7. Soleimany, H., Bagheri, N., Hadipour, H., Ravi, P., Bhasin, S., Mansouri, S.: Practical multiple persistent faults analysis. IACR Trans. Cryptogr. Hardw. Embed. Syst. 367–390 (2022). https://doi.org/10.46586/tches.v2022.i1.367-390
8. Zhang, F., et al.: Persistent fault analysis on block ciphers. IACR Trans. Cryptogr. Hardw. Embed. Syst. 150–172 (2018). https://doi.org/10.13154/tches.v2018.i3.150-172
9. Zhang, F., et al.: Persistent fault attack in practice. IACR Trans. Cryptogr. Hardw. Embed. Syst. 172–195 (2020). https://doi.org/10.13154/tches.v2020.i2.172-195

Big Brother Is Watching You: A Closer Look at Backdoor Construction

Anubhab Baksi[1]([✉]), Arghya Bhattacharjee[2], Jakub Breier[3], Takanori Isobe[4], and Mridul Nandi[2]

[1] Nanyang Technological University, Singapore, Singapore
anubhab001@e.ntu.edu.sg
[2] Indian Statistical Institute, Kolkata, India
[3] Silicon Austria Labs, Graz, Austria
jbreier@jbreier.com
[4] University of Hyogo, Kobe, Japan
takanori.isobe@ai.u-hyogo.ac.jp

Abstract. With the advent of Malicious (Peyrin and Wang, Crypto'20), the question of a cipher with an intentional weakness which is only known to its designer has gained its momentum. In their work, the authors discuss how an otherwise secure cipher can be broken by its designer with the help of a secret backdoor (which is not known to the user/attacker). The contribution of Malicious is to propose a cipher-level construction with a backdoor, where it is computationally infeasible to retrieve the backdoor entry despite knowing how the mechanism works.

In this work, we revisit the work done by Peyrin and Wang in a greater depth. We discuss the relevant aspects with more clarity, thereby addressing some of the important issues connected to a backdoor construction. The main contribution, however, comes as a new proof-of-concept block cipher with an innate backdoor, named ZUGZWANG. Unlike Malicious, which needs new/experimental concepts like partially non-linear layer; our cipher entirely relies on concepts which are well-established for decades (such as, using a one-way function as a Feistel cipher's state-update), and also offers several advantages over Malicious (easy to visualise, succeeds with probability 1, and so on). Having known the secret backdoor entry, one can recover the secret key with only 1 plaintext query to our cipher; but it is secure otherwise.

Keywords: Backdoor · Hash function · XOF · Block cipher · Feistel · Low-MC · Malicious · Low-MC-M · Provable security · SPRP · White-box

1 Introduction

One of the problems that comes with designing a cipher is to gain the collective trust of the community. The cipher must satisfy certain security requirement with sufficient margin to prevent a malicious attacker (who has the full knowledge of

© The Author(s), under exclusive license to Springer Nature Switzerland AG 2022
L. Batina et al. (Eds.): SPACE 2022, LNCS 13783, pp. 81–96, 2022.
https://doi.org/10.1007/978-3-031-22829-2_5

the cipher specification) from getting information secured by the cipher under a secret key. At the same time, it is also essential that the cipher designer will fail to retrieve the data secured by the cipher under a secret key. Stated in other words, the designers of a cipher have to convince the rest of the community that the cipher does not have a hidden vulnerability that evades known cryptanalytic methods (thus, it is known only to the designers). As we have seen, this is not always the situation. Case in point, it has long been speculated that the SIMON and SPECK [4] family of block ciphers have some form of hidden backdoor (see [9] or Schneier's blog[1]. among other sources[2]), which are only known to the designers[3]. Despite years of speculation, the presence of any backdoor is not determined.

Amidst such situation, it is not surprising that the cryptographic community will take interest in the prospect of designing a cipher with an implanted backdoor. We have recently seen this happening in the Crypto'20 paper [9] where the designers take an otherwise secure cipher family and implant a backdoor in it. They present their contribution in the form of a framework, named, Malicious. It works by querying the cipher with a chosen tweak difference on a variant of the LOWMC [1] family of ciphers (this tweak difference is secret and known only by the cipher designer). Ultimately, this tweak difference propagates through the cipher in such a way that the resulting ciphertext difference allows the cipher designer to retrieve the secret key (the secret key is chosen by, and only known to the user) with a certain probability. They also describe a Malicious based tweakable block cipher, named LOWMC-M.

1.1 Contribution

A big part of the inspiration of our work goes to the Crypto'20 paper by Peyrin and Wang [9]. More precisely, we take a deeper look at the Malicious framework (and its instance LOWMC-M), and improve the state-of-the-art in a number of ways.

To begin with, we show a provably secure construction of backdoor that improves from LOWMC-M [9]. Our method of the backdoor construction relies entirely on pre-existing notions of security, which are well-known/well-analysed for decades. The construction of Malicious is more on the experimental side, that relies on lesser studied concepts such as partially non-linear layer. Apart from that, our backdoor requires only 1 plaintext query (works with probability 1), unlike the LOWMC-M that requires a number of chosen (plaintext, tweak) queries. We do not need any tweak, and the overall idea is generic – it can be implemented atop virtually any encryption and hash algorithm[4]. Thus, making it possible to have a backdoor without any tweak and not tied to LOWMC [1].

---

[1] https://www.schneier.com/blog/archives/2018/04/two_nsa_algorit.html.

[2] It is also worth pointing out that problem is partly exacerbated due to the absence of any cryptanalytic result in the introducing paper [4].

[3] In this case, the designers are a group of researchers from the American government's National Security Agency (NSA), possibly hinting at a government-level initiative in the background.

[4] Depending on the hash output size and the state size of the encryption algorithm, we may need to pad/truncate.

The coverage/contribution of our paper does not end there. We ask several relevant questions, which have not been answered yet. We argue that no matter how cleverly the backdoor is designed, it is not possible for the designer to access it without the user's cooperation (as the user can always cross-check if some secret information is revealed – and if so – can deny the request); or one backdoor entry cannot be used more than once (as the attacker will get to know as soon as it is used). The elephant in the room, however, lurks in hiding the key which is released as a result of the backdoor access—the key is not encrypted in any way, meaning the attacker gets to know about it no later than the designer does.

1.2   Prerequisite

As discussed in [9, Section 1], the concept of backdoor itself is not new. In our context, we directly follow [9]. For clarity, the terms/ideas used are briefly described here.

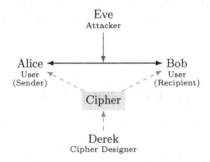

Fig. 1. Schematic of backdoor work-flow

The cipher designer, whom we refer to as *Derek* for simplicity, designs a cipher with an intentional backdoor (which is known only by him). The cipher (the public description of the cipher, to be more precise) is then used by the users, Alice and Bob, to communicate sensitive information. The attacker, Eve, watches the channel between Alice and Bob closely and knows all the (publicly available) specification/cryptanalysis regarding the cipher. Figure 1 shows a schematic representation.

Now, at some point during communication, Derek can use the backdoor to retrieve sensitive information, this incidence (if happens) is indicated by backdoor *access*. The backdoor *mechanism* lets Derek to access sensitive information (this works as a weakened version of the cipher). The mechanism is activated with the help of a backdoor *entry* (e.g., a 128-bit string when used as the plaintext to the cipher), which is known only to Derek (it will likely become a public knowledge after it has been used once).

For the interest of brevity, we assume the reader's familiarity with the basic terms/concepts, including; CSPRNG, LFSR, block cipher (along with padding, and mode of operation like CTR), stream cipher (along with IV and nonce), hash function, MAC, AE, AEAD; PRP, SPRP; OWF ; cipher families (Feistel, SPN and ARX); and ciphers (DES, AES, RC4, RSA). We also use XOF[5] (eXtended Output Function). An XOF is a one-way function that takes a message of arbitrary length and returns a message of desired length (i.e., $\{0,1\}^{\star} \rightarrow \{0,1\}^{\star}$).

1.3 Organisation

The background information is covered in Sect. 2 (particularly Sect. 2.2 contains some previously unreported observations). Section 3.1 goes through the practical aspects of a backdoor, and Sect. 3.2 covers two related notions of security.

In Sect. 4, we present our block cipher named "ZUGZWANG"[6] that has a backdoor[7]. After the fundamental idea is stated in Sect. 4.1, we show a concrete instance by using AES-128 and SHAKE-128[5] in Sect. 4.2. Apart from that, a comparison with Malicious is given in Sect. 4.3.

The conclusion can be found in Sect. 5. For more discussion (along with security proof and test cases) one may refer to the extended version available at [3].

2 Background

2.1 Implementation Level and Cipher Level Backdoors

The term, 'backdoor' is generally more common in the cyber-security or hacking communities. Here it typically refers to an intentionally implanted weakness[8]. This process is done at the fabrication/implementation level and transparent at the cipher design level[9]. See [10] for a recent example.

Our interest, however, lies on the other type of backdoor, which works at the cipher design level. In this case, the cipher is so designed that, it has a secret backdoor which is known only by its designers. It is long been speculated that some ciphers, whose entire specification is available in public, may contain some secret backdoor.

---

[5] See https://nvlpubs.nist.gov/nistpubs/FIPS/NIST.FIPS.202.pdf.

[6] It is a German word (translates to 'a compulsion to move'), used in context of Chess to describe wherein all the available moves for a player make the situation worse.

[7] As it has a backdoor, any practical application of ZUGZWANG is not recommended (to be used mostly, if not only, as an interesting proof-of-concept).

[8] For instance, one may look at the "politically correct" backdoor: https://www.kb.cert.org/vuls/id/247371.

[9] This is noted in [9, Section 1]: "There are two categories of backdoors. The first one is the backdoor implemented in a security product at the protocol or key-management level, which is generally considered in practice.".

2.2 Context

The cipher level backdoors can be theoretically divided into the following categories:

(1) A cipher so craftily designed that nobody is able to find the presence of a backdoor after few years of speculation and testing. So far it passes all the known methods of cryptanalysis. It is not known whether there is actually a backdoor or this is just a myth. If/when this cipher is made a standard and adopted as a global standard, it is in theory possible for its designers to access the backdoor and retrieve sensitive information.

The SIMON and SPECK [4] family contain few block ciphers which are suspected to have this kind of backdoor (see, e.g., [9]). It is not known if there is any backdoor, or how the backdoor mechanism works; if there is any in the first place. If there is some backdoor in those ciphers, it is never accessed, to the best of our knowledge/understanding.

(2) A cipher where the designers publicly claim there is a backdoor. The cipher is secure except when the backdoor is accessed. The designers make no attempt to hide the backdoor; rather they claim upfront that there is a backdoor – this is how the backdoor mechanism works – so on and so forth.

This category is recently popularised through the Malicious framework [9]. This framework can create such a cipher by tinkering with some otherwise secure cipher, given the base cipher satisfies some criteria. By accessing the backdoor, the cipher designer can retrieve the key by analysing the cipher output. The LOWMC-M [9] is an instance of this framework, which takes a secure instance of LOWMC as the base cipher.

One may notice the following characterisation of this category:

(α) The presence of the backdoor is made public by the designers. This also nullifies the question of whether it is hard to spot the presence of the backdoor had it not been known[10].

(β) Except when the backdoor is accessed, the cipher is secure. When the backdoor is accessed, the secret key is released from the cipher output (assuming the user does not prevent that, see Inference (B)) – at least in theory, satisfying the "practicality" condition of [9, Section 2.2].

(γ) Though the backdoor mechanism is public, it is infeasible to find out what the secret backdoor entry that activates the mechanism is. This is called the "undiscoverability" condition [9, Section 2.2].

By observing the Category (2) design in the literature (namely, [9]), the following inferences can be drawn (see Sect. 3.1 for more discussion):

(A) The backdoor can be accessed at most once. The backdoor mechanism is public, therefore anyone can check the incoming requests to the user to see if the backdoor is activated. Once it is found, the secret backdoor access

---

[10] It may be hard to spot the backdoor for someone who does not know beforehand, but here it does not matter as the designers have already made it public.

becomes visible to everyone. Basically, one can monitor all the incoming traffic to the user and attempt to reverse-engineer the backdoor entry, and will eventually succeed as soon as the backdoor entry is used.

This can be done by the user (Alice) or the attacker (Eve[11]) alike. Though Eve does not know the actual secret key (which is chosen and kept secret by Alice), she can still choose an arbitrary key, and then follow-through the steps of the backdoor mechanism to see if information about the arbitrarily chosen key is released.

(B) It is not possible to extract the secret key without the user's (Alice's) cooperation. Alice can always keep an eye out for activation of the backdoor mechanism. Based on that, she may return an invalid output or something random (if the backdoor mechanism is activated), instead of the actual output from the cipher.

(C) The key which is released from the cipher output (as a consequence of the backdoor access) is not encrypted[12], meaning pretty much everyone on the network (including the attacker) can access it.

In this work, we aim at improving Category (2) backdoors; i.e., we are interested to create improved design that satisfies Criteria (2α), (2β) and (2γ). It is important to note that those criteria are adopted from [9], and are not conceived by us. It is perhaps worth noting that Inferences (A) and (B) violate the "untraceability" condition which is described in [9, Section 2.2] (Inference (B) is already acknowledged in [9, Section 5.3] as a violation of "untraceability"). Whether or not it is possible to design a Category (1) backdoor is left as an open problem.

Remark 1. The closest to Category (1) the designers of Malicious could have gone is to present a new cipher/framework/mode and make a vague claim about presence/absence of a backdoor. Then it would be up to the community to figure out if there is a backdoor, how to activate the backdoor/how the backdoor mechanism works, etc.

Remark 2. In theory, it is possible to design a cipher in Category (1) if the designer manages to find an attack not yet known to the (mainstream) community[13]. The backdoor in this case will be activated through this new attack, and will (more than likely) be missed by the community (at least until this attack

---

[11] As per [9, Section 2.1], the attacker/eavesdropper Eve is considered within the Malicious framework.

[12] If the released key is encrypted with another key, that means the cipher designer and the user have to know the other key beforehand. In that case, they can simply use any cipher (with the other key) to communicate the key released through the backdoor instead, thus completely cutting off the need for a backdoor.

[13] For instance, some of the public-key ciphers (including RSA) are now known to be vulnerable against quantum computers, but those attacks were not known when those ciphers were designed. In a less restricted sense, the quantum attacks can be considered as backdoors to those ciphers.

is discovered or the backdoor mechanism is reverse-engineered). For perspective, the construction of `Malicious` [9] depends on the well-studied differential attack; thus the backdoor, in a very high likelihood, would be spotted by the community (had it not been known already).

3 Basic Concepts

3.1 Practical Application of a Backdoor

Status Quo. The first problem that arises while talking about the practicality of backdoor is to convince the users to adopt it. There is no shortage of efficient ciphers in the public domain; with well-described design rationale and which are well-analysed by the community. The users, Alice and Bob, may simply refuse to adopt any new/experimental cipher (for example, any cipher from the `LOWMC` family [1] altogether, or the unusual choice of using an XOF to design an encryption as in `LOWMC-M` [9]), suspecting there could potentially be a backdoor. Therefore, in a loose sense, they agree for the designer to retrieve the secret key if they agree to adopt a new cipher. Thus, the design and study of backdoor appears to be purely an academic interest than a pragmatic one.

Anyway, as far the technical problems are concerned with the current concept of backdoor [9] (which we call Category (2), see Sect. 2.2), we note the following: Since the identity of the cipher designer (whom we call Derek for simplicity, as indicated in Sect. 1.2) is known to everybody in the network; including Alice (sender), Bob (recipient) and Eve (attacker). Therefore Alice (as well as Bob) can be extra cautious when a request comes from Derek, implying the limitations:

(i) Alice can simply deny any request from Derek, preventing him to access the backdoor.

(ii) If Alice complies with Derek's requests and lets him access the backdoor, this can be noticed by Eve. Now the secret key is leaked through the response from Alice and the key is not encrypted[14], thus Eve can effectively recover the key.

Overall, the Limitations (i) and (ii) mostly, if not fully, diminish any real-life application for a Category (2) backdoor. The cipher designer (Derek) cannot use it without active cooperation from the user (Alice or Bob). Even if Derek can obtain anonymous identity or spoof a fake identity, it is still up to the mercy of Alice. All the information is coming from Alice, so she can simply check the output from the cipher before sending it[15]; and discard the request or give a random output; should she suspect the backdoor is being accessed. On

---

[14] There is practically no way to encrypt this key, at least within the realm of symmetric-key cryptography; as this would require exchange of another secret key between Alice and Derek. This invalidates the need for a backdoor in the first place.

[15] For instance, Alice can check if the XOR of two consecutive cipher outputs equals to the key. Given the backdoor mechanism is public, she already knows exactly what to look out for.

the other hand, if Alice agrees Derek to access the backdoor, they can instead create a secure channel between them (no need for a backdoor). Besides, letting Eve know the secret key is a miserable flaw, since the whole purpose of any cryptographic system is to ensure the attacker cannot access the key.

The point to note here is, we are heavily implying that the notion of backdoor, at least in its current form, suffers from severe limitation that comes from lack/absence of trust for Derek. If Alice does not respond to anyone she does not trust, anonymous/fake identity by Derek is meaningless. We are not saying either of the assumptions is objectively true/untrue. We are simply saying, in order for Derek to succeed in utilising the backdoor; he needs to circumvent those real-life problems at first, which may turn out to be challenging.

Uncertain Future Prospect. While it does not seem possible to extract the secret key without cooperation from the user, it may be possible with some cipher in the future where the designer can extract the key in a way that the attacker cannot get it. One potential concept to achieve this in the future (that may or may not work) can be stated as follows.

Suppose, instead of only one backdoor entry, it is split into q backdoor shares[16] (somewhat comparable with the concept of secret-sharing [11]), where the cipher output from all the shares are required to retrieve the key. Say, by querying with the b_i backdoor entry, c_i is obtained, for $i = 0, \ldots, q-1$. Each c_i contains some information about the secret key, but all of those are required to get the key.

Not only that, each c_i is connected in secret way (which is only known to Derek) so that the connection is to be respected in order to find the key. With some suspension of disbelief, say, $k = \mathbf{f}(c_{j_0}, c_{j_1}, \ldots, c_{j_{q-1}})$ where the function $\mathbf{f}$ is secret (only known to Derek) and is not symmetric, for $(j_0, j_1, \ldots, j_{q-1})$ being secret a permutation of $(0, 1, \ldots, q-1)$. Thus, despite knowing all the public information as Derek does, Eve may not be able to actually uncover the key given certain regularity assumptions (like, q is sufficiently large) as she would need to cover the search-space of $q!$.

This concept is shared here only to pique the interest of the future researchers. Whether or not this will turn out to be a feasibility is unclear as of now.

3.2 Associated Notions of Security

Undetectability. The authors of Malicious in of [9, Section 2.2] mention one desirable security notion for a Category (2) backdoor, "undetectability". It is defined as *"the inability for an external entity to realize the existence of the hidden backdoor"*. Here we argue that this is a bit tricky.

Note from Criterion (2α), the backdoor designers of Malicious [9] have already made the presence of the backdoor a public knowledge. Thus, it is a pre-conceived knowledge that a backdoor exists, thus violating the "undetectability".

---

[16] Possibly something similar is laid out by Peyrin: https://thomaspeyrin.github.io/web/assets/docs/invited/TII_CRC_21_slides.pdf, Slide 63.

We further notice that the notion about whether the cipher has an embedded backdoor does not seem to hold either. This is because we are not aware of any possible way to ascertain a cipher does not contain a backdoor ("*How do you know* AES *does not have a backdoor?*"). The ciphers which are broken can be (arguably) considered to have a backdoor, but it does not seem possible to comment on non-existence of a backdoor about those ciphers which are deemed secure. As a consequence, it is not possible to say an arbitrary instance of LOWMC-M does not contain a backdoor (regardless of an intentional backdoor following Malicious is implanted or not).

Need for White-box Security. Given the analysis in Sects. 2.2 and 3.1; it stands to reason that, Alice (as well as Bob) and Eve can reverse-engineer the backdoor mechanism as soon as the first query is made by Derek as long as the cipher specification is public. Indeed, no matter how the backdoor mechanism works, it has to trigger something (such as, some variable has to become 0, some loop has to terminate, and so on). If the cipher specification is known, then anybody can utilise such information no later than the correct backdoor entry is used.

Therefore, if we want the backdoor mechanism will not be revealed even after a backdoor entry is queried with, a basic condition is that the cipher specification is to be kept secret by Derek. However, this alone is not enough, since it is possible to reverse-engineer the cipher specification given its (unprotected) implementation (cf. the well-known cases of reverse-engineering RC4[17] or CRYPTO-1 in Mifare Classic RFID tag [8]). Thus, the implementations of the cipher (which are prepared and shared by Derek to Alice and Bob) practically have to be secure against the *white-box* [5,6] attacks. In a white-box setting, the secret key is embedded in the cipher implementation in a way that it cannot be recovered. That said, one may notice the following differences from the usual white-box setting (cf. *obfuscation*[18]):

1. The cipher specification itself is secret in a backdoor setting, which is a more stringent requirement than usual white-box (where it is public).
2. The cipher designer supplies the implementations to the users, but he does not know the secret key. This contrasts the usual white-box setting where the implementer knows and embeds the key. It is not clear whether this is a more stringent requirement.

At this point, it is perhaps safe to assume, there is no proper real-life application of the concept of backdoor introduced in [9], at least in the mainstream academic community. Somebody may still use a cipher like that if it is enforced[19].

---

[17] https://web.archive.org/web/20010722163902/http://cypherpunks.venona.com/date/1994/09/msg00304.html.

[18] https://www.esat.kuleuven.be/cosic/blog/program-obfuscation/.

[19] One may compare with the government-issued (closed-source) applications to trace COVID-19 to some extent, though there is no separate recipient (Derek = Bob) and there is no secret key to recover.

For instance, assume the situation where there a push from the government to implant some intentional backdoor to compromise the security of products used by the common people. In that case, it is in theory possible to use a Category (2) cipher, with its full specification being available in public (and with no white-box protection). Our cipher ZUGZWANG can be in theory used in such a situation; but as academic researchers with a moral compass, we do not condone that. To the best of our finding, the only incident similar to this is rumoured in Australia back in 2018, but it seems to be officially denied[20].

4   ZUGZWANG: Constructing a Block Cipher with a Backdoor

One major observation from Malicious [9] is that, the only reason the user/attacker cannot retrieve the backdoor is the one-way property of the XOF. As it is known, a Feistel block cipher can use an OWF as its state-update (see, DES for an example), we adopt the idea to finally extend it to ZUGZWANG. Whether or not a similar construction is possible with SPN and ARX families, and whether some other idea is possible that does not involve any OWF, are left open for future research.

4.1   Fundamental Idea of ZUGZWANG

In its simplest form, ZUGZWANG is a 2-branch balanced Feistel network based block cipher that runs for n rounds (counting of rounds goes from 0 to $n - 1$). It uses $f_i(K_i, c_L)$ as the round function for the ith round; where K_i is the corresponding round key, c_L is the plaintext or the intermediate ciphertext currently at the left branch. Each f_i has the property that it collapses if $c_L = \hat{p_0}$ (if i is even) or $c_L = \hat{p_1}$ (if i is odd), for some predefined $\hat{p_0}$ and $\hat{p_1}$. In this case, $\hat{p} = \hat{p_0}||\hat{p_1}$ constitutes the secret backdoor. Also note that, the last Feistel round does not have any swap operation between the two branches (so there are $n - 1$ branch swaps).

Now, notice that, $\hat{p_0}$ and $\hat{p_1}$ cannot be used directly in the specification of f_i's (those cannot be passed as parameters of f_i's); otherwise Alice and Eve would trivially retrieve these. Thus, we run an OWF, $H(\cdot)$ first. This leads to pre-computing and storing $H(\hat{p_0})$ (respectively, $H(\hat{p_1})$) where i is even (respectively, odd) in the cipher specification as constants. Now that $H(\cdot)$ is used to $\hat{p_0}$ and $\hat{p_1}$, we need to apply it to c_L too. Ultimately, instead of directly checking whether $c_L = \hat{p_0}$ or $c_L = \hat{p_1}$, we are now checking if $H(c_L) = H(\hat{p_0})$ or $H(c_L) = H(\hat{p_1})$.

Although $H(\hat{p_0})$ and $H(\hat{p_1})$ are stored and accessible in the cipher specification, the following claims hold due to the property of $H(\cdot)$:

- **Pre-image resistance:** It is hard to retrieve $\hat{p_0}$ and $\hat{p_1}$.
- **Second pre-image resistance:** It is hard to find another $\hat{p_i}'$ ($\neq \hat{p_i}$) such that $H(\hat{p_i}') = H(\hat{p_i})$ for $i = 0, 1$.

---

[20] https://www.homeaffairs.gov.au/about-us/our-portfolios/national-security/lawful-access-telecommunications/myths-assistance-access-act.

Notice that the birthday-bound security for collision does not apply here. These claims constitute the secrecy of the backdoor entry given its H; i.e., no algorithm better than the brute-force search is known.

Next, we need to use an encryption, $E_{K_i}(\cdot)$ inside f_i's to make the overall Feistel cipher secure. As some form of the check $H(c_L) = H(\hat{p}_j)$ for $j = i$ (mod 2) has to be inside f_i, a natural choice is $f_i = E_{K_i}(H(c_L)) \oplus \alpha_i$ where $\alpha_i = E_{K_i}(H(\hat{p}_j))$. After n rounds of update are done, post-whitening keys (K_L, K_R) are XORed to the branches.

Notice that when $\hat{p}_0$ and $\hat{p}_1$ are fed to the left and right branches respectively, f_i's are always 0, and this holds irrespective of number of rounds. Basically, f_i (which is 0) is XORed to the right branch, making the content of the right branch going to the left branch in the next round. As the content of the right branch is what makes f_{i+1} collapse, the pattern continues. This allows us to create an arbitrary number of rounds, though for proper security in two directions (and with the assumption that E and H have desirable cryptographic properties) the number of rounds is required to be ≥ 4. Therefore, when fed with the secret backdoor $\hat{p} = \hat{p}_0 \| \hat{p}_1$, the ciphertext from the cipher does not depend on the Feistel round keys (K_i's). Rather it always follows the simple invariant relationship with the post-whitening keys (K_L, K_R), which leads to direct key recovery with 1 plaintext query as:

$$(c_L, c_R) = \begin{cases} (\hat{p}_0 \oplus K_L, \hat{p}_1 \oplus K_R) & \text{if number of Feistel rounds is odd,} \\ (\hat{p}_1 \oplus K_L, \hat{p}_0 \oplus K_R) & \text{if number of Feistel rounds is even.} \end{cases}$$

On the other hand, when a p ($\neq \hat{p}$) is used as the plaintext, the cipher works as secure Feistel block cipher. At each round, the state update can be compared to a Boolean derivative of E – it resembles a form of differential attack on E (but weaker since $H(\hat{p}_0)$ and $H(\hat{p}_0)$ constants). Given E is secure, any differential attack on E does not give any usable information. We thus conclude, 4 rounds of the ZUGZWANG construction can be considered to provide adequate security in two directions.

Extension to Other Symmetric-key Primitives. It may be possible to extend the core idea of ZUGZWANG to other primitives in the symmetric-key cryptography (viz., stream cipher, hash function, MAC, AE and AEAD). However, it is not immediately apparent how such extension will pan out. For instance, it is possible to get a stream cipher from a block cipher by using a number of modes (e.g., CTR); but it is to be noted that the plaintext does not enter the state of a stream cipher per-se. As such, we may have to use a secret IV/nonce so that, (say) the key-stream becomes all-zero regardless of the secret key. This requires elaborate discussion, and hence is kept out-of-scope for this work.

Feistel Types, Branches and Rounds. The basic idea can be generalised to more Feistel branches, wherein the secret backdoor entry is split into multiple branches. In that case, one also needs to decide on the type of the Feistel Network and the minimum number of rounds required. Analysis such such options is left open for future research.

Table 1. Complexity of whitening key recovery in 128-bit ZUGZWANG construction

(a) 2-branch Feistel

Whitening		Backdoor Complexity	
#Pre	#Post	Encryption	Decryption
$0^{\ddagger}$	$2^{\ddagger}$	2^0	2^{128}
1	1	2^{64}	2^{64}
2	0	2^{128}	2^0
2	2	2^{128}	2^{128}

‡: Instantiated in Sect. 4.2

(b) 4-branch Feistel

Whitening		Backdoor Complexity	
#Pre	#Post	Encryption	Decryption
0	4	2^0	2^{128}
1	3	2^{32}	2^{96}
2	2	2^{64}	2^{64}
3	1	2^{96}	2^{32}
4	0	2^{128}	2^0
4	4	2^{128}	2^{128}

Location of Whitening Keys/Backdoor on Decryption. Note that, the key recovery through backdoor access in ZUGZWANG does not retrieve any Feistel round key, rather it retrieves the whitening keys (the post-whitening keys for encryption, to be more precise). If we take all the Feistel branches have a whitening key XOR (for maximum key recovery), then the question is whether to use pre- or post-whitening keys.

For simplification of notation, assume that we have a 128-bit and 2-branch ZUGZWANG construction with n-rounds. First, let us study the situation for encryption where the left branch has a pre-whitening key (K'), the right branch does not have a pre-whitening key. In this case, $\hat{p}_0$ does not make the f_i's collapse for even rounds, but $\hat{p}_0 \oplus K'$ does. Since the designer does not know which K', he has to brute-force over 64-bits. Therefore, he has to query with $\hat{p}_0 \oplus K' \| \hat{p}_1$ for all possible 2^{64} choices of K'. The correct guess of K' can be identified by the output at the end (which will depend on presence/absence of whitening keys and if n is even/odd).

Reflecting on this, we observe that the construction with post-whitening keys helps in backdoor access in encryption, but not in decryption. Similarly, pre-whitening helps in decryption, but not in encryption. The invariant property that the product of the complexities for the whitening key recovery at both sides remains the same as the brute-force search. This is an inherent property of the ZUGZWANG construction. As shown in Table 1, this cannot be improved by increasing the number of Feistel branches. Improving the whitening key recovery complexity from two sides can be considered as a future work. Further, as indicated in Table 1, if both the pre- and post-whitening keys are used; this particular backdoor mechanism ceases to exist.

To the best of our finding, no claim about the backdoor access from Bob's side (i.e., decryption) is available in Malicious [9]. Thus, the notion of "practicability", which is introduced in [9, Section 2.2], is unclear for Malicious/LOWMC-M decryption.

4.2   A Concrete Instance of ZUGZWANG (Using AES and SHAKE)

We show an instance of ZUGZWANG[21] that uses a 2-branch balanced Feistel structure, 128-bit state, runs for 4 Feistel rounds, and uses 0 pre-whitening and 2 post-whitening keys. We choose AES-128 for encryption (E), and SHAKE-128 as XOF (H). See Algorithm 1 for its formal description.

The basic construction for ZUGZWANG is as shown in Fig. 2. The 128-bit master key K and the 128-bit backdoor entry $\hat{p}$ are split into two 64-bit post-whitening keys: $K = K_4 \| K_5$, $\hat{p} = \hat{p}_0 \| \hat{p}_1$ respectively. The 128-bit Feistel round keys (K_i for $i = 0, 1, 2, 3$) are generated by running AES in CTR mode with key k (i.e., with i as the plaintext).

As per the construction, the $H(\cdot)$ of $\hat{p}_0$ and $\hat{p}_1$ are computed and stored. Since these are to be used as the plaintext for AES-128 (Line 10), we take 128-bit output for these. Similarly, the plaintext/intermediate ciphertexts are to be used in AES as plaintexts (Line 11), so the outputs from SHAKE for these are also taken as 128 bits long. However, since each Feistel branch is 64 bits long (see Line 12), we truncate the last 64 bits of these 128-bit SHAKE outputs.

If $\hat{p}$ is not known, then we claim this concrete instance offers 128-bit security. On the other hand, if queried with $\hat{p}$ as the plaintext, then the post-whitening keys (K_4, K_5) are revealed.

ZUGZWANG is not meant to be used in practice, rather its primary function is to work as a proof-of-concept. Thus, we acknowledge the device footprint for the concrete instance can be significantly lowered (say, using less number of rounds for AES, replacing AES with a lightweight encryption, using an LFSR to generate Feistel round keys, etc.) but do not make any attempt to do so. For the same reason, we do not present any benchmark.

4.3   Comparison of ZUGZWANG with Malicious/LOWMC-M

In essence, the fundamental concept in Malicious [9] can be as described as follows. The backdoor entry is accessed through a (secret) difference at the (public) tweak and the (public) plaintext. The backdoor access works by cancelling the differences with one another in such a way that ultimately there is a high probability differential trail at the end, which potentially leaks the key. However, if just this much would be implemented, the attacker/user would (likely) notice the differences applied through the tweak and the plaintext, which would in turn reveal the backdoor entry. To prevent the attacker/user from obtaining the differences, the designers of Malicious [9] pass the differences through an XOF.

In essence, the fundamental concept in Malicious [9] can be as described as follows. The backdoor entry is accessed through a (secret) difference at the (public) tweak and the (public) plaintext. The backdoor access works by cancelling the differences with one another in such a way that ultimately there is a high probability differential trail at the end, which potentially leaks the key. However, if just this much would be implemented, the attacker/user would (likely)

---

[21] We use the same term, 'ZUGZWANG', to indicate the overall construction idea as well as the concrete instance.

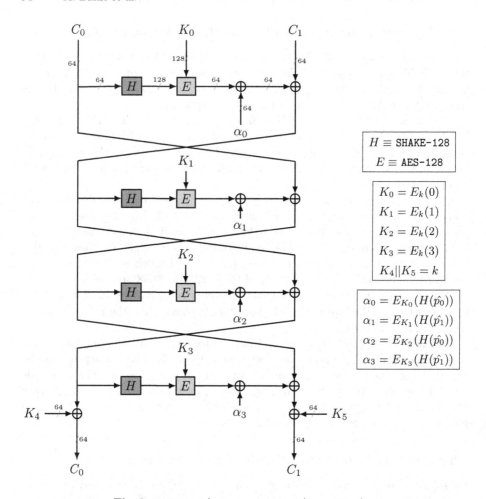

Fig. 2. ZUGZWANG (concrete instance/encryption)

notice the differences applied through the tweak and the plaintext, which would in turn reveal the backdoor entry. To prevent the attacker/user from obtaining the differences, the designers of Malicious [9] pass the differences through an XOF.

The following comparative points can be noted:

1. Malicious is based on relatively novel and not so much analysed design principles. It cannot be implemented atop of any pre-existing cipher. Effectively, Malicious is reliant on the security of LOWMC [1]. Besides, being a new design type, itself requires its own analysis (in particular, LOWMC-M is revised in [9, Section 4.3] after a new analysis is presented in [7] where 7 instances of LOWMC-M with original parameters are broken without finding backdoor by algebraic attacks on LOWMC). ZUGZWANG can be designed using already

---

Algorithm 1 : ZUGZWANG – concrete instance/encryption (128 bits, 2-branch Feistel, 4 rounds; AES-128 as encryption, SHAKE-128 as XOF)

Input: $\hat{p}$ (backdoor entry, 128 bits), p (plaintext, 128 bits), k (master key, 128 bits)
Output: Secure encryption with key k and plaintext p if $p \neq \hat{p}$; k if $p = \hat{p}$

1: $n \leftarrow 4$ ▷ Number of Feistel rounds
2: **for** $i \leftarrow 0$ to $n - 1$ **do**
3: $K_i \leftarrow \mathtt{AES}_k(i)$ ▷ Generate Feistel round keys by using AES in CTR mode
4: $K_4, K_5 \leftarrow k[0 : 63], k[64 : 127]$ ▷ Split k to use as post-whitening keys
5: $\hat{p_0}, \hat{p_1} \leftarrow \hat{p}[0 : 63], \hat{p}[64 : 127]$ ▷ Split $\hat{p}$ into 2 parts
6: Pre-compute and store $\mathtt{SHAKE}(\hat{p_0})$, $\mathtt{SHAKE}(\hat{p_1})$ ▷ Both are of 128-bits
7: $C_0, C_1 \leftarrow p[0 : 63], p[64 : 127]$ ▷ Split p into 2 parts
8: **for** $i \leftarrow 0$ to $n - 1$ **do**   ▷ Iterate over Feistel rounds
9: $j \leftarrow i \pmod 2$
10: $\alpha_i \leftarrow \mathtt{AES}_{K_i}(\mathtt{SHAKE}(\hat{p_j}))[0 : 63]$
11: $\beta_i \leftarrow \mathtt{AES}_{K_i}(\mathtt{SHAKE}(C_0))[0 : 63]$ ▷ $\mathtt{SHAKE}(C_0)$ is of 128-bits
12: $f_i \leftarrow \beta_i \oplus \alpha_i$ ▷ $f_i = 0$ when $C_0 = \hat{p_j}$
13: $C_1 \leftarrow C_1 \oplus f_i$ ▷ Update right Feistel branch with f_i
14: **if** $i \leq n - 2$ **then**   ▷ No branch swap in last Feistel round
15:   $C_0, C_1 \leftarrow C_1, C_0$ ▷ Swap two Feistel branches
16: $C_0, C_1 \leftarrow C_0 \oplus K_4, C_1 \oplus K_5$ ▷ XOR post-whitening keys
17: **return** $C_0 || C_1$ ▷ $(C_0, C_1) = (\hat{p_1} \oplus K_4, \hat{p_0} \oplus K_5)$ when $p = \hat{p}$

---

well-analysed primitives—all the concepts used in its construction/analysis are known for decades. Its security can be formally proven.

2. Malicious requires a tweak. Tweak is said to be relatively new, less efficient, and any standard does not appear to exist [2, Section II.B]. ZUGZWANG does not require a tweak.

3. The key recovery using the secret backdoor entry in ZUGZWANG is deterministic in nature, which requires only one call to the cipher with the secret backdoor entry equated with the plaintext; whereas LOWMC-M requires multiple calls, and the key recovery is not guaranteed even if its queries satisfy all the requisite conditions.

4. The overall idea of ZUGZWANG is easier to visualise, analyse and implement. It is not clear whether the designers [9] actually have constructed the full cipher, or have left it as a wishful thinking – thus it is further not clear whether Malicious would work in real life.

5 Conclusion

Taking inspiration from Peyrin and Wang's Crypto'20 paper [9], we partake in a deeper dive at backdoor construction and related security concerns. A major contribution in our work is to present a block cipher concept, ZUGZWANG, that has an internal backdoor it. We also show a concrete instance of the concept. Our construction answers some of the open problems of Malicious/LOWMC-M [9], thus considerably improving from it.

To make ourselves clear, we do not support the government or any organisation forcing/tricking anybody to use any cipher that has a backdoor. We believe the intentional design a cipher with a hidden backdoor should be done as an academic curiosity (and not for any practical application).

References

1. Albrecht, M., Rechberger, C., Schneider, T., Tiessen, T., Zohner, M.: Ciphers for MPC and FHE. Cryptology ePrint Archive, Report 2016/687 (2016). https://eprint.iacr.org/2016/687
2. Baksi, A., Bhasin, S., Breier, J., Khairallah, M., Peyrin, T.: Protecting block ciphers against differential fault attacks without re-keying (extended version). Cryptology ePrint Archive, Report 2018/085 (2018). https://eprint.iacr.org/2018/085
3. Baksi, A., Bhattacharjee, A., Breier, J., Isobe, T., Nandi, M.: Big brother is watching you: a closer look at backdoor construction. Cryptology ePrint Archive, Paper 2022/953 (2022). https://eprint.iacr.org/2022/953
4. Beaulieu, R., Shors, D., Smith, J., Treatman-Clark, S., Weeks, B., Wingers, L.: The Simon and speck families of lightweight block ciphers. Cryptology ePrint Archive, Report 2013/404 (2013). https://eprint.iacr.org/2013/404
5. Chow, S., Eisen, P., Johnson, H., van Oorschot, P.C.: A white-box DES implementation for DRM applications. In: Feigenbaum, J. (ed.) DRM 2002. LNCS, vol. 2696, pp. 1–15. Springer, Heidelberg (2003). https://doi.org/10.1007/978-3-540-44993-5_1
6. Chow, S., Eisen, P., Johnson, H., Van Oorschot, P.C.: White-box cryptography and an AES implementation. In: Nyberg, K., Heys, H. (eds.) SAC 2002. LNCS, vol. 2595, pp. 250–270. Springer, Heidelberg (2003). https://doi.org/10.1007/3-540-36492-7_17
7. Liu, F., Isobe, T., Meier, W.: Cryptanalysis of full LowMC and LowMC-M with algebraic techniques. Cryptology ePrint Archive, Paper 2020/1034 (2020). https://eprint.iacr.org/2020/1034
8. Nohl, K., Evans, D., Starbug, Plötz, H.: Reverse-engineering a cryptographic RFID tag. In: van Oorschot, P.C. (ed.) Proceedings of the 17th USENIX Security Symposium, July 28–August 1, 2008, San Jose, CA, USA, pp. 185–194. USENIX Association (2008). https://www.usenix.org/events/sec08/tech/full_papers/nohl/nohl.pdf
9. Peyrin, T., Wang, H.: The malicious framework: Embedding backdoors into tweakable block ciphers. Cryptology ePrint Archive, Report 2020/986 (2020). https://eprint.iacr.org/2020/986
10. Ravi, P., Deb, S., Baksi, A., Chattopadhyay, A., Bhasin, S., Mendelson, A.: On threat of hardware trojan to post-quantum lattice-based schemes: a key recovery attack on saber and beyond. In: Batina, L., Picek, S., Mondal, M. (eds.) SPACE 2021. LNCS, vol. 13162, pp. 81–103. Springer, Cham (2022). https://doi.org/10.1007/978-3-030-95085-9_5
11. Shamir, A.: How to share a secret. Commun. ACM. **22**, 612–613 (1979). https://dl.acm.org/doi/10.1145/359168.359176

Public-Key Cryptography,
Post-quantum Cryptography, Zero
Knowledge Proofs

KEMTLS vs. Post-quantum TLS:
Performance on Embedded Systems

Ruben Gonzalez[1]([✉]) and Thom Wiggers[2]

[1] Neodyme AG, Garching, Germany
`mail+kemtls@ruben-gonzalez.de`
[2] Radboud University, Nijmegen, The Netherlands

Abstract. TLS is ubiquitous in modern computer networks. It secures transport for high-end desktops and low-end embedded devices alike. However, the public key cryptosystems currently used within TLS may soon be obsolete as large-scale quantum computers, once realized, would be able to break them. This threat has led to the development of post-quantum cryptography (PQC). The U.S. standardization body NIST is currently in the process of concluding a multi-year search for promising post-quantum signature schemes and key encapsulation mechanisms (KEMs). With the first PQC standards around the corner, TLS will have to be updated soon. However, especially for small microcontrollers, it appears the current NIST post-quantum signature finalists pose a challenge. Dilithium suffers from very large public keys and signatures; while Falcon has significant hardware requirements for efficient implementations.

KEMTLS is a proposal for an alternative TLS handshake protocol that avoids authentication through signatures in the TLS handshake. Instead, it authenticates the peers through long-term KEM keys held in the certificates. The KEMs considered for standardization are more efficient in terms of computation and/or bandwidth than the post-quantum signature schemes.

In this work, we compare KEMTLS to TLS 1.3 in an embedded setting. To gain meaningful results, we present implementations of KEMTLS and TLS 1.3 on a Cortex-M4-based platform. These implementations are based on the popular WolfSSL embedded TLS library and hence share a majority of their code. In our experiments, we consider both protocols with the remaining NIST finalist signature schemes and KEMs, except for Classic McEliece which has too large public keys. Both protocols are benchmarked and compared in terms of run-time, memory usage, traffic volume and code size. The benchmarks are performed in network settings relevant to the Internet of Things, namely low-latency broadband, LTE-M and Narrowband IoT. Our results show that KEMTLS can reduce handshake time by up to 38%, can lower peak memory consumption and can save traffic volume compared to TLS 1.3.

Keywords: Post quantum cryptography · KEMTLS · Transport layer security · Embedded systems · Cortex-M4 · NIST PQC

© The Author(s), under exclusive license to Springer Nature Switzerland AG 2022
L. Batina et al. (Eds.): SPACE 2022, LNCS 13783, pp. 99–117, 2022.
https://doi.org/10.1007/978-3-031-22829-2_6

1   Introduction

Transport Layer Security (TLS) is ubiquitous in modern computer networks. It adds confidentiality, authenticity and integrity to application-layer protocols. We trust it, among other things, with securing connections to websites, emails, instant messages and virtual private networks. In its most recent version, TLS 1.3 [31], ephemeral (elliptic curve) Diffie-Hellman is used to establish encryption keys. Server (and optionally client) authentication is achieved by using digital signatures. To verify the signatures, public keys are transmitted in certificates during the TLS handshake. These certificates are in turn signed by certificate authorities, which are pre-installed on the verifying device.

As TLS is an integral part of today's internet security architecture, it is vital to integrate post-quantum cryptography soon. This promises to mitigate the increasingly grave threat of large quantum computers to cryptography. The United States National Institute of Standards and Technologies (NIST) launched a multi-year standardization project for post-quantum algorithms [28]. The project is calling for key encapsulation mechanisms (KEMs) and digital signature algorithms that withstand large quantum computers.

While standardization of the primitives is ongoing, work on post-quantum TLS (PQTLS) has also begun. This began with academic experiments in 2015, demonstrating R-LWE key exchange in TLS 1.2 [5]. Like the previous work, many have focused on the ephemeral key exchange in TLS, often using so-called "hybrid" algorithms. These essentially perform a classic elliptic-curve key and a post-quantum key exchange in parallel, to increase the confidence in the security. Google and Cloudflare have already conducted large-scale industry studies employing hybrid algorithms within TLS [21–23]. Amazon already includes experimental support for post-quantum schemes in its S2N TLS implementation and its Key Management Services product [16]. While previous works have mainly focused on post-quantum confidentiality; there have been fewer experiments deploying post-quantum authentication. Sikideris et al. [36] have measured the performance of post-quantum signature schemes between servers in two data centers. They concluded that out of the (NIST Round 2) schemes they tested, only two (Falcon [30] and Dilithium [24]) seem viable for deployment in TLS 1.3. Experiments by Cloudflare [38], that added dummy data to TLS connections to measure the impact of the larger sizes of post-quantum signature schemes, seem to support these results. Still, when using Dilithium as a drop-in replacement for all of the signatures in TLS (which adds 17 kB to the handshake), Cloudflare reports an expected 60–80% slowdown for the Linux default congestion window of 10 packets. Falcon has much more favorable public key and signature sizes but requires hardware support for double-precision floating-point operations. Without this, Sikideris et al. report signing handshakes with Falcon is not viable.

There has also been some work investigating embedded devices rather than large-scale, high-performance computers. Bürstinghaus-Steinbach et al. have experimented with Kyber and stateless hash-based signature scheme SPHINCS$^+$. They integrated SPHINCS$^+$ in mbedTLS's [25] TLS 1.2 implementation and showed the performance on various Arm boards [6]. More recently,

George et al. have evaluated the performance of post-quantum TLS 1.3 on embedded systems [13]. They investigated the performance of the NIST finalist KEMs and the Dilithium and Falcon signature algorithms in WolfSSL's TLS 1.3 implementation.

To mitigate the difficulties with post-quantum signatures, Wiggers et al. proposed KEMTLS [33]. Instead of authenticating the handshake through a signature, KEMTLS performs authentication through KEM key exchange with KEM public keys in the certificates. As the KEMs currently considered for standardization are generally smaller and/or more computationally efficient than the post-quantum signature schemes, this can be more efficient. Additionally, it reduces the size of the trusted code base: the code that facilitates the ephemeral key exchange can also be used for authentication. Knowledge of the server's long-term key is imaginable in e.g. session resumption, or perhaps in IoT applications where the clients speak to a single server. We note that the certificates are still signed by a certificate authority using post-quantum signatures. We thus still need to verify post-quantum signatures; we might however choose signature algorithms that are optimized for size or verification time rather than signing time.

While KEMTLS and PQTLS have been compared, these studies focused on high-end hardware and high bandwidth connections [7,33,34]. However, TLS is used for more than just protecting web browsing on desktop computers. The Internet of Things (IoT) increasingly interconnects embedded devices over the internet. Especially device-to-cloud communication is an omnipresent IoT use case. New communication protocols like Matter [10] (formerly Connected Home over IP) mark a new trend by using IPv6 and forcing every embedded device to establish its own end-to-end-secure connection. From a security perspective, this makes perfect sense. However, for embedded software developers this poses a challenge. Key establishment, digital signatures and certificate transmission are already problematic for low-cost, resource-constrained devices. With the advent of post-quantum cryptography, it will become even more challenging to establish TLS connections from those embedded devices.

1.1   Contribution

This work investigates if KEMTLS' advantages transfer to the embedded realm by comparing KEMTLS and PQTLS in an embedded setting. For this purpose, KEMTLS and PQTLS were implemented including all NIST finalist signature schemes and KEMs, except for Classic McEliece which has too large public keys. As the PQTLS and KEMTLS implementation share large parts of their code base, a direct performance comparison is possible. Our analysis focuses on the relevant trade-offs embedded systems engineers face. To our knowledge, this is the first work to investigate KEMTLS in an embedded setting. We benchmark runtime, memory usage, code size and bandwidth consumption of our KEMTLS and PQTLS instantiations. The benchmark results were obtained by running our implementations on a Cortex-M4-based platform. Our experiments were conducted with a technology stack that is typically used in real-world deployments, in which the embedded device is a TLS client talking to a TLS server running on a high-end computer. This computer also simulated different network technologies throughout the experiments. After a brief introduction of post-quantum cryptography, previous work and the ongoing standardization process, the PQTLS and KEMTLS protocols will be presented. The differences between these protocols will be outlined afterward. To support our results, the implementation and experimental setup will then be explained in detail. Finally, the results will be presented and concluded.

2   Background

In this section, we will give some background on the development of post-quantum cryptography, providing some history and summarizing the NIST standardization process. We will also detail the impact post-quantum cryptography has on TLS 1.3 and the development of KEMTLS.

2.1   Post-quantum Cryptography

In 1994 Peter Shor published his famous quantum algorithms for discrete logarithms and factoring [35]. Virtually all of today's deployed public-key cryptography is based on the difficulty of computing discrete logarithms or integer factorization. Shor's algorithm, therefore, poses a severe threat to information security. This affects key-exchange methods and signature algorithms alike. Unfortunately, all of today's TLS key exchange and signature algorithms would be broken once an adversary has access to a large quantum computer. Moreover, advances in quantum computing give reason to believe that the arrival of large quantum computers is on the horizon [26,27]. Since development, standardization and adaptation of cryptographic algorithms is a slow process, preparations against quantum computers have to be started now.

The NIST standardization project for post-quantum cryptography started in 2017 [28]. From over 60 proposed candidates, four KEMs and three signature algorithms have proceeded as *finalists* to the competition's third round. There are an additional five KEMs and three signature algorithms still in the competition as *alternate candidates*. NIST has announced that they will select at most one of the lattice-based KEMs Kyber, SABER or NTRU as a standard, as well as one of the two lattice-based signature schemes Falcon and Dilithium. They will also be opening up an on-ramp for new signature schemes in the next round for signature schemes based on other assumptions.

The algorithms in the NIST competition propose parameters at three security levels, called *I*, *III* and *V*. Algorithms in these security levels should be at least as hard to break as AES-128, AES-192 and AES-256. Due to the resource constraints of embedded devices, we will only consider parameters of security level I.

NIST Finalists. Three signature schemes remained as finalists in the third round of the NIST standardization project. Two of them are lattice-based constructions, and both were selected for standardization at the end of Round 3 in July 2022. **Falcon** [30]'s security assumptions are based on NTRU, while **Dilithium** [24]'s assumptions are based on the Module-LWE and the Short Integer Solution problems. **Rainbow** [12] is a multivariate signature algorithm that is a variant of UOV [18]. Its security is based on the hardness of finding solutions to systems of equations in many variables over finite fields. Rainbow was recently broken by Beullens [4], and later eliminated from the standardization process. However, Rainbow is a good representative of UOV-based multivariate signature schemes in terms of size and performance. In these schemes, public keys are very large, but the very small signature sizes lead to interesting trade-offs. Since other UOV-like multivariate schemes will likely be proposed during NIST's next call for post-quantum signatures, we choose to include Rainbow in this our analysis.

Key encapsulation mechanisms (KEMs) are used for key exchange. Within TLS they can serve the same role as the Diffie-Hellman ephemeral key exchange. Similar to public-key encryption (PKE), a KEM public key is used to generate an encapsulated shared secret key. Only the corresponding private key can then decrypt this ciphertext into the right shared secret key.

Four KEMs proceeded as finalists into the third round of NIST's PQC competition. Among them are the lattice-based schemes **Kyber** [32], **Saber** [11] and **NTRU** [8]. Although these schemes are all based on lattices, their underlying lattice structure and implementation details differ substantially. **Classic McEliece** [3] is the only non-lattice-based finalist; its security relies on the hardness of decoding random linear codes instead. Code-based cryptography has been around since the 1970s. Therefore, it has a longer history of cryptanalysis than lattice-based cryptography. Because of this body of literature around Classic McEliece, it is often considered the most conservative choice. However, Classic McEliece's parameter choices make for very large public key sizes. Also in terms of speed, it can not compete with the lattice-based algorithms. Kyber was chosen to be the next NIST standard for key exchange in July 2022, while Classic McEliece was moved forward into the fourth round of the competition [2].

PQC on Embedded Device. Public-key cryptography was already challenging for embedded systems in a pre-quantum setting. The more expensive post-quantum algorithms will make this worse. To gain a better understanding of PQC algorithm performance on embedded systems, the PQM4 [17] project collects implementations for the Cortex-M4 platform and benchmarks them. Table 1 shows size and performance tradeoffs between the NIST PQC finalists based on numbers from [17] and [9]. Here it is important to mention that these numbers are accomplished on a clocked-down Cortex-M4. Using such a slowed-down embedded processor is customary for measuring algorithm run times because it avoids flash wait states. In a real deployment, code would be fetched from a fast ROM instead of a flash. For our experiments, we are not exclusively interested in PQC algorithm run-time, but in the performance of the overall system. Therefore, we do not clock down our CPU. The ramifications of this are detailed in Subsect. 3.1.

Table 1. Comparison of NIST PQC Round 3 finalists at security level I. We show the size (in bytes) of data transmitted during a handshake (public key, signature and ciphertext), offline data (secret keys) and operation timings (from [9,17]) on M4.

	bytes transmitted			stored	computation ($\approx$Kcycles)		
Signatures	pubkey	sig	sum	secret	keygen	sign	verify
Dilithium ★	1 312	2 420	3 732	2 528	1 597	4 095	1 572
Falcon ★	897	690	1 587	1 281	163 994	39 014	473
Rainbow †	161 600	66	161 666	103 648	94	907	238
KEMs	pubkey	ciph	sum	secret	keygen	encaps	decaps
Kyber ★	800	768	1 568	1 632	440	539	490
NTRU †	699	699	1 398	953	2 867	565	538
SABER †	672	736	1 408	1 568	352	481	453

★: Scheme was selected for standardization.
†: Scheme was eliminated from the NIST standardization project.

2.2   Post-quantumtls TLS

We will briefly explain how TLS 1.3 post-quantum can be made post-quantum and summarize the KEMTLS proposal for an alternatively authenticated TLS handshake.

(Post-quantumtls). TLS is a protocol that has seen widespread deployment, famously as part of HTTPS. Its most recent iteration is TLS 1.3 [31]. In the most common uses, it offers unilateral authentication of the server to the client. Optionally, it also allows mutual, client-to-server authentication. The protocol authenticates the peers through signatures, which are in turn verified using public keys that are contained in (CA-signed) certificates. There is optional support for pre-shared, symmetric keys in place of certificate authentication as well.

The unilateral, certificate-authenticated TLS 1.3 handshake consists of an ephemeral, Diffie–Hellman (DH) key exchange followed by a signature over the handshake to authenticate. Finally, the handshake is additionally authenticated by a MAC. It is possible to make this handshake post-quantum, simply by replacing the server's DH key generation with KEM$_e$.Encapsulate, to encapsulate against the client's ephemeral public key, and sending the ciphertext instead of the server's ephemeral DH public key. The client would derive the shared secret by decapsulating the ciphertext. For authentication, we simply use post-quantum signature algorithms in place of RSA or elliptic curve signatures. The TLS 1.3 handshake has been very carefully designed to be very efficient in the number of round-trips and is a single round-trip (1-RTT) protocol. As we can see on the left-hand side of Fig. 1, the server can already send data to the client in its first response flow. The client can send it first message after the server's first flow, after 1.5 RTT.

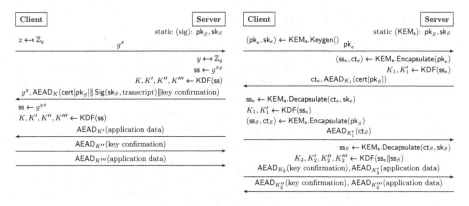

Fig. 1. Simplified protocol flow diagrams of: (left) the TLS 1.3 handshake, using signatures for server authentication; and (right) the KEMTLS handshake, using KEMs for server authentication.

KEMTLS. The post-quantum KEMs and signature algorithms are further apart than their classic variants were. KEMTLS is an alternative proposal for a PQTLS handshake, which allows using KEMs (which are typically much smaller and/or more computationally efficient than post-quantum signatures) instead of signatures in the online handshake. In KEMTLS, the certificates contain public keys for a KEM instead of a signature scheme. There are still signatures for the verification of the certificate chain, but these only need to be verified. As those signatures are done offline, it is also possible to use algorithms optimized for public key and signature size, rather than signing time. For example, [33, Appendix D] gives parameters for such a variant of XMSS^{MT}.

KEMTLS is inspired by the OPTLS proposal by Krawczyk and Wee [19]. OPTLS was an early proposal for TLS 1.3, where the authentication would be done via Diffie–Hellman key exchange. However, as observed by Kuhnen [20], OPTLS requires the non-interactive key exchange properties of DH, which KEMs do not offer. To authenticate a server via KEM, the client encapsulates a ciphertext to the long-term public key contained in the server's certificate. This would naively result in a 2-RTT protocol. KEMTLS avoids the performance penalty this would imply by observing that, in many applications including HTTP, for a *useful* response from the server, it first needs to receive a request from the client. For example, which page the client is requesting from the server. KEMTLS allows the client to send its request in the same flow as it would in TLS 1.3, returning the protocol to 1.5-RTT. This is achieved by encrypting the data with a key that is derived from both the ephemeral key exchange and the shared secret encapsulated to the server's long-term key. This key is *implicitly* authenticated, as the client can not be sure of the server's presence before it receives a message (`ServerFinished`) in which the server uses the encapsulated secret. The right-hand side of Fig. 1 describes a simplified version of a (unilaterally authenticated) KEMTLS handshake.

3 Experimental Setup

The following section describes the experimental setup used to acquire our results. Both protocols were benchmarked for handshake times, run-times of algorithms, peak memory usage, code size, and network traffic. Handshake times were measured in three network environments relevant to the IoT domain. This includes regular "broadband" internet, as well as two low-power wide-area network standards, LTE-Machine Type Communication (LTE-M) and Narrowband-IoT (NB-IoT), developed by the 3rd Generation network Partnership Project (3GPP). We give the characteristics employed for these environments in Table 2. While the performance characteristics of LTE-M and NB-IoT are based on numbers of the 3GPP [1], the broadband scenario is based on realistic round-trip times of client-to-cloud communication within West Europe using a consumer-grade connection [29].

Table 2. Connection characteristics according to 3GPP [1]

Name	Abbrev.	Bandwidth	RTT time
Broadband	BB	1 Mbit	26 ms
LTE machine type communication	LTE-M	1 Mbit	120 ms
Narrowband-IoT	NB-IoT	46 kbit	3 s

Cryptographic Primitives. As KEMTLS is a post-quantum protocol, it is not specifically designed for transitional security. Although KEMTLS does not preclude their use, we do not consider mixed classic/post-quantum certificates or hybrid (post-quantum plus elliptic curve) key-exchange methods in our experiments. For comparability, our PQTLS implementation is also exclusively using post-quantum algorithms. We evaluated all combinations of NIST finalists, except for the KEM *Classic McEliece*. Classic McEliece's public keys are too large to fit into memory and do not fit in the ClientHello's KeyShareEntry extension [31, Sec. 4.2.8].

Both KEMTLS and PQTLS make use of a certificate authority (CA) that signs certificates. The CA's certificate, containing the CA's public key used for signature verification, is stored on the client device. Only leaf certificates, transmitted by the server during the handshake, differ in KEMTLS and TLS 1.3. For PQTLS they include the public key of a signature algorithm, in KEMTLS a KEM public key.

We only evaluate primitives at the lowest security level, NIST level I. These are the smallest and most efficient parametersets.

3.1 Implementation

All benchmarks were conducted on a Silicon Labs STK3701A board, also known as the "Giant Gecko". This board was chosen because it features a 72 MHz ARM

Cortex-M4F embedded processor and offers large enough memory (2 MB flash storage, 512 kB SRAM) to fit Rainbow public keys. As Cortex-M4 is the designated NIST PQC reference platform for embedded devices, there are optimized assembly implementations available for most finalist algorithms. The PQM4 project collects these implementations and provides extensive benchmarks [17]. All PQC implementations used for benchmarking were taken from the PQM4 project. Only minor modifications, such as adding *verify* functions to signature schemes, fixing alignment issues and name-spacing symbol names had to be conducted. The code was compiled using GCC version 11.1, with the -O3 speed optimization flag. In contrast to experiments run within the PQM4 project, we do not clock down the processor to avoid wait states. Instead, the processor runs at full speed. This makes sense since we are not exclusively interested in the run times of the primitives, but the performance of the overall system. Running the processor at full speed makes the PQC algorithms consume more cycles due to flash wait states and higher costs of memory accesses. However, since the PQC algorithms do not consume more wall-clock time, the actual handshake durations are not negatively affected. The Giant Gecko board exclusively takes on the role of an embedded (KEM)TLS client, wanting to connect to a backend server. To validate certificates send in the handshake, we flash the CA's root certificate into the Giant Gecko's persistent memory during setup. For efficiency, the CA directly signs the server's certificate. This avoids the need for transmitting intermediate CAs, reducing the size of the certificate chain. As both endpoints in embedded scenarios are usually under some level of manufacturer control, this is a common deployment. Communication to the backend server is done via the Giant Gecko's Ethernet port, which is directly connected to a high-end computer. This host computer simulates different network environments by using Linux's *netem* network emulation framework [15]. The network emulation framework is set up to throttle bandwidth and delay round trip times (RTTs) according to the aforementioned network environments. Wiggers' original KEMTLS implementation [33,34] is used as server software. When running an iteration of the experiment, the corresponding PQC algorithms and the CA certificate are linked into the binary using Zephyr's *West* build tool. We then flash the binary onto the board via JLink. Benchmark results are received via serial communication.

Platform. To have a realistic setup, we employed a typical embedded systems software stack. In our case that includes an embedded real-time operating system (RTOS) with an open-source TCP/IP stack and added TLS support. For reproducibility, we used the Apache-licensed Zephyr RTOS [39]. Zephyr supports over 200 boards and is backed by the Linux Foundation and multiple large corporations involved with developing embedded systems, such as NXP, NORDIC or Memfault. It provides its own optimized embedded network stack and allows cycle-accurate run time measurements (given a board's hardware supports it). Our application code runs as the exclusive Zephyr thread, eliminating scheduling costs. PQTLS and KEMTLS support was added to the operating system via a custom WolfSSL module. All code, including reproducible build system and server software, used in this work is publicly available.[1] KEMTLS certificate generation was conducted using a customized Python script based on Wiggers et al. code. Post-quantum certificates for PQTLS were generated using a fork of OpenSSL's command-line tool maintained by the Open Quantum Safe project [37]. The TLS 1.3 cipher suite `TLS_CHACHA20_POLY1305_SHA256` was used in all experiments.

Wolfssl Integration. Previous work [6,13] also uses WolfSSL for running benchmarks on embedded systems. We decided to use WolfSSL for the same reasons as the mentioned works and to make comparisons with our results easier. WolfSSL is designed to be memory efficient and fast on embedded systems. On top, it already supports TLS 1.3 and has a clean implementation of TLS's state machine. This makes it an ideal basis for implementing PQTLS and KEMTLS. Adding post-quantum algorithms to WolfSSL is straightforward. WolfSSL's crypto provider, called WolfCrypt, has a clean API that can be extended easily. As the KEM Kyber was already included in WolfSSL by [6], we did not need to make changes to the TLS 1.3 state machine. Apart from including the relevant ASN.1 object identifiers for KEMs and post-quantum signatures, only small changes such as increasing the maximum size of certificates had to be applied. Our embedded KEMTLS implementation is based on the same WolfSSL version as our PQTLS implementation. The majority of the code is identical in the PQTLS and KEMTLS implementation. However, adding support for KEMTLS to WolfSSL still required significant effort. Apart from altering the certificate/ASN.1 parser to allow KEM keys in certificates (and using those), WolfSSL's internal state machine, key derivations and state structures had to be modified. In both our PQTLS and KEMTLS experiments the client only performs signature verification, so no code for signing was linked into the final binary.

4   Results

For developers of embedded systems, the trade-offs between ROM (code size), RAM (memory usage), network traffic and CPU time (run-time of code) are most crucial. In this section, we present our findings regarding the consumption of these resources by KEMTLS and TLS 1.3 using NIST PQC finalists.

The run-time of algorithms impacts the device's energy consumption. This is especially relevant for battery-powered devices that rely on the possibility to hibernate when inactive. Network traffic also affects energy consumption, as operating an antenna is usually a very energy-consuming operation. Depending on the underlying wireless technology, network traffic can also be expensive in terms of network provider fees. Our results are representative for Cortex-M4-based platforms in general. Hence we focus on benchmarks that are independent of our specific evaluation board. As energy consumption varies heavily based on a board's

---

[1] Source code is available at https://github.com/rugo/wolfssl-kemtls-experiments/tree/paperv1.

design, choice of peripherals and transmission technology we did not include direct energy measurements into our results. Instead, we present code size, consumed memory, handshake traffic, handshake duration and run-time of PQC primitives. All KEMTLS and PQTLS instantiations were run 1000 times, with each run using a different CA and leaf certificate. The presented benchmarks are averaged over all runs. The NIST signature finalist Rainbow, which is included as a representative for multivariate-based cryptography, is only present in the KEMTLS results. This is because Rainbow public keys are very large. There was not enough memory to fit Rainbow as well as another signature scheme. It could therefore not be included into the PQTLS benchmarks. We emphasize that all employed PQC algorithms were optimized for speed, and not stack consumption.

4.1   Storage and Memory Consumption

Both protocol implementations are roughly the same size. Without post-quantum primitives, they have a code size of around 111 kB. Table 3 shows combinations of PQC algorithms with their measured code size. For KEMTLS, only instantiations with one KEM used for both ephemeral key exchange and authentication are shown. Including two KEMs does not give an advantage, but increases code size. However, for completeness, a table with all combinations can be found in Appendix A. Similarly, PQTLS instantiations with the same signature algorithm used for CA and leaf certificates are shown. Additionally, we include the combination of Dilithium and Falcon, where Dilithium is used as the handshake signature algorithm. This combination was suggested by Sikideris et al. [36] to make use of Dilithiums faster signing times for servers without hardware support for Falcon's double-precision floating-point operations.

The table also shows the PQC code's share of the overall code size as a percentage. Also included in Table 3 is memory consumption. Shown is the peak of consumed memory, in both heap and stack, during the handshake. This includes the memory consumed by the protocol implementation and PQC primitives.

In contrast to TLS 1.3, KEMTLS uses a KEM encapsulation instead of a signature verification to authenticate the connection. KEMTLS, therefore, needs code for KEM encapsulation, whereas TLS 1.3 does not. TLS 1.3 on the other hand needs the code for two distinct verification algorithms if different signature algorithms are used for CA and leaf certificates. Instantiations with NTRU ephemeral key exchange are notable outliers in terms of code size, requiring over 200 kB of code. This is in line with results reported by PQM4 [17]. Interestingly, this big increase in code size can not be observed when NTRU is used exclusively for authentication. This is because the client requires key generation and decapsulation code for ephemeral key exchange, whereas authentication via KEM only requires encapsulation functionality. Whenever Rainbow is used, the CA certificate containing a Rainbow public key takes up between 33% and 53% of the overall consumed storage space. This, however, does not disqualify Rainbow from usage on embedded systems, due to its small signature and very fast verification times (see Sect. 4.2).

Further, the results show that the lattice-based schemes perform well in terms of memory consumption. The consumed memory is mainly driven by stack usage

Table 3. Code and CA certificate sizes (and as percentage of total ROM size), and peak memory usage in the experiments. Parametersets used are NIST level I.

	KEX	Auth.	CA	PQC code (%)	CA size (%)	Memory
KEMTLS	Kyber	Kyber	Dilithium	29.0 kB (20.1%)	3.9 kB (2.7%)	49.7 kB
	Kyber	Kyber	Falcon	25.7 kB (18.6%)	1.7 kB (1.2%)	52.8 kB
	Kyber	Kyber	Rainbow	29.8 kB (9.8%)	161.8 kB (53.4%)	167.0 kB
	NTRU	NTRU	Dilithium	203.4 kB (63.9%)	3.9 kB (1.2%)	49.7 kB
	NTRU	NTRU	Falcon	200.0 kB (63.9%)	1.7 kB (0.6%)	52.8 kB
	NTRU	NTRU	Rainbow	204.0 kB (42.8%)	161.8 kB (33.9%)	182.9 kB
	SABER	SABER	Dilithium	31.5 kB (21.5%)	3.9 kB (2.7%)	49.7 kB
	SABER	SABER	Falcon	28.2 kB (20.0%)	1.7 kB (1.2%)	52.8 kB
	SABER	SABER	Rainbow	32.2 kB (10.5%)	161.8 kB (53.0%)	167.9 kB
PQTLS	Kyber	Dilithium	Dilithium	29.0 kB (20.1%)	4.0 kB (2.8%)	58.0 kB
	Kyber	Falcon	Dilithium	34.4 kB (23.0%)	4.0 kB (2.7%)	60.7 kB
	Kyber	Falcon	Falcon	25.8 kB (18.6%)	1.8 kB (1.3%)	56.2 kB
	NTRU	Dilithium	Dilithium	203.4 kB (63.8%)	4.0 kB (1.3%)	56.6 kB
	NTRU	Falcon	Dilithium	208.7 kB (64.4%)	4.0 kB (1.2%)	59.3 kB
	NTRU	Falcon	Falcon	200.1 kB (63.9%)	1.8 kB (0.6%)	54.8 kB
	SABER	Dilithium	Dilithium	31.5 kB (21.5%)	4.0 kB (2.7%)	58.0 kB
	SABER	Falcon	Dilithium	36.8 kB (24.2%)	4.0 kB (2.6%)	60.7 kB
	SABER	Falcon	Falcon	28.2 kB (20.0%)	1.8 kB (1.3%)	56.2 kB

of the PQC signature algorithms. Only Rainbow is an exception here. With a Rainbow-powered CA certificate, the very large public key has to be loaded into memory and held during signature verification. This requires a large allocation of heap space. In a custom certificate loader implementation it would be possible to store the public key in an already usable form in flash. Then the public key could directly be streamed in from flash (similar to [14]), without the need to hold it in memory entirely. However, since we present comparable results of reusable code, we did not include this kind of optimization for an individual algorithm.

4.2 Handshake Times

Apart from storage and memory consumption, handshake times are key in an embedded environment. Table 4 shows handshake times for different transmission technologies measured in millions of cycles. A complete table, with all possible instantiations, can be found in Appendix A. In Fig. 2 we show the handshake times and traffic for the broadband and NB-IoT scenarios. In a real deployment, the device would likely go into a low power mode or sleep instead of actively polling data during a slow transmission. This behavior however depends highly on the specifics of the embedded system and its transmission technology. Therefore, to achieve reproducible results, the CPU was running at a constant speed of 72MHz during all experiments. This also makes a direct translation to wall time possible. The table also shows the percentage of cycles spend on the underlying PQC primitives. The remaining cycles are spent in the TLS state machine, memory operations or waiting for I/O.

Time spent in crypto operations is significant in the broadband and LTE-M setting. Whereas the NB-IoT transmission is so slow, that the share of cycles spent in cryptographic operations is very low (0.8%–1.7%). In low-bandwidth/high-RTT settings like NB-IoT, the transmission size of certificates and public keys is the main driving factor of run time. Loading large public keys from storage into memory is a relevant factor as well, slowing down the otherwise fast Rainbow signature algorithm. Cycles spent to access memory and storage also become increasingly negligible when using slow transportation mediums. This is visible in Fig. 2b, where the instantiations with similarly sized handshake traffic clearly form clusters.

Table 4. TLS handshake traffic and runtime for various scenarios. Parametersets used are NIST level I.

	KEX	Auth.	CA	Handshake traffic	Handshake time in Mcycles (% of crypto)		
					BB (%)	LTE-M (%)	NB-IoT (%)
KEMTLS	Kyber	Kyber	Dilithium	6.3 kB	17.1 (30.2%)	34.0 (15.2%)	593.6 (0.9%)
	Kyber	Kyber	Falcon	4.5 kB	12.3 (27.2%)	25.7 (13.0%)	467.8 (0.7%)
	Kyber	Kyber	Rainbow	3.9 kB	11.3 (25.1%)	20.4 (13.9%)	459.0 (0.6%)
	NTRU	NTRU	Dilithium	6.0 kB	21.3 (46.0%)	38.1 (25.6%)	595.8 (1.6%)
	NTRU	NTRU	Falcon	4.2 kB	16.6 (47.8%)	25.9 (30.6%)	469.7 (1.7%)
	NTRU	NTRU	Rainbow	3.6 kB	15.7 (47.4%)	24.7 (30.1%)	361.6 (2.1%)
	SABER	SABER	Dilithium	6.0 kB	16.3 (29.4%)	33.3 (14.4%)	590.8 (0.8%)
	SABER	SABER	Falcon	4.2 kB	11.6 (25.5%)	21.0 (14.1%)	464.8 (0.6%)
	SABER	SABER	Rainbow	3.6 kB	10.7 (23.1%)	19.8 (12.5%)	356.8 (0.7%)
PQTLS	Kyber	Dilithium	Dilithium	8.4 kB	19.9 (35.9%)	36.8 (19.5%)	818.1 (0.9%)
	Kyber	Falcon	Dilithium	6.3 kB	15.5 (33.0%)	29.0 (17.6%)	586.4 (0.9%)
	Kyber	Falcon	Falcon	4.5 kB	10.9 (30.1%)	21.0 (15.6%)	464.6 (0.7%)
	NTRU	Dilithium	Dilithium	8.3 kB	24.3 (47.6%)	41.1 (28.1%)	821.3 (1.4%)
	NTRU	Falcon	Dilithium	6.1 kB	19.9 (47.8%)	33.4 (28.5%)	590.6 (1.6%)
	NTRU	Falcon	Falcon	4.3 kB	15.2 (50.3%)	25.4 (30.2%)	468.0 (1.6%)
	SABER	Dilithium	Dilithium	8.3 kB	19.7 (35.2%)	36.6 (19.0%)	817.3 (0.8%)
	SABER	Falcon	Dilithium	6.1 kB	15.3 (32.0%)	28.8 (17.0%)	586.2 (0.8%)
	SABER	Falcon	Falcon	4.3 kB	10.7 (28.5%)	20.9 (14.6%)	464.0 (0.7%)

Both PQTLS and KEMTLS use a KEM for key exchange. While the performance of the module lattice KEMs Kyber and SABER is similar, they both outperform NTRU for this task. This is mainly due to the rather slow key generation of NTRU increasing handshake time. Slow key generation is also the reason why PQTLS and KEMTLS instantiations using NTRU have the highest percentage of cycles spent in PQC operations.

All KEMs outperform Dilithium when used for authentication. This makes sense as Dilithium's verify routine is slower than the encapsulation routine of all investigated KEMs. Dilithium's performance also suffers from its large public key and signature that increase the required transmission size. In slow, bandwidth-constrained network environments, such as NB-IoT, this drawback becomes even more apparent. Rainbow performs well in terms of handshake times when used as a CA certificate. Not only because it has a fast, bitsliced Cortex-M4 implementation. Since the large Rainbow public key is stored on the client device, only the small signature has to be transmitted during the handshake. Rainbow's small signature and fast runtime make it a good fit for CA certificates if the storage and memory demands can be afforded. The instantiations with Rainbow offer the fastest KEMTLS handshake times throughout all transmission mediums. Additionally, the shortest NB-IoT handshake times use KEMTLS with Rainbow and SABER. Falcon on the other hand performs very well on the Cortex-M4 platform in our experiments. In terms of runtime, it even outperforms KEMs for server authentication. However, this is only true for the client side. Signing operations using Falcon are considerably more expensive than KEM decapsulations. But these operations are conducted on the server side, increasing server load, which is not part of our measurements. Additionally, Falcon's public key and signature sizes are comparable to the sizes of the KEM's public keys and ciphertexts. So it is not surprising that PQTLS instantiations using Falcon perform well. In the broadband and LTE-M setting, PQTLS with Falcon and SABER performs as well as KEMTLS with Rainbow and SABER.

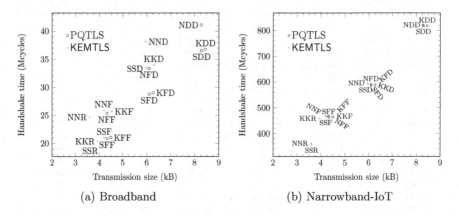

Fig. 2. Handshake times and traffic for instantiations of KEMTLS and PQTLS. Letters represent the algorithms <u>D</u>ilithium, <u>F</u>alcon, <u>K</u>yber, <u>N</u>TRU, <u>R</u>ainbow, and <u>S</u>ABER in the roles of ephemeral key exchange, handshake authentication and CA, in that order.

5   Discussion

Our results show that KEMTLS with server-only authentication uses less memory than PQTLS and has similar code sizes. Due to Falcon's verification algorithm being very efficient, in terms of bandwidth and computation time, PQTLS with Falcon performs as well as or better than any KEMTLS instantiation. The only exception are the KEMTLS instantiations using SABER or NTRU with Rainbow, where the ability of KEMTLS to use Rainbow due to lower memory usage saves a few bytes and thus become the best-performing instantiations in the NB-IoT scenario. Falcon also performs better than Dilithium on the client side, in any scenario.

Although we have not measured client authentication or an embedded server, we can extrapolate from our results. As reported by PQM4 [17] and Sikideris et al. [36], Falcon's signing algorithm, especially without hardware support, is significantly more costly than Dilithium's or any of the KEM operations. This suggests that Falcon is perhaps not generically suitable for post-quantum authentication.

Sikideris et al. also suggested a combination of Dilithium and Falcon for PQTLS, in scenarios where there is no hardware support for Falcon's double-precision floating-point operations. Dilithium would be put in the leaf certificate, to make use of its efficient signing times for online handshake signatures. Falcon's smaller public key and signature sizes would be beneficial for the CA certificate algorithm, which signs the leaf certificate only once, but the signature is transmitted many times. However, our results show that for embedded clients that only need to do signature validation Falcon is preferable over Dilithium, especially in very low bandwidth scenarios like NB-IoT.

6   Conclusion and Future Work

In this paper, we compared the performance of KEMTLS and TLS 1.3 using NIST PQC finalists in an embedded environment. This environment was represented by a Cortex-M4-based client communicating with a desktop-class server. We showed that a KEMTLS client consumes less memory than TLS 1.3, due to the smaller memory footprint of KEMs. The code size did not differ between KEMTLS and TLS 1.3. Since only server authentication was used, both protocols require a signature verify function and KEM for key exchange. Our run times show that in both protocols PQC primitives require a significant amount of computational time during the handshake, sometimes requiring over 50% of the entire handshake time. Even in the LTE-M setting, the percentage of cycles spent in PQC computations is considerable. However, in the bandwidth-constrained NB-IoT setting, handshake times are mostly driven by handshake size. In these conditions, Rainbow's very small signatures are an advantage. While Dilithium is generally outperformed by KEMs when used for authentication, Falcon performs very well due to its efficient verification algorithm. However, signing in Falcon is a very costly operation. Future work should therefore investigate KEMTLS and TLS 1.3 using client authentication, and embedded KEMTLS and post-quantum TLS 1.3 servers. In both of these applications, the embedded TLS 1.3 client needs to produce handshake signatures. This would increase the cost of using signatures instead of KEMs significantly, leading to new trade-offs. Another avenue of research is the pre-distributed key setting, where the client already knows the server's public key. In this setting, bandwidth can be reduced even further, which may be compelling for the NB-IoT application.

Acknowledgements. This work has been supported by Neodyme AG, the European Research Council through Starting Grant No. 805031 (EPOQUE) and by an NLnet Assure grant for the project "Standardizing KEMTLS".

A   Extended Benchmark Tables

In Table 5 we report code sizes, CA certificate sizes and memory usage for all experiments we ran. Table 6 provides all results for the handshake traffic and handshake timing metrics.

Table 5. Code and CA certificate sizes (and as percentage of total ROM size), and peak memory usage in the experiments.

	KEX	Auth.	CA	PQC code	(%)	CA size	(%)	Memory
	Kyber	Kyber	Dilithium	29.0 kB	(20.1%)	3.9 kB	(2.7%)	49.7 kB
	Kyber	Kyber	Falcon	25.7 kB	(18.6%)	1.7 kB	(1.2%)	52.8 kB
	Kyber	Kyber	Rainbow	29.8 kB	(9.8%)	161.8 kB	(53.4%)	167.0 kB
	Kyber	NTRU	Dilithium	41.0 kB	(26.3%)	3.9 kB	(2.5%)	49.7 kB
	Kyber	NTRU	Falcon	37.7 kB	(25.0%)	1.7 kB	(1.1%)	52.8 kB
	Kyber	NTRU	Rainbow	41.7 kB	(13.3%)	161.8 kB	(51.4%)	182.9 kB
	Kyber	SABER	Dilithium	44.9 kB	(28.1%)	3.9 kB	(2.4%)	49.7 kB
	Kyber	SABER	Falcon	41.7 kB	(26.9%)	1.7 kB	(1.1%)	52.8 kB
	Kyber	SABER	Rainbow	45.7 kB	(14.3%)	161.8 kB	(50.8%)	167.9 kB
	NTRU	Kyber	Dilithium	216.3 kB	(65.3%)	3.9 kB	(1.2%)	49.7 kB
	NTRU	Kyber	Falcon	213.0 kB	(65.4%)	1.7 kB	(0.5%)	52.8 kB
KEMTLS	NTRU	Kyber	Rainbow	217.1 kB	(44.3%)	161.8 kB	(33.0%)	182.9 kB
	NTRU	NTRU	Dilithium	203.4 kB	(63.9%)	3.9 kB	(1.2%)	49.7 kB
	NTRU	NTRU	Falcon	200.0 kB	(63.9%)	1.7 kB	(0.6%)	52.8 kB
	NTRU	NTRU	Rainbow	204.0 kB	(42.8%)	161.8 kB	(33.9%)	182.9 kB
	NTRU	SABER	Dilithium	219.7 kB	(65.6%)	3.9 kB	(1.2%)	49.7 kB
	NTRU	SABER	Falcon	216.4 kB	(65.7%)	1.7 kB	(0.5%)	52.8 kB
	NTRU	SABER	Rainbow	220.4 kB	(44.7%)	161.8 kB	(32.8%)	182.9 kB
	SABER	Kyber	Dilithium	44.5 kB	(27.9%)	3.9 kB	(2.4%)	49.7 kB
	SABER	Kyber	Falcon	41.3 kB	(26.8%)	1.7 kB	(1.1%)	52.8 kB
	SABER	Kyber	Rainbow	45.3 kB	(14.2%)	161.8 kB	(50.8%)	167.9 kB
	SABER	NTRU	Dilithium	43.9 kB	(27.6%)	3.9 kB	(2.5%)	49.7 kB
	SABER	NTRU	Falcon	40.6 kB	(26.4%)	1.7 kB	(1.1%)	52.8 kB
	SABER	NTRU	Rainbow	44.6 kB	(14.0%)	161.8 kB	(50.9%)	182.9 kB
	SABER	SABER	Dilithium	31.5 kB	(21.5%)	3.9 kB	(2.7%)	49.7 kB
	SABER	SABER	Falcon	28.2 kB	(20.0%)	1.7 kB	(1.2%)	52.8 kB
	SABER	SABER	Rainbow	32.2 kB	(10.5%)	161.8 kB	(53.0%)	167.9 kB
	Kyber	Dilithium	Dilithium	29.0 kB	(20.1%)	4.0 kB	(2.8%)	58.0 kB
	Kyber	Dilithium	Falcon	34.4 kB	(23.3%)	1.8 kB	(1.2%)	60.0 kB
	Kyber	Falcon	Dilithium	34.4 kB	(23.0%)	4.0 kB	(2.7%)	60.7 kB
	Kyber	Falcon	Falcon	25.8 kB	(18.6%)	1.8 kB	(1.3%)	56.2 kB
	NTRU	Dilithium	Dilithium	203.4 kB	(63.8%)	4.0 kB	(1.3%)	56.6 kB
PQTLS	NTRU	Dilithium	Falcon	208.7 kB	(64.9%)	1.8 kB	(0.6%)	58.6 kB
	NTRU	Falcon	Dilithium	208.7 kB	(64.4%)	4.0 kB	(1.2%)	59.3 kB
	NTRU	Falcon	Falcon	200.1 kB	(63.9%)	1.8 kB	(0.6%)	54.8 kB
	SABER	Dilithium	Dilithium	31.5 kB	(21.5%)	4.0 kB	(2.7%)	58.0 kB
	SABER	Dilithium	Falcon	36.8 kB	(24.6%)	1.8 kB	(1.2%)	60.0 kB
	SABER	Falcon	Dilithium	36.8 kB	(24.2%)	4.0 kB	(2.6%)	60.7 kB
	SABER	Falcon	Falcon	28.2 kB	(20.0%)	1.8 kB	(1.3%)	56.2 kB

Table 6. TLS handshake traffic and runtime for various scenarios

	KEX	Auth.	CA	Handshake traffic	Handshake time in Mcycles (% of crypto)					
					BB	(%)	LTE-M	(%)	NB-IoT	(%)
KEMTLS	Kyber	Kyber	Dilithium	6.3 kB	17.1	(30.2%)	34.0	(15.2%)	593.6	(0.9%)
	Kyber	Kyber	Falcon	4.5 kB	12.3	(27.2%)	25.7	(13.0%)	467.8	(0.7%)
	Kyber	Kyber	Rainbow	3.9 kB	11.3	(25.1%)	20.4	(13.9%)	459.0	(0.6%)
	Kyber	NTRU	Dilithium	6.1 kB	17.1	(31.5%)	34.1	(15.8%)	592.2	(0.9%)
	Kyber	NTRU	Falcon	4.4 kB	12.4	(28.8%)	21.7	(16.4%)	466.2	(0.8%)
	Kyber	NTRU	Rainbow	3.8 kB	11.4	(27.0%)	20.5	(15.0%)	358.1	(0.9%)
	Kyber	SABER	Dilithium	6.1 kB	16.8	(30.0%)	33.6	(15.0%)	591.5	(0.8%)
	Kyber	SABER	Falcon	4.4 kB	12.0	(26.6%)	21.5	(14.9%)	465.4	(0.7%)
	Kyber	SABER	Rainbow	3.8 kB	11.0	(24.5%)	20.2	(13.4%)	357.4	(0.8%)
	NTRU	Kyber	Dilithium	6.1 kB	21.3	(44.8%)	38.2	(25.0%)	596.9	(1.6%)
	NTRU	Kyber	Falcon	4.4 kB	16.6	(46.4%)	25.9	(29.7%)	470.8	(1.6%)
	NTRU	Kyber	Rainbow	3.8 kB	15.5	(46.3%)	24.7	(29.1%)	462.4	(1.6%)
	NTRU	NTRU	Dilithium	6.0 kB	21.3	(46.0%)	38.1	(25.6%)	595.8	(1.6%)
	NTRU	NTRU	Falcon	4.2 kB	16.6	(47.8%)	25.9	(30.6%)	469.7	(1.7%)
	NTRU	NTRU	Rainbow	3.6 kB	15.7	(47.4%)	24.7	(30.1%)	361.6	(2.1%)
	NTRU	SABER	Dilithium	6.0 kB	20.8	(45.1%)	37.7	(24.9%)	594.9	(1.6%)
	NTRU	SABER	Falcon	4.2 kB	16.2	(46.6%)	25.6	(29.5%)	468.9	(1.6%)
	NTRU	SABER	Rainbow	3.6 kB	15.3	(46.3%)	24.3	(29.1%)	360.9	(2.0%)
	SABER	Kyber	Dilithium	6.1 kB	16.8	(29.4%)	33.6	(14.7%)	593.0	(0.8%)
	SABER	Kyber	Falcon	4.4 kB	11.9	(26.1%)	22.7	(13.7%)	466.8	(0.7%)
	SABER	Kyber	Rainbow	3.8 kB	11.0	(23.7%)	20.2	(12.8%)	458.3	(0.6%)
	SABER	NTRU	Dilithium	6.0 kB	16.8	(30.8%)	33.7	(15.3%)	591.5	(0.9%)
	SABER	NTRU	Falcon	4.2 kB	12.0	(27.9%)	21.5	(15.5%)	465.6	(0.7%)
	SABER	NTRU	Rainbow	3.6 kB	11.0	(25.8%)	20.2	(14.1%)	357.6	(0.8%)
	SABER	SABER	Dilithium	6.0 kB	16.3	(29.4%)	33.3	(14.4%)	590.8	(0.8%)
	SABER	SABER	Falcon	4.2 kB	11.6	(25.5%)	21.0	(14.1%)	464.8	(0.6%)
	SABER	SABER	Rainbow	3.6 kB	10.7	(23.1%)	19.8	(12.5%)	356.8	(0.7%)
PQTLS	Kyber	Dilithium	Dilithium	8.4 kB	19.9	(35.9%)	36.8	(19.5%)	818.1	(0.9%)
	Kyber	Dilithium	Falcon	6.7 kB	14.7	(35.4%)	31.0	(16.8%)	595.8	(0.9%)
	Kyber	Falcon	Dilithium	6.3 kB	15.5	(33.0%)	29.0	(17.6%)	586.4	(0.9%)
	Kyber	Falcon	Falcon	4.5 kB	10.9	(30.1%)	21.0	(15.6%)	464.6	(0.7%)
	NTRU	Dilithium	Dilithium	8.3 kB	24.3	(47.6%)	41.1	(28.1%)	821.3	(1.4%)
	NTRU	Dilithium	Falcon	6.5 kB	19.0	(50.3%)	35.3	(27.2%)	599.2	(1.6%)
	NTRU	Falcon	Dilithium	6.1 kB	19.9	(47.8%)	33.4	(28.5%)	590.6	(1.6%)
	NTRU	Falcon	Falcon	4.3 kB	15.2	(50.3%)	25.4	(30.2%)	468.0	(1.6%)
	SABER	Dilithium	Dilithium	8.3 kB	19.7	(35.2%)	36.6	(19.0%)	817.3	(0.8%)
	SABER	Dilithium	Falcon	6.5 kB	14.5	(34.2%)	30.7	(16.2%)	595.2	(0.8%)
	SABER	Falcon	Dilithium	6.1 kB	15.3	(32.0%)	28.8	(17.0%)	586.2	(0.8%)
	SABER	Falcon	Falcon	4.3 kB	10.7	(28.5%)	20.9	(14.6%)	464.0	(0.7%)

References

1. 3rd Generation Partnership Project (3GPP): The mobile broadband standard specification release 13. Tech. rep., 3GPP Sep 2015 https://www.gpp.org/ftp/Information/WORK_PLAN/Description_Releases/Rel-13_description_20150917.zip
2. Alagic, G., et al.: Status report on the third round of the NIST post-quantum cryptography standardization process. Tech. Rep. NISTIR 8413, National Institute of Standards and Technology (2022). https://doi.org/10.6028/NIST.IR.8413

3. Albrecht, M.R., et al.: Classic McEliece. Tech. rep., National Institute of Standards and Technology (2020). https://csrc.nist.gov/projects/post-quantum-cryptography/round-3-submissions
4. Ding, J., Schmidt, D.: Rainbow, a new multivariable polynomial signature scheme. In: Ioannidis, J., Keromytis, A., Yung, M. (eds.) ACNS 2005. LNCS, vol. 3531, pp. 164–175. Springer, Heidelberg (2005). https://doi.org/10.1007/11496137_12
5. Bos, J.W., Costello, C., Naehrig, M., Stebila, D.: Post-quantum key exchange for the TLS protocol from the ring learning with errors problem. In: 2015 IEEE Symposium on Security and Privacy, pp. 553–570. IEEE Computer Society Press (2015). https://doi.org/10.1109/SP.2015.40
6. Bürstinghaus-Steinbach, K., Krauß, C., Niederhagen, R., Schneider, M.: Post-quantum TLS on embedded systems: integrating and evaluating KYBER and SPHINCS+ with mbed TLS. In: Sun, H.M., Shieh, S.P., Gu, G., Ateniese, G. (eds.) ASIACCS 20, pp. 841–852. ACM Press (2020). https://doi.org/10.1145/3320269.3384725
7. Celi, S., et al.: Implementing and measuring KEMTLS. In: Longa, P., Ràfols, C. (eds.) LATINCRYPT 2021. LNCS, vol. 12912, pp. 88–107. Springer, Cham (2021). https://doi.org/10.1007/978-3-030-88238-9_5
8. Chen, C., et al.: NTRU. Tech. rep., National Institute of Standards and Technology (2020). https://csrc.nist.gov/projects/post-quantum-cryptography/round-3-submissions
9. Chou, T., Kannwischer, M.J., Yang, B.Y.: Rainbow on cortex-M4. IACR TCHES 2021(4), 650–675 (2021). https://doi.org/10.46586/tches.v2021.i4.650-675. https://tches.iacr.org/index.php/TCHES/article/view/9078
10. Connectivity Standards Alliance: Build with Matter (2022). https://buildwithmatter.com. Accessed 16 May 2022
11. D'Anvers, J.P., et al.: SABER. Tech. rep., National Institute of Standards and Technology (2020). https://csrc.nist.gov/projects/post-quantum-cryptography/round-3-submissions
12. Ding, J., et al.: Rainbow. Tech. rep., National Institute of Standards and Technology (2020). https://csrc.nist.gov/projects/post-quantum-cryptography/round-3-submissions
13. George, T., Li, J., Fournaris, A.P., Zhao, R.K., Sakzad, A., Steinfeld, R.: Performance evaluation of post-quantum TLS 1.3 on embedded systems. Cryptology ePrint Archive, Report 2021/1553 (2021). https://eprint.iacr.org/2021/1553
14. Gonzalez, R., et al.: Verifying post-quantum signatures in 8 kB of RAM. In: Cheon, J.H., Tillich, J.-P. (eds.) PQCrypto 2021 2021. LNCS, vol. 12841, pp. 215–233. Springer, Cham (2021). https://doi.org/10.1007/978-3-030-81293-5_12
15. Hemminger, S., Ludovici, F., Pfeiffer, H.P.: (Nov 2011). https://man7.org/linux/man-pages/man8/tc-netem.8.html, man ip netem
16. Hopkins, A.: Post-quantum TLS now supported in AWS KMS. Amazon AWS Security Blog (2019). https://aws.amazon.com/blogs/security/post-quantum-tls-now-supported-in-aws-kms/. Accessed 20 May 2022
17. Kannwischer, M.J., Rijneveld, J., Schwabe, P., Stoffelen, K.: PQM4: post-quantum crypto library for the ARM Cortex-M4. https://github.com/mupq/pqm4
18. Nie, X., Liu, B., Xiong, H., Lu, G.: Cubic unbalance oil and vinegar signature scheme. In: Lin, D., Wang, X.F., Yung, M. (eds.) Inscrypt 2015. LNCS, vol. 9589, pp. 47–56. Springer, Cham (2016). https://doi.org/10.1007/978-3-319-38898-4_3
19. Krawczyk, H., Wee, H.: The OPTLS protocol and TLS 1.3. In: 2016 IEEE European Symposium on Security and Privacy (EuroS&P), pp. 81–96 (2016). https://doi.org/10.1109/EuroSP.2016.18

20. Kuhnen, W.: OPTLS revisited. Master's thesis, Radboud University (2018). https://www.ru.nl/publish/pages/769526/thesis-final.pdf
21. Kwiatkowski, K., Langley, A., Sullivan, N., Levin, D., Mislove, A., Valenta, L.: Measuring TLS key exchange with post-quantum KEM (2019). https://csrc.nist. gov/Presentations/2019/measuring-tls-key-exchange-with-post-quantum-kem
22. Langley, A.: CECPQ2. ImperialViolet (2018). https://www.imperialviolet.org/ 2018/12/12/cecpq2.html. Accessed 16 Feb 2021
23. Langley, A.: Real-world measurements of structured-lattices and supersingular iso-genies in TLS. In: ImperialViolet (2019). https://www.imperialviolet.org/2019/10/ 30/pqsivssl.html. Accessed 16 Feb 2021
24. Langley, A.: Real-world measurements of structured-lattices and supersingular iso-genies in TLS. In: ImperialViolet (2019). https://www.imperialviolet.org/2019/10/ 30/pqsivssl.html. Accessed 16 Feb 2021
25. mbed TLS. https://www.trustedfirmware.org/projects/mbed-tls/. Accessed 29 Apr 2022
26. Mosca, M.: Cybersecurity in an era with quantum computers: will we be ready? Cryp-tology ePrint Archive, Report 2015/1075 (2015). https://eprint.iacr.org/2015/1075
27. Mosca, M., Piani, M.: Quantum threat timeline. Tech. rep., Global Risk Institute (2019). https://globalriskinstitute.org/publications/quantum-threat-timeline/
28. National Institute for Standards and Technology: Submission requirements and evaluation criteria for the post-quantum cryptography standardiza-tion process (2016). https://csrc.nist.gov/CSRC/media/Projects/Post-Quantum-Cryptography/documents/call-for-proposals-final-dec-2016.pdf
29. Paul, S., Kuzovkova, Y., Lahr, N., Niederhagen, R.: Mixed certificate chains for the transition to post-quantum authentication in TLS 1.3. Cryptology ePrint Archive, Report 2021/1447 (2021). https://eprint.iacr.org/2021/1447
30. Prest, T., et al.: FALCON. Tech. rep., National Institute of Standards and Tech-nology (2020). https://csrc.nist.gov/projects/post-quantum-cryptography/round-3-submissions
31. Rescorla, E.: The Transport Layer Security TLS Protocol Version 1.3. RFC 8446, RFC Editor (2018). https://doi.org/10.17487/RFC8446
32. Schwabe, P., et al .: CRYSTALS-KYBER. Tech. rep., National Institute of Standards and Technology (2020). https://csrc.nist.gov/projects/post-quantum-cryptography/round-3-submissions
33. Schwabe, P., Stebila, D., Wiggers, T.: Post-quantum TLS without handshake sig-natures. In: Ligatti, J., Ou, X., Katz, J., Vigna, G. (eds.) ACM CCS 2020, pp. 1461–1480. ACM Press (2020). https://doi.org/10.1145/3372297.3423350
34. Schwabe, P., Stebila, D., Wiggers, T.: More efficient post-quantum KEMTLS with pre-distributed public keys. In: Bertino, E., Shulman, H., Waidner, M. (eds.) ESORICS 2021. LNCS, vol. 12972, pp. 3–22. Springer, Cham (2021). https://doi. org/10.1007/978-3-030-88418-5_1
35. Shor, P.W.: Algorithms for quantum computation: Discrete logarithms and factor-ing. In: 35th FOCS, pp. 124–134. IEEE Computer Society Press (1994). https:// doi.org/10.1109/SFCS.1994.365700
36. Sikeridis, D., Kampanakis, P., Devetsikiotis, M.: Post-quantum authentication in TLS 1.3: A performance study. In: NDSS 2020. The Internet Society, Feb 2020
37. The Open Quantum Safe project: Open Quantum Safe. https://openquantumsafe. org/. Accessed 20 May 2022
38. Westerbaan, B.: Sizing up post-quantum signatures (2021). https://blog.cloudflare. com/sizing-up-post-quantum-signatures/
39. Zephyr Project: Zephyr project. https://www.zephyrproject.org

Protecting the Most Significant Bits in Scalar Multiplication Algorithms

Estuardo Alpirez Bock[1]([✉]), Lukasz Chmielewski[2,3], and Konstantina Miteloudi[3]

[1] Aalto University, Espoo, Finland
estuardo.alpirezbock@aalto.fi
[2] Masaryk University, Brno, Czechia
chmiel@fi.muni.cz
[3] Radboud University, Nijmegen, The Netherlands
konstantina.miteloudi@ru.nl

Abstract. The Montgomery Ladder is widely used for implementing the scalar multiplication in elliptic curve cryptographic designs. This algorithm is efficient and provides a natural robustness against (simple) side-channel attacks. Previous works however showed that implementations of the Montgomery Ladder using Lopez-Dahab projective coordinates easily leak the value of the most significant bits of the secret scalar, which led to a full key recovery in an attack known as *LadderLeak* [3]. In light of such leakage, we analyse further popular methods for implementing the Montgomery Ladder. We first consider open source *software* implementations of the X25519 protocol which implement the Montgomery Ladder based on the ladderstep algorithm from Düll et al. [15]. We confirm via power measurements that these implementations also easily leak the most significant scalar bits, even when implementing Z-coordinate randomisations. We thus propose simple modifications of the algorithm and its handling of the most significant bits and show the effectiveness of our modifications via experimental results. Particularly, our re-designs of the algorithm do not incurring significant efficiency penalties. As a second case study, we consider open source *hardware* implementations of the Montgomery Ladder based on the complete addition formulas for prime order elliptic curves, where we observe the exact same leakage. As we explain, the most significant bits in implementations of the complete addition formulas can be protected in an analogous way as we do for Curve25519 in our first case study.

Keywords: ECC · Montgomery Ladder · Curve25519 · Complete addition formulas · Side-channel analysis

1 Introduction

Elliptic curve and isogeny based cryptographic implementations commonly make use of the Montgomery Ladder for performing the scalar point multiplication

E. Alpirez Bock—Work partially done while at Radboud University.
L. Chmielewski—This work was partially supported by the Technology Innovation Institute (https://www.tii.ae/) and by Ai-SecTools (VJ02010010) project.

L. Batina et al. (Eds.): SPACE 2022, LNCS 13783, pp. 118–137, 2022.
https://doi.org/10.1007/978-3-031-22829-2_7

[13,21]. The preference for the Montgomery Ladder comes from its efficiency and also from its natural robustness against simple side channel attacks, such as timing, simple power analysis (SPA), and simple electromagnetic analysis. Its robustness comes from the fact that for each loop iteration, we always perform a point addition followed by a point doubling, independent of the bit value we are processing for the scalar (see Algorithm 1). Nevertheless, previous works have shown that implementations of the Montgomery Ladder based on Lopez-Dahab projective coordinates [22] easily leak at least one bit of the scalar via simple side channel observations [3,9]. Lopez-Dahab projective coordinates represent the points on the curve only by means of their x-coordinate in the form $x = \frac{X}{Z}$ and allow for fast computation of the Montgomery Ladder since no divisions need to be performed during the main loop. The leakage in the implementations is caused by the initialisation phase of the algorithm, where the projective representation of the input point is defined as $x = \frac{x}{1}$ and thus one set of input variables of the algorithm is initialised as $X_1 = x$ and $Z_1 = 1$. The other input variables are initialised with the values $X_2 = x^4 + b$ and $Z_2 = x^2$. As we then enter the main loop of the algorithm, we perform some multiplications with $Z_1 = 1$ as operand. However the number of such multiplications varies depending on the value of the key bit we are processing: if the first loop iteration is performed for a key bit with value 1, we perform only one multiplication with $Z_1 = 1$ as operand. On the other hand if the first loop iteration is performed for a key bit with value 0, then we perform three multiplications with $Z_1 = 1$ as operand. Multiplications with operands with value 1 usually consume a notably smaller amount of power than multiplications between two larger values.[1] Thus, if we observe the region of a power trace corresponding to the first loop iteration of the Montgomery Ladder using Lopez-Dahab projective coordinates, we can easily tell the value of the key bit being processed. This value corresponds to the second most significant bit of the key, assuming that the most significant bit is always 1.

Although we are only talking about one bit, the LadderLeak attack [3] took advantage of this leakage to fully break the ECDSA protocol implemented in recent OpenSSL versions. They showed how this small leakage can be exploited together with advanced approaches for solving the *hidden number problem* [11], leading thus to a complete recovery of the secret scalar. In an earlier work, the authors of [9] also identified the same leakage on a hardware implementa-

---

Algorithm 1. Montgomery Ladder

Inputs: $k = (k_{n-1}, ..., k_0)$,
$G = (G_x, G_y, G_z)$
Output: $R_0 \leftarrow k \cdot G$
  $R_0 \leftarrow \mathcal{O}, \quad R_1 \leftarrow G$
  for i **from** $n-1$ **downto** 0 **do**
    if $k_i = 1$ **then**
      $R_0 \leftarrow R_0 + R_1, \quad R_1 \leftarrow 2R_1$
    else
      $R_1 \leftarrow R_0 + R_1, \quad R_0 \leftarrow 2R_0$
    end if
  end for

---

[1] In this paper we will use the term *balanced value* to refer to large values or bitstrings containing similar amounts of 0s and 1s. While we expect operations on such values to consume a notably larger amount of power than operations on small values like zero or one, this may not always be clearly visible due, e.g. to software optimisations.

tion of the Montgomery Ladder. They showed the leakage via simulated power traces and proposed a simple countermeasure: a re-design of the initialisation phase of the algorithm as well as a special treatment of the first loop iteration. The idea is that no registers are initialised with a value equal 1 and when the loop is entered for the first time; we do not need to perform multiplications with operands equal to 1 since the results of such operations are already known. The authors showed that implementing the Montgomery Ladder in this alternative way barely implies any additional costs in terms of execution time, area and power consumption.

In this paper we consider further case studies of the Montgomery Ladder when implemented with other projective coordinates or other point addition and doubling algorithms. We consider both, software and hardware ECC implementations over prime fields and explore whether the aforementioned leakage is present. We confirm its presence, even when Z-coordinate randomisation is employed, and propose corresponding countermeasures to mitigate the easy extraction of the most significant scalar bit(s). Our work is motivated by the results of the LadderLeak attack, which showed how such leakage could be exploited, but also by the fact that previous works showed that mitigating such leakage could be done in a simple and efficient way. Below we elaborate on the implementations we study and modify in this paper.

1.1 Software Implementations of Curve25519

We begin our studies with a software implementation of Curve25519 based on the ladderstep algorithm introduced in [15] (see Algorithm 3 below). This algorithm is a popular choice for implementing the X25519 key-exchange protocol in software [7] (see [25] for alternative implementations of this algorithm and [14] for a tutorial on implementations of Curve25519 on ARM Cortex-M0). Concretely, we consider a recent open source implementation of X25519 from [4][2]. This implementation performs the scalar multiplications via the Montgomery Ladder as described in Algorithm 2 and the ladderstep function is implemented according to Algorithm 3.[3] Note that Algorithm 2 does not assume that the most significant bit of the scalar has a value equal to 1. Instead, the algorithm initialises the registers X_1, Z_1, X_2, Z_2 with values corresponding to the point at infinity and the input point x_P respectively, and then the algorithm executes the ladderstep function for the most significant bit of k, independently of its value. Clearly, if the first loop iteration(s) is (are) executed for scalar bits with value 0, we know that the resulting outputs of the loops are basically equal to their input values, and thus, such loop iterations are not really necessary. However,

---

[2] The source code from [4] is located in the following repository: https://github.com/sca-secure-library-sca25519/sca25519.

[3] Note that in the X25519 protocol, the most significant (254th) bit of the secret scalars is always set to 1; this is done by anding the most significant scalar byte with 0x7F|0x40 in [4]. However, since we consider the ECDSA protocol then the most significant scalar bits can be 0 and we need to consider fully random scalars.

the algorithm is implemented in this way with the scope of protecting the length of the key with respect to timing and side channel attacks. That is, if we only start executing the main loop of the algorithm once we've reached the first key bit with value 1, we would obtain power traces of different sizes, depending on where this first 1 is located. Implementing the Montgomery Ladder according to Algorithm 2 also relaxes the assumption that the most significant bit of the scalar is always 1, and thus we always talk about a key space of size $2^{|k|}$ and not of size $2^{|k|-1}$.

However as we show in this paper, this approach does not really protect the values of the most significant bits (MSBs) of the scalar when considering SPA. Namely, loop iterations for MSBs with value 0 can be easily distinguished from the rest of the loop iterations, and thus it is easy for an adversary to extract all MSBs of the scalar up to (and including) the first 1. This happens because the loop iterations for MSBs with value 0 have a notably different power consumption than the rest, given that many operations performed within those loops use operands with the value 0 or 1. Such operands are only overwritten with larger, balanced values once we finally iterate a loop for a key bit with value 1.

Leakage on DPA-Protected Implementations. We also verify the presence of this leakage on the second implementation from [4] (see their Algorithm 2), which is an SCA-protected implementation of ephemeral X25519 that randomises the projective representation of the input value. However, the leakage is still present since the input coordinates representing the point at infinity are initialised with the values of 0 and 1. We thus show that projective coordinate randomisation does not protect the MSBs of Curve25519 implementations.

Countermeasure. We modify Algorithm 2 to remove the aforementioned leakage in a simple, but effective way (see Algorithm 6). Our approach relies on always executing the ladderstep function using balanced operands as inputs. This way, the corresponding measurements always have similarly looking patterns and it is not easy to determine when the first loop iteration for a key bit with value 1 is executed. Our approach is implemented as follows. We initialise all input variables X_1, Z_1, X_2, Z_2 with randomly chosen, balanced values. Additionally, we use two new variables W_1 and W_2 initialised with values needed for the first ladderstep execution for a scalar bit with value 1. These values are the result of additions and subtractions with operands with value 1, and we pre-calculate them to avoid performing such operations during ladderstep. Now, if the most significant scalar bit is 0, we execute the normal ladderstep from Algorithm 3, but with balanced input variables. Note also that the outputs of these loops are irrelevant for the actual calculation of kP. We repeat this process for all key bits until we reach the first scalar bit with value 1. For this scalar bit, we execute a special version of ladderstep (see Algorithm 7), where we use the pre-calculated W_1 and W_2. After this loop iteration, we finally have all variables X_1, Z_1, X_2, Z_2 overwritten with correct, balanced values. Thus from this point on, we can simply continue with the regular execution of the Montgomery Ladder using the standard ladderstep from Algorithm 3. We avoid potential operation leakage by ensuring that the special and regular ladderstep both consist of the same operation sequence, and by using only constant-time operations.

For implementing the countermeasure described above, we consider two alternative software techniques and compare the costs of each. First we make use of arithmetic constant-time "conditional swap" operations (referred to as cswap operations in this paper) for alternating between the two versions of the ladderstep function as described above. The cswap(X, Y, c) routine simply swaps the first two inputs if and only if $c = 1$. This is achieved without traditional conditional statements in the following way. First $c \in \{0, 1\}$ is converted to the form $c' = -c$ (now $c' = 0$ if $c = 0$ and $c' = 0xFF...$, otherwise). Then, the conditional swap on the first argument (and similarly on the second one) is performed arithmetically: $X\ \hat{}= c'\ \&\ (X\hat{}Y)$. Thus, the value of X remains the same for $c' = 0$ and is overwritten with Y, otherwise.

The resulting re-design using cswap, while secure, incurs a notable performance penalty due to the extra arithmetic operations. However, our second re-design alternative is based on secret-memory access and incurs a much smaller performance penalty. Here, instead of doing a swap depending on c, we put X and Y into an array and we access them through memory access depending on the value of c. Note that in our implementation, c depends directly on the secret scalar, hence the name *secret-memory* access. We note that the security of our second re-design may be dependent on the architecture used for running the code. Namely if memory access is not always constant-time (as is the case for architectures equipped with memory caching, for example), some small key dependencies may be visible on power consumption traces.

We would like to underline that the above countermeasures aim to efficiently protect against SPA, but not against more sophisticated single-trace attacks, like [26], for which extra costly countermeasures are required.

1.2   Hardware Implementations of the Complete Addition Formulas

Our second case study is performed analogously to our first one, but we consider *hardware* implementations based on the complete addition formulas from Renes, Costello and Batina [28]. These formulas gained popularity since they allow addition of any two points on Weierstrass curves and avoid thus exceptions during the computations. Moreover, these formulas can be used for implementing both the point addition and point doubling operations within the main loop of the Montgomery Ladder. We consider an open-source implementation presented in [27] which is based on Algorithm 7 in [28]. This implementation does not assume that the MSB of the scalar is equal to 1 and for each loop iteration, it executes Algorithm 7 of [28] twice: once for a point addition and once for a point doubling. As for our first case study on Curve25519, we show via power consumption measurements that the MSBs of the scalar can be (very) easily extracted from this hardware implementation. We believe that a countermeasure in the same style as for Curve25519 can be proposed and we leave that for future work.

Algorithm 2. Montgomery Ladder for x-coordinate-based scalar multiplication on $E \; : \; y^2 = x^3 + 486662x^2 + x$ [4]

Inputs: $k \in \{0, ..., 2^{255} - 1\}, x_P$

   $X_1 \leftarrow 1; \quad Z_1 \leftarrow 0; \quad X_2 \leftarrow x_P; \quad Z_2 \leftarrow 1; \quad p \leftarrow 0$
   for $i \leftarrow 254$ **downto** 0 **do**
      $c \leftarrow k[i] \oplus p; \quad p \leftarrow k[i]$ ▷ $k[i]$ denotes bit i of k
      $(X_1, Z_1, X_2, Z_2) \leftarrow \mathsf{cswap}(X_1, Z_1, X_2, Z_2, c)$
      $(X_1, Z_1, X_2, Z_2) \leftarrow \mathsf{ladderstep}(x_p, X_1, Z_1, X_2, Z_2)$
   end for
   return (X_1, Z_1)

Exploiting the Leakage. The leakage discussed int this paper may be particularly useful for preparing template [5,23] and single-trace horizontal attacks [17,20], since it easily reveals the length of loop executions. It also may reveal time interval cycles when specific operations such as multiplications take place, which is useful information for performing fault injection [10]. On implementations of the complete addition formulas, the leakage might let an adversary distinguish a point addition from a doubling (see Sect. 5). Finally, this leakage can be used for *zero value attacks* [1,16], which require the knowledge of some initial scalar bits.

2 Background and Experimental Setup

In [24] Montgomery introduced efficient x-coordinate-only formulas for computing addition and doubling operations between points in elliptic curves. These formulas would later be simply referred to as the *Montgomery Ladder*, described in Algorithm 2. The ladderstep process corresponds to a point addition and a point doubling operation. There exist different formulas for implementing the ladderstep process using projective coordinates (e.g. [15,22,28]), and the choice of the formulae is usually determined by the type of implementation we are considering (software vs hardware, type of curve used, etc.). In [15] the authors proposed Algorithm 3 for efficient software implementations of Curve25519. Implementations based on this algorithm only need to make use of two extra variables (T_1 and T_2) for the ladderstep processes. Additionally, each ladderstep process consists of only 6 multiplications and 4 squarings, plus a few addition and subtraction operations. This method of implementing the ladderstep has also been embraced on a recent work [4], where the authors implement the X25519 key exchange protocol in combination of a large amount of side-channel countermeasures.

Curve25519. The X25519 key-exchange protocol is based on Curve25519 defined over $\mathbb{F}_{2^{255}-19}$ as: $E : y^2 = x^3 + 486662x^2 + x$. The protocol uses 255 bit long public and secret keys, where the secret key is a randomly generated scalar k and the public key corresponds to a little-endian encoding of the x-coordinate

Algorithm 3. Single Montgomery ladder step on Curve25519 from [15]

Inputs: x_P, X_1, Z_1, X_2, Z_2

1: $T_1 \leftarrow X_2 + Z_2$	8: $X_1 \leftarrow X_1 \cdot X_1$	15: $Z_2 \leftarrow Z_2 \cdot Z_2$
2: $X_2 \leftarrow X_2 - Z_2$	9: $T_2 \leftarrow Z_2 - X_1$	16: $Z_2 \leftarrow Z_2 \cdot x_P$
3: $Z_2 \leftarrow X_1 + Z_1$	10: $Z_1 \leftarrow T_2 \cdot a24$	17: $X_2 \leftarrow T_1 + X_2$
4: $X_1 \leftarrow X_1 - Z_1$	11: $Z_1 \leftarrow Z_1 + X_1$	18: $X_2 \leftarrow X_2 \cdot X_2$
5: $T_1 \leftarrow T_1 \cdot X_1$	12: $Z_1 \leftarrow T_2 \cdot Z_1$	
6: $X_2 \leftarrow X_2 \cdot Z_2$	13: $X_1 \leftarrow Z_2 \cdot X_1$	**return** (X_1, Z_1, X_2, Z_2)
7: $Z_2 \leftarrow Z_2 \cdot Z_2$	14: $Z_2 \leftarrow T_1 - X_2$	

of a point P on the curve. In the protocol, the shared secret corresponds to the resulting point on the curve from the scalar multiplication of kP. For calculating kP, we use the Montgomery Ladder algorithm. Note that in X25519, the most significant scalar bit is always set to 1, and if the scalar needs to be a multiple of word length (that is 256 bits for many architectures) then it is extended with zeroes. However, note that Curve25519 is also used in EdDSA protocols, which are ECC-based signature schemes [8].[4] Here, the scalar is the resulting hash of the message to be signed together with an auxiliary parameter b. Thus in this case, the resulting scalar does not have a fixed value for its most significant bits.

Complete Addition Formulas. Renes et al. [28] introduced the *complete addition formulas for prime order elliptic curves*, which are optimisations on formulas presented earlier by Bosma and Lenstra in [12]. These formulas are said to be *complete* on prime order Weirstrass curves of the form $y^2 = x^3 + ax + b$ since they can compute the sum of any two points on these curves. Moreover, these addition formulas can be used for implementing both, the point addition and point doubling operations within an implementation of the Montgomery Ladder. It is believed that using the same addition formula for implementing both operations may provide additional robustness in light of SCA attacks, since it becomes more difficult to distinguish a point addition from a point doubling operation, and behavioural effects of branching can be easily mitigated.

These formulas also use projective representation of the input points, in the form $P = (X, Y, Z)$. Thus, we additionally use the y-coordinate of the input points for these formulas. The authors present one general addition formula and further optimisations for special families of curves, in cases where the constant a has the values -3 or 0. In this paper, we will focus on an open source implementation of Algorithm 7 of [28]. This flavour of the formula is applicable for short Weierstrass curves which set the constant $a = 0$. As the authors explain, such a curve has appeared in Certicom's SEC-2 standard [29] which specifies the curve secp256k1, used in the Bitcoin protocol.

---

[4] We refer to EdDSA with the parameters of Curve25519 as Ed25519 [7].

2.1 Experimental Setup and Side-Channel Evaluation

We perform our experiments and verifications with respect to three open source implementations. The first two correspond to implementations from [4], which are designs of X25519 using Montgomery Ladder for performing scalar multiplications. For simplicity and for obtaining a general result, we first focus on the plain and unprotected design from the repository, which is an implementation of the Montgomery Ladder according to Algorithm 2, and implements the ladderstep according to Algorithm 3. We will then show that the second design from the repository, which implements some SCA countermeasures, also leaks the most significant bits of the scalar. We run these designs on a Cortex-M4 on an STM32F407IGT6 board clocked at 168 MHz. For side-channel evaluation of the designs, we measure current using the Riscure Current Probe [30] and we collect the traces using the PicoScope 3406D oscilloscope with the sampling frequency of 10^9 samples per second. Finally for side-channel analysis we use the Inspector software by Riscure [31]. Subsequently, we re-design Algorithms 2 and 3 and propose countermeasures. We test our new designs by performing experiments on the same experimental setup as described above.

We conduct our second case study on the hardware accelerator implementing the Montgomery Ladder using the complete addition formulas [27]. We run the design on an FPGA SAKURA-G board [19] and measure its power consumption via a Teledyne Lecroy Waverunner 8404M oscilloscope with the sampling of frequency 10^8 samples per second.

3 Leakage on Curve25519

In this section we analyse the Montgomery Ladder implemented according to Algorithms 2 and 3 and explain how the most significant scalar bits can be extracted via SPA. We confirm our intuitions via experimental results by measuring the power consumption of the algorithm when running on a microcontroller.

3.1 Initial Loop Iterations

We now focus on Algorithm 2, whereby the ladderstep process is defined in Algorithm 3. As we see, the input variables are initialised as $X_1 \leftarrow 1$, $Z_1 \leftarrow 0$, $X_2 \leftarrow x_P$, and $Z_2 \leftarrow 1$. If the most significant scalar bit equals 0 then all variables will hold these values when we enter the ladderstep process. Otherwise, the cswap operation will be executed and the variables will have the values $X_1 = x_P, Z_1 = 1, X_2 = 1, Z_2 = 0$. We first focus on the former case. In the following, we refer to $k[0]$ as the most significant bit of the scalar. Observe that in Algorithm 4 (and in all algorithms in this paper) "=" denotes only the equality relation and "←" is used for assignment.

Case $k[0] = 0$. Algorithm 4 shows the explicit operand values that will be used during the first execution of ladderstep if the most significant bit of the scalar

Algorithm 4. Ladder step when entered just after the initialisation for $k[0] = 0$

Inputs: $x_P, X_1 = 1, Z_1 = 0, X_2 = x_P, Z_2 = 1$

1: $T_1 \leftarrow x_P + 1$
2: $X_2 \leftarrow x_P - 1$
3: $Z_2 \leftarrow 1 + 0$
4: $X_1 \leftarrow 1 - 0$
5: $T_1 \leftarrow T_1 \cdot 1$
6: $X_2 \leftarrow X_2 \cdot 1$
7: $Z_2 \leftarrow 1 \cdot 1$
8: $X_1 \leftarrow 1 \cdot 1$
9: $T_2 \leftarrow 1 - 1 = 0$
10: $Z_1 \leftarrow 0 \cdot a24$

11: $Z_1 \leftarrow 0 + 1$
12: $Z_1 \leftarrow 0 \cdot 1$
13: $X_1 \leftarrow 1 \cdot 1$
14: $Z_2 \leftarrow (x_P + 1) - (x_P - 1) = 2$
15: $Z_2 \leftarrow 2 \cdot 2 = 4$
16: $Z_2 \leftarrow 4 \cdot x_P$
17: $X_2 \leftarrow (x_P + 1) + (x_P - 1) = 2x_P$
18: $X_2 \leftarrow 2x_P \cdot 2x_P = 4x_P^2$
    return $(X_1 = 1, Z_1 = 0)$;
    $(X_2 = 4x_P^2, Z_2 = 4x_P)$

has a value of 0. We highlight in gray all operations that will be performed with a variable with value 1 or 0 as operand, or operations where the variables are not overwritten with any new values. Particularly interesting are the multiplications performed in steps 5 through 8 and in step 13, which are all multiplications with at least one operand with value 1. In steps 10 and 12, we perform multiplications with operands with value 0. We can expect to see very small power consumption peaks in the power trace regions corresponding to the execution of these steps.

Note that by the end of the process, i.e. by the end of this first loop iteration, the variables X_1 and Z_1 preserve their values of 1 and 0 respectively. Moreover, for X_2 and Z_2, note that $\frac{X_2}{Z_2} = \frac{4x^2}{4x} = \frac{x}{1}$, i.e. these projective coordinates preserve their original value as well. Thus, the input values for the next loop iteration (for the second bit of the scalar) are equivalent to the input values for the first iteration. If the second loop iteration is executed again for a key bit with value 0, i.e. if $k[1] = 0$, we have basically the same situation as the one described in Algorithm 4. Namely, although variable Z_2 enters the loop with a value different from 1, Z_2 is quickly overwritten in step 3 with a value equal to 1. This holds for all following loop iterations until we finally process a key bit with value 1.

Case $k[0] = 1$. We now analyse the first ladderstep execution for a key bit with value equal to 1. Recall that when executing the ladderstep for a key bit with value 1, we first swap the content of the variables via the cswap operation. Thus the variables enter the loop with values $X_1 = x_P, Z_1 = 1, X_2 = 1, Z_2 = 0$. Recall that the values of X_2 and Z_2 may vary from x_P and 1 respectively if the ladderstep function was previously executed for a key bit with value 0. However, the variables will retain the relation $\frac{X_1}{Z_1} = \frac{x}{1}$. For simplicity, we assume here that $Z_1 = 1$. Algorithm 5 shows the explicit operand values that will be used during this loop execution. In this algorithm, the variables w_i denote some operand value larger than 1 (usually, some balanced operand value). As we can see, only steps 5 and 6 consist of multiplications with operands with value 1.

We can expect higher power consumption peaks on the power trace region corresponding to this execution of the ladderstep, in comparison to the regions corresponding to the $k[0] = 0$ case. Moreover, note that by the end of the loop,

---

Algorithm 5. Ladder step executed for the first scalar bit equal to 1 $(k[i] = 1)$

Inputs: $x_P, X_1 = x_P, Z_1 = 1, X_2 = 1, Z_2 = 0$

1: $T_1 \leftarrow 1 + 0$
2: $X_2 \leftarrow 1 - 0$
3: $Z_2 \leftarrow x_P + 1$
4: $X_1 \leftarrow x_P - 1$
5: $T_1 \leftarrow 1 \cdot (x_P + 1)$
6: $X_2 \leftarrow 1 \cdot (x_P - 1)$
7: $Z_2 \leftarrow (x_P + 1) \cdot (x_P + 1) = (x_P + 1)^2$
8: $X_1 \leftarrow (x_P - 1) \cdot (x_P - 1) = (x_P - 1)^2$
9: $T_2 \leftarrow (x_P + 1)^2 - (x_P - 1)^2 = w_1$
10: $Z_1 \leftarrow w_1 \cdot a24 = w_2$
11: $Z_1 \leftarrow w_2 + (x_P - 1)^2 = w_3$

12: $Z_1 \leftarrow w_1 \cdot w_3 = w_4$
13: $X_1 \leftarrow (x_P + 1)^2 \cdot (x_P - 1)^2$
14: $Z_2 \leftarrow (x_P - 1) - (x_P + 1) = w_5$
15: $Z_2 \leftarrow w_5 \cdot w_5 = w_6$
16: $Z_2 \leftarrow w_6 \cdot x_P$
17: $X_2 \leftarrow (x_P - 1) + (x_P + 1) = w_7$
18: $X_2 \leftarrow w_7 \cdot w_7 = w_8$
return
$(X_1 = (x_P + 1)^2 \cdot (x_P - 1)^2, Z_1 = w_4);$
$(X_2 = w_8, Z_2 = w_6 x_P)$

---

all variables have been overwritten with some more balanced values. Thus in all following executions of ladderstep, we can expect to see high power consumption peaks. Next, we verify our assumptions via power consumption measurements.

3.2 Experimental Verification

We run the implementation of the Montgomery Ladder with selected scalar values, and record its power consumption as described in Sect. 2.1. We consider cases where the most significant bit(s) of the scalar are 0s and cases where the most significant bit of the scalar is 1. More concretely, we consider two keys with the following values for their first bits: $k_1[0..7] = $ 0x04 $ = $ 00000100 and $k_2[0..7] = $ 0x7F $ = $ 01111111.[5] When comparing the power traces generated for each key, we expect notably different power consumption profiles for the regions corresponding to the processing of the first 5 bits of the scalars. After that, we expect to see very similar power consumption profiles.

Figure 1 shows two power traces overlapped. The blue coloured trace corresponds to the execution of the algorithm on k_1 and a fixed input point P.[6] The yellow coloured trace corresponds to the execution with k_2 and the same input P. We mark in the red box the regions corresponding to the most significant bits of the scalars. As we can observe, these regions differ notably from each other and they do not align. The remaining regions of the power traces align very well with each other, since they correspond to executions of the ladderstep where we always use operands with balanced values. We repeated the experiment in a similar setting but with random input points and the result was very similar.

In Fig. 2 we include power traces measured on the second implementation from [4], which is also an implementation of Algorithm 2, but additionally protected with projective Z-coordinate randomisation. We can observe a very

---

[5] Note that 256th bit of the scalar is always set to 0 since $p = 2^{255} - 19$.

[6] $P_x = $ 0x67C5590EF5591AEEE312308D155579DC042E497FEC764BB3CAF3DE88597B8C24.

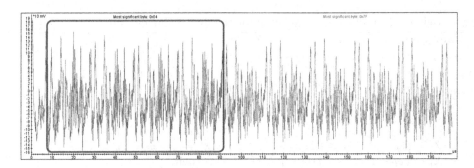

Fig. 1. Comparison of power profiles with scalars starting with 0x04 and 0x7F.

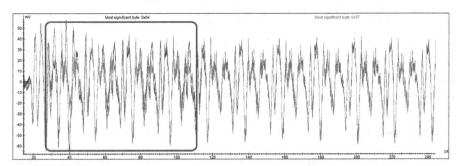

Fig. 2. Comparison of power profiles with scalars starting with 0x04 and 0x7F when the Z-coordinate is randomized.

similar leakage as in Fig. 1.[7] As explained in the introduction, the projective randomisation is applied only to the variables corresponding to the input point P, but not to the variables corresponding to the point at infinity and thus, many operations with operands equal to 1 or 0 are performed during the initial loops.

4   Protecting the Most Significant Bits in Curve25519

We now present our proposed modification of the Montgomery Ladder, which protects the most significant bits of the scalar.[8] As mentioned before, our idea consists on always using balanced operands during all executions of the ladder-step process. For this, we initialise the input variables with dummy, balanced values and use these values for all executions of the main loop until we reach the first 1 of the scalar. For the loop iteration corresponding to the first 1 of the

---

[7] We acknowledge that the traces in Fig. 2 look different than the ones collected from the first implementation. This is caused not only by differences in implementations, but also due to the fact that these new traces were collected later on with a new physical setup (although probes and oscilloscopes were equivalent models).

[8] We will provide a link to the code repository in the final version of the paper.

Algorithm 6. Modified x-coordinate-based Montgomery Ladder

Inputs: $k \in \{0, ..., 2^{255} - 1\}, x_P$

$\quad X_1 \leftarrow\!\!\$\ \mathbb{F}_p; \quad Z_1 \leftarrow\!\!\$\ \mathbb{F}_p; \quad X_2 \leftarrow\!\!\$\ \mathbb{F}_p; \quad Z_2 \leftarrow\!\!\$\ \mathbb{F}_p;$

$\quad W_1 \leftarrow x_P + 1; \quad W_2 \leftarrow x_P - 1; \quad p, s \leftarrow 0;$

$\quad$**for** $i \leftarrow 254$ **downto** 0 **do**

$\quad\quad t \leftarrow (k[i] \vee s) \oplus s \qquad\qquad\qquad\qquad \triangleright\ k[i]$ denotes bit i of k

$\quad\quad c \leftarrow k[i] \oplus p; \quad p \leftarrow k[i]$

$\quad\quad (X_1, Z_1, X_2, Z_2) \leftarrow \mathsf{cswap}(X_1, Z_1, X_2, Z_2, c)$

$\quad\quad (X_1, Z_1, X_2, Z_2) \leftarrow \mathsf{ladderstep}(x_p, X_1, Z_1, X_2, Z_2, W_1, W_2, t)$

$\quad\quad s \leftarrow s \vee t$

$\quad$**end for**

$\quad$**return** (X_1, Z_1)

---

scalar, we execute a special version of the ladderstep, where we finally use the operand values necessary for a correct calculation of kP.

Algorithm 6 describes our proposed modification of the Montgomery Ladder. All input variables $X_1, Z_1, X_2,$ and Z_2 are initialised with randomly chosen balanced values. These are 32-byte values which represent elements of $\mathbb{F}_p$. Note that these values can either be chosen at random for each execution, they can be derived from the input point P or they can also just be hardcoded in the implementation. Additionally, we also use two new variables W_1 and W_2 that we initialise as follows: $W_1 \leftarrow x_P + 1, W_2 \leftarrow x_p - 1$. Both W_1 and W_2 contain values needed when we execute ladderstep for the first 1 in the scalar. Note that in Algorithm 5 these two values ($x_P + 1$ and $x_P - 1$) are obtained from an addition and subtraction with value 1, performed in steps 3 and 4. These are the first operations in the loop which actually depend on the input point value x_P. Moreover, these two values are used as operands in steps 7, 8, 14 and 17 in Algorithm 5.

We now describe the operation flow of Algorithm 6 when processing the scalar bits. If the most significant bit is 0 then we execute the normal ladderstep as described in Algorithm 3. Note that in this case, the inputs to the ladderstep process will be (dummy) balanced variables, set in the second line of the algorithm. We repeat this process until we reach the first scalar bit with the value 1. When we reach the first 1 of the scalar, we execute a special variation of the ladderstep function (Algorithm 7), where we make use of the pre-calculated values W_1 and W_2. After this iteration, we have all variables X_1, Z_1, X_2, Z_2 overwritten with correct values and we simply continue the regular execution of the Montgomery Ladder using the standard ladderstep function (Algorithm 3).

4.1 Implementing Our Proposed Modification

For implementing Algorithm 6, we need to take special care of the two following aspects. First, we need to determine *when* we encounter the first non-zero scalar bit so we can execute the modified ladderstep (for $t = 1$). Second, the modified ladderstep loop should be executed only once. Naturally, all operations

Algorithm 7. Single Montgomery ladder step for the case $t = 1$

Inputs: $x_P, X_1, Z_1, X_2, Z_2, W_1, W_2$

1: $T_1 \leftarrow X_2 + Z_2$	8: $X_1 \leftarrow W_2 \cdot W_2$	15: $Z_2 \leftarrow Z_2 \cdot Z_2$
2: $X_2 \leftarrow X_2 - Z_2$	9: $T_2 \leftarrow Z_2 - X_1$	16: $Z_2 \leftarrow Z_2 \cdot x_P$
3: $Z_2 \leftarrow X_1 + Z_1$	10: $Z_1 \leftarrow T_2 \cdot a24$	17: $X_2 \leftarrow W_2 + W_1$
4: $X_1 \leftarrow X_1 - Z_1$	11: $Z_1 \leftarrow Z_1 + X_1$	18: $X_2 \leftarrow X_2 \cdot X_2$
5: $T_1 \leftarrow T_1 \cdot X_1$	12: $Z_1 \leftarrow T_2 \cdot Z_1$	
6: $X_2 \leftarrow X_2 \cdot Z_2$	13: $X_1 \leftarrow Z_2 \cdot X_1$	**return** (X_1, Z_1, X_2, Z_2)
7: $Z_2 \leftarrow W_1 \cdot W_1$	14: $Z_2 \leftarrow W_2 - W_1$	

need to be implemented in constant-time, else we might observe small scalar-dependent operation leakages in the power traces. In the following we explain how we identify the first non-zero bit of the scalar and how we ensure that the modified ladderstep algorithm (Algorithm 7) is executed only once and is hard to distinguish from a regular ladderstep.

Note that the variable s is initialised to 0. Then, if $k[0] = 0$ (at the beginning of the scalar multiplication), variable t is set to 0. This follows for all subsequent scalar bits that equal to 0 because at the end of the loop s retains the value 0 ($s = 0 \vee 0$). When $k[i] = 1$ for the first time, t is set to 1 right at the beginning of the loop. Namely, $s = 0$ and thus we calculate $t \leftarrow (1 \vee 0) \oplus 0$. Now we will execute the special case for ladderstep since $t = 1$. Note that at the end of this loop, right after executing the special ladderstep, s will be set to 1: $s \leftarrow 0 \vee 1$. In all subsequent loops t will be set to 0 regardless the value of $k[i]$ because $(k[i] \vee 1) \oplus 1$ always equals 0. By ensuring that $t = 0$ for all subsequent loop iterations, we ensure that we execute the standard ladderstep process from Algorithm 3.

Note that the original ladder step (for $t = 0$) executes the exact same instructions as the modified one (for $t = 1$). Their only difference is the use of some registers as operands as we explain in the next subsection. Thus, there may *still* be data leakage present in the above operations, but there is no operation leakage. Moreover, as we show later in Sect. 4.3 via side-channel evaluation, the present data leakage is small and not visible by SPA means.

4.2   Implementations of the Ladder Step

Our proposed Montgomery Ladder described in Algorithm 6 needs to switch seamlessly between both Algorithm 3 and Algorithm 7. Note that the algorithms execute the same operations but differ only on how the following steps are implemented: 7, 8, 14, and 17—see Table 1 for details. As we see from the table, we need to seamlessly alternate between parameters Z_2 and W_1 in step 7, X_1 and W_2 in step 8, and T_1, X_2 and W_2, W_1 in steps 14 and 17 respectively.

We now describe how we implement the ladderstep from Algorithm 6 alternating smoothly between both versions of the ladderstep. Essentially, we want to ensure that the same sequence of operations is always performed, regardless of the used ladderstep version in order to stop SPA. To achieve this, we combine Algorithms 3 and 7 into one software implementation since both algorithms use

Table 1. Different Steps between Algorithm 3 and Algorithm 7.

Step	Algorithm 3	Algorithm 7
7	$Z_2 \leftarrow Z_2 \cdot Z_2$	$Z_2 \leftarrow W_1 \cdot W_1$
8	$X_1 \leftarrow X_1 \cdot X_1$	$X_1 \leftarrow W_2 \cdot W_2$
14	$Z_2 \leftarrow T_1 - X_2$	$Z_2 \leftarrow W_2 - W_1$
17	$X_2 \leftarrow T_1 + X_2$	$X_2 \leftarrow W_2 + W_1$

the same sequence of operations and only their operands differ. When the most significant scalar bit is 1, we choose operands as in Algorithm 7. When the bit is 0, we choose operands as in Algorithm 3. We propose two alternatives for implementing this operand switch:

1. a cswap-based implementation and
2. an implementation based on secret-memory accesses.

These methods differ in provided security guarantees and performance impact as we explain bellow.

cswap Based Implementation. Our first design is based on conditional swap (cswap). The cswap(X, Y, c) routine swaps the content of the inputs X and Y if and only if $c = 1$. For the sake of simplicity let us consider 32-bit values. In this case cswap can be implemented as follows:

```
c' = - c; //now c'=0xFFFFFFFF if c=1 and 0 otherwise
TMP = X;
X ^= c' & (X ^ Y);
Y ^= c' & (TMP ^ Y);
```

Since in our implementation the operands are 255-bit values, the last 3 lines need to be repeated multiple times to swap all words of the operands.

While this implementation is not very fast, it has the following advantage: the sequence of addresses accessed by the algorithm does not depend on the secret scalar. Therefore, the implementation is constant-time even on a target equipped with data caching and we obtain a design which is constantly robust against SPA, independently of the platform we are running it on. For implementing, we use the same extra memory as for our secret memory access-based method (described below), but instead of accessing the memory directly we perform cswaps (depending on the t value from Algorithm 6) twice: just before and just after the operations from Table 1.

Secret-Memory Accesses. Our second proposed re-design uses secret scalar-dependent access to memory locations. The memory locations correspond to the operands we are using within the loop. The bit t from Algorithm 6 indicates which operands we use. We access the memory corresponding to the operands from Algorithm 7 if $t = 1$, and according to Algorithm 3 otherwise.

Table 2. Performance Evaluation.

Implementation	Time (milliseconds):	Extra Memory (bytes):
Unprotected Imp.:	5.62	-
Cswap-based Imp.:	7.6 (+35.2%)	$8 * 32 = 256$
Secret-Memory Access Imp.:	5.81 (+3.4%)	$8 * 32 = 256$

This implementation is fast but it is constant-time only if the access to the memory by the microcontroller is constant-time. Thus, the robustness of this countermeasure depends on the used platform. Since, our target, a Cortex-M4 on an STM32F407IGT6 board, does not have data caches, the memory access is expected to be constant-time as long as the same SRAM region is accessed;[9] as shown in [2] this target has 2 different regions with different characteristics. To increase the probability that the memory accesses are to the same region, we declare the alternating operands as global variables next to each other. In particular, we keep pairs of the values in an array with two elements and access either the original value for $t = 0$ or W_1 and W_2 for $t = 1$. There are 4 values in total for which we need to keep the corresponding pre-computed values. Additionally, there are 4 balanced values that we pre-calculate and which are hard-coded in our implementation. Thus, we increase the memory usage by 8 coordinates of 32-bytes each.

4.3 Evaluation of Our Countermeasures

We now present our benchmark results comparing our two proposed re-designs with the original one from [4]. We later perform a side-channel evaluation and confirm the effectiveness of our proposed countermeasures. All experiments presented in this section are performed as described in Sect. 2.1.

Performance Evaluation. The performance evaluation results are presented in Table 2. We have checked that all implementations are constant-time. Sometimes, minimal jitter takes place due to instruction caching.[10] As expected, the SCA countermeasure against SPA comes at a cost in our re-designs since we are performing additional arithmetic operations on each loop execution when setting the values of the variables s and t. For our implementation using cswap operations, the overhead is of 35.2%. However for our re-design using secret memory access, the overhead is only of about 3.4%. The memory overheard is small: for both implementations it consists of 256 extra bytes, which come from 8 extra global variables in the finite field $\mathbb{F}_p$, where $p = 2^{255} - 19$.

---

[9] The target has however an instruction cache. This caching mechanism is randomized, but since the sequence of instructions is always the same in our algorithms, this potential timing difference is independent from the scalar.

[10] The sequence of instructions performed by our algorithms is always the same but the instruction caching of our target seems to be random.

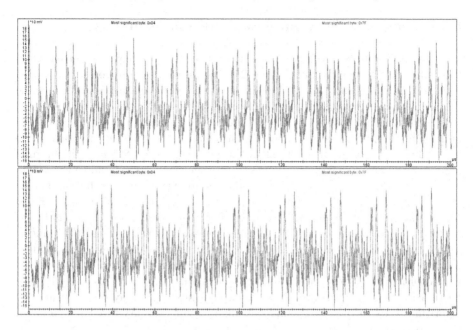

Fig. 3. Comparison of power profiles scalars starting with 0x04 and 0x7F for the cswap-based implementation (top) and the secret-memory access implementation (bottom).

Side-Channel Evaluation. We run both of our modified implementations using the same inputs as in Sect. 3.2. Namely, we consider scalars k_1 and k_2 starting with 0x04 and 0x7F, and the same fixed point for each case. Figure 3 shows the resulting power traces for both implementations. We conduct the experiment a total of 20 times for verification, obtaining always the same result for both cases. The top plot in Fig. 3 shows that indeed the cswap-based implementation is protected against SPA. The bottom plot confirms that different memory-access does not generate an SPA-detectable leakage on our evaluation target. We also repeated the experiment in a similar setting but with random input points and the result was very similar for both implementations. Therefore, we can confirm the effectiveness of our designs.

Note that as expected (given our performance evaluation), the secret-memory access implementation is visibly faster than the cswap-based one. This is visible from the repeating pattern in the traces, which corresponds to a loop iteration in the Montgomery Ladder. This pattern is notably longer in the traces corresponding to the cswap-based implementation.

Evaluation Limitations. Since we only consider SPA, we use visual means to determine the leakage. We are aware that even for our protected implementations, automated leakage detection like TVLA [6,18] would indicate leakage exploitable by more advanced side-channel attacks. This is expected since we do not use randomisations and we do not consider such attacks in this work.

5   Leakage on the Complete Addition Formulas

We now analyse *hardware* implementations of the Montgomery Ladder based on the complete addition formulas from [28]. We provide a more compact analysis as for our previous case study, since the reasons for the leakage and its possible mitigation can be explained and proposed analogous. We will focus on an open source implementation from [27]. This design implements the point addition and doubling operations based on Algorithm 7 in [28] (for space reasons we do not include a description of the algorithm and refer the reader to the original paper). For point addition, the inputs to the algorithm correspond to the points we want to add (i.e. R_0 and R_1). For point doubling we provide the same point twice as input and perform thus $R_0 + R_0$ or $R_1 + R_1$. This implementation also relaxes the assumption that the most significant bit of the secret scalar is 1, and performs a loop iteration for each MSB of the scalar, even if it has the value 0. To this scope, the first register R_0 is initialised with coordinates corresponding to the point at infinity, i.e. $R_0 = (0, 1, 0)$, and the second register R_1 is initialised with coordinates corresponding to the input point P, i.e. $R_1 = (x_P, y_P, 1)$, (see Section IV D in [27]). However as we explain next, this way of executing the algorithm leads to the exact same side-channel vulnerability discussed so far in this paper.

We now describe what happens if the MSB of the scalar has a value of 0, with focus on the point doubling step, since this is the part of the algorithm where the most leakage will be visible. If the MSB of the scalar is equal to 0, we will perform a point doubling with values corresponding to the point at infinity. That is, both inputs to the algorithm will have the values $R_0 = (0, 1, 0)$. Consequently, the first 5 operations of the algorithm are executed as follows: $t_0 \leftarrow 0 \cdot 0; t_1 \leftarrow 1 \cdot 1; t_2 \leftarrow 0 \cdot 0; t_3 \leftarrow 0 + 1; t_4 \leftarrow 0 + 1$. We are thus performing multiplications and additions exclusively with operands equal to 0 and 1 in the beginning of the algorithm. Moreover, the registers t_0 and t_2 are overwritten with 0 and registers t_1, t_3 and t_4 are overwritten with a 1 which leads to a very large amount of leaky additions, subtractions and multiplications throughout the rest of the algorithm execution. Note that equally as for our previous case studies, such a leakage will be visible in the next loop iteration if the next bit of the scalar also has a value of 0, and the leakage will only be gone once we execute a loop iteration for a key bit with a value of 1. Figure 4 shows power traces from this implementation running first on a scalar whose initial bits are 0xFF and then with a scalar whose initial bits are 0x08, both times with the same input point. These power trace measurements confirm the presence of the leakage. We repeated the experiment in a similar setting but with random input points and also with enabled Z-coordinate randomisation. For all cases, the leakage was still very present.

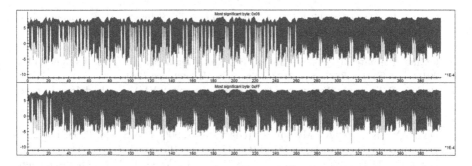

Fig. 4. Power profiles of the hardware implementation using complete addition formulas with scalars starting with `0x08` (above) and `0xFF` (below).

6 Conclusions and Future Work

In this paper we studied and verified an SCA leakage commonly found in ECC implementations. We studied the leakage on implementations of Curve25519 and proposed re-designs of its scalar multiplication algorithm with the goal of removing this leakage. We verified the effectiveness of our re-designs via experimental results in Sect. 4.

It remains to propose a complete re-design for the implementations using the complete addition formulas, which we studied in Sect. 5. To remove the leakage of these implementations, we can outline a similar re-design as the one presented for Curve25519. Namely, we can initialise all input registers with random values, and execute "dummy" loops for all MSBs with value equal 0. Once we reach the first key bit with value 1, we can perform a special variation of the loop iteration, where we plug-in pre-calculated values depending on the input point P. We can alternate between the two possible loop iterations by means of a final state machine, as usually done for VHDL designs. We leave a complete description of a re-design for our second case study (and its evaluation) as future work.

Acknowledgments. The work of Estuardo Alpirez Bock was in part supported by MATINE, Ministry of Defence of Finland.

References

1. Akishita, T., Takagi, T.: Zero-value point attacks on elliptic curve cryptosystem. In: Boyd, C., Mao, W. (eds.) ISC 2003. LNCS, vol. 2851, pp. 218–233. Springer, Heidelberg (2003). https://doi.org/10.1007/10958513_17
2. Andrikos, C., et al.: Location, location, location: revisiting modeling and exploitation for location-based side channel leakages. In: Galbraith, S.D., Moriai, S. (eds.) ASIACRYPT 2019. LNCS, vol. 11923, pp. 285–314. Springer, Cham (2019). https://doi.org/10.1007/978-3-030-34618-8_10
3. Aranha, D.F., Novaes, F.R., Takahashi, A., Tibouchi, M., Yarom, Y.: LadderLeak: breaking ECDSA with Less than One Bit of Nonce Leakage, pp. 225–242. Association for Computing Machinery, New York (2020)

4. Batina, L., Chmielewski, L., Haase, B., Samwel, N., Schwabe, P.: Sca-secure ECC in software - mission impossible? IACR Cryptol. ePrint Arch., p. 1003 (2021)
5. Batina, L., Chmielewski, L., Papachristodoulou, L., Schwabe, P., Tunstall, M.: Online template attacks. In: Meier, W., Mukhopadhyay, D. (eds.) INDOCRYPT 2014. LNCS, vol. 8885, pp. 21–36. Springer, Heidelberg (2014)
6. Becker, G.T., et al.: Test vector leakage assessment (TVLA) methodology in practice. In: International Cryptographic Module Conference (2013)
7. Bernstein, D.J.: Curve25519: new Diffie-Hellman speed records. In: Yung, M., Dodis, Y., Kiayias, A., Malkin, T. (eds.) PKC 2006. LNCS, vol. 3958, pp. 207–228. Springer, Heidelberg (2006). https://doi.org/10.1007/11745853_14
8. Bernstein, D.J., Duif, N., Lange, T., Schwabe, P., Yang, B.-Y.: High-speed high-security signatures. In: Preneel, B., Takagi, T. (eds.) CHES 2011. LNCS, vol. 6917, pp. 124–142. Springer, Heidelberg (2011). https://doi.org/10.1007/978-3-642-23951-9_9
9. Alpirez Bock, E., Dyka, Z., Langendoerfer, P.: Increasing the robustness of the montgomery kP-algorithm against SCA by modifying its initialization. In: Bica, I., Reyhanitabar, R. (eds.) SECITC 2016. LNCS, vol. 10006, pp. 167–178. Springer, Cham (2016). https://doi.org/10.1007/978-3-319-47238-6_12
10. Boneh, D., DeMillo, R.A., Lipton, R.J.: On the importance of checking cryptographic protocols for faults. In: Fumy, W. (ed.) EUROCRYPT 1997. LNCS, vol. 1233, pp. 37–51. Springer, Heidelberg (1997). https://doi.org/10.1007/3-540-69053-0_4
11. Boneh, D., Venkatesan, R.: Hardness of computing the most significant bits of secret keys in Diffie-Hellman and related schemes. In: Koblitz, N. (ed.) CRYPTO'96. LNCS, vol. 1109, pp. 129–142. Springer, Heidelberg (1996)
12. Bosma, W., Lenstra, H.W.: Complete system of two addition laws for elliptic curves. J. Number Theory (1995)
13. Castryck, W., Lange, T., Martindale, C., Panny, L., Renes, J.: CSIDH: an efficient post-quantum commutative group Action. In: Peyrin, T., Galbraith, S. (eds.) ASIACRYPT 2018. LNCS, vol. 11274, pp. 395–427. Springer, Cham (2018). https://doi.org/10.1007/978-3-030-03332-3_15
14. CryptoJedi. Micro salt: μnacl - the networking and cryptography library for microcontrollers. http://munacl.cryptojedi.org/curve25519-cortexm0.shtml
15. Düll, M., et al.: High-speed curve25519 on 8-bit, 16-bit, and 32-bit microcontrollers. Des. Codes Cryptogr. **77**(2–3), 493–514 (2015)
16. De Feo, L., et al.: Sike channels. Cryptology ePrint Archive, Paper 2022/054 (2022). https://eprint.iacr.org/2022/054
17. Genêt, A., Kaluđerović, N.: Single-trace clustering power analysis of the point-swapping procedure in the three point ladder of cortex-M4 SIKE. In: Balasch, J., O'Flynn, C. (eds.) COSADE 2022. LNCS, vol. 13211, pp. 164–192. Springer, Cham (2022). https://doi.org/10.1007/978-3-030-99766-3_8
18. Goodwill, G., Jun, B., Jaffe, J., Rohatgi, P.: A testing methodology for side-channel resistance validation, niat. Workshop record of the NIST Non-Invasive Attack Testing Workshop (2011). csrc.nist.gov/CSRC/media/Events/Non-Invasive-Attack-Testing-Workshop/documents/08Goodwill.pdf
19. Guntur, H., Ishii, J., Satoh, A.: Side-channel attack user reference architecture board sakura-g. In: 2014 IEEE 3rd Global Conference on Consumer Electronics (GCCE), pp. 271–274 (2014)

20. Heyszl, J., Ibing, A., Mangard, S., De Santis, F., Sigl, G.: Clustering algorithms for non-profiled single-execution attacks on exponentiations. In: Francillon, A., Rohatgi, P. (eds.) CARDIS 2013. LNCS, vol. 8419, pp. 79–93. Springer, Cham (2014). https://doi.org/10.1007/978-3-319-08302-5_6
21. Jao, D., De Feo, L.: Towards quantum-resistant cryptosystems from supersingular elliptic curve isogenies. In: Yang, B.-Y. (ed.) PQCrypto 2011. LNCS, vol. 7071, pp. 19–34. Springer, Heidelberg (2011). https://doi.org/10.1007/978-3-642-25405-5_2
22. López, J., Dahab, R.: Fast multiplication on elliptic curves over $GF(2^m)$ without precomputation. In: Koç, Ç.K., Paar, C. (eds.) CHES 1999. LNCS, vol. 1717, pp. 316–327. Springer, Heidelberg (1999). https://doi.org/10.1007/3-540-48059-5_27
23. Medwed, M., Oswald, E.: Template attacks on ECDSA. In: Chung, K.-I., Sohn, K., Yung, M. (eds.) WISA 2008. LNCS, vol. 5379, pp. 14–27. Springer, Heidelberg (2009). https://doi.org/10.1007/978-3-642-00306-6_2
24. Montgomery, P.L.: Speeding the pollard and elliptic curve methods of factorization. Math. Comput. **48**(177), 243–264 (1987)
25. Nascimento, E., Chmielewski, Ł: Applying horizontal clustering side-channel attacks on embedded ECC implementations. In: Eisenbarth, T., Teglia, Y. (eds.) CARDIS 2017. LNCS, vol. 10728, pp. 213–231. Springer, Cham (2018). https://doi.org/10.1007/978-3-319-75208-2_13
26. Nascimento, E., Chmielewski, L., Oswald, D.F., Schwabe, P.: Attacking embedded ECC implementations through cmov side channels. In: Selected Areas in Cryptography - SAC 2016–23rd International Conference, St. John's, NL, Canada, 10–12 August, 2016, Revised Selected Papers, pp. 99–119 (2016)
27. Pirotte, N., Vliegen, J., Batina, L., Mentens, N.: Design of a fully balanced ASIC coprocessor implementing complete addition formulas on weierstrass elliptic curves. In: 2018 21st Euromicro Conference on Digital System Design (DSD), pp. 545–552 (2018)
28. Renes, J., Costello, C., Batina, L.: Complete addition formulas for prime order elliptic curves. In: Fischlin, M., Coron, J.-S. (eds.) EUROCRYPT 2016. LNCS, vol. 9665, pp. 403–428. Springer, Heidelberg (2016). https://doi.org/10.1007/978-3-662-49890-3_16
29. Certicom Research. Sec 2: Recommended elliptic curve domain parameters, version 2.0. www.secg.org/sec2-v2.pdf
30. Riscure. Current probe. security test tool for embedded devices (2018). www.riscure.com/product/current-probe/. Accessed 05 May 2021
31. Riscure. Side channel analysis security tools (2021). www.riscure.com/security-tools/inspector-sca/

Combining Montgomery Multiplication with Tag Tracing for the Pollard Rho Algorithm in Prime Order Fields

Madhurima Mukhopadhyay[1]($\boxtimes$) ⓘ and Palash Sarkar[2] ⓘ

[1] Indian Institute of Technology, Kanpur, India
mukhopadhyaymadhurima@gmail.com
[2] Indian Statistical Institute, Kolkata, India
palash@isical.ac.in

Abstract. In this short paper we show how to apply Montgomery multiplication to the tag tracing variant of the Pollard rho algorithm applied to prime order fields. This combines the advantages of tag tracing with those of Montgomery multiplication. In particular, compared to the previous version of tag tracing, the use of Montgomery multiplication entirely eliminates costly modular reductions and replaces these with much more efficient divisions by a suitable power of two.

Keywords: Cryptography · Discrete logarithm problem · Pollard's Rho · Tag tracing · Montgomery multiplication

1 Introduction

Let G be the finite cyclic group and g be a generator of G. The discrete logarithm problem (DLP) in G is the following. Given a non-zero element h of G, find i such that $g^i = h$. This i is called the discrete logarithm of h to base g which is written as $i = \log_g h$. Over suitably chosen groups, the DLP is considered to be a computationally hard problem and forms the basis for security of various cryptosystems.

The best known generic algorithm for solving the DLP is the Pollard rho algorithm [5]. The resources required by the algorithm are $O(\sqrt{\#G})$ time and $O(1)$ space. For the DLP on finite fields, faster algorithms, namely the function field sieve and the number field sieve, are known. Nevertheless, improving the performance of the Pollard rho algorithm in prime order fields can be relevant for DLP computations in smaller prime fields, even though it does not improve the state of the art of DLP cryptanalysis over finite fields.

Since its introduction, several variants of the Pollard rho algorithm have been proposed. In particular, the tag tracing variant [2] showed the possibility of obtaining practical speed-up of the Pollard rho algorithm for certain groups. Concrete speed-ups were demonstrated for prime order subgroups of multiplicative groups of finite fields. Two kinds of fields were considered in [2], namely,

ⓒ The Author(s), under exclusive license to Springer Nature Switzerland AG 2022
L. Batina et al. (Eds.): SPACE 2022, LNCS 13783, pp. 138–146, 2022.
https://doi.org/10.1007/978-3-031-22829-2_8

prime order fields and small characteristic, large extension degree fields. We focus on the application of tag tracing to prime order fields.

Let p be a prime, $\mathbf{F}_p$ be the finite field of p elements. The group G where DLP is considered is typically a prime order subgroup of $\mathbf{F}_p^*$.

The Pollard rho algorithm performs a pseudo-random walk. For solving DLP in $\mathbf{F}_p$, each step of the walk requires performing a multiplication in $\mathbf{F}_p$. The improvement achieved by the tag tracing method is to ensure that a field multiplication is required after every ℓ steps for a suitable choice of the parameter ℓ. In the intermediate steps between two field multiplication steps, a special computation is performed by the tag tracing method. This computation is significantly faster than a field multiplication. So tag tracing speeds up the Pollard rho algorithm by a factor of about ℓ.

A field multiplication in $\mathbf{F}_p$ consists of two phases. The first phase is an integer multiplication while the second phase is a reduction modulo p operation. For primes p not having a special structure, the reduction operation can require a substantial portion of the overall time for a field multiplication. The technique of Montgomery multiplication [1,3] works with Montgomery representation of elements and replaces a field multiplication by a Montgomery multiplication. The advantage of Montgomery multiplication is that all divisions are by certain powers of two and so can be implemented using right shift operations. The expensive modulo p operation is no longer required.

In this work, we show how the Montgomery multiplication can be combined with the tag tracing method. The goal is to retain the advantages achieved by tag tracing and also simultaneously replace the field multiplications required after every ℓ steps by a Montgomery multiplication. All the time consuming modulo p operations are completely eliminated. Consequently, the Montgomery multiplication version of tag tracing achieves further speed-up compared to the usual tag tracing algorithm. The combination of Montgomery multiplication and tag tracing is achieved without any trade-offs. In particular, the storage space required remains the same in both cases.

2   Background

We provide brief descriptions of the Pollard rho algorithm, tag tracing and Montgomery multiplication.

The Pollard Rho Algorithm: The Pollard rho algorithm [5] is a well known method for solving DLP in prime order fields. Several variants of this algorithm have been studied. We briefly mention the variant introduced in [6].

Let r be a small positive integer. For $i = 1, \ldots, r$, randomly choose integers $\alpha_i, \beta_i \in \{0, \ldots, p-2\}$ such that both α_i and β_i are not zeros. Define $m_i = g^{\alpha_i} h^{\beta_i}$, $i = 0, \ldots, r-1$. A pre-computed table T stores the entries $(i, m_i, (\alpha_i, \beta_i))$ for $i = 0, \ldots, r-1$. Define an indexing function $s : G \to \{0, \ldots, r-1\}$. Using s, a sequence of elements of G is defined as follows. Choose $a_0, b_0 \in \{0, \ldots, \#G - 1\}$ and set $g_0 = g^{a_0} h^{b_0}$. For $j \geq 0$, define $g_{j+1} = g_j m_{s(g_j)}$. The computation of the sequence $g_0, g_1, g_2, \ldots$ is considered to be a pseudo-random walk on G.

Writing $g_j = g^{a_j} h^{b_j}$ for $j \geq 0$, we have $a_{j+1} = a_j + \alpha_{s(g_j)}$ and $b_{j+1} = b_j + \beta_{s(g_j)}$. So it is easy to obtain a_{j+1} and b_{j+1} from a_j and b_j. Since G is finite, there must be some j and k, with $j < k$ such that $g_j = g_k$, i.e., the pseudo-random walk must lead to a collision. Denoting $\log_g h$ by $\eth$, the condition $g_j = g_k$ leads to the relation $a_j + \eth b_j = a_k + \eth b_k$. Under the condition that $b_j - b_k$ is invertible modulo $\#G$ (which holds with high probability for large p and appropriate group G), we have $\eth = (a_j - a_k)(b_k - b_j)^{-1} \bmod \#G$.

There are several methods for detecting collisions. The distinguished point method [4] is the most practical of these methods and allows parallelisation.

Tag Tracing: In the pseudo-random walk defining the Pollard rho algorithm, the computation of g_{j+1} from g_j is done by multiplying g_j and $m_{s(g_j)}$. So each step requires a field multiplication. The tag tracing method was introduced in [2]. The essential idea is to increase the size of the pre-computed table so that a field multiplication is required after every ℓ steps for a suitable choice of the parameter ℓ. The computation done in the intermediate steps between two field multiplications is significantly faster than a field multiplication.

The set of multipliers $\{m_i : m_i = g^{\alpha_i} h^{\beta_i}, i = 0, \ldots, r-1\}$ is defined as in the case of the original Pollard rho algorithm. Choose a parameter ℓ and let $\mathcal{M}_\ell$ be the set of all possible products of at most ℓ elements from $\mathcal{M}$. The elements of $\mathcal{M}_\ell$ can be indexed by vectors of the form $(i_1, \ldots, i_k)$ where $i_1, \ldots, i_k \in \{0, \ldots, r-1\}$ and $0 \leq k \leq \ell$. Given $\mathbf{x} = (i_1, \ldots, i_k)$, the element of $\mathcal{M}$ indexed by $\mathbf{x}$ is $m_{\mathbf{x}} = m_{i_1} \cdots m_{i_k}$. Note that if $\mathbf{x}'$ is obtained by permuting the components of $\mathbf{x}$, then $m_{\mathbf{x}'} = m_{\mathbf{x}}$. So we will assume that the vector $\mathbf{x}$ satisfies $i_1 \leq i_2 \leq \cdots \leq i_k$. A pre-computed table Tab is created. The rows of Tab are as follows.

$$(\mathbf{x}, m_{\mathbf{x}}, (a, b), (\hat{m}_0, \ldots, \hat{m}_{d-1}))$$

where

- $\mathbf{x} = (i_1, \ldots, i_k)$, with $0 \leq k \leq \ell$, $i_1, \ldots, i_k \in \{0, \ldots, r-1\}$,
- $m_{\mathbf{x}} = m_{i_1} \cdots m_{i_k} \bmod p$,
- (a, b) is such that $m_{\mathbf{x}} = g^a h^b$.

We explain the component $(\hat{m}_0, \ldots, \hat{m}_{d-1})$ later. The table Tab is stored as a hash table (or, some other suitable data structure), so that given an appropriate vector $\mathbf{x}$, it is easy to locate the corresponding row of Tab.

The indexing function $s : G \to \{0, \ldots, r-1\}$ defines the pseudo-random walk. Tag tracing requires an auxiliary indexing function $\bar{s} : G \times \mathcal{M}_\ell \to \{0, \ldots, r-1\} \cup \{\mathsf{fail}\}$, such that

$$\text{if } \bar{s}(y, m) \neq \mathsf{fail}, \text{ then } \bar{s}(y, m) = s(ym).$$

Suppose the element at the j-th step of the pseudo-random walk is g_j. The elements in the next ℓ steps are $g_{j+1}, \ldots, g_{j+\ell}$. For $1 \leq i < \ell$, recall that in the Pollard rho algorithm $g_{j+i} = g_{j+i-1} m_{s(g_{j+i-1})}$. Iterating leads to the following.

$$g_{j+i} = g_{j+i-1}m_{s(g_{j+i-1})}$$
$$= g_{j+i-2}m_{s(g_{j+i-2})}m_{s(g_{j+i-1})}$$
$$= \cdots$$
$$= g_j m_{s(g_j)}m_{s(g_{j+1})}\cdots m_{s(g_{j+i-1})}.$$

The goal of the tag tracing method is to avoid computing the intermediate elements $g_{j+1},\ldots,g_{j+\ell-1}$ and instead jump directly from g_j to $g_{j+\ell}$. This requires obtaining the element $m_{s(g_j)}m_{s(g_{j+1})}\cdots m_{s(g_{j+\ell-1})}$ and so in particular, the index values $s(g_j), s(g_{j+1}),\ldots,s(g_{j+\ell-1})$. Since g_j is available, $s(g_j)$ can be directly obtained. For $i > 1$, the value of $s(g_{j+i})$ is obtained using the auxiliary tag function $\bar{s}$ as

$$s(g_{j+i}) = s(g_j m_{s(g_j)}m_{s(g_{j+1})}\cdots m_{s(g_{j+i-1})})$$
$$= \bar{s}(g_j, m_{s(g_j)}m_{s(g_{j+1})}\cdots m_{s(g_{j+i-1})}).$$

The elements $m_{s(g_j)}m_{s(g_{j+1})}\cdots m_{s(g_{j+i-1})}$ for $i = 0,\ldots,\ell-1$ are elements of $\mathcal{M}_\ell$ and are part of the pre-computed table.

In the tag tracing method, a tag set $\mathcal{T}$ is identified. The index function s is defined as the composition of a tag function $\tau : G \to \mathcal{T}$ and a projection function $\sigma : \mathcal{T} \to \{0,\ldots,r-1\}$, i.e., for $y \in G$, $s(y) = \sigma(\tau(y))$. Similarly, the auxiliary index function $\bar{s}$ is defined as the composition of an auxiliary tag function $\bar{\tau} : G \times \mathcal{M}_\ell \to \mathcal{T}$ and a projection function $\bar{\sigma} : \mathcal{T} \to \{0,\ldots,r-1\}\cup\{\text{fail}\}$, i.e., for $y \in G$ and $m \in \mathcal{M}_\ell$, $\bar{s}(y,m) = \bar{\sigma}(\bar{\tau}(y,m))$.

The definitions of $\tau, \sigma, \bar{\tau}$ and $\bar{\sigma}$ depend on a number of parameters. The two basic parameters are the prime p and the size of the index set r. The tag set is $\mathcal{T} = \{0,\ldots,t-1\}$ which also defines the parameter t. The parameter u is taken to be a suitable word size and d is defined to be $d = \lceil \log_u(p-1) \rceil$. An integer $\bar{t}$ is chosen such that $\bar{t} > d(u-1)$ and $t\bar{t} < p^{1/3}$. The parameter w is defined to be $w = t\bar{t}$. Finally, the parameter $\bar{r}$ is defined so that $r\bar{r} = t$. As shown in [2], it is possible to choose all the parameters (other than p) to be a power of 2. Based on these parameters, the functions τ and σ are defined as follows.

$$\tau(y) = \left\lfloor \frac{y \bmod p}{t w} \right\rfloor \;;\; \sigma(x) = \lfloor x/\bar{r} \rfloor.$$

To define the function $\bar{\tau}$, elements of $y \in \mathbf{F}_p^\star$ are represented in base u as $y \bmod p = y_0 + y_1 u + \cdots + y_{d-1}u^{d-1}$. Given $m \in \mathcal{M}_\ell$, for $i = 0,\ldots,d-1$, define $\hat{m}_i = \lfloor (u^i m \bmod p)/\overline{w} \rfloor$. Since u is fixed, for each $m \in \mathcal{M}_\ell$, the values $\hat{m}_0,\ldots,\hat{m}_{d-1}$ are pre-computed and stored in the table Tab along with m (as mentioned earlier).

Given $y \in G$ and $m \in \mathcal{M}_\ell$, the value of $\bar{\tau}(y,m)$ is defined to be the following.

$$\bar{\tau}(y,m) = \left\lfloor \frac{\left(\sum_{i=0}^{d-1} y_i \hat{m}_i\right) \bmod w}{\bar{t}} \right\rfloor.$$

Given $x \in \mathcal{T}$, the function $\overline{\sigma}$ is defined as follows.

$$\overline{\sigma}(x) = \begin{cases} \text{fail} & \text{if } x \equiv -1 \bmod \overline{r}, \\ \lfloor x/\overline{r} \rfloor & \text{otherwise.} \end{cases}$$

The proof of correctness of the tag tracing procedure based on the above definitions of s and $\overline{s}$ is complex. We refer to [2] for details. The use of tag tracing for the Pollard rho algorithm requires a suitable definition of distinguished point. Again, we refer to [2] for details.

The computation of $\overline{s}$ has a chance of failure. In case of failure, a field multiplication is required. Otherwise, a field multiplication is required after every ℓ steps. The computation of $\overline{s}$ require the computations of $\overline{\tau}$ and $\overline{\sigma}$. The quantities $\hat{m}_0, \ldots, \hat{m}_{d-1}$ are part of the pre-computed table. So for the computation of $\overline{\tau}$, the d multiplications $y_i \hat{m}_i$, $i = 0, \ldots, d-1$ are required. Apart from these, all other computations are divisions by w, $\overline{t}$ and $\overline{r}$. Since these are chosen to be powers of 2, such computations are very fast. Overall, the computation of $\overline{s}$ is significantly faster than a field multiplication.

Our description of tag tracing has been in the context of DLP computation in a multiplicative subgroup of $\mathbf{F}_p^\star$ as given in [2]. A general description of the method applicable to any finite cyclic group for which suitable tag and projection functions can be defined has been provided in [2]. Further, the application of the method to small characteristic, large extension degree fields has also been described in [2].

Montgomery Multiplication: Let x and y be two elements of $\mathbf{F}_p$ and the requirement is to compute the product $x \cdot y \in \mathbf{F}_p$. Typically, this is a two-stage process, where in the first stage the integer multiplication of x and y is carried out and then the result is reduced modulo p. The reduction operation can take a substantial fraction of the total time to perform the field multiplication. This is especially true if p does not have a special form. Montgomery multiplication was introduced [3] to replace the costly reduction operation modulo p by much cheaper divisions by powers of two. Below we provide a brief description of Montgomery multiplication based on [1].

Following the notation used in the context of tag tracing, let u be a power of two representing a word size and d be such that the elements of $\mathbf{F}_p^\star$ have a d-digit representation to base u. Choose $R = u^d$ such that $u^{d-1} \le p < u^d$. Since p is odd and u is a power of two, there exists μ satisfying $\mu = -p^{-1} \bmod u$.

The core of Montgomery multiplication is a procedure called Montgomery reduction. Given an integer x having a d-digit representation to base u, Montgomery reduction computes $xR^{-1} \bmod p$. The Montgomery multiplication is a generalisation which given two integers x and y computes $xyR^{-1} \bmod p$. Suppose x and y satisfy $0 \le x, y < R$ and x is written as $x = \sum_{i=0}^{d-1} x_i u^i$ with $0 \le x_i < u$ for $i = 0, \ldots, d-1$. From [1], the basic Montgomery multiplication procedure is the following.

$z \leftarrow 0$
for $i = 0$ to $d - 1$ do
$\quad z \leftarrow z + x_i y$
$\quad q \leftarrow \mu z \bmod u$
$\quad z \leftarrow (z + pq)/u$
end for
if $z \geq p$ then $z \leftarrow z - p$
output z.

It can be shown that the output z satisfies $z \equiv xyR^{-1} \bmod p$. For a proof of this statement and for a discussion on improvements to the above algorithm, we refer to [1]. The point to be noted here is that the only divisions in the above procedure are by u which is a power of two. So these divisions are simply right shift operations and are very fast.

Given two field elements x and y, one way to multiply them is to first convert them to Montgomery representation by computing $\tilde{x} = xR \bmod p$ and $\tilde{y} = yR \bmod p$, then performing a Montgomery multiplication of $\tilde{x}$ and $\tilde{y}$ to obtain $\tilde{z} = \tilde{x}\tilde{y}R^{-1} = xyR \bmod p$ and then performing a Montgomery reduction (or, performing Montgomery multiplication of $\tilde{z}$ and 1) on $\tilde{z}$ to obtain $\tilde{z}R^{-1} \bmod p = xy \bmod p$. This procedure has the overhead of converting x and y to Montgomery representation and at the end applying a Montgomery reduction to $\tilde{z}$. So for performing a single multiplication, this procedure is not very useful. Instead, Montgomery multiplication turns out to be effective when a sequence of multiplications can be done in the Montgomery representation.

3   Combining Montgomery Multiplication with Tag Tracing

The Pollard rho algorithm in G consists of a sequence of multiplications modulo p. So it is an ideal application case for Montgomery multiplication. Let us first consider how this can be done.

As described earlier, the pseudo-random walk of the Pollard rho algorithm starts with g_0 and continues by computing $g_1, g_2, \ldots$, where for $j \geq 0$, $g_{j+1} = g_j m_{s(g_j)}$. Recall that for each $i \in \{0, \ldots, r - 1\}$, the values α_i and β_i are known such that $m_i = g^{\alpha_i} h^{\beta_i}$. As before, a pre-computed table T stores $(i, m_i, (\alpha_i, \beta_i))$ for $i = 0, \ldots, r - 1$.

To perform the Pollard rho algorithm using Montgomery multiplication, the multipliers are converted to Montgomery representation. This requires a change in the pre-computed table T. Denote the modified table by modT. Then the rows of modT are $(i, \tilde{m}_i, (\alpha_i, \beta_i))$ for $i = 0, \ldots, r - 1$, where $\tilde{m}_i = m_i R \bmod p$.

As in the Pollard rho algorithm described above, randomly choose a_0 and b_0 and define $z_0 = g^{a_0} h^{b_0}$. Let $\tilde{z}_0 = z_0 R \bmod p$ be the Montgomery representation of z_0. For $j \geq 0$, we define $z_{j+1} = z_j m_{s(\tilde{z}_j)} \bmod p$. Note that in this case, the indexing function s is applied to $\tilde{z}_j$ instead of being applied to z_j. This is because the element computed at the $(j + 1)$-th step of the walk is $\tilde{z}_{j+1}$. The quantity $\tilde{z}_{j+1}$ is computed by applying Montgomery multiplication to $\tilde{z}_j$ and $\tilde{m}_{s(\tilde{z}_j)}$, i.e., $\tilde{z}_{j+1} = \tilde{z}_j \tilde{m}_{s(\tilde{z}_j)} R^{-1} \bmod p = z_j m_{s(\tilde{z}_j)} R \bmod p = z_{j+1} R \bmod p$.

With the above modification, all the multiplications required in the pseudo-random walk are Montgomery multiplications. So at no stage the reduction operation modulo p is required.

The exponent information can be obtained from the walk. For $j \geq 0$, let $z_j = g^{a_j} h^{b_j}$. Note that a_0 and b_0 are known. Let $i = s(\tilde{z}_j)$. Then from the pre-computed table, it is possible to obtain (m_i, α_i, β_i). By definition, we have $z_{j+1} = z_j m_i$ and so, $a_{j+1} = a_j + \alpha_i$ and $b_{j+1} = b_j + \beta_i$.

Now, suppose there is a collision in the pseudo-random walk, i.e., there are j and k with $j < k$ such that $\tilde{z}_j = \tilde{z}_k$. Using the definition of $\tilde{z}_j$ and $\tilde{z}_k$, we have $z_j R = z_k R \bmod p$ implying $z_j = z_k \bmod p$ since R is co-prime to p. Using $z_j = z_k \bmod p$, we obtain $a_j + \mathfrak{d} b_j = a_k + \mathfrak{d} b_k$, where $\mathfrak{d} = \log_g h$. From this relation, it is possible to obtain $\mathfrak{d}$ as mentioned earlier.

The distinguished point method for detecting collisions can be applied to this modified pseudo-random walk by defining distinguished points based on $\tilde{z}_j$ for $j \geq 0$.

The above description shows that using Montgomery multiplication to define the pseudo-random walk for the Pollard rho algorithm results in replacing all the relatively expensive modulo p operations with divisions by powers of two. We next consider, how the tag tracing method can be applied to this version of the Pollard rho algorithm.

Let us first consider the difficulties in applying Montgomery multiplication to the setting of tag tracing. Suppose the pseudo-random walk is at an element $\tilde{z}_j$ for some $j \geq 0$. The goal of tag tracing is to perform a single field multiplication to move to the element $\tilde{z}_{j+\ell}$. For the intermediate points of the walk, the index values $s(\tilde{z}_j), s(\tilde{z}_{j+1}), \ldots, s(\tilde{z}_{j+\ell-1})$ are required.

The goal is to replace the usual field multiplication with a Montgomery multiplication. On the other hand, recall that the function s is obtained from the auxiliary function $\bar{s}$, such that for $y \in G$ and $x \in \mathcal{M}_\ell$, if $\bar{s}(y, m) \neq$ fail, then $s(y \cdot m) = \bar{s}(y, m)$. The product $y \cdot m$ in the argument of s is the usual field multiplication. So there are two apparently conflicting requirements. For the movement from $\tilde{z}_j$ to $\tilde{z}_{j+\ell}$, a Montgomery multiplication is to be applied, while the indexing function s is defined with respect to the usual field multiplication.

We show a simple resolution of this problem. The first thing to note is that the product in the argument of s is not actually performed. Instead, $s(y \cdot m)$ is computed as $\bar{s}(y, m)$. For $1 \leq i \leq \ell$, we have

$$
\begin{aligned}
s\left(\tilde{z}_{j+i}\right) &= s\left(\tilde{z}_{j+i-1} \tilde{m}_{s(\tilde{z}_{j+i-1})} R^{-1} \bmod p\right) \\
&= s\left(\tilde{z}_{j+i-1} m_{s(\tilde{z}_{j+i-1})} R R^{-1} \bmod p\right) \\
&= s\left(\tilde{z}_{j+i-1} m_{s(\tilde{z}_{j+i-1})} \bmod p\right) \\
&= s\left(\tilde{z}_{j+i-2} \tilde{m}_{s(\tilde{z}_{j+i-2})} R^{-1} m_{s(\tilde{z}_{j+i-1})} \bmod p\right) \\
&= s\left(\tilde{z}_{j+i-2} m_{s(\tilde{z}_{j+i-2})} m_{s(\tilde{z}_{j+i-1})} \bmod p\right) \\
&= \cdots \\
&= s\left(\tilde{z}_j m_{s(\tilde{z}_j)} \cdots m_{s(\tilde{z}_{j+i-2})} m_{s(\tilde{z}_{j+i-1})} \bmod p\right) \\
&= \bar{s}\left(\tilde{z}_j, m_{s(\tilde{z}_j)} \cdots m_{s(\tilde{z}_{j+i-2})} m_{s(\tilde{z}_{j+i-1})} \bmod p\right).
\end{aligned}
$$

Let $m = m_{s(\tilde{z}_j)} \cdots m_{s(\tilde{z}_{j+i-2})} m_{s(\tilde{z}_{j+i-1})} \bmod p$. The element m is in the set $\mathcal{M}_\ell$. For computing $\overline{\tau}$, the quantities $\hat{m}_0, \dots, \hat{m}_{d-1}$ derived from m are required, but, the actual value of m is not required. The fourth component of the pre-computed table Tab corresponding to the entry for m has the values $\hat{m}_0, \dots, \hat{m}_{d-1}$. So using the entries in Tab, it is possible to compute $\overline{\tau}(\tilde{z}_j, m)$ and hence $\overline{s}(\tilde{z}_j, m)$ which provides the value for $s(\tilde{z}_{j+i})$.

Now let us consider the computation of $\tilde{z}_{j+\ell}$ from $\tilde{z}_j$.

$$\tilde{z}_{j+\ell} = \tilde{z}_{j+\ell-1} \tilde{m}_{s(\tilde{z}_{j+\ell-1})} R^{-1} \bmod p$$
$$= \cdots$$
$$= \tilde{z}_j m_{s(\tilde{z}_j)} \cdots m_{s(\tilde{z}_{j+\ell-2})} m_{s(\tilde{z}_{j+\ell-1})} \bmod p$$
$$= \tilde{z}_j m_{s(\tilde{z}_j)} \cdots m_{s(\tilde{z}_{j+\ell-2})} m_{s(\tilde{z}_{j+\ell-1})} R R^{-1} \bmod p$$
$$= \tilde{z}_j \mathsf{m} R R^{-1} \bmod p$$
$$= \tilde{z}_j \tilde{\mathsf{m}} R^{-1} \bmod p$$

where $\mathsf{m} = m_{s(\tilde{z}_j)} \cdots m_{s(\tilde{z}_{j+\ell-2})} m_{s(\tilde{z}_{j+\ell-1})}$. So $\tilde{z}_{j+\ell}$ is obtained by applying Montgomery multiplication to $\tilde{z}_j$ and $\tilde{\mathsf{m}}$. The element m is in the set $\mathcal{M}_\ell$ and so is in the pre-computed table Tab. Note however, the value of $\tilde{\mathsf{m}}$ is required which is not present in Tab. One may, of course, obtain $\tilde{\mathsf{m}}$ from m by performing the product $\mathsf{m}R \bmod p$. This would be costly and would defeat the whole purpose of utilising Montgomery multiplication. So a better option would be to include the element $\tilde{\mathsf{m}}$ in the table Tab as part of the entry corresponding to the row for m. This would increase the size of the table Tab. Instead, we propose that in the table Tab, the entry $\tilde{\mathsf{m}}$ is to be stored in place of m.

Let us denote the modified table by modTab. Based on the above discussion, the rows of the table modTab are as follows.

$$(\mathbf{x}, \tilde{m}_{\mathbf{x}}, (a.b), (\hat{m}_0, \dots, \hat{m}_{d-1}))$$

where

- $\mathbf{x} = (i_1, \dots, i_k)$, with $0 \le k \le \ell$, $i_1, \dots, i_k \in \{0, \dots, r-1\}$,
- $m_{\mathbf{x}} = m_{i_1} \cdots m_{i_k} \bmod p$ and $\tilde{m}_{\mathbf{x}} = m_{\mathbf{x}} R \bmod p$,
- (a, b) is such that $m = g^a h^b$,
- $\hat{m}_i = \lfloor (u^i m \bmod p)/\overline{w} \rfloor$ for $i = 0, \dots, d-1$.

So modTab stores $\tilde{m}$ instead of m while the quantities $\hat{m}_0, \dots, \hat{m}_{d-1}$ in modTab are derived from m and not from $\tilde{m}$. In particular, the only difference between Tab and modTab is that Tab stores m whereas modTab stores $\tilde{m}$. All other entries of Tab and modTab are identical. So the storage requirements of both Tab and modTab are also the same.

Using modTab, tag tracing can proceed as follows. For the jump from $\tilde{z}_j$ to $\tilde{z}_{j+\ell}$, the entry $\tilde{m}$ is to be used, whereas for the computations of the outputs of the function s, the entries $\hat{m}_0, \dots, \hat{m}_{d-1}$ are to be used. Consequently, the advantage of tag tracing is retained, i.e., all computations required for computing the output of s are divisions by powers of two. Additionally, there is an efficiency gain where the field multiplication required in tag tracing for the jump from the j-th step of the walk to the $(j+\ell)$-th step of the walk is replaced by a Montgomery multiplication. As explained earlier, this replaces the costly reduction operations modulo p by inexpensive divisions by powers of two.

Acknowledgements. We thank Ruben Niederhagen and the reviewers for helpful comments and suggestions on how to improve the presentation of the paper.

References

1. Bos, J.W., Montgomery, P.L.: Montgomery arithmetic from a software perspective. In: Bos, J.W., Lenstra, A.K. (eds.) Topics in Computational Number Theory Inspired by Peter L. Montgomery, pp. 10–39. Cambridge University Press (2017)
2. Cheon, J.H., Hong, J., Kim, M.: Accelerating Pollard's rho algorithm on finite fields. J. Cryptol. **25**(2), 195–242 (2012)
3. Montgomery, P.L.: Modular multiplication without trial division. Math. Comput. **44**(170), 519–521 (1985)
4. van Oorschot, P., Wiener, M.: Parallel collision search with cryptanalytic applications. J. Cryptol. **12**, 1–28 (1999)
5. Pollard, J.M.: A Monte Carlo method for index computation (mod p). Math. Comput. **32**(143), 918–924 (1978)
6. Schnorr, C., Lenstra, H.W.: A Monte Carlo factoring algorithm with linear storage. Math. Comput. **43**(167), 289–311 (1984)

Card-Based Zero-Knowledge Proof for the Nearest Neighbor Property: Zero-Knowledge Proof of ABC End View

Takuro Fukasawa and Yoshifumi Manabe[⊠][ID]

Kogakuin University, Shinjuku, Tokyo 163-8677, Japan
manabe@cc.kogakuin.ac.jp

Abstract. This paper shows a zero-knowledge proof protocol of a solution to ABC end view puzzle using physical cards. Card-based cryptographic protocols are proposed to execute a secure multi-party calculation using physical cards instead of computers. This paper shows a card-based zero-knowledge proof of the ABC end view puzzle. The puzzle needs a new technique to prove the nearest neighbor from an end. We show a new zero-knowledge proof protocol to securely calculate the nearest neighbor using physical cards.

Keywords: Card based cryptographic protocols · Zero-knowledge proof · ABC end view · Nearest neighbor

1 Introduction

This paper shows a zero-knowledge proof protocol of a solution of ABC end view puzzle [6] using physical cards. Card-based cryptographic protocols [2,18] are proposed to execute a secure multi-party calculation using physical cards instead of computers. These protocols can be used when the users cannot trust the software on the computer. Many protocols were shown to calculate any boolean functions [10,13,32] and specific problems such as voting [1,17] and millionaires' problem [14,20,21] and so on.

As another usage of card-based cryptographic protocols, zero-knowledge proof of puzzle solutions was proposed. The protocol proves that a user has a solution to the puzzle without leaking any information about the solution.

A zero-knowledge proof of Sudoku [8] was first considered. The proof has a soundness error, thus improved zero-knowledge proofs were shown [26,31]. Zero-knowledge proofs of the other puzzles are shown, for example, Akari [3], Flow Free [9], Heyawake [23], Hitori [23], Juosan [15], Kakuro [3,16], KenKen [3], Makaro [4,29], Masyu [12], Nonogram [5,25], Norinori [7], Numberlink [27], Nurikabe [23], Nurimisaki [24], Ripple Effect [28], Shikaku [30], Slitherlink [12], Suguru [22], Takuzu [3,15], Topswops [11], and so on.

This paper shows a zero-knowledge proof of the ABC end view puzzle. The proof needs a new technique to prove the nearest neighbor from an end. We show a new protocol to securely calculate the nearest neighbor using physical cards.

L. Batina et al. (Eds.): SPACE 2022, LNCS 13783, pp. 147–161, 2022.
https://doi.org/10.1007/978-3-031-22829-2_9

Section 2 shows the problem definition. Section 3 shows the protocol. Section 4 concludes the paper.

2   Definition of Problem

A zero-knowledge proof for a language L is a protocol executed by two players, called prover P and verifier V. The prover has an element x.

- (Completeness) If $x \in L$, an honest verifier V is convinced that $x \in L$ by an honest prover P.
- (Soundness) If $x \notin L$, no cheating prover P can convince an honest verifier V that $x \in L$.
- (Zero-knowledge) If $x \in L$, no verifier V learns anything other than the fact that $x \in L$.

For the problem of a solution to a puzzle, if the prover has a solution, an honest verifier is convinced that the prover has a solution. If the prover does not have a solution, the prover cannot convince an honest verifier that the prover has a solution. By the execution of the protocol, the verifier has no information about the solution.

ABC end view (aka "Easy as ABC" or "Last man standing") [6] is a pencil puzzle. The problem is given as a grid and a range of letters, for example, A-E. Each different letter must occur exactly once in each row and column. The letters outside the grid show which letter comes across first from that direction. An example of the problem of a 5 * 5 grid and range A-C is shown in the left of Fig. 1. The solution to the problem is shown on the right of Fig. 1, where "×" means no letter is written in the space.

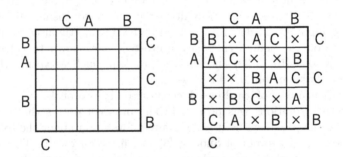

Fig. 1. An example of ABC end view problem and its solution

Card-based cryptographic protocols use physical cards to securely calculate values. For calculations of boolean functions, two kinds of cards, ♣ and ♡ are used. Cards of the same marks cannot be distinguished. In addition, the back of both types of cards is ?. It is impossible to determine the mark on the back of a given card of ?. Some additional cards are used for the zero-knowledge proof protocols. The first type of card is the number card, whose marks are $\boxed{1}$, $\boxed{2}$,..., $\boxed{n}$, where n is the size of the grid. The second type of card is the letter card, whose marks are $\boxed{A}$, $\boxed{B}$, $\boxed{C}$, and so on. The last type of card is the empty card, whose mark is $\boxed{\times}$, which means "no letter". Cards of the same marks cannot be distinguished. In addition, the back of all types of cards is $\boxed{?}$. Note that any kind of card can be represented by an appropriate encoding using the two kinds of cards $\boxed{\clubsuit}$ and $\boxed{\heartsuit}$. For example, a number card can be represented by $\lceil \log n \rceil$ $\boxed{\clubsuit}$ and $\boxed{\heartsuit}$ cards. Each bit of the number is represented by the encoding rule $\boxed{\clubsuit}\boxed{\heartsuit} = 0$ and $\boxed{\heartsuit}\boxed{\clubsuit} = 1$. For the letter cards and the empty card, a similar encoding rule can be introduced and one card is represented by several numbers of $\boxed{\clubsuit}$ and $\boxed{\heartsuit}$ cards. For the simplicity of the discussion, this paper uses additional cards.

3   Protocol for ABC End View

Zero-knowledge proof of a solution to an ABC end view puzzle is executed as follows. First, the prover P sets the solution of the given puzzle in a committed manner, that is, V cannot see the values of the solution. Then P and V execute the verification protocol to prove the solution is correct without knowing the values. They need to prove the following two properties

- nearest neighbor property: The letter in the grid that is nearest to the letter written outside of the grid must be correct.
- uniqueness property: Every row and column has just one letter for the given range of letters.

For an example of the uniqueness property, if the range is A-C, A, B, and C appear once in the squares of each row and column. All the other squares have $\times$ as the example in Fig. 1.

Initially, we show card-based cryptographic protocols used in this paper. One-bit data is represented by two cards as follows: $\boxed{\clubsuit}\boxed{\heartsuit} = 0$ and $\boxed{\heartsuit}\boxed{\clubsuit} = 1$.

One pair of cards that represents one bit $x \in \{0,1\}$, whose face is down, is called a commitment of x, and denoted as $commit(x)$. It is written as $\underbrace{\boxed{?}\boxed{?}}_{x}$.

Note that when these two cards are swapped, $commit(\bar{x})$ can be obtained. Thus, logical negation can be easily calculated.

A set of cards placed in a row is called a sequence of cards. A sequence of cards S whose length is n is denoted as $S = s_1, s_2, \ldots, s_n$, where s_i is i-th card of the sequence. $S = \underbrace{\boxed{?}}_{s_1} \underbrace{\boxed{?}}_{s_2} \underbrace{\boxed{?}}_{s_3} \ldots \underbrace{\boxed{?}}_{s_n}$.

A shuffle is executed on a sequence of cards S. Its parameter is $(\Pi, \mathcal{F})$, where Π is a set of permutations on S and $\mathcal{F}$ is a probability distribution on Π. For a given sequence S, each permutation $\pi \in \Pi$ is selected by the probability distribution $\mathcal{F}$ and π is applied to S. If π is applied on $S = s_1, s_2, \ldots, s_n$, the result is $s_{\pi^{-1}(1)}, s_{\pi^{-1}(2)}, \ldots, s_{\pi^{-1}(n)}$. Since π is selected from Π, the result is not deterministic. Non-deterministic shuffles are necessary for card-based cryptographic protocols to make the protocols secure at opening cards. As shown in the below protocol, cards on each row are randomly shuffled and then opened to show that A, B, and C appear once. If the shuffle is deterministic, the players know the initial position where the A card was set as the answer. Therefore, a random shuffle whose result is unknown to the players is necessary.

We show examples of shuffles used in the protocols shown below. A random shuffle is randomly changing the positions of the cards for the given sequence of cards. When $S = s_1, s_2, s_3$, the result of a random shuffle is $S_1 = s_1, s_2, s_3$, $S_2 = s_1, s_3, s_2$, $S_3 = s_2, s_1, s_3$, $S_4 = s_2, s_3, s_1$, $S_5 = s_3, s_1, s_2$, or $S_6 = s_3, s_2, s_1$. The probability of obtaining each result is $1/|S|!$.

A random bisection cut is swapping the left half and the right half of a given even-length sequence. When $S = s_1, s_2, s_3, s_4, s_5, s_6$, the result of a random bisection cut is $S_0 = s_1, s_2, s_3, s_4, s_5, s_6$ or $S_1 = s_4, s_5, s_6, s_1, s_2, s_3$. The probability of obtaining each result is $1/2$. The random bisection cut is considered as selecting a random bit $b \in \{0, 1\}$ and obtaining S_b.

Next, we introduce piles of cards. A pile of cards is a sequence of cards whose order cannot be changed using some additional tools such as clips or envelopes. For example, consider a case when cards $x_{i,j}(i = 1, 2, \ldots, n, j = 1, 2, \ldots m)$ are given. The players make piles of cards such that $plie_i = x_{i,1}, \ldots, x_{i,m}(i = 1, 2, \ldots, n)$ using clips or envelopes. The players treat each pile $pile_i$ just like a single card during shuffle operations. The order of cards in a pile cannot be changed because of the clip or envelope. For a pile y, let $y(i)$ be i-th card in y. Players can rearrange piles by removing clips, setting new sequences of cards, and making new piles. Let $y[2-]$ be the new pile that $y(1)$ is removed from y.

The shuffles can be executed for piles of cards. Consider the case shuffle π is executed on the above piles $pile_i(i = 1, 2, \ldots, n)$. The result is $pile_{\pi^{-1}(1)}$, $pile_{\pi^{-1}(2)}, \ldots, pile_{\pi^{-1}(n)}$, where $pile_{\pi^{-1}(i)} = x_{\pi^{-1}(i),1}, x_{\pi^{-1}(i),2}, \ldots, x_{\pi^{-1}(i),m}$. Random shuffles on piles are called pile-scramble shuffles.

Next, we show logical AND and copy protocols used in this paper.

Protocol 1 *(AND protocol) [19]*
   Input: commit(x) and commit(y).
   Output: commit(x ∧ y).

1. *Input commit(x) and commit(y) are set as Fig. 2 (a).*
2. *The positions of the cards are changed as Fig. 2 (b).*
3. *Execute a random bisection cut on the sequence of the cards. The result can be written as follows: select a random bit $b \in \{0, 1\}$, that is unknown to the players. If $b = 0$, there is no change in the order of the cards. If $b = 1$, the left half and the right half are swapped as Fig. 2 (c).*
4. *Change the sequence of the cards as Fig. 2 (d).*

5. *Open the left two cards. If the sequence is* ♣♡ *, the center two cards are commit(x ∧ y). Otherwise, the right two cards are commit(x ∧ y), as Fig. 2 (e).*

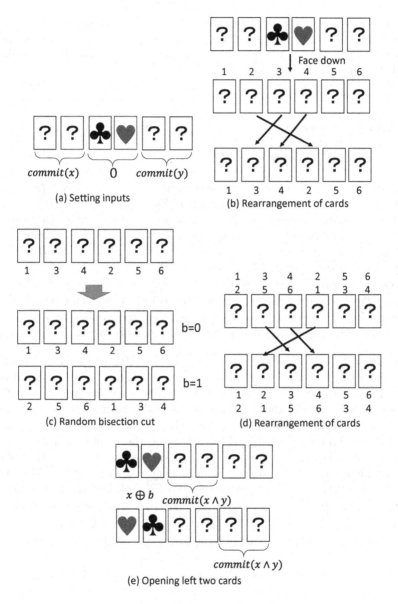

(a) Setting inputs

(b) Rearrangement of cards

(c) Random bisection cut

(d) Rearrangement of cards

(e) Opening left two cards

Fig. 2. AND protocol in [19] .

The protocol outputs

$$x \wedge y = \begin{cases} y & \text{if } x = 1 \quad (\boxed{\heartsuit}, \boxed{\clubsuit}) \\ 0 & \text{if } x = 0 \quad (\boxed{\clubsuit}, \boxed{\heartsuit}) \end{cases} \tag{1}$$

That is, the output is the right two cards if $x = 1$. The output is the center two cards if $x = 0$. The protocol opens two cards $x \oplus b$. Since b is a random number unknown to the players, the security of the private input data is achieved. The detailed proof is shown in [19].

Next, we show copy protocol, which gives multiple copies of a given input commitment.

Protocol 2 *(copy protocol using random bisection cuts) [19]*
   Input: commit(x).
   Output: two copies of commit(x).

1. *Input commit(x) and two copies of commit(0) are set as Fig. 3 (a).*
2. *The positions of the cards are changed as Fig. 3 (b).*
3. *Execute a random bisection cut on the sequence of the cards. The result can be written as follows: select a random bit $b \in \{0,1\}$, that is unknown to the players. If $b = 0$, there is no change in the order of the cards. If $b = 1$, the left half and the right half are swapped as Fig. 3 (c).*
4. *Change the sequence of the cards as Fig. 3 (d).*
5. *Open the left two cards. If the sequence is $\boxed{\clubsuit}\boxed{\heartsuit}$, the remaining pairs are commit(x). Otherwise, the remaining pairs are commit($\bar{x}$), as Fig. 3 (e). In this case, commit(x) can be obtained by swapping the two cards of commit($\bar{x}$).*

We show the zero-knowledge proof protocol for ABC end view in Algorithms 1–3. Algorithm 1 is the main routine and Algorithm 2 is the subroutine to verify the nearest neighbor property. Algorithm 3 is the subroutine to verify the uniqueness property. In the following protocol description, the corresponding code at Line j of Algorithm i is written as "(L. $j(i)$)". The outline of the protocol is as follows. Suppose that the grid is $n * n$ and the number of letters is c. In the example in Fig. 1, $n = 5$ and $c = 3$. First, the prover P sets the solution in a committed manner as follows. For the square at i-th row and j-th column (denoted as square (i,j)), P puts face-down $\boxed{\heartsuit}$, $\boxed{\clubsuit}$, and $\boxed{L}$ in this order if the solution is letter L. P puts face-down $\boxed{\clubsuit}$, $\boxed{\heartsuit}$, and $\boxed{\times}$ in this order if the solution is "no letter" (L. 3–5(1)). Thus the sequence $\boxed{\heartsuit}$, $\boxed{\clubsuit}$ means the solution is a letter. These cards are denoted as $x_{i,j(1)}$, $x_{i,j(2)}$, and $x_{i,j(3)}$ (L. 6(1)).

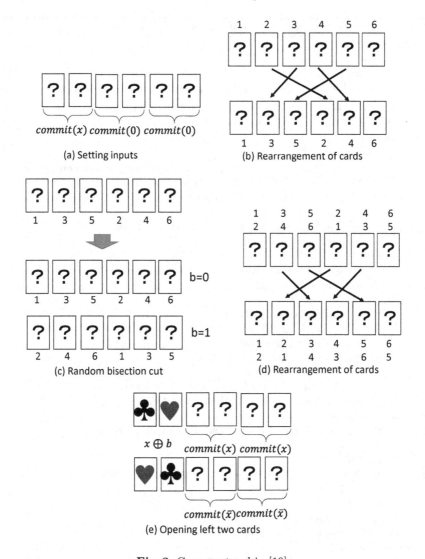

Fig. 3. Copy protocol in [19].

P and V set number cards to remember the positions of the cards, since the positions are changed by the verification. P and V publically put face-up card $\boxed{j}$ to the right of three cards on square (i, j) and then face down the card (L. 9(1)). The card is denoted as $x_{i,j(4)}$(L.10(1)). The four cards form a pile $x_{i,j}$ (L. 11(1)).

Algorithm 1. Zero knowledge proof protocol of ABC end view

```
1: procedure MAIN
2:     Let k = n − c + 1
3:     At square (i, j), P sets
4:     face-down ♡ , ♣ , and L in this order if the solution is letter L,
5:     face-down ♣ , ♡ , and × in this order if the solution is 'no letter'.
6:     These cards are denoted as x_{i,j}(1), x_{i,j}(2), and x_{i,j}(3).
7:     for i=1 to n do
8:         for j=1 to n do
9:             P and V put face-up card  j  to the right of three cards on square (i, j).
10:            They face down the card. The card is denoted as x_{i,j}(4).
11:            The pile of cards at (i, j) is denoted as x_{i,j}.
12:        end for
13:        if There is a letter at the left end of i-th row then
14:            Execute nearestneighbor.
15:        end if
16:        if There is a letter at the right end of i-th row then
17:            Execute nearestneighbor.
18:        end if
19:        Execute uniqueness at i-th row.
20:        Face-down x'_j(1), x'_j(2), and x'_j(3) for each pile x'_j.
21:        Execute pile scramble shuffle on x'_1, . . . , x'_n.
22:        Let the results be x''_1, . . . , x''_n.
23:        Open x''_j(4) of each pile.
24:        If x''_j(4) = l, put x''_j(1), x''_j(2), and x''_j(3) to square (i, l).
25:    end for/* Each row check is finished. */
26:    for i=1 to n do
27:        if There is a letter at the top end of i-th column then
28:            Execute nearestneighbor.
29:        end if
30:        if There is a letter at the bottom of i-th column then
31:            Execute nearestneighbor.
32:        end if
33:        Execute uniqueness at i-th column.
34:    end for/* Each column check is finished. */
35: end procedure
```

First, we show the procedure to verify the neighborhood property(called at L. 14(1), 17(1), 28(1), and 31(1)). Let i be the current row to verify and consider the case when there is a letter L at the left end. Let $k = n - c + 1$. The candidate of the nearest square that has a letter is $(i, 1), (i, 2) \ldots (i, k)$, since the number of "no letter" squares is $n - c$ (L. 2(2)).

Algorithm 2. Subroutine: nearest neighbor verification

```
1: procedure NEARESTNEIGHBOR
2:     Select k plies on the squares in the current row or column.
3:     Let y_i(1 ≤ i ≤ k) be the piles, where y_1 is the closest to the end.
4:     Let z be y_k.
5:     for j = k − 1 downto 1 do
6:         Execute copy protocol on (y_j(1), y_j(2)).
7:         Let the obtained pair be (y'_j(1), y'_j(2)).
8:         Execute AND protocol using (y'_j(1), y'_j(2), y_j(1), y_j[2−], z(1), z[2−]).
9:         if The left two opened cards are (♣, ♡) then
10:            Set the right card-pile pair as new z.
11:            Set the center card-pile pair as new y_{j+1}.
12:        else
13:            Set the center card-pile pair as new z.
14:            Set the right card-pile pair as new y_{j+1}.
15:        end if
16:    end for
17:    Open z(3) and verify that the letter is the same as the one written outside.
18:    Face-down z(3) and set pile z to new y_1.
19:    Put y_1, y_2, . . . , y_k to the original squares.
20: end procedure
```

Algorithm 3. Subroutine: uniqueness verification

```
1: procedure UNIQUENESS
2:     Let x_1, . . . , x_n be the piles in the current row or column.
3:     Execute pile scramble shuffle on x_1, . . . , x_n.
4:     Let the results be x'_1, . . . , x'_n.
5:     Open x'_j(1), x'_j(2), and x'_j(3) of each pile x'_j.
6:     Verify that (1) if x'_j(3) is a letter, (x'_j(1), x'_j(2)) is (♡, ♣), otherwise
       (x'_j(1), x'_j(2)) is (♣, ♡) and (2) all letters on the letter cards differ from each
       other and the number of ×  cards is n − c.
7: end procedure
```

The procedure to obtain the nearest neighbor is as follows:

1. Let $y_j = x_{i,j}(1 \leq j \leq k − 1)$ and $z = y_k$.
2. For $j = k − 1$ down to 1 Do
3. If $(y_j(1), y_j(2)) = ($♡, ♣$)$ then $z = y_j$
4. EndFor
5. Return z

Initially, the candidate z is y_k, the farthest from the border (L. 4(2)). If the nearer square has a letter (that is, $(y_j(1), y_j(2)) = ($♡, ♣$)$), replace the candidate. After the test at $j = 1$ is finished, z has the nearest letter. For example, consider the case when the players verify the left end "B" in the first row in Fig. 1. Since $k = 3$, the players set $y_i = x_{1,i}(1 \leq i \leq 2)$, and $z = x_{1,3}$. Execute the for loop and when $j = 2$, $(y_j(1), y_j(2)) = (\clubsuit, \heartsuit)$ and z is unchanged. When $j = 1$, $(y_j(1), y_j(2)) = (\heartsuit, \clubsuit)$ and $z = y_1$ is executed. Thus the final $z = y_1$ and the letter is "B".

We need to execute the above procedure without knowing the value $(y_j(1), y_j(2))$. We use AND protocol to solve the problem. The if statement in step 3 can be written as follows:

$$new \ z = \begin{cases} y_j & \text{if } y_j = 1 & (\heartsuit, \clubsuit) \\ z & \text{if } y_j = 0 & (\clubsuit, \heartsuit) \end{cases} \tag{2}$$

Comparing this equation and Eq. (1), we can obtain the result using AND protocol if we set $y_j(1), y_j(2), z(1), z[2-], y_j(1), y_j[2-]$ in this order[1] at the first step in Fig. 2(a) (L. 8(2)). We need a copy of $(y_j(1), y_j(2))$, thus the copy protocol is executed to $(y_j(1), y_j(2))$ in advance (L. 6(2)). Another difference between the AND protocol is that $z[2-]$ and $y_j[2-]$ are a pile of cards. This change does not reveal the secret random value b of the AND protocol, because the positions of piles are the fourth and sixth positions in Fig. 2(b) and (c), The piles come to the same positions when $b = 0$ and $b = 1$. Thus, the difference between a card and a pile does not reveal the secret random value b.

When a new z is selected, the unused pile (old z or y_j) is put to the square $(i, j + 1)$ for further verification from the other side(L. 11(2), L. 14(2)).

When the procedure is finished, the players open $z(3)$ to see the final result (L. 17(2)). If the letter on the card is the same as the letter written outside of the grids, the verification succeeds.

The final z is put to the square $(i, 1)$ (L.18(2)). Though the positions of the piles differ from the initial position set by P, the change does not affect the next verification from the other side. The reason is as follows. Pile z with some letter might go left (to the position of the smaller index), but it will not go left further to the position where another letter exists. If y_j has a letter, new z becomes y_j, and old z is put to the position of $(i, j+1)$, the relative order of the letters in the i-th row does not change. For example, consider the case when the players verify the left end "B" in the first row in Fig. 1. After the verification, the letters in the first row become "B A×C×", but the relative order of "B" and "A" is not changed. Thus, the verification for the right end works with this modified sequence.

After the right and left nearest neighbor verifications of i-th row, uniqueness verification of i-th row is executed(L. 19(1)). Note that the position of each pile differs from the initial positions P set, but the change does not affect the verification since the set of letters in i-th row does not change during the nearest neighbor verifications.

The verification technique is just the same as the one used for Sudoku [31]. Execute a pile-scramble shuffle to the piles $x_{i,1}, \ldots, x_{i,n}$ in i-th row(L. 3(3)). Let

---

[1] It is unnecessary to divide the piles as $z(1)$ and $z[2-]$. We set $y_j(1), y_j(2), z, y_j$ in this order, swap the second and the third, execute a random bisection cut, swap the second and the third, open the left two cards, and obtain the result as the AND protocol. The result is the same as the protocol shown in this paper.

the results be $x'_1, x'_2, \ldots, x'_n$ (L. 4(3)). Then open $x'_j(l)(1 \le j \le n, 1 \le l \le 3)$ (L. 5(3)). V verifies that all the letters in $x'_j(3)$ differ and the number of $\boxed{\times}$ in $x'_j(3)$ is $n - c$. In addition, V checks the consistency of cards, that is, $(x'_j(1), x'_j(2)) = (\boxed{♡}, \boxed{♣})$ or $(\boxed{♣}, \boxed{♡})$ must be satisfied. If $(x'_j(1), x'_j(2)) = (\boxed{♡}, \boxed{♣})$, $x'_j(3)$ must be a letter card, otherwise $x'_j(3)$ must be $\boxed{\times}$ (L. 6(3)).

After the verification is finished, P and V face-down $x'_j(l)(1 \le j \le n, 1 \le l \le 3)$ (L. 20(1)). Then the players execute a pile-scramble shuffle on $x'_1, x'_2, \ldots, x'_n$ (L. 21(1)). Let the results be $x''_1, x''_2, \ldots, x''_n$ (L.22(1)). Then open $x''_j(4)(1 \le j \le n)$ (L.23(1)). If $x''_j(4) = l$, put x''_j to square (i, l) (L.24(1)). Each pile is moved to the original square P set. Note that the number cards are no more necessary for the verifications of each column because it is unnecessary to move the plies to the original squares again.

For each column, execute the above nearest neighbor check and uniqueness check (L.26–34(1)). The only difference is each pile consist of three cards. Since the number cards are used only for resetting the positions of piles and are not used in the verification itself, there is no change in the procedure.

(Example) We show the steps for the first row of the problem in Fig. 1. P sets the solution by face-down cards as in Fig. 4 (a). Since the solution is "B×A C×", P sets $(x_{1,1}(1), x_{1,1}(2), x_{1,1}(3)) = (\boxed{♡}, \boxed{♣}, \boxed{B})$, $(x_{1,2}(1), x_{1,2}(2), x_{1,2}(3)) = (\boxed{♣}, \boxed{♡}, \boxed{\times})$, $(x_{1,3}(1), x_{1,3}(2), x_{1,3}(3)) = (\boxed{♡}, \boxed{♣}, \boxed{A})$, $(x_{1,4}(1), x_{1,4}(2), x_{1,4}(3)) = (\boxed{♡}, \boxed{♣}, \boxed{C})$, and $(x_{1,5}(1), x_{1,5}(2), x_{1,5}(3)) = (\boxed{♣}, \boxed{♡}, \boxed{\times})$ in the face-down manner (Note that in Fig. 4, the sequence of cards at each square are written from the top to bottom).

Then P and V sets $x_{1,1}(4) = \boxed{1}$, $x_{1,2}(4) = \boxed{2}$, $x_{1,3}(4) = \boxed{3}$, $x_{1,4}(4) = \boxed{4}$, and $x_{1,5}(4) = \boxed{5}$. These cards are turned face-down. They make piles $x_{1,1}, x_{1,2}, x_{1,3}, x_{1,4}$ and $x_{1,5}$ as Fig. 4 (a). Then they execute the nearest neighbor verification algorithm. Since $n = 5$ and $c = 3$, $k = n - c + 1 = 3$. Thus, the players select three piles from the left end. $y_1 = x_{1,1}$, $y_2 = x_{1,2}$, and $y_3 = x_{1,3}$. Then set $z = y_3$. First, the modified AND protocol is executed between y_2 and z, as shown in Fig. 4(b). Execute the copy protocol on $(y_2(1), y_2(2))$. Note that since the cards are face-down, the marks of the cards are unknown, but they are written in Fig. 4(b) by small marks for the explanation. In this example, $(y_2(1), y_2(2)) = (\boxed{♣}, \boxed{♡})$. Set sequence $y_2(1), y_2(2), y_2(1), y_2[2-], z(1), z[2-]$ and execute AND protocol. Suppose that $b = 1$ by the random bisection cut. In the case, the final sequence becomes $y_2(2), y_2(1), z(1), z[2-], y_2(1), y_2[2-]$. The left two cards are opened. Since they are $(\boxed{♡}, \boxed{♣})$, the center two elements are selected as the new z. The left two elements are set as y_3. In this case, z remains at the position of z and y_2 is moved to y_3 as in Fig. 4(b).

Next, the players execute the modified AND protocol between z and y_1. Since $(y_1(1), y_1(2)) = (\boxed{♡}, \boxed{♣})$, y_1 becomes the new z. Old z is moved to y_2. The final value of z is obtained. Since it is y_1, $\boxed{B}$ appears when $z(3)$ is opened. Thus, the verification succeeds. z is then set at the position of y_1. The piles are then

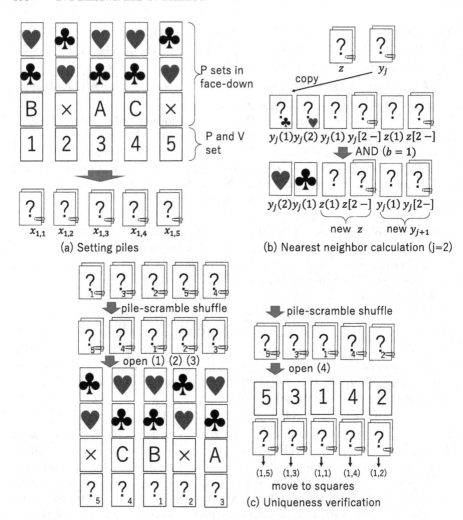

Fig. 4. Example of execution in the first row.

moved to the squares. Thus, the letter cards of $(x_{1,1}, x_{1,2}, x_{1,3})$ are changed as $(\boxed{\mathrm{B}}, \boxed{\mathrm{A}}, \boxed{\times})$.

Next, the players verify the right end card. $k = 3$ and $y_1 = x_{1,5}$, $y_2 = x_{1,4}$ and $y_3 = x_{1,3}$. Note that the letter card of $x_{1,3}$ is currently $\boxed{\times}$ by the above procedure. Initially, $z = y_3$ and execute modified AND protocol between z and y_2. Since $(y_2(1), y_2(2)) = (\boxed{\heartsuit}, \boxed{\clubsuit})$, y_2 becomes the new z. Old z is set as y_3. Next, the modified AND protocol is executed between z and y_1. Since $(y_1(1), y_1(2)) = (\boxed{\clubsuit}, \boxed{\heartsuit})$, z remains unchanged. y_1 is set as new y_2. Thus, when $z(3)$ is opened, the card is $\boxed{\mathrm{C}}$ and the letter is correct.

Then the uniqueness verification is executed. After the nearest neighbor verifications, the letter cards of $(x_{1,1}, x_{1,2}, x_{1,3}, x_{1,4}, x_{1,5})$ are changed as ($\boxed{\text{B}}$, $\boxed{\text{A}}$, $\boxed{\times}$, $\boxed{\times}$, $\boxed{\text{C}}$), that is, the number cards are ($\boxed{1}$, $\boxed{3}$, $\boxed{2}$, $\boxed{5}$, $\boxed{4}$). Note that in Fig 4(c), the numbers are written in a small font for the explanation, but the players cannot see the cards. Then the players execute a pile-scramble shuffle. The order of the piles is randomly changed. Suppose that the order is changed as $(5, 4, 1, 2, 3)$ as Fig. 4(c). Let the result as $x_1', x_2', x_3', x_4', x_5'$. The players open $x_j(1), x_j(2)$, and $x_j(3)$ for every $j (j = 1, 2, \ldots, 5)$. The players verify that the numbers of each card of $\boxed{\text{A}}$, $\boxed{\text{B}}$, and $\boxed{\text{C}}$ are one. Pile x_i with a letter card has $(x_i(1), x_i(2)) = (\boxed{\heartsuit}, \boxed{\clubsuit})$. Pile x_j with $\boxed{\times}$ card has $(x_j(1), x_j(2)) = (\boxed{\clubsuit}, \boxed{\heartsuit})$. Thus the uniqueness verification is finished. The players face down the opened cards and make piles again. The players execute a pile-scramble shuffle again. Let the result be $x_1'', x_2'', x_3'', x_4'', x_5''$. The players open $x_j''(4)$ for every $j (j = 1, 2, \ldots, 5)$. If $x_j''(4) = i$, $x_j''(1), x_j''(2), x_j''(3)$ are moved to square $(1, i)$. Each pile is moved to the original square P set as in Fig. 4(c). The piles are used for the verification of each column.

The number of cards used by the algorithm is as follows: $n^2 + 4$ cards for each of $\boxed{\heartsuit}$ and $\boxed{\clubsuit}$, n cards for each of $\boxed{\text{A}}$$\boxed{\text{B}}$, $\ldots$, $\boxed{\text{L}}$ card when the range of letters is $A - L$. $n^2 - n * c$ cards of $\boxed{\times}$ and one card for each of $\boxed{1}$, $\boxed{2}$, $\ldots$, $\boxed{\text{n}}$. Thus the total number of cards is $3n^2 + n + 8$.

Last, we show the correctness of the protocol.

Theorem 1. *The procedure is a zero-knowledge proof of solutions to the ABC end view problem.*

(Proof)

(Completeness) When P has a solution to the given problem and correctly sets the cards, the nearest neighbor verification and uniqueness verification succeeds in each row and column as shown above.

(Soundness) When P sets the cards that are not a solution, the fact can be detected by V. The reason is as follows. At the uniqueness verification, all cards in a row or a column are simultaneously opened. Thus, if the cards are not correct, the fact can be detected by V. In addition, the nearest neighbor verification protocol outputs the letter nearest to the end, thus if the letter is not correct, V can detect that.

(Zero-knowledge) During the uniqueness verification, V gets no information other than the fact that each row and column has one letter for each A-L. During the nearest neighbor verification, V gets no information other than the nearest letter is correct. The protocol uses AND protocol and copy protocol. They leak no information from the opened cards, as shown in [19].

During the uniqueness verification protocol, all cards in a row or a column are opened. However, they leak no information since the positions are randomized by the pile-scramble shuffles. □

4   Conclusion

This paper showed a card-based zero-knowledge proof of a solution of the ABC end view puzzle. The nearest neighborhood calculation is a new technique to solve the problem. Zero-knowledge proof to the other puzzle problems is one of the further studies.

References

1. Abe, Y., et al.: Efficient card-based majority voting protocols. New Gener. Comput. **40**(1), 173–198 (2022)
2. den Boer, B.: More efficient match-making and satisfiability *The Five Card Trick*. In: Quisquater, J.-J., Vandewalle, J. (eds.) EUROCRYPT 1989. LNCS, vol. 434, pp. 208–217. Springer, Heidelberg (1990). https://doi.org/10.1007/3-540-46885-4_23
3. Bultel, X., Dreier, J., Dumas, J.G., Lafourcade, P.: Physical zero-knowledge proofs for Akari, Takuzu, Kakuro and Kenken. In: Proceedings of 8th International Conference on Fun with Algorithms, vol. 49, pp. 1–8. Schloss Dagstuhl-Leibniz-Zentrum fuer Informatik (2016)
4. Bultel, X., et al.: Physical zero-knowledge proof for Makaro. In: Izumi, T., Kuznetsov, P. (eds.) SSS 2018. LNCS, vol. 11201, pp. 111–125. Springer, Cham (2018). https://doi.org/10.1007/978-3-030-03232-6_8
5. Chien, Y.-F., Hon, W.-K.: Cryptographic and physical zero-knowledge proof: from Sudoku to Nonogram. In: Boldi, P., Gargano, L. (eds.) FUN 2010. LNCS, vol. 6099, pp. 102–112. Springer, Heidelberg (2010). https://doi.org/10.1007/978-3-642-13122-6_12
6. crossa@list.ru: Puzzles: Abc end view. http://www.cross-plus-a.com/puzzles.htm#EasyAsABC. Accessed 31 Aug 2022
7. Dumas, J.-G., Lafourcade, P., Miyahara, D., Mizuki, T., Sasaki, T., Sone, H.: Interactive Physical Zero-Knowledge Proof for Norinori. In: Du, D.-Z., Duan, Z., Tian, C. (eds.) COCOON 2019. LNCS, vol. 11653, pp. 166–177. Springer, Cham (2019). https://doi.org/10.1007/978-3-030-26176-4_14
8. Gradwohl, R., Naor, M., Pinkas, B., Rothblum, G.N.: Cryptographic and physical zero-knowledge proof systems for solutions of Sudoku puzzles. Theor. Comput. Syst. **44**(2), 245–268 (2009)
9. Hart, E., McGinnis, J.A.: Physical zero-knowledge proofs for flow free, Hamiltonian cycles, and many-to-many k-disjoint covering paths (2022) arXiv preprint arXiv:2202.04113
10. Kastner, J., et al.: The minimum number of cards in practical card-based protocols. In: Takagi, T., Peyrin, T. (eds.) ASIACRYPT 2017. LNCS, vol. 10626, pp. 126–155. Springer, Cham (2017). https://doi.org/10.1007/978-3-319-70700-6_5
11. Komano, Y., Mizuki, T.: Physical zero-knowledge proof protocol for topswops. In: Proceedings of 17th International Conference on Information Security Practice and Experience (ISPEC 2022), LNCS. Springer (2022) https://doi.org/10.1007/978-3-031-21280-2_30
12. Lafourcade, P., Miyahara, D., Mizuki, T., Robert, L., Sasaki, T., Sone, H.: How to construct physical zero-knowledge proofs for puzzles with a "single loop" condition. Theor. Comput. Sci. **888**, 41–55 (2021)
13. Manabe, Y.: Survey: card-based cryptographic protocols to calculate primitives of boolean functions. Int. J. Comput. Softw. Eng. **27**(1), 178 (2022)

14. Miyahara, D., Hayashi, Y.I., Mizuki, T., Sone, H.: Practical card-based implementations of Yao's millionaire protocol. Theoret. Comput. Sci. **803**, 207–221 (2020)
15. Miyahara, D., et al.: Card-based ZKP protocols for Takuzu and Juosan. In: Proceedings of 10th International Conference on Fun with Algorithms (FUN 2020). Schloss Dagstuhl-Leibniz-Zentrum für Informatik (2020)
16. Miyahara, D., Sasaki, T., Mizuki, T., Sone, H.: Card-based physical zero-knowledge proof for kakuro. IEICE Trans. Fundam. Electron. Commun. Comput. Sci. **102**(9), 1072–1078 (2019)
17. Mizuki, T., Asiedu, I.K., Sone, H.: Voting with a logarithmic number of cards. In: Mauri, G., Dennunzio, A., Manzoni, L., Porreca, A.E. (eds.) UCNC 2013. LNCS, vol. 7956, pp. 162–173. Springer, Heidelberg (2013). https://doi.org/10.1007/978-3-642-39074-6_16
18. Mizuki, T., Shizuya, H.: A formalization of card-based cryptographic protocols via abstract machine. Int. J. Inf. Secur. **13**(1), 15–23 (2014)
19. Mizuki, T., Sone, H.: Six-card secure AND and four-card secure XOR. In: Deng, X., Hopcroft, J.E., Xue, J. (eds.) FAW 2009. LNCS, vol. 5598, pp. 358–369. Springer, Heidelberg (2009). https://doi.org/10.1007/978-3-642-02270-8_36
20. Nakai, Takeshi, Misawa, Yuto, Tokushige, Yuuki, Iwamoto, Mitsugu, Ohta, Kazuo: How to Solve Millionaires' Problem with Two Kinds of Cards. New Gener. Comput. **39**(1), 73–96 (2021). https://doi.org/10.1007/s00354-020-00118-8
21. Ono, H., Manabe, Y.: Efficient card-based cryptographic protocols for the millionaires problem using private input operations. In: Proceedings of 13th Asia Joint Conference on Information Security(AsiaJCIS 2018), pp. 23–28 (2018)
22. Robert, L., Miyahara, D., Lafourcade, P., Libralesso, L., Mizuki, T.: Physical zero-knowledge proof and np-completeness proof of Suguru puzzle. Inf. Comput. **285**, 104858 (2022)
23. Robert, L., Miyahara, D., Lafourcade, P., Mizuki, T.: Card-based ZKP for connectivity: applications to nurikabe, Hitori and Heyawake. New Gener. Comput. **40**(1), 149–171 (2022)
24. Robert, L., Miyahara, D., Lafourcade, P., Mizuki, T.: Card-based ZKP protocol for Nurimisaki. In: Proceedings of 24th International Symposium on Stabilization, Safety, and Security of Distributed Systems (SSS 2022), LNCS. Springer (2022)
25. Ruangwises, S.: An improved physical ZKP for nonogram. arXiv preprint arXiv:2106.14020 (2021)
26. Ruangwises, S.: Two standard decks of playing cards are sufficient for a ZKP for sudoku. New Gener. Comput. **40**(1), 49–65 (2022)
27. Ruangwises, Suthee, Itoh, Toshiya: Physical Zero-Knowledge Proof for Number link Puzzle and k Vertex-Disjoint Paths Problem. New Generation Computing **39**(1), 3–17 (2021). https://doi.org/10.1007/s00354-020-00114-y
28. Ruangwises, Suthee, Itoh, Toshiya: Physical zero-knowledge proof for Ripple Effect. Theor. Comput. Sci. **895**, 115–123 (2021). https://doi.org/10.1016/j.tcs.2021.09.034
29. Ruangwises, S., Itoh, T.: Physical ZKP for Makaro using a standard deck of cards. arXiv preprint arXiv:2112.12042 (2021)
30. Ruangwises, S., Itoh, T.: How to physically verify a rectangle in a grid: a physical ZKP for shikaku (2022). arXiv preprint arXiv:2202.09788
31. Sasaki, T., Miyahara, D., Mizuki, T., Sone, H.: Efficient card-based zero-knowledge proof for Sudoku. Theoret. Comput. Sci. **839**, 135–142 (2020)
32. Shinagawa, Kazumasa, Nuida, Koji: A single shuffle is enough for secure card-based computation of any Boolean circuit. Discrete Applied Mathematics **289**, 248–261 (2021). https://doi.org/10.1016/j.dam.2020.10.013

Hardware Security and AI

What Do You See? Transforming Fault Injection Target Characterizations

Marina Krček[✉]

Delft University of Technology, Delft, The Netherlands
`m.krcek@tudelft.nl`

Abstract. In fault injection attacks, the first step is to evaluate the target behavior for various fault injection parameters. Showing the results of such a characterization (commonly known as target cartography) is informative and allows researchers to assess the target's behavior better. Additionally, it helps understand the performance of new search methods or attacks. Thus, publishing obtained results is essential to provide relevant information for reproducibility and benchmarking, improving state-of-the-art results and general security. Unfortunately, publishing the results also allows malicious parties to reverse engineer the information and potentially mount an attack easier.

This work discusses how various transformations can be used to occlude sensitive information but, at the same time, still be useful for interested researchers. Our results show that even simple 2D transformations, such as rotation, scaling, and shifting, significantly increase the effort required to reverse engineer the transformed data but maintain the interesting data distribution. Consequently, this work provides a method to allow publishers to share more data in a confidential setting.

Keywords: Fault injection · Target characterization · 2D Transformations

1 Introduction

Secure hardware devices should be designed to operate with confidential data so that the information does not leak and cannot be altered by an adversary. While the algorithms running on such devices might be secure, it has been shown that various attacks on hardware can be powerful [6,12]. Such attacks do not attack the algorithms but the weaknesses in the implementation. Those attacks are called implementation attacks and are commonly divided into side-channel and fault injection (FI) attacks. While these attacks are powerful, there are still challenges to improving the attacks to be more efficient.

When considering fault injection, one main challenge is improving the target characterization. Indeed, to mount a successful fault injection campaign, one needs to recognize where the fault should be inserted. Due to the many parameters that need to be tested, this problem can become a very challenging task.

© The Author(s), under exclusive license to Springer Nature Switzerland AG 2022
L. Batina et al. (Eds.): SPACE 2022, LNCS 13783, pp. 165–184, 2022.
https://doi.org/10.1007/978-3-031-22829-2_10

New, more powerful attacks are needed to improve state-of-the-art research and contribute to the further security and more efficient evaluation of products. Findings should be shared in a reproducible manner to enable this process. There are cases where the research is done on open public targets, and the results can be shared entirely without restrictions. However, sometimes the data and the actual vulnerabilities of the products must be kept secret as sharing them could pose an economic, privacy, or security threat to target stakeholders. At the same time, it becomes difficult to reproduce the results or even fairly compare them against others without providing sufficient details. Thus, there is a need to enable the community to share the findings publicly without compromising stakeholders.

In this work, we consider sharing data from FI target characterization. We showcase our proposals on data from several types of fault injection - electromagnetic fault injection (EMFI) [19], laser fault injection (LFI) [27], and voltage glitching [3]. Usually, the results of target characterization are shown in a 2D figure with specific FI parameters on the x and y axis. For example, $x - y$ location of the laser or EM probe, or *pulse width* and *intensity* of the laser. We propose several methods to alter the obtained data from the characterization. Accordingly, we allow sharing results publicly while hiding the real vulnerabilities so malicious adversaries cannot directly abuse published information. Publishers can choose the modifications they desire to perform on the data. In this manner, the results of the fault injections and attacks can be published and discussed while the data remains secret. At the same time, transformed data should maintain the original distribution to remain relevant. We propose to use two known metrics to measure the similarity and relation to actual data. Our main contributions are:

1. We showcase that it is easy to recover the exact data points from the cartography (target characterization) figures.
2. We discuss several possible transformations and their effects. We define specific 2D transformations to transform data from 2D plots. We also propose polynomial transformations for transforming more dimensions when not considering the visual representation of the results.
3. We provide two techniques to evaluate the similarity of the original and transformed data and discuss how difficult it would be to reverse engineer the transformed data.

2   Background

2.1   Fault Injection and Target Characterization

Fault injection (FI) can be done physically at the hardware level [5]. Additionally, nowadays, it can also be done on software. However, we focus on fault injection for introducing faults at the hardware level. The idea is to expose the device to various harmful conditions and observe the behavior to determine its response. There are multiple ways to introduce the faults. For example, there are voltage [3] and clock glitching [2,9], temperature variations [26], optical injections [27], and electromagnetic radiation [22,25]. These techniques differ in equipment and cost, precision, and the number of parameters necessary to tune for a successful attack. Once the target is subjected to abnormal conditions (i.e., the external stimuli are introduced), we observe the effects on the device's behavior. Specifically, as analysts, we are interested in at what point the device would fail so that the device can be designed to be more resilient. That is especially important for security-critical devices, such as smartcards. Using previously mentioned techniques for injecting faults, the attacker can change the memory state in a device, cause a mistake in the computation (intermediate values), or skip instructions. Then, the attackers can exploit the faulty results to extract information about confidential data. Examples of these attacks are differential fault analysis (DFA) [4], fault sensitivity analysis (FSA) [15], differential fault intensity analysis (DFIA) [10], and statistical fault attacks (SFA) [8]. Not all faults can be used to reach the malicious goal with these attacks. Thus, the attackers must find a way to inject a fault that can be exploited. Consequently, the fault injection procedure can be divided into two phases: finding faults and using those faults to achieve some (malicious) goal. In this work, we need to be familiar with the first step of finding parameters from the search space that cause faults, i.e., producing the target characterization.

Numerous parameters must be defined for injecting the faults for all the mentioned injection methods. Optimal parameters (parameters that cause the target to show faulty behavior) can be searched manually or with an exhaustive or random search. However, manual testing and a random search are unreliable, as the optimal solutions can be easily overlooked. On the other hand, the exhaustive search is usually very time-consuming. There are many proposed alternatives for finding the optimal set of parameters for different types of fault injection. For example, methods from evolutionary optimization are utilized to improve voltage glitching [7,20,21], EMFI [16], and LFI [13]. Other techniques were also used, e.g., hyperparameter optimization techniques [28] and reinforcement learning [17]. However, while these methods provide a good approximation of specific points (regions), the search space for FI is complex. The issue when using such (intelligent) approaches is that the problem of coverage remains. The obtained optimal parameters are also specific to the setup and target. Finally, the methods need adjustments between different FI techniques. Improvements for conducting target characterization are also proposed in [29]. The methodology is based on finding a sensitivity curve whose generation is fast and compatible with different FI techniques and targets. Additionally, the authors discussed an approach based on deep learning to predict the complete target characterization based on limited data from the sensitivity curve.

2.2 Polynomial Functions

A polynomial with a single indeterminate x can be written in the form:

$$a_n x^n + a_{n-1} x^{n-1} + \cdots + a_2 x^2 + a_1 x + a_0 = \sum_{k=0}^{n} a_k x^k, \tag{1}$$

where $a_0, \ldots, a_n$ are coefficients of the polynomial, and x is indeterminate and can be replaced by any value. For example, x can be substituted with the FI parameters we desire to transform. Thus, we consider a function defined by the polynomial where x is the function's argument and is referred to as a variable:

$$f(x) = \sum_{k=0}^{n} a_k x^k.$$ (2)

2.3   Kullback-Leibler Divergence (KLD)

Kullback-Leibler Divergence (KLD) measures how one probability distribution differs from a second, reference probability distribution [14]. For example, one can consider two probability distributions, P and Q. P usually represents the data, the observations, or a measured probability distribution. On the other hand, distribution Q represents a theory, a model, or an approximation of P. KL divergence calculates how one distribution differs from another and is not symmetrical. Calculating the divergence for distributions P and Q would give a different score from Q and P. KLD is the non-negative measure that equals 0 if and only if $P = Q$. For discrete probability distributions P and Q defined on the same probability space, $\mathcal{X}$, KLD is defined as:

$$D_{KL}(P \parallel Q) = \sum_{x \in \mathcal{X}} P(x) \log\left(\frac{P(x)}{Q(x)}\right).$$ (3)

2.4   Canonical Correlation Analysis (CCA)

Canonical Correlation Analysis (CCA) is a method of correlating linear relationships between two multidimensional variables [11]. Proposed by Hotelling in 1936, CCA can be seen as the problem of finding basis vectors for two sets of variables. The correlations between the projections of the variables onto these basis vectors are mutually maximized. However, it has been used for measuring the similarity between different neural network layers [18,23]. CCA is invariant to linear transformations and can find shared structures across superficially dissimilar representations. If CCA converges to one, the two compared variables are highly correlated.

3   Motivation and Application

Let us assume that an Evaluator wants to share target characterization data with the general public, including interested researchers in academia, evaluation and certification labs, companies, and malicious parties. The Evaluator can be from academia, an evaluation lab, or a company. They want to either share that they successfully found vulnerabilities in a system previously considered secure or propose new methods for FI target analysis or attack. Sharing all the data helps the community find countermeasures and solutions for the observed vulnerabilities. Consequently, we improve the security of existing systems. Additionally, it is crucial for a fair comparison of the new methods. The data can be used for a public database with realistic data that can help to generalize solutions and benchmark methods and attacks. We can opt for using open public targets, but often these do not represent realistic scenarios. Therefore, the community tends to use targets used by the general public to work in a more realistic and relevant setting. The manufacturer can limit the amount of information shared from such research, which also applies to internal evaluation labs. Sharing data that directly exposes vulnerabilities to malicious parties can raise public concerns and economic threats.

To bridge this gap, we propose to use transformations and explore them in FI analysis. The data in the FI setup is the mentioned target characterization results, parameter values, and device responses to injections with those parameters. This data can be accompanied by target and bench setup information, parameter intervals, and utilized method. Sharing target information and parameter intervals with target characterization data directly reveals vulnerabilities for exploitation and are usually kept secret. With transformations, we motivate to share data at this level as it enables reproducibility and fair comparison. If data is transformed, the attacker cannot directly abuse reported data and speed up the attack process. They will still have to search the parameter space.

In our examples, we consider using brute force for reversing the transformations, as we assume that the authors provide all information on the transformations they applied and fault injection data. However, in a realistic scenario, we expect the author to report that the data is transformed. Still, we do not deem it necessary to report which specific transformations were used as long as data distribution remains close to the original.

4   Proposed Transformations

We consider transformations for altering and hiding results from fault injections. Multiple parameters define the injection during target characterization with any type of FI. For example, in LFI, the parameters can be x, y, *delay*, *pulse width*, and *intensity*. Usually, the results of target characterization are published in a 2D plot with two selected FI parameters on the x and y-axis [13,16,21]. We aim to hide the real vulnerabilities of the target with transformations, but we want to keep the transformed data relevant for publication. We propose 2D transformations on the interesting (vulnerable) points to keep their relative positions (shape they create), but we scale, rotate, and translate the shape.

Since we change only the interesting points, depending on the data, replacing the interesting data with a non-interesting class or randomizing non-interesting points over the whole region will be necessary. We consider both cases in the experiments and explain the choices. Another issue to consider when applying transformations is the possible assumptions that could exist between two parameters that are displayed. Thus, we adjust the transformations so that the resulting transformed data still conforms to the assumptions. For example, analysts expect normal behavior from the device with low absolute values for glitch voltage and length in voltage glitching. Contrary, with high values, we expect the device to reset or stop communication. Interesting responses are usually found between the two regions, and described relative positioning should be kept in transformed data. In our experiments, we use voltage glitching to showcase the changes in the transformations.

These transformations are only used for the selected two parameters shown as the target cartography in a 2D graph. However, we mentioned that all FI types have multiple parameters to set, so if we want to transform all of them and use more than two dimensions, then we propose to use polynomial transformations. These transformations keep the fault class distribution but randomize the data. Therefore, these are unsuitable for cases where we visually must keep the relative position of the classes as in the described voltage glitching case.

In the FI campaign, usually, an interval is defined for each of the parameters with a corresponding step. The step size usually corresponds to the physical properties of the setup. Consequently, we cannot use any value from the interval but only those allowed according to the step size. For the proposed transformations, to ensure we use the specific values, we transform the index of the parameter value instead of the value itself. The code is publicly available[1].

4.1   2D Transformations

Every point in the 2D plot is defined with the x and y coordinates. Note that any two parameters of any FI technique can be set on the x and y-axis. This can be *intensity* and *pulse width* in LFI or EMFI, or x and y location of the laser spot or EM probe on the target. As mentioned, we will rotate, scale, and translate our interesting area (shape) over the target area. We perform rotation with expressions $x_t = x \cos\theta - y \sin\theta$ and $y_t = x \sin\theta + y \cos\theta$. Here, θ is the angle of the rotation. While rotation can be done around any specified point, this formula and what we use in our transformations rotate points around the coordinate system's $(0,0)$ point. We allow scaling to a minimum of 20% of the entire range for x and y, so the area does not become overly small. For the maximum, we can scale the interesting set of parameters to the entire area. However, we do not necessarily scale equally on both axes, so we can also get the stretching effect. The percentage for the minimum size can be adjusted depending on the real results. To perform the scaling and shifting, we select the starting points (lower bounds) for x and y. The upper bound is then defined with the lower bound and interval size. This way, depending on the lower bound, we have the shift, and depending on the interval, we have scaling.

As mentioned, we need to adjust the transformations for the cases where we must conform to the assumptions we described. Firstly, we limit the angles for the rotation of the interesting area. Secondly, instead of scale and shift, we stretch over both axes and cause a more dense area on other parts. We show this in our experiments with the voltage glitching results, and the reasons are more apparent when we can see the effects visually in the plotted results.

---

[1] The code is available at https://github.com/marinakrcek/transformations_FI.

4.2   Polynomial Transformations

The explained 2D transformations are used only on two FI parameters shown in a 2D graph within the publication. However, if we want to consider altering the data using all the parameters, then we propose polynomial transformations. We consider these transformations to randomize the non-interesting points or interesting points to lose shape but keep the distribution of fault classes.

We can transform each parameter using a polynomial with different coefficients. We refer to these transformations as *local transformations*. These are used to break the relative positioning of the points. We can also run a *global transformation* that simultaneously transforms all data using the same coefficients for the whole set of parameter combinations. These are used to shift and scale the points. During transformations, the values may get out of bounds, so we have three options for resolving those situations. First, we can *clip* the values, meaning that if the transformed index is out of bounds, we clip it to a lower or higher bound depending on which is closer. Another option is the *modulo* operation (remainder of a division), where if the value is out of bounds, we will calculate a modulo with the number of possible values. Lastly, we have *scale*, where the values are scaled to the original parameter interval. While *modulo* and *clip* can be done immediately after transforming each parameter combination, scaling is done after we transform all the data. This way, we obtain the transformed intervals for the parameters used to scale to the original intervals.

To define the polynomial, the user sets the degree of the polynomial, and the coefficients are selected uniformly at random from user-defined intervals or expressions to define the interval. We can also define a specific polynomial function that controls the output of the transformation, but as we want to randomize the data, we keep the coefficients random. We report the coefficient intervals we used in the presented experimental results. We have a coefficient a_0 not multiplied by the variable x, allowing larger values for this coefficient. We limit the possible values by a maximum of 20% of the allowed values of the parameter. Thus, there is a different interval for the coefficient for each parameter. For global transformation, we use a parameter with the least possible values. For the next coefficient, a_1, we set the allowed interval to $[-2, 2)$. The issue is that the changes will be small with the small indexes, even if the number of allowed values for that parameter is large. We, therefore, allow negative coefficients, as we can still have larger changes depending on the chosen way of handling the out-of-scope values. Other coefficients are defined to achieve lower coefficients for higher polynomial coefficients with the expression $0.5^{(degree-2-i)}$, where $degree$ is the defined polynomial degree. We add the term -2 as intervals for coefficients a_1 and a_0 are already defined. i is the counter from $degree - 2$ to zero. These coefficients must get smaller as x has larger exponents because, in our case, x is an index, a positive value that can get rather large as the exponents get larger.

We noticed that the polynomial of degree 1 is sufficient, and larger polynomial degrees do not change the data in any other different pattern than visible with the polynomial of degree 1. The difference is that the changes are more significant, which is quite prominent with clipping, as more points get clipped to maximum or minimum values for the parameters. We tested several other combinations of the coefficient intervals and expressions with smaller and larger values. Our search is not exhaustive, but we noticed similar behavior with larger coefficients as with larger polynomial degrees. Also, the benefit of using the global transformation after the local one is that the data is not spread over the whole parameter 2D space but usually occupies a smaller region of a rectangular or oval shape.

5   Utilized Data Examples

To allow evaluation of the proposed transformations, we need relevant examples of target characterizations. We do not use real confidential data because we cannot show the original data and its transformed data. Instead, we use published work and one simulated example.

First, we use an example from [16] with a graph of Electromagnetic FI (EMFI) showing x-y locations on the target and corresponding fault classes. The authors use RESET, NORMAL, CHANGING, and SUCCESS fault classes. Since we investigate different examples, we use the fault class names MUTE, PASS, CHANGING, and FAIL, which correspond to the mentioned fault classes. As we did not have the original data, we extracted it from the pixels of the image. Similarly, attackers could obtain results from published figures to get precise data points. Note that the attacker can take the interval and search only in that area, which is more efficient than mounting a complete characterization. However, extracting from the pixels is more specific and speeds up an attack. With transformations, we want to prevent this. Additionally, we show another example that corresponds well with possible LFI or EMFI campaign results, showing x-y locations on the target in the 2D plots. For this example, we also show 3D plots with intensity on the z-axis. The third example is somewhat different, where glitch voltage and length are on the x and y-axis. The data is obtained in the same manner as for the EMFI data example from [21]. This example represents parameters for which analysts have some assumptions. Specifically, in this case, the assumption is that we expect normal behavior from the device (PASS) with a low values combination of those parameters. Contrary, with high values for that combination of parameters, one would expect the device to reset or stop communication (MUTE). The interesting FAIL responses are usually situated on a border between the two regions which analysts try to find during characterization. Another example of such parameters would be laser intensity and pulse width for LFI.

Reverse Engineering Data Points from Figures. There are online tools, such as Webplotdigitizer[2] [24] or PlotDigitizer[3] [1], where one can upload an image, and after aligning the x and y axes, it is possible to extract the information

---

[2] https://automeris.io/WebPlotDigitizer/.
[3] https://plotdigitizer.com/.

about certain points from the plot. However, we used Python Imaging Library to read the pixels as it was easier to save the data for later transformations. Each pixel defined with its location has an RGB (Red Green Blue) code - an array with three values for determining the color. From the legend, we can learn the color of each fault class in the plot. From the range information on each axis, we can scale the data from pixels to the actual scope of the parameters. In this manner, we obtain the parameter values from the image and the device's response per parameter combination.

6   Experimental Results

6.1   Electromagnetic Fault Injection (EMFI) Case

Transformations. We start with the EMFI case, where the authors presented information about the device, its size, used intervals, and the obtained results [16]. The results from the original paper are presented in Fig. 1a. As previously explained, we extracted the data from pixels in the image, and the result is visible in Fig. 1b. As mentioned, we recommend polynomial transformations for randomizing the data, and they are specifically useful for more than two dimensions when we do not care about visual results. Nevertheless, we first show results using polynomial transformations to showcase their issue when using them for the visual representation of the results. Transformed data is visible in Fig. 2. We transform the interesting points while the non-interesting (PASS) remain the same. In Fig. 2a, we show a polynomial of degree 1 with the clip method for values out of bounds. Here, the original interesting area is visible as an empty area as we did not replace the points, neither we alter the rest of the non-interesting points. The clip method is noticeable in the edges of the rectangular shape. In the setting without global transformation, the values are on the borders of the plot. The global transformation translated and scaled the interesting area after local transformations. With larger polynomial degrees (2 and 3), more values

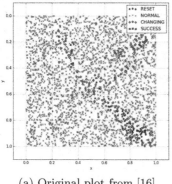 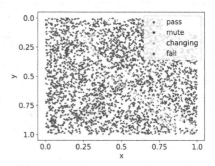

(a) Original plot from [16].   (b) Extracted data from Figure 1a.

Fig. 1. Original cartography from [16] and extracted data from the image.

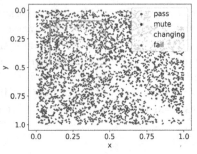 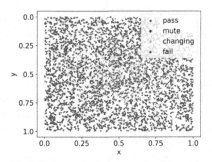

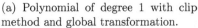

(a) Polynomial of degree 1 with clip method and global transformation.

(b) Polynomial of degree 1 with scale method and global transformation.

Fig. 2. Polynomial transformations on cartography shown in Fig. 1.

are clipped and end in the image's corners. Next, we show the results with the scale method in Fig. 2b, which rounds the interesting points around the central point in the image. Also, we replace the interesting points in the original data with a non-interesting class as we want to cover the empty space in the plot that indicates where the interesting points were located. The difference between results with and without global transformations is the translation of the central point and scaling. The points converge more to the central point with a higher polynomial degree and larger coefficients. We also tested the modulo method with the same example. The transformation results with modulo are that the data is fully randomized over the whole area if global transformation is not used. Similarly, global transformation can shift and scale the area, and the interesting area can become a smaller rectangular shape. The resulting shapes of the interesting area are very different from the original data. Still, if we do not consider the visual shapes, we can use the transformations on more dimensions for statistical analysis.

We now show two different 2D transformations on the extracted data from [16]. First, we have the transformation results shown in Fig. 3a we refer to as transformation T1. The issue with the result of T1 is the overlap with the interesting area in the original cartography. An example without such an overlap is preferred and visible in Fig. 3b as transformation T2. Non-interesting points replace the original interesting area as before. Transformation preserves the shape from the original cartography, but it is rotated, scaled, and moved to another region. Thus, the attacker could focus on the area shown in the figure and miss the actual interesting area. Finally, the actual values of x and y on corresponding axes are hidden by normalizing the data. Without knowing the parameter intervals, we do not know if the whole target was tested or only a specific smaller part.

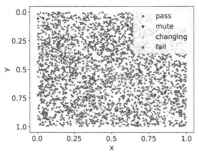
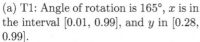

(a) T1: Angle of rotation is 165°, x is in the interval [0.01, 0.99], and y in [0.28, 0.99].

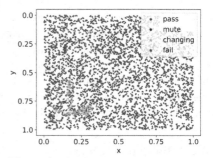

(b) T2: Angle of rotation is 310°, x is in the interval [0.05, 0.32], and y in [0.55, 0.93].

Fig. 3. 2D transformations on cartography shown in Fig. 1.

Note that x-y target characterizations can end in different unique shapes. Therefore, one can consider that knowing the shape can still help the attackers make more efficient attacks. So, depending on the wanted level of security, we can change the shape with local polynomial transformations or with more specific transformations for different shapes.

Reversing Transformed Data. Now, we discuss how an attacker could find the correct transformation presented in a certain work. We consider that the attacker knows what transformations are used, and we also assume that the attacker knows the intervals for the parameters. We investigate how many possible transformations there are and how long it would take to reach the original cartography with a brute-force approach.

Since we use rotations on the interesting area, we have 360 possible rotations. For scale and shift, the number of possibilities depends on the number of possible values of the parameters for the x and y axes. The number of possible transformations is calculated with the following formula for each parameter:

$$\frac{n(n+1)}{2}, n = \lceil 0.8 \cdot nb\_values \rceil + 1. \tag{4}$$

nb_values is the number of possible values for a specific parameter. As previously explained, we select the interval size and the lower bound to define the shift and scaling. The possibilities for the interval size are between 20% of the possible values and all possible values. Depending on the selected size, there are more or fewer possibilities to set the lower bound of the new interval. For example, if we uniformly at random select that the size of the interval is 20% of all possible values for that parameter, then the number of possibilities for the lower bound is the highest - 80% of the total number of possible values for the parameter. If, on the other hand, the selected size is all the possible values of the parameter, then there is only one possibility for choosing the lower bound. In the end, we have a sum of options calculated with the expression above.

In the case of EMFI cartography, with 481 possible values for both x and y, we have 74 691 possibilities for each, which in combination gives $\approx 5.58 \times 10^9$ options. With rotations, we have $\approx 2.01 \times 10^{12}$ possible transformations in this setting. If it takes 1 ms to test one possible transformation, it will take around 63 years to test all combinations. Therefore, if we consider the attack setting as described, it would take too long for the attacker to test all transformations and find the correct one in a reasonable time.

6.2   Simulated Case

We test the transformations on another example of a specific shape found with a fault injection campaign. We consider it to represent the x-y cartography of the EMFI or LFI campaign. The example does not correspond to any target or real cartography but is a good example as it highlights possible issues with the current transformations.

Transformation. We refer to the cartography presented in Fig. 4a as the original cartography, and we transform the data shown in that plot. We initially transform the data in the same way as in the previous example, and the result is visible in Fig. 4b. We replace the originally interesting area with a non-interesting area. However, since the area has a specific shape and many interesting points when replaced by a non-interesting fault class, we still see where the previous location was. In the following transformation in Fig. 4c do not replace the interesting area with a non-interesting fault class. Additionally, the interesting area is far from the original, interesting area, which is the desired result. However, we still notice that the non-interesting points are denser in the area close to the originally interesting area, which could help attackers find the real vulnerabilities. Since polynomial transformations are good for randomizing the data, we perform the local polynomial transformation of degree 1 with the modulo method, but only for the non-interesting fault class. We selected modulo as it was shown in our previous experiments that it had the best ability to spread the points over the entire target area. The result is a plot in Fig. 4d, where we see that the points are randomized over the whole target area, and there are no particularly dense areas to attract attention. In this transformation, the new interesting area is again not close to the actual interesting area hiding the real vulnerable locations. Here, we do not disclose the coefficients of the polynomials as they are selected uniformly at random from previously described intervals for each non-interesting x-y combination.

Reversing Transformed Data. In this setting, we have 32 896 interval combinations for x, and 61 075 for y, which equals $\approx 2.01 \times 10^9$ combinations in total. Again, we add the rotations and reach $\approx 7.23 \times 10^{11}$ combinations. In this case, we would need 22.94 years to test all transformation combinations if testing one transformation takes 1 ms. While we need less time to test all the transformations, it is still unreasonable to consider brute force.

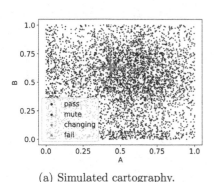

(a) Simulated cartography.

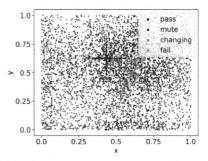

(b) T1: Angle of rotation is **239°**, x is in the interval [0, 0.97], and y in [0.01, 0.95].

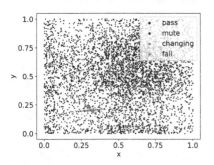

(c) T2: Angle of rotation is **15°**, x is in the interval [0.14, 0.56], and y in [0.08, 0.28].

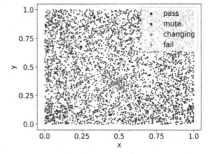

(d) T3: Angle of rotation is **134°**, x is in the interval [0.17, 0.99], and y in [0.01, 1]. The polynomial transformation is used for non-interesting points.

Fig. 4. Simulated cartography with its transformations.

3D Plot. Additionally, we show that we can transform data for figures that display three different parameters in a 3D plot. We use transformed data shown in a 2D plot in Fig. 4c and add the intensity to the z-axis. Figure 5a shows the data in 3D with the original intensity values without showing the non-interesting points for better visibility of the interesting area. As with other parameters, we also normalize the data for the z-axis. Hiding the actual intensity values by normalizing them could be enough. If we do not specify the range we used and disclose the information about the bench and the laser, it would be hard for an attacker to reverse the intensity values. However, we can randomize the intensity as well. Figure 5b shows the transformation of intensity in a way that for every point, a new random intensity was selected. On the other hand, in Fig. 5c, we map all possible values of the intensity to another intensity value. Then, the original intensity value gets replaced by the preselected random intensity value for every point. The values of the intensity can repeat in this setting. Thus, we add another option where we create unique mappings and use those to alter the intensity values. This transformation is visible in Fig. 5d.

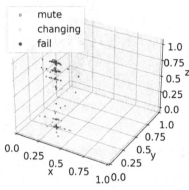

(a) Original intensity values.

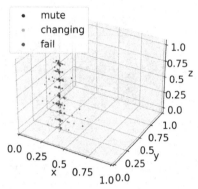

(b) Intensity values set uniformly at random for each data point.

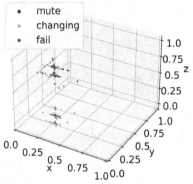

(c) Intensity values mapped to intensity values with possible repetition.

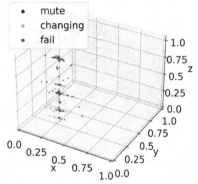

(d) Intensity values mapped to unique intensity values.

Fig. 5. T2 (Fig. 4c) of simulated cartography with transformations for the intensity on z-axis.

6.3   Voltage Glitching Case

The last use case is based on voltage glitching experiments presented in [21]. The original results are in Fig. 6a. There is glitch voltage on the x-axis, and on the y-axis is the glitch length. In this case, contrary to x-y locations, there are generally applicable assumptions for the target's responses depending on the glitch voltage/length values we already described. The analysts search for the boundary between the two regions. Therefore, we want to adhere to the assumptions by keeping the relations with transformed data but hiding the actual border between the classes where the device behaves as expected (PASS) and resets or stops communication (MUTE).

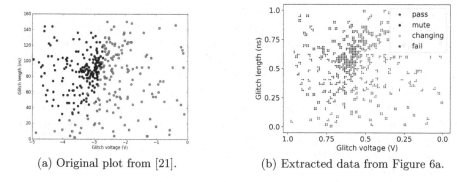

(a) Original plot from [21].   (b) Extracted data from Figure 6a.

Fig. 6. Original cartography from [21] and extracted data from the image.

Transformation. First, we extract the data from the original plot (Fig. 6a), and the result is visible in Fig. 6b. Note that the real parameter values are visible in the original plot, but we display plots with normalized values. Considering the assumptions, we care about absolute values, so the value −5 for the glitch voltage is replaced with 1.

The issue with the transformation we used for x-y characterization is that the boundary between interesting and non-interesting areas would not align with the mentioned assumptions. Suppose we can rotate the interesting area with any of the 360 angles. In that case, we can get a transformation where the border is not between the regions but at the plot's far left. On the other hand, if we rotate all the points, we can get a plot indicating the opposite response of the target - lowest values lead to MUTE and highest to PASS class. Moreover, it might be enough for these types of parameters to normalize the data. If we do not specify the range we used, it would be hard for an attacker to reproduce the injections. However, we still slightly adjusted the transformations by limiting the possibilities of previous transformations to conform with the assumptions for the glitch voltage-length parameters. Firstly, we do not allow all possible angle rotations but only from $[-80°, 30°]$, which we defined using the trial-and-error approach by visually checking if the assumptions still hold. The parameter combinations with FAIL fault class stay close to the border with a non-interesting area and do not invert to the opposite side using defined rotations. Previously, if we scaled and shifted only the interesting area, we lost the relative positioning of the MUTE and PASS classes. Instead, we make data points more dense or sparse by splitting the data below and above certain values on the x and y-axis. Then, we select new splitting x and y values and scale the data. Scaling is done so that the points above the first selected value remain above the newly selected splitting value and analogously for points below the selected values. Let us assume we selected a value x_1 and then x_2. In this case, the points below x_1 will be scaled from 0 to x_2. The value of x_2 can be lower or higher than the x_1. If x_2 is lower than x_1, the points will be denser; otherwise, the points will be more stretched as the interval increases. The results of these transformations are visible in Fig. 7. We can see that the relative positions of the different areas remain in both figures. In the T1 transformation in Fig. 7a, the FAIL points are close to the original border but rotated so that lower glitch length leads to those points. In the T2 transformation, the MUTE area is stretched, while the PASS area is denser since the border is moved to the right. As the data is stretched, the points become sparse in some areas. The exploration with algorithms is usually random over the whole search space, so one cannot expect such sparse testing in specific regions. Thus, we need to consider this for publishing the results. However, an algorithm used in this example converges to FAIL outcomes. The sparseness is explained by convergence in the algorithm, also visible in the original cartography.

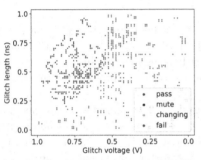

(a) T1: Angle of rotation is -53°. No change on x. y moved from 0.36 to 0.44.

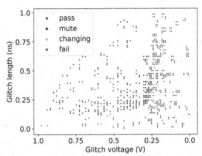

(b) T2: Angle of rotation is -4°. x moved from 0.67 to 0.31 and y from 0.44 to 0.27.

Fig. 7. Transformations of the glitching example (Fig. 6a).

Reversing Transformed Data. With the described transformations, we have even fewer possible transformations. The reason is fewer possible values for the parameters and limited possibilities because the transformations need to conform to the assumptions. We allow 110 possible rotations, and the splitting points are between 20% and 80% of all possible voltage or glitch length values. From 100 possible values for voltage, we allow 60, and from 75 possibilities for length, we have 45. In total, that is 7.29×10^6 possibilities, and after adding the rotations we have 8.019×10^8 possible transformations. It will take 9.28 days to try all combinations if one takes 1ms. That is much less time to test all combinations than in the previous examples. However, as already mentioned, hiding the parameter ranges, in this case, could be enough.

6.4   Evaluating the Effect of Transformations

To evaluate the effect of transformation, we use Kullback-Leibler divergence (KLD) and Canonical Correlation Analysis (CCA). KLD and CCA evaluate how similar the transformed data is to the original data. KLD is used to compare the distribution of fault classes and data points between original and transformed data, while CCA indicates the level of correlation between the two data sets. Since our transformations use randomness, with CCA, we measure if the transformed data has been randomized to a point where there is almost no correlation with the original data. While this was more critical for polynomial transformations, we kept it for the 2D transformations. Note that the implementation of CCA is taken from the public GitHub repository[4] [18,23].

Using the notation from the previous KLD definition, we consider the data from true cartography (target characterization) as the reference probability P and the probability of the transformed data as Q. We compute how the distribution from the transformed data differs from the true data for fault classes and utilized parameter values. The probability distribution for KLD is obtained by finding the frequency of each possible value for parameters in true and transformed data. We calculate KLD for each parameter and show the mean KLD in Table 1. Similarly, we calculate the KLD for fault class distribution. On the other hand, since we replace the original interesting area with a non-interesting fault class in some examples, we effectively add the newly transformed data to the existing one. For this reason, there is a different number of data points in the original and transformed data, and to calculate the CCA, we need to have the same number of data points. In most cases, we only transform the interesting area, so we calculate the CCA only on the interesting points. However, when possible, we show CCA on all data points, which is visible in the same Table 1. Occasionally, there could be overlaps and, with that, a possible change in fault class distribution, but this remains low, as visible by the KLD in all cases. The difference between the data's original and transformed distribution of parameter values remains low in the EMFI example. In the simulated example, with each transformation, the KLD increased. In T1, the original interesting area was replaced with non-interesting points. Then in T2, we removed this, and KLD increased. Lastly, we used polynomials to randomize the PASS fault class, resulting in a higher KLD because all the points have been modified. However, the worst situation is in the example with voltage glitching, as KLD is very high. This example's number of data points is lower than in other examples. Thus, many possible points are not tested, so the difference in the value distributions is high. CCA converges nicely to one, meaning original and transformed data are highly correlated. However, with the simulated example, when we calculate CCA for the interesting points, it is below 0.5. For T2, CCA calculated on all data points is close to 1 as points of the PASS class remain the same. On the other hand, with T3 transformation, CCA is almost zero because as the PASS is randomized, all data points are different. The issue might be the specific shape and the number of altered points. Visual inspection still provides the best indication for publishing, but these metrics offer good insight into the performed modifications. Metrics show that the transformations keep the fault class distributions and remain correlated with the original data.

---

[4] https://github.com/google/svcca.

Table 1. Kullback-Leibler Divergence (KLD) and Canonical Correlation Analysis (CCA). By default, CCA is calculated only on data points of interesting fault classes.

	EMFI			Simulated				Voltage glitching			
	KLD for classes	KLD for parameter values	CCA on interesting data	KLD for classes	KLD for parameter values	CCA on interesting data	CCA on all data points	KLD for classes	KLD for parameter values	CCA on interesting data	CCA on all data points
T1	0.0039	0.0138	0.9999	0.0069	0.0053	0.4243	/	0.0035	10.679	0.9953	0.9221
T2	0.0186	0.0275	0.9999	0.0045	0.2172	0.2895	0.9355	0.0035	4.6081	0.9851	0.8684
T3	/	/	/	0.0001	0.3503	0.3738	0.0275	/	/	/	/

7   Conclusion and Future Work

This work provides several techniques for transforming the target characterization results to hide sensitive information. Indeed, we show that from a figure (a typical representation of a characterization experiment), one could easily obtain the exact data points leading to a fault. We discuss various transformations and analyze the results for three different scenarios showing that using transformations significantly hinders the possibility of reverse-engineering the data from graphs. Additionally, we show that our transformations maintain the correct information about the data distribution and are highly correlated with the original data, making the transformed figures relevant. We show these transformations provide additional layers of hiding confidential data. We discuss potential cases where such transformations could be useful, and with that, we try to motivate Evaluators to share more data as it can lead to improved benchmarking and, consequently, the security of different systems against fault injections.

Proposed transformations are rather simple, which makes them easy to apply. However, more research should be done to provide guarantees on the effort to reverse the data. Furthermore, we aim to explore how to make automated transformations. Current experiments still require an expert with knowledge about the nature of parameters to select appropriate transformations. Building a rule-based system that can transform the data while maintaining the relevant assumptions would be interesting.

Acknowledgements. We thank the reviewers for their time and feedback, especially shepherd Shivam Bhasin.

References

1. PlotDigitizer: Version 2.2 (2022). https://plotdigitizer.com
2. Agoyan, M., Dutertre, J.-M., Naccache, D., Robisson, B., Tria, A.: When clocks fail: on critical paths and clock faults. In: Gollmann, D., Lanet, J.-L., Iguchi-Cartigny, J. (eds.) CARDIS 2010. LNCS, vol. 6035, pp. 182–193. Springer, Heidelberg (2010). https://doi.org/10.1007/978-3-642-12510-2_13
3. Aumüller, C., Bier, P., Fischer, W., Hofreiter, P., Seifert, J.-P.: Fault attacks on RSA with CRT: concrete results and practical countermeasures. In: Kaliski, B.S., Koç, K., Paar, C. (eds.) CHES 2002. LNCS, vol. 2523, pp. 260–275. Springer, Heidelberg (2003). https://doi.org/10.1007/3-540-36400-5_20

4. Biham, E., Shamir, A.: Differential fault analysis of secret key cryptosystems. In: Kaliski, B.S. (ed.) CRYPTO 1997. LNCS, vol. 1294, pp. 513–525. Springer, Heidelberg (1997). https://doi.org/10.1007/BFb0052259

5. Boneh, D., DeMillo, R.A., Lipton, R.J.: On the importance of checking cryptographic protocols for faults. In: Fumy, W. (ed.) EUROCRYPT 1997. LNCS, vol. 1233, pp. 37–51. Springer, Heidelberg (1997). https://doi.org/10.1007/3-540-69053-0_4

6. Breier, J., Hou, X.: How practical are fault injection attacks, really? Cryptology ePrint Archive, Paper 2022/301 (2022). https://eprint.iacr.org/2022/301

7. Carpi, R.B., Picek, S., Batina, L., Menarini, F., Jakobovic, D., Golub, M.: Glitch it if you can: parameter search strategies for successful fault injection. In: Francillon, A., Rohatgi, P. (eds.) CARDIS 2013. LNCS, vol. 8419, pp. 236–252. Springer, Cham (2014). https://doi.org/10.1007/978-3-319-08302-5_16

8. Fuhr, T., Jaulmes, E., Lomné, V., Thillard, A.: Fault attacks on AES with faulty ciphertexts only. In: 2013 Workshop on Fault Diagnosis and Tolerance in Cryptography, pp. 108–118. IEEE (2013)

9. Fukunaga, T., Takahashi, J.: Practical fault attack on a cryptographic LSI with iso/iec 18033-3 block ciphers. In: 2009 Workshop on Fault Diagnosis and Tolerance in Cryptography (FDTC), pp. 84–92. IEEE (2009)

10. Ghalaty, N.F., Yuce, B., Taha, M., Schaumont, P.: Differential fault intensity analysis. In: 2014 Workshop on Fault Diagnosis and Tolerance in Cryptography, pp. 49–58. IEEE (2014)

11. Hardoon, D.R., Szedmak, S., Shawe-Taylor, J.: Canonical correlation analysis: an overview with application to learning methods. Neural Comput. 16(12), 2639–2664 (2004). https://doi.org/10.1162/0899766042321814

12. Kocher, P., Jaffe, J., Jun, B.: Differential power analysis. In: Wiener, M. (eds.) Advances in Cryptology – CRYPTO 1999. CRYPTO 1999. LNCS, vol. 1666, pp. 388–397. Springer, Heidelberg (1999). https://doi.org/10.1007/3-540-48405-1_25

13. Krček, M., Fronte, D., Picek, S.: On the importance of initial solutions selection in fault injection. In: 2021 Workshop on Fault Detection and Tolerance in Cryptography (FDTC), pp. 1–12 (2021). https://doi.org/10.1109/FDTC53659.2021.00011

14. Kullback, S., Leibler, R.A.: On information and sufficiency. Ann. Math. Stat. 22(1), 79–86 (1951)

15. Li, Y., Sakiyama, K., Gomisawa, S., Fukunaga, T., Takahashi, J., Ohta, K.: Fault sensitivity analysis. In: Mangard, S., Standaert, F.-X. (eds.) CHES 2010. LNCS, vol. 6225, pp. 320–334. Springer, Heidelberg (2010). https://doi.org/10.1007/978-3-642-15031-9_22

16. Maldini, A., Samwel, N., Picek, S., Batina, L.: Genetic algorithm-based electromagnetic fault injection. In: 2018 Workshop on Fault Diagnosis and Tolerance in Cryptography (FDTC), pp. 35–42. IEEE (2018)

17. Moradi, M., Oakes, B.J., Saraoglu, M., Morozov, A., Janschek, K., Denil, J.: Exploring fault parameter space using reinforcement learning-based fault injection. In: 2020 50th Annual IEEE/IFIP International Conference on Dependable Systems and Networks Workshops (DSN-W), pp. 102–109. IEEE (2020)

18. Morcos, A., Raghu, M., Bengio, S.: Insights on representational similarity in neural networks with canonical correlation. In: Bengio, S., Wallach, H., Larochelle, H., Grauman, K., Cesa-Bianchi, N., Garnett, R. (eds.) Advances in Neural Information Processing Systems, vol. 31, pp. 5732–5741. Curran Associates, Inc. (2018). http://papers.nips.cc/paper/7815-insights-on-representational-similarity-in-neural-networks-with-canonical-correlation.pdf

19. Moro, N., Dehbaoui, A., Heydemann, K., Robisson, B., Encrenaz, E.: Electromagnetic fault injection: towards a fault model on a 32-bit microcontroller. In: 2013 Workshop on Fault Diagnosis and Tolerance in Cryptography, pp. 77–88. IEEE (2013)

20. Picek, S., Batina, L., Buzing, P., Jakobovic, D.: Fault injection with a new flavor: memetic algorithms make a difference. In: Mangard, S., Poschmann, A.Y. (eds.) COSADE 2014. LNCS, vol. 9064, pp. 159–173. Springer, Cham (2015). https://doi.org/10.1007/978-3-319-21476-4_11

21. Picek, S., Batina, L., Jakobović, D., Carpi, R.B.: Evolving genetic algorithms for fault injection attacks. In: 2014 37th International Convention on Information and Communication Technology, Electronics and Microelectronics (MIPRO), pp. 1106–1111. IEEE (2014)

22. Quisquater, J.J.: Eddy current for magnetic analysis with active sensor. Proc. Esmart **2002**, 185–194 (2002)

23. Raghu, M., Gilmer, J., Yosinski, J., Sohl-Dickstein, J.: SVCCA: singular vector canonical correlation analysis for deep learning dynamics and interpretability. In: Guyon, I., Luxburg, U.V., Bengio, S., Wallach, H., Fergus, R., Vishwanathan, S., Garnett, R. (eds.) Advances in Neural Information Processing Systems, vol. 30, pp. 6076–6085. Curran Associates, Inc. (2017). http://papers.nips.cc/paper/7188-svcca-singular-vector-canonical-correlation-analysis-for-deep-learning-dynamics-and-interpretability.pdf

24. Rohatgi, A.: Webplotdigitizer: Version 4.5 (2021). https://automeris.io/WebPlotDigitizer

25. Schmidt, J.M., Hutter, M.: Optical and EM fault-attacks on CRT-based RSA: Concrete results.na (2007)

26. Skorobogatov, S.: Low temperature data remanence in static RAM. Technical report. UCAM-CL-TR-536, University of Cambridge, Computer Laboratory, June 2002. https://doi.org/10.48456/tr-536

27. Picek, S., Batina, L., Buzing, P., Jakobovic, D.: Fault injection with a new flavor: memetic algorithms make a difference. In: Mangard, S., Poschmann, A.Y. (eds.) COSADE 2014. LNCS, vol. 9064, pp. 159–173. Springer, Cham (2015). https://doi.org/10.1007/978-3-319-21476-4_11

28. Werner, V., Maingault, L., Potet, M.L.: Fast calibration of fault injection equipment with hyperparameter optimization techniques. In: Grosso, V., Pöppelmann, T. (eds.) Smart Card Research and Advanced Applications. CARDIS 2021. LNCS, vol. 13173, pp. 121–138. Springer, Cham (2021). https://doi.org/10.1007/978-3-030-97348-3_7

29. Wu, L., Ribera, G., Beringuier-Boher, N., Picek, S.: A fast characterization method for semi-invasive fault injection attacks. In: Jarecki, S. (ed.) CT-RSA 2020. LNCS, vol. 12006, pp. 146–170. Springer, Cham (2020). https://doi.org/10.1007/978-3-030-40186-3_8

Dual-Tone Multi-Frequency Assisted Acoustic Side Channel Attack to Retrieve Dialled Call Log

Abhishek Revskar, Mahendra Rathor, and Urbi Chatterjee[✉]

Department of Computer Science and Engineering, Indian Institute of Technology
Kanpur, Kanpur, India
{abhishekdr,rmahendra,urbic}@cse.iitk.ac.in

Abstract. Acoustic side channel attack (SCA) is a type of SCA which exploits the sounds emitted by computers or other devices to retrieve the sensitive information, without requiring the adversary to perform any mathematical cryptanalysis. Recently, acoustic SCA has been exploited by attackers to breach the security of mobile devices. A malicious application installed in the mobile devices can access and take control of system components such as microphone, gyroscope, camera, etc. As users may not be aware of the security guarantee of the malicious applications, they can blindly trust and download such applications in their mobile phones and grant access to unnecessary permission. This security vulnerability can be exploited by an attacker to retrieve user sensitive information and compromise the user privacy. In this paper, a novel Dual-Tone Multi-Frequency (DTMF) assisted acoustic side channel attack is proposed to retrieve dialled call log from mobile devices. In this attack, an adversary can infer the call log or phone numbers dialed by the victims on their devices by gaining access to the in-built microphone. To the best of our knowledge, the proposed acoustic SCA is the first work in the literature that exploits the standards of DTMF to uniquely identify each key/digit dialed on the dialling keypad. In the proposed acoustic SCA methodology, we infer the keys/digits dialed by the victims by first analyzing the recordings of sounds produced from dialed digits and then finding the frequency distribution for each digit using Fast Fourier Transform (FFT). Further, the characteristic frequencies of the keys/digits are matched against the DTMF specifications to uniquely identify them. Further, we have trained the machine learning (ML) models to facilitate the prediction of the call log or the phone numbers dialed by the victim. The proposed attack is device-independent and is capable of predicting the phone numbers dialed in one device while training the ML models on the other. The prediction accuracy of the proposed approach is achieved to be 100% because of exploiting the standards of DTMF which are common for all the communication devices across the globe.

Keywords: Acoustic side channel attack · Dual-Tone
Multi-Frequency · Fast Fourier Transform · Machine learning

© The Author(s), under exclusive license to Springer Nature Switzerland AG 2022
L. Batina et al. (Eds.): SPACE 2022, LNCS 13783, pp. 185–203, 2022.
https://doi.org/10.1007/978-3-031-22829-2_11

1 Introduction

Side Channel Attacks (SCAs) have been analyzed rigorously and launched successfully on hardware and embedded systems to leak the secret key over the past two decades. Side channels bring forth the state information about the implementation which might not be captured by the classical adversaries [1]. For example, crypto-processors generally have variable execution time to process the data-dependent operations. By using the timing side channel, an adversary can measure the time required for the secret key operation and retrieve some important information about the secret key which can help the adversary to launch a successful SCA. In [2], it was shown that the adversary can extract the secret key of RSA [3] and Diffie-Hellman [4] key exchange by analyzing the timing information with known ciphertext. Similarly, other types of side channels can be exploited to leak some secret information (e.g. key) such as power side channel [5] and electromagnetic radiations (EM) etc. In power side channel [5], an adversary measures the power consumption of a hardware platform while running the cryptographic algorithms and try to relate it with the secret key (Simple Power Attacks) or the differential of an intermediate state between two consecutive rounds of the cipher depending upon the secret key (Differential Power Attacks). In EM side channel, an attacker tries to extract the secret key by collecting the EM radiations of an embedded system during the execution of the cipher using EM probe. Then the secret key can be extracted using the EM side channel traces.

Sometimes, the device platforms are so vulnerable that an attack can be launched to breach the privacy without even touching the crypto-module. This is possible because of some other types of side channels such as acoustic [6], thermal emission [7], magnetic [8] etc. Among these, acoustic-channels may be formed of audible or non-audible signals which are produced by a transmitter/speaker or executing specific processes on the processing unit of the computer [9]. Acoustic side channel attack leverages computer or device acoustics to get sensitive information without mathematical cryptanalysis. Recently, it has been found that the acoustic emanations produced by electronic devices can be used to infer the operations and data entered by the users in their systems and can present a serious threat to user privacy. Some existing works have highlighted that the sounds resulting from keyboard typing can be exploited to learn information about the entered data [10]. Asonov and Agrawal [11] have showed that the frequency features from the sound emanations of various keyboard clicks can be extracted to infer the different keys. Whereas in an another work, an acoustic side channel attack has been launched on additive manufacturing systems like 3D printers to infer the object that is being printed [12]. However, the above mentioned approaches of acoustic SCA did not target the security of smartphones or mobile devices. Instead, a number of techniques that leverage built-in smartphone sensors to leak users' private information through side channel attacks have been proposed in the literature [13–22]. However, some hardware, operating-system and application-level mechanisms can be employed to block this attack more effectively [22]. Moreover, these approaches also do not target the retrieval of 'call log' or '10-digit phone numbers' unlike the our proposed approach.

To be more specific, in [22], the acoustic SCA of retrieving the PINs/characters on mobile phones is device dependent. This is because, they have used the time-difference-of-arrival as the feature to classify the entered characters. The time-difference-of-arrival is measured between the signals received at the two microphones of the device which will vary across the devices. This leads to a question: *Can we can launch an attack that is generic to all mobile devices (i.e. system independent) and less complex to apply?* In order to cater the above mentioned issue, we have proposed a novel acoustic SCA which is independent of the type of mobile device as long as it supports dialling and calling function and have at least one microphone. In addition, the complexity of retrieving the dialed digits is comparatively lesser than the existing acoustic SCA on smartphones [22]. This is because in the proposed technique, the ML model needs to be trained only once and later it can be used to launch the attack on any type of device. Whereas in [22], the model is required to be trained separately for the type of device on which the attack is intended to be launched leading to higher implementation complexity and attack time.

The role of DTMF standards and ML models in the proposed approach are briefly described as follows:

- Dual-tone multi-frequency (DTMF) is used to produce the sound that is unique to each key on the dialling keypad. DTMF is a signaling system which is used for communication through telephone systems and mobile devices. It defines certain frequencies which are used to produce unique sound upon dialling each key. These frequencies are common across all the mobile devices which support calling function. Each key is composed of a pair of low frequency and high frequency which is unique and have no relation with other frequencies. Hence, it is possible to detect the key by analyzing the sound produced by that key. Table 1 shows the low and high frequencies associated with each key.
- In the proposed approach, we trained the ML models such as support vector machine (SVM), Random Forest, Artificial Neural Network (ANN) on only one device and the trained ML models are capable of predicting the phone numbers dialed on any type of device, making our attack device independent.

1.1   Main Intuition and Contributions

Further, the major intuitions behind the proposed attacking methodology are described as follows.

- When a user dials a phone number on dial pad, each key produces a sound which is composed of the frequencies specified by DTMF standards.
- If we record the sound through in-built microphone and analyze the frequencies present in it, we can predict the key which generated this sound.

- To do so, the recorded sound is converted from its time-domain to frequency-domain representation to find the frequencies present in it. We used a Discrete Fourier Transform (DFT) method to decompose a signal into its frequency components.
- Fast Fourier Transform (FFT) is an efficient algorithm to compute the discrete Fourier transform of a signal. Thus we can find the magnitude of each frequency present in the recorded signal.
- By finding the two frequencies which have the highest magnitudes, we can predict the key.

The top two frequencies will not be always exactly equal to what is shown in the Table 1, because of the noise present in the surrounding and limitations of the microphone hardware. However, the frequencies will certainly be somewhere around the characteristic frequencies with slight deviations. The frequencies corresponding to one key are unique and have no relation with the frequencies of the other keys. Now the problem statement boils down to a traditional classification problem wherein we classify the keys based on the frequencies present in them. In the proposed work, we trained several machine learning models to learn the mapping from frequencies to keys which accounts for the deviations in the frequencies as well. These models are later used to predict the keys by analyzing their sound recordings.

We performed this attack successfully on various devices like Samsung M31, Realme GT, Motorola, Lenovo Tablet and IPhone. The operating systems of all of the above devices are Android except for IPhone which uses iOS operating system. We used python libraries *librosa* and *numpy* to work with the recorded sound signals. The Numpy provides a function which computes the FFT of the given signal in order to find the magnitude of each frequency present in the recorded signal.

Table 1. DTMF keypad frequencies for each key

	1209 Hz	1336 Hz	1477 Hz	1633 Hz
697 Hz	1	2	3	A
770 Hz	4	5	6	B
852 Hz	7	8	9	C
941 Hz	*	0	#	D

In summary, the major contributions of our work are as follows:

- We have proposed a novel acoustic side channel attack methodology to retrieve the dialled call log by exploiting the in-built components of the victim's device such as microphone.
- The proposed approach leveraged the DTMF standards, to uniquely identify the phone number that is being dialed by the victim. The DTMF standards

being common across all the devices makes our proposed attack device independent, which we have also shown in the experimental results section.

- We have shown the use of ML models such as SVM, Random Forest and ANN for training with a number of samples of sounds corresponding to dialed digits and predicting the 10 digit phone number dialed by the victim with 100% accuracy.

The rest of the paper is organized as follows. In Sect. 2, we provide the background of the working principles of DTMF and FFT. We describe our attack methodology in Sect. 3 and provide the experimental setup and results of our work in Sect. 4. Finally, we conclude our paper in Sect. 5.

2   Background

This section briefly discusses the important terminologies used in the proposed methodology of acoustic SCA, such as DTMF, FFT and different ML models. First we discuss some background about DTMF and how it defines the frequencies for each key. Next, we discuss the FFT technique followed by the ML models such as SVM, Random Forest and ANN.

2.1   Dual-Tone Multi-Frequency (DTMF) Signals

DTMF is a signaling system which is used in communicating devices like telephone systems and mobile devices. The standards for DTMF signals have been developed by the Bell System Inc., US. These standards have been specified in the International Telecommunication Union ITU-T Recommendation Q.23 [27]. DTMF tones are produced by adding two sinusoidal signals having frequencies among the 8 defined frequencies. Each key is composed of a pair of low and high frequencies as shown in Table 1. The mathematical function to generate a pure DTMF tone for a particular key is given below.

$$x(t) = A\cos(2\pi f_L T + \phi) + A\cos(2\pi f_H T + \phi) \tag{1}$$

Where, A is the amplitude of the signal, f_L and f_H are the low and the high frequencies respectively from which the key signal is formed, $1/T$ is the sampling rate of the signal and ϕ is the phase of the signal. Figure 1 shows the time-domain representations of the DTMF tones of digit '0' and digit '1'. The DTMF tone corresponding to digit '0' is formed by combining signals of two distinct frequencies viz. 941 Hz and 1336 Hz whereas the DTMF tone corresponding to digit '1' is composed of the 697 Hz and 1209 Hz. As shown in Fig. 1, the combination of different frequencies results into distinct dial tones (signals) for different digits.

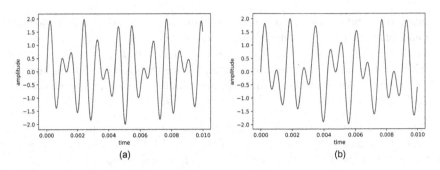

Fig. 1. Combination of two sine waves to produce (a) DTMF '0' and (b) DTMF '1'.

2.2   Fast Fourier Transform (FFT)

In this paper, we have employed the FFT to obtain the corresponding frequency-domain representation of the recorded dial tone in order to facilitate the features extraction for performing the attack. The FFT is an efficient algorithm to compute the discrete Fourier transform (DFT) of a signal. DFT is a method to decompose a signal into its frequency components. It is one of the easiest and commonly applied methods to get the frequency-domain representation of a given signal from its time-domain representation. The formula to compute the DFT of the sequence $x[n]$, corresponding to the continuous time signal $x(t)$, is given below.

$$\hat{x}(k) = \sum_{n=0}^{N-1} x(n)e^{\frac{-2\pi i n k}{N}}, \quad k = 0, ..., N-1 \tag{2}$$

Where, $\hat{x}(k)$ is a complex number in the form of $(a + ib)$ which represents the magnitude and the phase of the frequency $F(k)$ in the original signal $x(t)$. N is the number of samples in $x[n]$ and n is the sample number. The different frequencies given by $F(k)$ can be derived using the following equation.

$$F(k) = \frac{k.S_r}{N} \tag{3}$$

where, S_r is the sampling rate of the signal. The time complexity of finding Fourier transform using Eq. (2) is $O(N^2)$. However, it reduces to $O(NlogN)$ because of applying the FFT. We employ the FFT in our approach to translate the recorded dial tone into the corresponding frequency representation.

2.3 Machine Learning Models

The proposed work employs machine learning (ML) models to facilitate the prediction of the phone number digits dialed by the victim. Here, the objective of using an ML model is to classify the given sample into one of the 10 classes (10 digits from 0 to 9) which is a supervised learning task. Therefore, we have selected the classifiers namely, SVM, Random Forest and ANN which are widely used to solve classification problems.

The objective of SVM technique is to establish the best line or decision boundary that can divide n-dimensional space into classes, allowing us to quickly classify fresh data points in the future. A hyperplane is the name given to this optimal decision boundary. SVM selects the extreme vectors and points that aid in the creation of the hyperplane. Support vectors, which are used to represent these extreme instances, form the basis for the SVM method [23]. Further, random forest is also another supervised machine learning algorithm which is employed in classification problems. On various samples, it constructs decision trees and uses their majority vote to decide the class of the data point [24]. Additionally, we have also employed ANN based supervised learning model. A computational network based on biological neural networks, which create the structure of the human brain, is typically referred to as an Artificial Neural Network (ANN) [25]. It learns the weights for the edges connecting the neurons from one layer to the next layer to minimize the prediction loss/error at the output layer. We have used the softmax activation function in the output layer to predict the class of the sample. The formula for softmax activation function in given below.

$$\sigma(\overrightarrow{z})_i = \frac{e^{z_i}}{\sum_{j=1}^{K} e^{z_i}} \tag{4}$$

Here, σ is softmax, $\overrightarrow{z}$ is the input vector, e^{z_i} is standard exponential function for input vector, K is the number of classes in multi-class classifier (10 in our case) and e^{z_j} is standard exponential function for output vector. This softmax function outputs the probability distribution for all K classes.

Having this background on the core terminologies viz. DTMF, FFT and ML models used in our work, we present the proposed acoustic SCA methodology in the next section.

3 Proposed Acoustic Side Channel Attack Methodology

In this section, we present the acoustic SCA methodology of retrieving the 'call log' or inferring a '10-digit phone number' while being dialed by the victim on his mobile device. The main intuition behind the attacking methodology is

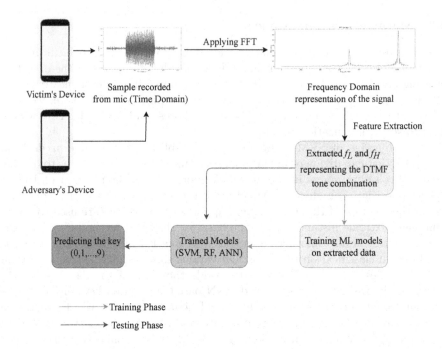

Fig. 2. The execution flow of the proposed attack methodology

based on the fact that the dial tone corresponding to each digit of a phone number is composed of the distinct frequencies specified by DTMF standards. Hence, if the frequencies present in the recorded dial tones are analyzed then the corresponding digit or key can be predicted by an attacker.

Adversarial Model: The adversarial model of our approach assumes that the victim downloads the malicious applications in his mobile phone and grants access to unnecessary permissions. For example, the victim can grant access to the device's microphone that in turn leads to recording of digits sound. We also assume that the sound of dialing digits on the device is enabled to get the tones. The malicious application installed in the mobile devices can access and take control of system's microphone. We assume that the malicious application which has been given the access to the microphone of victim's device sends the recording of dialling of a phone number by the victim to the adversary over the internet. This adversarial model is practical and complies with the standard adversarial models assumed for the state of the art attacks on smartphones [26].

The basic flow of our attack methodology is depicted in Fig. 2. This methodology is discussed in three major phases viz. (i) data collection and feature extraction (ii) training of ML models (ii) inference of dialed digits by attacker. In the *data collection and features extraction* phase, recording of the dialed digits are subjected to FFT technique followed by the features extraction with the help of DTMF standards. Further in the *training phase*, we use the features extracted in previous phase to train the ML models. Finally, in *prediction phase*, the recordings from the victim's device are processed and fed to the models to predict or infer the phone number dialed by the victim. The methodology is discussed in detail below.

3.1   Data Collection and Feature Extraction

We have collected 210 samples of recordings corresponding to 10 digits on the keypad with 21 samples for each digit from a mobile device which acts as the adversary's device. All these samples represent the signals in time-domain where we have time on the x-axis and amplitude on the y-axis as shown in Fig. 3.

Application of FFT: Since the attack exploits the features of recorded sounds in the from of fundamental frequency components, therefore we first need to perform translation of recorded signals from time-domain to frequency-domain. To do so, we apply the FFT technique which computes the DFT of the given signal. Applying FFT on the signal from time-domain gives us the frequency distribution in the signal. This frequency distribution tells us the magnitude of each frequency that is present in the original signal. The frequency-domain representation has frequencies on the x-axis and magnitude on the y-axis. Figure 3 (a) and (b) represents the time-domain representation of a sample recording when a user dials the key '0' and key '1' on the dial pad respectively. When we apply the FFT on this signal, we obtain its corresponding frequency-domain representation which is shown in Fig. 4 (a) and (b).

Role of DTMF: Each key will have different frequency-domain representation where the two frequencies that define the DTMF tone of the key will have higher magnitude as compared to any other frequency. Figure 4 (b) shows the frequency-domain representation of a sample recording when a user dials the key '1'. As shown, the two frequencies with the higher magnitudes lie somewhere around 700 Hz and 1200 Hz and the frequencies which represent the DTMF '1' are 697 Hz and 1209 Hz. If we calculate the exact values from the above representation, they come out to be 696 Hz and 1208 Hz which is very close to the DTMF standards. This property holds for every key on the keypad and is common across all the mobile devices. Hence, this property enables an attacker to detect the keys by training the models on only one device. This makes the attack device-independent.

Feature Extraction: Once we have the frequency-domain representation of the recorded samples, the next step is to extract the two characteristic frequencies based on the DTMF standards for each of the 210 samples. To do so, we find the frequency positions/indices which have the highest magnitudes and then find the frequencies which are present at these positions/indices. After extracting these two frequencies, we created a dataset with these frequencies as the features. In

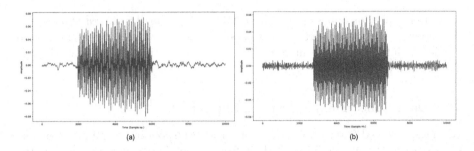

Fig. 3. Time-domain representation of (a) DTMF '0' and (b) DTMF '1'

this dataset, the key/digit which corresponds to these frequencies acts as the label for classification. Thus, we have 10 classes (one for each key) to classify the collected samples. A row in our dataset has 3 values (f_L,f_H,label) representing the low and high frequencies and the actual label of the sample.

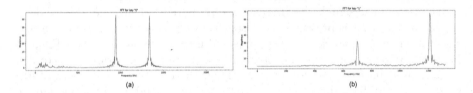

Fig. 4. Frequency-domain representation of (a) DTMF '0' and (b) DTMF '1'

3.2   Training ML Models with Extracted Features

Post obtaining the features of the recorded samples, we have trained our ML models viz. SVM, Random forest and ANN using the corresponding dataset. For SVM, we have used linear kernel for classification because our data is linearly separable. In other words, the data can be separated using a single line. Training an SVM with linear kernel is much faster than any other kernel. In Random forest regression, we have used 10 decision trees to classify the samples and then the majority prediction from these 10 decision trees is used as the final label for the sample. For ANN model, we have created a neural network with 3 hidden layers with 2-dimensional input layer and 10-dimensional output layer. ANN is widely used when the testing data is not much different than the training data and same is the case for our attack methodology, hence we decide to incorporate this model into our attack strategy.

3.3 Inference of Dialed Digits by Attacker

In the final phase of the acoustic SCA methodology, the trained models are used to predict the 10-digit phone number dialed by the victim. The prediction is accomplished in the following steps.

- The malicious application that has been granted the permission to access the microphone of victim's device can record while the victim is dialling a phone number.
- This recording can be sent to the adversary over the internet and then the adversary can perform the required operations on this recording to depict the phone number. Specifically, the recording contains a series of 10 DTMF tones representing the 10-digit phone number.
- Now, we need to separate the 10 DTMF tones from this recording and predict the digit for each tone. To do so, we have plotted the recorded signal in time-domain and observed the time instance at which a particular tone starts and ends.
- Further, we extract the signal containing only one tone from this original signal on the basis of these start and end times. We perform this process for all the 10-digits by observing their respective starting and ending times.
- Once we have the signal for one DTMF tone representing a digit from the phone number, we perform the steps viz. conversion into frequency-domain representation and feature extraction on this signal. These steps are similar to what we performed in the training phase discussed in the Sect. 3.2.
- Once we have created a feature vector from the test sample, we feed it as an input to the ML model to predict the respective key/digit.

Thus, the proposed SCA attack methodology is capable to infer a digit of the phone number in this phase. Similarly, we infer all the remaining digits of the phone number by following the same process.

4 Experimental Setup and Results

This section first discusses the required experimental setup to perform the proposed acoustic SCA for retrieving phone number from mobile devices. As discussed earlier, our attack methodology is performed in the different phases viz. data collection and feature extraction, training and inference. The necessary experimental setup in these phases has been discussed in this section. Later, we illustrate the results of our approach in terms of the accuracy of prediction of the dialed digits and implementation complexity or estimated attack time of the proposed acoustic SCA methodology using different ML models.

4.1 Experimental Setup for Data Collection, Feature Extraction and Training

We have recorded 210 samples of dialling a digit (21 samples for each digit) in one mobile device which will act as the adversary's device. In our case, we have used Samsung Galaxy M31 as the adversary's device. We have used the usual sound recorder application which comes pre-installed in almost all the devices. The recordings are sampled at a sampling rate of 44.1 kHz, which is very common in recent mobile applications. We recorded the samples in mono mode of recording which records from the main or default microphone. We have worked with these samples using python libraries (i) *librosa* which is very famous library for music and audio analysis, (ii) *numpy* to generate the frequency-domain representation from the time-domain representation using FFT method, (iii) *matplotlib* to plot various signal representations and results of our work.

Post obtaining the samples, we have transferred them to the machine on which all the processing will happen. Each acoustic signal (sample) has a duration of nearly one second which is long enough to capture the behavior of the signal. We then follow the below mentioned steps to create the dataset from the recorded samples.

- The time-domain signal is converted to frequency-domain by the FFT method of *numpy*.
- The frequency-domain representation of the signal has an array of frequencies present in the signal along with their magnitudes. We choose the two frequencies having the highest magnitudes.
- We have created a row in the dataset containing these two frequencies as the features and the key/digit to which these frequencies belong as the label.

We have performed the above steps for all the recorded samples and obtained a dataset in a comma separated values (csv) format which will be used to train the ML models. The dataset is of size 210×3 representing 210 samples, each having 3 values namely, low frequency, high frequency and its label. A few samples from the dataset have been shown in Fig. 5.

Once the dataset is obtained, it is used to train our ML models i.e. SVM, Random Forest and ANN. The SVM and Random forest models have training and testing data in $80 : 20$ ratio. For ANN model, we have used 3 hidden layers with 100 neurons in each layer. The input layer is 2-dimensional and the output layer is 10-dimensional, representing 10 classes. We have used rectified linear activation function or ReLU for the input and the hidden layers while softmax function for the output layer. The softmax function outputs the probability distribution for each of the 10 classes. The class with the highest probability is chosen as the label for the given sample. We have split the dataset into $9 : 1$ ratio representing the training and the testing set to train the ANN model. The number of epochs are taken as 100 which means that we feed the training data 100 times to the neural network and each time the weights are updated such that the loss will be minimized. We have saved all these models in .sav format using python library pickle so that we can directly use them in the future for prediction without having to train all of them again.

Index	Low Frequency	High Frequency	Label
0	944	1336	0
1	944	1336	0
...	...	...	...
22	696	1208	1
23	701	1208	1
...	...	...	...
208	851	1477	9
209	851	1477	9

Fig. 5. An excerpt of our Dataset used for training

4.2 Experimental Set-up for Inferring the Digits of a Phone Number

We assume that the malicious application which has been given the access to the microphone of victim's device sends the recording of dialling of a phone number by the victim to the adversary over the internet. We have recorded the dialling of phone numbers on a number of devices like Realme GT, Motorola, Iphone and Lenove tablet to validate the attack. These recordings contain a sequence of 10-digit DTMF tones for the 10 digits in a phone number. A typical recording of dialling a 10-digit phone number looks like that in Fig. 6. We can see multiple peaks in the signal, each of which represents a certain digit in the dialed phone number.

Further, we separate these 10 peaks by estimating their start and end time. We then obtain the frequency-domain representation of each peak/digit using FFT followed by finding the two characteristic frequencies that represent this digit. We also load the models which were saved after the training phase. When we obtain the two characteristic frequencies for each digit, we treat them as the test data for our models and feed them to the models to get their predicted digit as the output. When this process is repeated for each of the 10 digits, we retrieve the full 10-digit phone number which was dialed by the victim. The Fig. 7 shows the flow of proposed attack of inferring the phone digits that are being dialed in the victim's device. As shown, the recording of phone number retrieved by the malicious app from the victim's device is sent to the adversary's machine over the internet where the adversary executes the attack and predicts the phone number from the received recording.

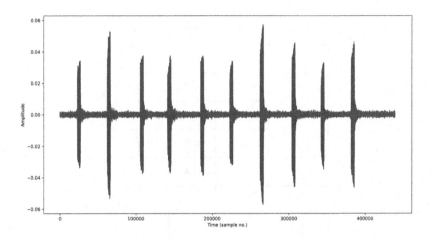

Fig. 6. Recording of a typical phone number

4.3   Accuracy of Prediction of the Dialed Digits Using the Proposed Acoustic SCA Methodology

The accuracy is measured as the ratio of the number of samples predicted correctly to the total number of samples in the testing set.

$$Accuracy = \frac{No.\ of\ samples\ predicted\ correctly}{Total\ no.\ of\ samples} \tag{5}$$

Figure 8 shows the loss and accuracy for all the 100 epochs in case of the ANN model. We have used the cross entropy loss as the loss function in our model and the optimizer we used is the adam optimizer. As shown in Fig. 8, the accuracy for this model reaches to 100% and the loss decreases to 0 when the training phase ends. The reported accuracy for all three models is 100%. For the accuracy analysis, we have varied the number of samples per digit from 3 to 21. However for each case, we are achieving 100% accuracy. The underlying reason is as follows. The two characteristic frequencies in the dial tone of corresponding digits differ by a large value. More explicitly, low frequencies are 70 Hz apart and high frequencies are 120 Hz apart. Therefore, it is highly unlikely that a digit would be predicted incorrectly. For example, the characteristic frequencies '770 Hz and 1209 Hz' corresponding to the digit '4' cannot be predicted to be any other digit by the model as its corresponding frequencies are far away from that of other digits. However, we still need to train the classifiers to capture the small difference between the frequencies. For example, in case of the digit '1' the low frequency might vary 697 Hz to 771 Hz due to the noise present in the recorded signal or the limitations of the device's microphone which might result in predicting it incorrectly. Hence, the goal of the classifiers is to capture these small differences using decision boundary and these differences will be captured better if we train with large number of samples.

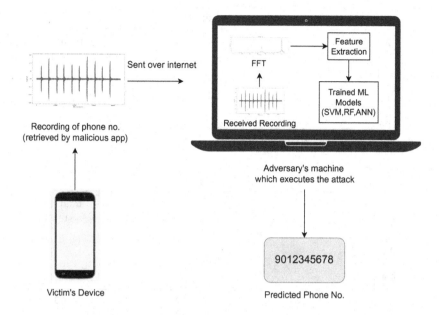

Fig. 7. The proposed attack flow of inferring the phone number from recording

Since, the DTMF tones and their corresponding fundamental frequencies remain the same irrespective of the type of mobile device. Hence, all the 10 digits predicted by the models represent the exact phone number dialed by the victim. We have successfully retrieved the dialed phone numbers on all the devices mentioned earlier by following this method. Hence, we propose that our attack methodology is device independent.

4.4 Implementation Complexity (Estimated Attack Time) of the Proposed Methodology

We have executed this attack on a system having 8 GB of RAM, AMD PRO A4-3350B APU 2 GHz Processor. The overall implementation complexity of the proposed attack methodology is divided in the following three time slices:

- implementation run time of finding FFT and feature extraction (T_f).
- implementation run time of training ML models (T_t).
- implementation run time of predicting dialed digits (T_p).

Hence, the total implementation complexity or overall attack time (T_A) is given using the following equation:

$$T_A = T_f + T_t + T_p \tag{6}$$

The implementation run time of finding FFT and feature extraction (T_f) is **12.49** s. This process is performed only once and is common for all the ML

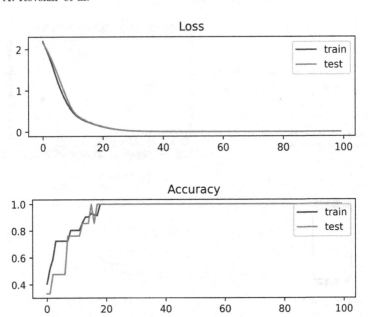

Fig. 8. Training loss and accuracy for ANN model

models. Further, the time required (in seconds) for training all the three ML models after performing the feature extraction and then testing them to predict the dialed digits is given in Table 2. Finally, the Table 2 also presents the total attack time computed using Eq. 6. The implementation complexity of retrieving the dialed digits is achieved to be very less. This is because, the ML model needs to be trained only once and later it can be used to launch the attack on any type of device. It does not required to be trained separately for the type of device on which the attack is intended to be launched. Hence, it leads to lower implementation complexity or attack time.

Table 2. Implementation run times in seconds (s) of the proposed attack for three different ML models

Model	Training time (T_t)	Testing time (T_p)	Overall attack time (T_A)
SVM	0.12 s	0.20 s	12.81 s
Random forest	0.08 s	0.28 s	12.85 s
ANN	9.17 s	0.75 s	22.41 s

5   Conclusion

Acoustic side channel attack has recently come up as a potential threat as it can breach the security of mobile devices and leak the user's sensitive data. In this work, we have shown how a malicious application in the victim's device can retrieve the phone numbers that are being dialed by him/her by recording the sounds through in-built microphone of the device. Since the DTMF tones of the keys/digits are common across all mobile devices, the adversary can exploit this property to launch a successful attack on the mobile devices making this attack device independent. The adversary just needs to train a machine learning model on his/her device to make this attack successful. The experimental results implied that an adversary can retrieve the phone number digits using the ML models with 100% accuracy. Moreover, the implementation complexity or the overall attack time of the proposed acoustic SCA methodology is very less. For a user to be less likely to fall victim to this kind of attack, he or she needs to pay close attention to the hardware and software requirements of the applications he or she wants to install. Demanding access by an application to an irrelevant component of the mobile device can be a big giveaway of such an attack.

References

1. Naik, P., Chatterjee, U.: Network data remanence side channel attack on SPREAD, H-SPREAD and reverse AODV. In: Batina, L., Picek, S., Mondal, M. (eds.) SPACE 2021. LNCS, vol. 13162, pp. 129–147. Springer, Cham (2022). https://doi.org/10.1007/978-3-030-95085-9_7
2. Kocher, P.C.: Timing attacks on implementations of Diffie-Hellman, RSA, DSS, and other systems. In: Koblitz, N. (ed.) CRYPTO 1996. LNCS, vol. 1109, pp. 104–113. Springer, Heidelberg (1996). https://doi.org/10.1007/3-540-68697-5_9
3. Rivest, R.L., Shamir, A., Adleman, L.M.: A method for obtaining digital signatures and public-key cryptosystems (reprint). Commun. ACM **26**(1), 96–99 (1983)
4. Diffie, W., Hellman, M.E.: New directions in cryptography. IEEE Trans. Inf. Theory **22**(6), 644–654 (1976)
5. Kocher, P., Jaffe, J., Jun, B.: Differential power analysis. In: Wiener, M. (ed.) CRYPTO 1999. LNCS, vol. 1666, pp. 388–397. Springer, Heidelberg (1999). https://doi.org/10.1007/3-540-48405-1_25
6. Carrara B.: Air-gap covert channels (2016)
7. Huang, H., Wang, X., Jiang, Y., Singh, A.K., Yang, M., Huang, L.: Detection of and countermeasure against thermal covert channel in many-core systems. IEEE Trans. Comput. Aided. Des. Integr. Circ. Syst. **42**, 252–265 (2021)
8. Ji, X., et al.: No seeing is also believing: electromagnetic-emission-based application guessing attacks via smartphones. IEEE Trans. Mob. Comput. (2021)
9. Carrara, B., Adams, C.: On acoustic covert channels between air-gapped systems. In: Cuppens, F., Garcia-Alfaro, J., Zincir Heywood, N., Fong, P.W.L. (eds.) FPS 2014. LNCS, vol. 8930, pp. 3–16. Springer, Cham (2015). https://doi.org/10.1007/978-3-319-17040-4_1
10. Halevi, T., Saxena, N.: Keyboard acoustic side channel attacks: exploring realistic and security-sensitive scenarios. Int. J. Inf. Secur. **14**, 443–456 (2015)

11. Asonov, D., Agrawal, R.: Keyboard acoustic emanations. In: Proceedings of IEEE Symposium on Security and Privacy, pp. 3–11 (2004). https://doi.org/10.1109/SECPRI.2004.1301311

12. Al Faruque M. A., Chhetri S. R., Canedo A. and Wan J.: Acoustic side-channel attacks on additive manufacturing systems. In: 2016 ACM/IEEE 7th International Conference on Cyber-Physical Systems (ICCPS), pp. 1–10 (2016). https://doi.org/10.1109/ICCPS.2016.7479068

13. Al-Haiqi, A., Ismail, M., Nordin, R.: On the best sensor for keystrokes inference attack on android. Procedia Technol. **11**, 989–995 (2013). (4th International Conference on Electrical Engineering and Informatics, ICEEI 2013)

14. Cai, L., Chen, H.: TouchLogger: inferring keystrokes on touch screen from smartphone motion. In: Proceedings of the 6th USENIX Conference on Hot Topics in Security, HotSec 2011, p. 9. USENIX Association, Berkeley, CA, USA (2011)

15. Goller, G., Sigl, G.: Side channel attacks on smartphones and embedded devices using standard radio equipment. In: Mangard, S., Poschmann, A.Y. (eds.) Constructive Side-Channel Analysis and Secure Design: 6th International Workshop, COSADE 2015, Berlin, Germany, 13–14 April 2015. Revised Selected Papers, pp. 255–270 (2015)

16. Li, M., et al.: When CSI meets public WiFi: inferring your mobile phone password via WiFi signals. In: Proceedings of the 2016 ACM SIGSAC Conference on Computer and Communications Security, CCS 2016, pp. 1068–1079, New York, NY, USA (2016)

17. Negulescu, M., McGrenere, J.: Grip change as an information side channel for mobile touch interaction. In: Proceedings of the 33rd Annual ACM Conference on Human Factors in Computing Systems, CHI 2015, pp. 1519–1522, New York, NY, USA (2015)

18. Sarkisyan, A., Debbiny, R., Nahapetian, A.: WristSnoop: smartphone pins prediction using smartwatch motion sensors. In: 2015 IEEE International Workshop on Information Forensics and Security (WIFS), pp. 1–6, November 2015

19. Simon, L., Anderson, R.: Pin skimmer: inferring pins through the camera and microphone. In: Proceedings of the Third ACM Workshop on Security and Privacy in Smartphones, vol. 38; Mobile Devices, SPSM 2013, pp. 67–78, New York, NY, USA (2013)

20. Xu, Z., Bai, K., Zhu, S.: TapLogger: inferring user inputs on smartphone touchscreens using on-board motion sensors. In: Proceedings of the Fifth ACM Conference on Security and Privacy in Wireless and Mobile Networks, WISEC 2012, pp. 113–124, New York, NY, USA (2012)

21. Yan, L., Guo, Y., Chen, X., Mei, H.: A study on power side channels on mobile devices. In: Proceedings of the 7th Asia-Pacific Symposium on Internetware, Internetware 2015, pp. 30–38, New York, NY, USA (2015)

22. Shumailov, I., Simon, L., Yan, J., Anderson, R.: Hearing your touch: A new acoustic side channel on smartphones (2019)

23. Schuldt, C., Laptev, I., Caputo, B.: Recognizing human actions: a local SVM approach. In: Proceedings of the 17th International Conference on Pattern Recognition, 2004. ICPR 2004, vol. 3, pp. 32–36. IEEE, 26 August 2004

24. Sarica, A., Cerasa, A., Quattrone, A.: Random forest algorithm for the classification of neuroimaging data in Alzheimer's disease: a systematic review. Front. Aging Neurosci. **6**(9), 329 (2017)

25. Jain, A.K., Mao, J., Mohiuddin, K.M.: Artificial neural networks: a tutorial. Computer **29**(3), 31–44 (1996)

26. Narain, S., Sanatinia, A., Noubir, G.: Single-stroke language-agnostic keylogging using stereo-microphones and domain specific machine learning. In: Proceedings of the 2014 ACM conference on Security and privacy in wireless and mobile networks (WiSec 2014). Association for Computing Machinery, New York, NY, USA, pp. 201–212 (2014). https://doi.org/10.1145/2627393.2627417
27. International Telecommunication Union: ITU-T Recommendation Q.23, Technical features of pushbutton telephone sets, Fascicle VI.1, Blue Book (1993)

Machine Learning Attacks on Low-Cost Reconfigurable XRRO and XRBR PUF Designs

Manthan Kojage, Neelofar Hassan, and Urbi Chatterjee[✉]

Department of Computer Science and Engineering, Indian Institute of Technology Kanpur, Kanpur, India
{manthank,neelofar,urbic}@cse.iitk.ac.in

Abstract. Physically unclonable functions (PUFs) can be seen as hardware circuits whose output does not only depend upon the inputs fed to it, but also on the random variation in the integrated circuits (ICs) during its manufacturing process. As a result of their unique hardware fingerprinting, these circuits can be used to authenticate devices among a population of identical silicon chips, much like a human being can be authenticated by their biometrics. In ACM TECS 2019, two low-cost reconfigurable Strong PUF designs namely XOR-based Reconfigurable Bistable Ring PUF (XRBR PUF) and XOR-based Reconfigurable Ring Oscillator PUF (XRRO PUF) have been proposed as a promising low-cost solution for IoT security. The two notable features of these architectures are: i) both of them exploit the logic reconfigurability which is efficient in terms of hardware cost, and ii) they exhibit good uniqueness and reliability properties. These make XRRO and XRBR PUFs good candidates for Strong PUF-based authentications and an interesting target for the machine learning (ML) adversaries as the machine learning resiliency was never discussed for both the cases in the proposal. In this paper, we develop a mathematical model for both of the designs by exploiting a common flaw of not having any non-linear component in the structure. Hence they are proven to be as vulnerable as their forerunner designs such as Configurable Ring Oscillator PUF and Bistable Ring PUFs. Finally, we show through experimental analysis that 128-bit XRBR PUFs can be broken with $10K$ CRPs with an accuracy of approximately 99%. On the other hand, for 127-stage XRRO PUFs having $8, 16, 32, 64$ layers of XRROs can be broken with $200K, 1M, 3M, 8M$ CRPs with an accuracy of approximately 97%–99%.

Keywords: Physically unclonable functions · Machine learning · XOR gate · Bistable ring · Configurable Ring Oscillator

1 Introduction

Over the past two decades, Physically Unclonable Functions (PUFs) have garnered significant attention from the research community worldwide [6,14]. They

© The Author(s), under exclusive license to Springer Nature Switzerland AG 2022
L. Batina et al. (Eds.): SPACE 2022, LNCS 13783, pp. 204–224, 2022.
https://doi.org/10.1007/978-3-031-22829-2_12

have been employed in a number of authentication protocols as building blocks. As a component of hardware-based security primitive, PUFs create a distinct digital fingerprint for a circuit or device using manufacturer process variations. PUFs cannot be physically replicated because of its unpredictable, small-scale manufacturing variances. Even the manufacturer is unable to deliberately duplicate a PUF instance. As a result, producing physically identical specimens is infeasible. PUFs use a challenge-response mechanism to serve as hardware primitive. We provide the PUF with *"challenge"* (denoted as C), which act as a trigger or excitation signal, causing them to react by producing a *"response"* (denoted as R_C). The produced response depends on the physical characteristics of the PUF and the challenge fed to it. The challenge fed, and the response generated by the PUF is called the challenge-response pair (CRP) of the PUF. Based on the size of the challenge-response space of the PUF circuit, it can classified in two categories, namely Weak PUFs and Strong PUFs.

- **Weak PUFs:** Weak PUFs [7,8,22,23], are generally used for on-device secret key generation. It is generally assumed that the response generated by this kind of PUFs never leave the hardware platform.
- **Strong PUFs:** Strong PUFs [4–6,16,25] possess huge challenge-response pairs which are mainly used for device authentication. It is not feasible to construct all the 2^N challenge-response pairs (CRPs) for N-bit Strong PUF and to search the particular response for any arbitrary challenge in polynomial time. In the state-of-the-art literature, the Strong PUFs architectures such as Arbiter PUF (APUF), XOR-Arbiter PUF (XOR-APUF), Configurable Ring Oscillator PUF (CRO PUF) and Bistable Ring PUF (BR PUF) have proven to be versatile cryptographic primitives with a wide set of applications, such as key establishment and identification protocols [18]. However, the Strong PUFs suggested in the literature consume significant hardware resources, and thus, are not scalable for lightweight applications in IoT framework. To address this problem, recently two lightweight PUF architectures such as XOR-based Reconfigurable Ring Oscillator PUF (XRRO PUF) and XOR-based Reconfigurable Bistable Ring PUF (XRBR PUF) [13] have been proposed which incur lesser hardware overhead while retaining good uniqueness and reliability values.

But, due to the emergence of classical and reliability-based machine learning (ML) attacks, most of the PUF compositions are proven to be vulnerable in recent state-of-the-art literature [3,17,19–21,24]. Ruhrmair *et al.* proposed the first ML attacks against strong PUFs in 2010 [19,20], based on a mathematical delay model [12] of the APUF, RO PUF, XOR-APUF, Feed Forward APUF, and LSPUF. A similar kind of delay-based modelling is done for CRO PUF in which the delays of the oscillation of the CROs are exploited [17]. Memory-based Strong PUFs such as Bistable Ring PUF has also been modelled in which the pull strengths of the logic gates are exploited [24]. Several machine learning techniques, such as Support Vector Machine (SVM), Logistic Regression (LR), and Covariance Matrix Adaptation Evolution Strategies(CMA-ES), have been used to demonstrate these models [11,19]. Hence, while assessing the quality of a Strong PUF candidate, it is of paramount importance that we not only estimate the uniqueness, uniformity and reliability properties of the design but also evaluate the robustness of the circuit against ML-based attacks.

Hence, in this paper, we try to answer the question that: *Though XRRO and XRBR PUFs are suitable for generating hardware fingerprints for lightweight applications, how vulnerable are they against ML-based modelling attacks?* The intuition for modelling these PUF architectures is that they inherit the similar flaws as CRO PUF and BR PUF that make them vulnerable against the ML attacks [17,24]. Though the vulnerabilities are similar, but due to the change in the construction of XRRO and XRBR PUF, the exact model for CRO PUF and BR PUF might not be directly applied to these two architectures. Hence the main crux of this work is to use the knowledge of the mathematical model formation of the former and build the same specifically for the XRRO and XRBR PUF. To the best of our knowledge, no prior works have been done to perform a security analysis on XRRO and XRBR constructions so far.

Overall, this paper's main contributions can be summed up as follows:

- We examine the security vulnerability and machine learning resiliency of XRRO and XRBR PUF architecture which was missing in the actual proposal [13]. We propose a mathematical model of the same to successfully launch ML-based attacks.
- We also implement the attack on simulated XRRO and XRBR PUF and evaluate the security architectures against SVM and LR algorithms. We further show the efficiency of the proposed attack by successfully modeling both the designs with 97%–99% accuracy.

The rest of the paper is organized in the following manner. In Sect. 2 we provide the background related to the proposed mathematical model and the machine learning attacks. The novel mathematical model proposed in this paper is illustrated in Sect. 3. The machine learning attacks and the experimental results are presented in Sect. 4. Finally, we conclude the paper with Sect. 5.

2   Background

In this section, we first discuss the basic working principles of Configurable Ring Oscillator PUF (CRO PUF) [16] and Bistable Ring PUF (BR PUF) [4]. Then we briefly discuss mathematical models that are used to perform machine learning attacks on these architectures.

2.1   CRO PUFs and BR PUFs

The basic building block of CRO PUF is a Ring oscillator PUF (RO PUF). The RO PUF is generally made of an identically laid-out loop of an odd number of logically inverting delay elements (as shown in Fig. 1). An RO generally continues to oscillate between 0 and 1 when triggered because the output of the last buffer is always the logical "NOT" of the input fed. An RO PUF [22] utilizes this non-settling property of RO to introduce randomness in the circuit and it can be exploited for hardware fingerprinting. Figure 2 shows the circuit diagram of a traditional RO PUF. There are two multiplexers MUX1 and MUX2, each of which has N selection lines. There are 2^N ROs that are connected to both these multiplexers. The oscillating frequency of each oscillator in RO PUF is unique across devices due to the manufacturing process variations and can not be predicted apriori. The challenges are divided into two parts and provided to the select lines of multiplexers of RO PUF respectively in order to select a pair of ROs, and then, their frequencies are calculated using the counters. Finally, these two counter values are compared to generate an output. If RO selected by MUX1 has a higher oscillation frequency, the output is 1, otherwise, the output is 0.

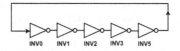

Fig. 1. Traditional 5-stage RO.

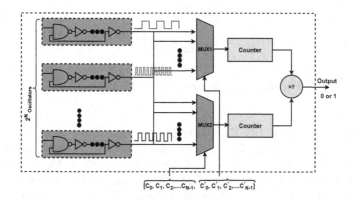

Fig. 2. Ring Oscillator PUF [22].

Now, from the implementation perspective, it has been found that if we increase the challenge space, the number of ROs need to be added to the circuit grows exponentially. Hence the hardware overhead will be very high if we try to use RO PUF as a *Strong PUF candidate*. On the other hand, the RO PUFs have higher reliability compared to other Strong PUF architectures [15]. To balance this trade-off, the Configurable Ring Oscillator PUF(CRO PUF) circuit [16] has been proposed as a variant of the RO PUF. We show its circuit design as well in Fig. 3. Here each RO can be reconfigured by using a multiplexer to select one of two inverters at each stage. The selection bit (S_i) for the multiplexer at the ith stage acts as a configurable signal which determines whether the upper or lower

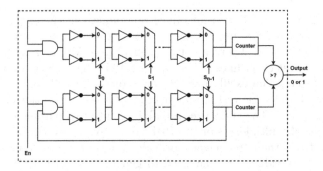

Fig. 3. The architecture of the CRO PUF [16].

delay element will be used at that stage. Finally, the output frequencies of the two CROs are compared to derive the PUF response. The main advantage of using CRO PUF is that we can do away with 2^N layers of ROs as in RO PUF (please ref to Fig. 2). Hence it is more efficient in terms of hardware overhead and can be considered as a Strong PUF as well.

Fig. 4. Schematic diagram of a SRAM cell [8].

On the other hand, BR PUF is comprised of a cycle of an even number of logically inverted delay elements. Its main principle is the same as that of SRAM PUF [9] i.e. it exploits the unstable properties of SRAM cell transience. Whenever it is powered on, every SRAM cell (as shown in Fig. 4) results in invariably random deviations in the threshold voltages. This variation is extracted in the startup values of "uninitialized" SRAM memory. Consequently, an SRAM response produces a unique, random binary bit patterns. Now, A n-bit BR PUF (as shown in Fig. 5) is composed of n stages, where each stage has two inverting delay elements (e.g. NOR gates). The challenge bits $\{C_0, C_1, ..., C_{n-1}\}$ applied to the multiplexer and demultiplexer of every stage selects the NOR gates used in each bistable ring configuration. Once triggered, the BR PUF works like a memory cell and will enter either "101010..." or "010101..." as one of its two stable states. An n-bit BR PUF can have a total of 2^n different configurations as each NOR gate has a distinct process variation and each challenge vector generates a distinct bistable ring configuration.

Before allowing the ring to stabilise and produce a response, a synchronous RESET signal is applied to every stage in order to start with an all-0 state. When RESET is low and the ring starts to oscillate through the selected NOR gates,

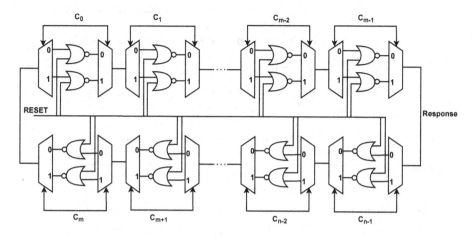

Fig. 5. Schematic diagram of a n-bit BR PUF [4, 24]

the response is evaluated. Once the ring reaches a stable state, the outputs of any two neighboring stages will be opposite to each other. In the ring configuration, the noise and process variation of the NOR gates are utilised to determine which of the two probable stable states of the ring is selected. Moreover, an output port can be created at any node that connects two stages.

We next briefly discuss the mathematical models of CRO and BR PUFs.

2.2 ML Attacks on CRO PUFs and BR PUFs

ML-based modeling attacks on Strong PUF candidates are very prominent in the state-of-the-art literature. The adversarial model that is assumed over here is that a small subset of the challenge-response pairs (CRPs) are given to the adversary for a particular PUF design. The hurdle is whether (s)he can build a mathematical model of the same using the given CRPs to achieve high prediction accuracy while guessing responses for an unknown challenge.

First we briefly discuss the mathematical model of the CRO PUF. Each stage of a CRO PUF consists of four delay components: $(\delta_{i1}, \delta_{i2})$ for the upper and lower delay line of the top CRO (as shown in Fig. 6) and $(\delta'_{i1}, \delta'_{i2})$ for the upper and lower delay line of the bottom CRO. Now the oscillation frequency of the top and bottom CROs will be decided by the configuration of the paths through which the signal propagates and their delay contributes to the overall summation. And the choice of paths depends on the challenge bit selection. If the upper CRO is faster, i.e., the oscillation frequency is more than the lower CRO, we get a response of 1; otherwise, the response is 0. Now, the delay difference for every stage can be formulated as given below [17]:

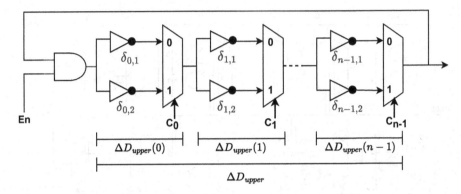

Fig. 6. CRO PUF diagram showing delay components of upper CRO [17].

$$\Delta D(i) = \Delta D_{upper}(i) - \Delta D_{lower}(i) \tag{1}$$

$$\Delta D_{upper}(i) = \frac{1 - C_i}{2}\delta_{i1} + \frac{1 + C_i}{2}\delta_{i2}$$
$$\Delta D_{lower}(i) = \frac{1 - C_i}{2}\delta'_{i1} + \frac{1 + C_i}{2}\delta'_{i2} \tag{2}$$

$$\Delta D(i) = \frac{1 - C_i}{2}(\delta_{i1} - \delta'_{i1}) + \frac{1 + C_i}{2}(\delta_{i2} - \delta'_{i2}) \tag{3}$$

Please note that for i-th stage of the CRO, the challenge bits $C_i \in \{-1, 1\}$ is bipolar-encoded. Let,

$$\delta_i^\alpha = \delta_{i1} - \delta'_{i1}$$
$$\delta_i^\beta = \delta_{i2} - \delta'_{i2}$$

Now similar to the mathematical modelling of Arbiter PUF [21], the overall delay difference between the oscillation of upper and lower CRO for an n-stage CRO-PUF can be described as a linear sum of vector dot products.

$$\Delta D = \sum_{i=0}^{n-1} \Delta D(i) = \overrightarrow{P_\alpha}.\overrightarrow{W_\alpha} + \overrightarrow{P_\beta}.\overrightarrow{W_\beta} \tag{4}$$

where,

$$\overrightarrow{P_\alpha} = \left\{ \frac{1 - C_0}{2}, \frac{1 - C_1}{2} ..., \frac{1 - C_{n-1}}{2} \right\}$$

$$\overrightarrow{P_\beta} = \left\{ \frac{1 + C_0}{2}, \frac{1 + C_1}{2} ..., \frac{1 + C_{n-1}}{2} \right\}$$

$$\overrightarrow{W_\alpha} = \left\{ \delta_0^\alpha, \delta_1^\alpha, ..., \delta_{n-1}^\alpha \right\}, \overrightarrow{W_\beta} = \left\{ \delta_0^\beta, \delta_1^\beta, ..., \delta_{n-1}^\beta \right\}$$

This model can be used to launch CMA-ES and LR based ML attacks on the CRO PUF [17]. We have used the similar idea in Sect. 3 to model XRRO PUF as proposed in [13].

Similarly, an additive model has been put forth in the literature for predicting the resolution of metastability [10], with weights representing the strength with which different cells pull toward a particular outcome. Using this idea, a mathematical model of the BR PUF has been made [24]. Each gate in the BR PUF has weight associated with it representing difference between the pull-up strength and pull-down strength of the same. The overall response given a specific challenge(C) is determined by the summation of the weights across all the gates in accordance with the path that the applied challenge has selected. A positive sum indicates that the configured ring provides a "1", whereas a negative sum indicates that ring provides "−1" value. As the pull-up strength of even stages and the pull-down strength of odd stages favour a overall positive response, the summation of weights requires negative and positive polarities.

Let t_i and b_i represent the difference in the pull-up and pull-down strength of the top and bottom NOR gates in the ith stage respectively (please ref to Fig. 5).

The total strength pulling toward the positive response for a given n-bit challenge is the summation of n number of t_i or b_i weights (depending on whether C_i is +1 or −1) and can be given as [24],

$$R_C = sgn(\sum_{i=0}^{n-1} \left(-1^i . \frac{t_i - b_i}{2}\right) + C_i \left(-1^i . \frac{t_i + b_i}{2}\right) \tag{5}$$

where C_i is the challenge bit of the ith stage and is bipolar-encoded i.e. $C_i \in \{-1, 1\}$. The sign of R_C could be used to predict the response. For convenience, α_i and β_i can be defined as $\left(-1^i . \frac{t_i - b_i}{2}\right)$ and $\left(-1^i . \frac{t_i + b_i}{2}\right)$ respectively. Then,

$$R_C = sgn(\sum_{i=0}^{n-1} \alpha_i + C_i . \beta_i) \tag{6}$$

Given that the weights α_i and β_i are not known and since a BR PUF has only two possible responses, The response prediction of a BR PUF can be converted into a classification problem based on the given equation. We have exploited similar notion in Sect. 3 to model XRBR PUF.

3   Modelling XOR-Based Reconfigurable PUFs

In this section we first briefly describe the working principle of XRBR PUF and XRRO PUF followed by our proposed mathematical models for the same.

To start with, XOR gate is the basic building block for both the designs. It has a property that it can act as both buffer and inverter relying on the input values. The mechanism of XOR-based Reconfigurable PUFs [13] is based the above property of XOR gates. Let A and B be the inputs to an XOR gate. When B = "0", the XOR gate acts as a buffer relaying the input value A to the output following a delay. When B = "1", the XOR gate's output value is the logic inverse of the input A, hence it acts as an inverter. Thus by controlling one of its bits, an XOR gate can be switched from a buffer to an inverter and vice-versa.

3.1   Mechanism of XRBR PUF

As discussed in Sect. 2.1, every stage of BR PUF consists of two inverting delay elements. The gate is chosen in each bistable ring configuration by providing the challenge bit at the select line of the MUX and DEMUX of that particular stage (please refer to Fig. 5). The XRBR PUF replaces each stage of BR PUF with an XOR gate (as shown in Fig. 7). The stages of XRBR PUF thus can be configured as buffers or inverters by controlling one of the inputs to the XOR gate of that stage. The selection bit is provided to each stage of a XRBR PUF to configure it into a unique circuit. As the number of stages in the BR PUF is even which makes it act like a memory circuit, The XOR gates configured as inverters in the XRBR PUF must be even in number. It implies that the configuration bits to the XRBR PUF should have an even number of 1's, which in turn configures an even number of XOR gates as inverters befitting it to behave like a memory circuit similar to BR PUF. Now there are variations due to the hardware intrinsic properties such as delay and driving capabilities of the XOR gate for every buffers and inverters of the XRBR PUF. This property is absolutely similar to SRAM PUF as the impurities are induced in the platform due to the random process variations in the manufacturing phase. Additionally, different configuration of the XRBR PUF adds to the variation in the output to the circuit and results in different responses of the PUF instance.

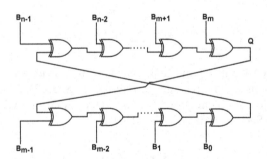

Fig. 7. The schematic diagram of an n-bit XRBR PUF [13].

The uniqueness and reliability values for the XRBR PUF are 40.67% and 98.22% respectively as shown in [13], which are very close to the ideal values. The comparison between the uniqueness and reliability values of BR PUF and XRBR PUF in [13] shows that XRBR PUF achieves better values. Also, XRBR PUF is a low-cost PUF design. As a memory-based PUF, the XRBR PUF is feasible, and it can generate a comparably higher number of CRPs while reducing the hardware overheads. Now we proceed with the modelling attack.

3.2   Modelling XRBR PUF

The intuition behind the modeling of XRBR PUF will be of using an additive model for predicting the response. We have used an additive model where each XOR gate has weights that correspond to the difference between its pull-up strength and pull-down strength. To find the overall favoured response for a specific challenge, the weights are summed across all the XOR gates configured as an inverter. A higher preference for a positive response is indicated by a positive sum. The overall positive response is favoured by the pull-up strength of even positioned inverters and the pull-down strength of odd positioned inverters. Thus, the summation of weights requires negative and positive polarities.

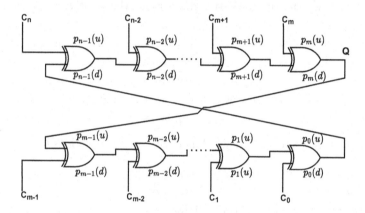

Fig. 8. XRBR PUF diagram showing the pull strengths of an XOR gate at each stage.

Let the the pull-up strength, pull-down strength and the difference between them for the ith stage XOR gate be $p_i(u)$, $p_i(d)$ and p_i respectively (as shown in Fig. 8). On feeding the challenge (C) to the PUF circuit, the XOR gate of each stage will either be configured as a buffer or an inverter. The XOR gates that are configured as buffers will not contribute toward the response in any way. The XOR gates that are configured as inverters will contribute depending upon their position in the circuit. If an ith stage XOR gate (configured as an inverter) is also an even positioned inverter in the PUF circuit, then it contributes towards the positive response with strength p_i, otherwise it contributes towards the positive response with strength $-p_i$.

Let us assume that the challenge bit for the ith stage $C_i \in [-1, 1]$ is bipolar-encoded. Then we define the parity bit corresponding to the challenge bit as, $\Phi_i = -1^{s_i}.(1 + C_i)/2$. Here, s_i is the number of stages configured as inverters till stage i. This provides the even or odd positioning of the stages that are configured as inverters.

The strength toward the positive response for any stage given a challenge bit C_i will be $\Delta S(i)$ and is given in Eq. 7,

$$\Delta S(i) = p_i.(-1^{s_i}\frac{1+C_i}{2}) \implies \Delta S(i) = p_i.\Phi_i \qquad (7)$$

where the variable s_i is defined as:

$$s_i = \begin{cases} \frac{1+C_i}{2} & \text{if } i = 0 \\ s_{i-1} + \frac{1+C_i}{2} & \text{if } i = 1, ..., n-1 \end{cases}$$

The above mentioned notation not only nullifies the contribution of the stage configured as a buffer, but also lets the stage configured as an inverter contribute according to its position in the PUF circuit. For any challenge vector $C = \{C_0, C_1, ..., C_{n-1}\}$, the summed strengths toward the positive response is given in Eq. 8,

$$\Delta S = \sum_{i=0}^{n-1} \Delta S(i)$$
$$\Delta S = p_0.\Phi_0 + p_1.\Phi_1 + ... + p_{n-1}.\Phi_{n-1}$$
$$\Delta S = \mathbf{p}.\Phi^T \qquad (8)$$

where the feature vector Φ is defined as parity of challenge bits C:

$$\Phi_i = -1^{s_i}.\frac{1+C_i}{2}$$

The weight vector $\mathbf{p}$ is defined as follows:

$$\mathbf{p} = \{p_0, p_1, ..., p_{n-1}\}$$

According to our formulation, if the weight vector $\mathbf{p}$ (pull strengths) was known explicitly, then the sign of R_C could be used to predict the PUF response (Eq. 9).

$$R_C = sgn(\mathbf{p}.\Phi^T) \qquad (9)$$

We will be using this additive model to simulate XRBR PUF and to evaluate it against SVM and LR algorithms in Sect. 4.

3.3   Mechanism of XRRO PUF

Next we proceed with the working principle of XRRO PUF. As discussed in Sect. 2.1, in CRO PUF, both the rings have stages consisting of two inverting delay elements and a multiplexer. The use of a inverter in a stage is dependent on the selection bit of the multiplexer of that stage. Now, to reduce the hardware overhead, XRRO PUF [13] employs single XOR gate at every stage in place

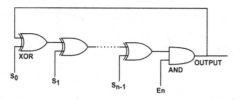

Fig. 9. The schematic diagram of an XRRO [13].

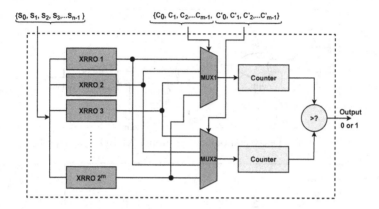

Fig. 10. The architecture of the XRRO PUF [13].

of the two inverters and a multiplexer. One input to the XOR gate acts as a configuration signal and the other input is connected to the output of the previous XOR gate, forming an XOR-based Ring Oscillator (as shown in Fig. 9).

Now, as shown in Fig. 1, a RO is generally made of odd number of logically inverting delay components. Thus the output of the last component is always logical "NOT" of the first input. Therefore the output of the RO oscillates between 0 and 1. Similarly for an XRRO, to oscillate, the number of inverting components should be odd. That is why, the configuration bits to all the XOR gates of an XRRO ring must contain an odd number of 1's so that odd number of XOR gates can be configured as inverters. The XRRO can construct up to $2^n/2$ different ROs from different configuration patterns, where n is the number of stages in the XRRO.

The architecture of the XRRO PUF is given in Fig. 10. We consider 2^m number of XRRO layers and all of them are configured using the same configuration signals ($S_0, S_1, ..., S_{n-1}$). The selection bits for both top ($C_0, C_1, ..., C_{m-1}$) and bottom ($C'_0, C'_1, ..., C'_{m-1}$) multiplexers chooses two different XRROs. The selected pair of XRROs only participate in the response generation process. The oscillation frequencies for both of them are compared based on which the response gets generated. If an XRRO selected by MUX1 has more oscillation frequency than the one selected by MUX2, response 1 is generated, otherwise response 0 is generated.

The uniqueness and reliability values for the XRRO PUF are 48.76% and 97.72% respectively as shown in [13], which are very close to the ideal values. The comparison between uniqueness and reliability values of RO PUF, CRO PUF and XRRO PUF in [13] shows that, XRRO PUF achieves better values.

3.4   Modelling XRRO PUF

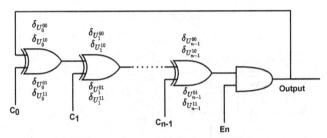

(a) Delay components of upper XRRO.

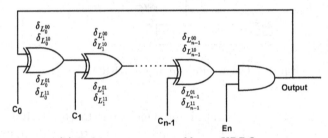

(b) Delay components of lower XRRO.

Fig. 11. Delay components of the selected XRROs.

Next, we build up the mathematical model of the XRRO PUF. For upper and lower XRRO, there are two XOR gates. Every XOR gate contributes four delay elements corresponding to input values of '00', '01', '10' and '11'. So, every stage of XRRO PUF contains total eight delay elements based on the input values of the two XOR gates. Let the delay elements associated with stage i of the upper XRRO of be $\delta_{U_i^{00}}$, $\delta_{U_i^{01}}$, $\delta_{U_i^{10}}$ and $\delta_{U_i^{11}}$ for the inputs AB = "00", "01", "10" and "11" respectively (as shown in Fig. 11a). Similarly for stage i of the lower XRRO, the delays be, $\delta_{L_i^{00}}$, $\delta_{L_i^{01}}$, $\delta_{L_i^{10}}$ and $\delta_{L_i^{11}}$ (as shown in Fig. 11b). Consider the input C_i to the XOR gates be the configuration bit.

Now the main crux of our attack is to find out how the computation of the oscillation frequency of XRRO is different from RO/CRO PUF. In RO/CRO PUF, whatever be the input signal (0/1), it simply gets passed through the buffer depending on the multiplexer selection. But this is not the case in XRRO. Here two inputs of the XOR gate are involved at every stage. Now, selection bit is fixed for a particular stage, i.e. either 0/1. Now, depending on the output of the previous stage, the inputs of the current stage can be either [00/10] or [01/11] and XOR logic is evaluated. And for every input pattern, the delay will be different. Thus two consecutive oscillation delays for the XRRO will be different due to the complement of the previous input. Finally, the frequency of the XRRO will be determined by the sum of the delay components that are selected by the configuration bits in two consecutive oscillations.

Hence, the delays selected for stage i for both upper and lower XRRO in two consecutive oscillations is given by the following equation where a challenge bit $C_i \in [-1, 1]$ is bipolar-encoded.

$$\Delta D_{upper}(i) = \frac{1 - C_i}{2}(\delta_{U_i^{00}} + \delta_{U_i^{10}}) + \frac{1 + C_i}{2}(\delta_{U_i^{01}} + \delta_{U_i^{11}})$$
$$\Delta D_{lower}(i) = \frac{1 - C_i}{2}(\delta_{L_i^{00}} + \delta_{L_i^{10}}) + \frac{1 + C_i}{2}(\delta_{L_i^{01}} + \delta_{L_i^{11}})$$

(10)

The total delays across stages for both upper and lower XRROs will be (for two consecutive oscillations),

$$\Delta D_{upper} = \sum_{i=0}^{n-1} \left[\frac{1 - C_i}{2}(\delta_{U_i^{00}} + \delta_{U_i^{10}}) + \frac{1 + C_i}{2}(\delta_{U_i^{01}} + \delta_{U_i^{11}}) \right]$$
$$\Delta D_{lower} = \sum_{i=0}^{n-1} \left[\frac{1 - C_i}{2}(\delta_{L_i^{00}} + \delta_{L_i^{10}}) + \frac{1 + C_i}{2}(\delta_{L_i^{01}} + \delta_{L_i^{11}}) \right]$$

(11)

The XRRO PUF response is generated by the comparison of ΔD_{upper} and ΔD_{lower}, generating a binary 1 if ΔD_{upper} has lesser value than ΔD_{lower} and 0 if it is the opposite. Let the difference be ΔD,

$$\Delta D = \sum_{i=0}^{n-1} \left[\frac{1 - C_i}{2}(\delta_{U_i^{00}} + \delta_{U_i^{10}}) + \frac{1 + C_i}{2}(\delta_{U_i^{01}} + \delta_{U_i^{11}}) \right]$$
$$- \sum_{i=0}^{n-1} \left[\frac{1 - C_i}{2}(\delta_{L_i^{00}} + \delta_{L_i^{10}}) + \frac{1 + C_i}{2}(\delta_{L_i^{01}} + \delta_{L_i^{11}}) \right] \quad (12)$$

$$\Delta D = \left[\sum_{i=0}^{n-1} \frac{1 - C_i}{2}(\delta_{U_i^{00}} + \delta_{U_i^{10}}) - \sum_{i=0}^{n-1} \frac{1 - C_i}{2}(\delta_{L_i^{00}} + \delta_{L_i^{10}}) \right]$$
$$+ \left[\sum_{i=0}^{n-1} \frac{1 + C_i}{2}(\delta_{U_i^{01}} + \delta_{U_i^{11}}) - \sum_{i=0}^{n-1} \frac{1 + C_i}{2}(\delta_{L_i^{01}} + \delta_{L_i^{11}}) \right] \quad (13)$$

$$\Delta D = \left[\sum_{i=0}^{n-1} \frac{1 - C_i}{2}(\delta_{U_i^{00}} + \delta_{U_i^{10}} - \delta_{L_i^{00}} - \delta_{L_i^{10}}) \right]$$
$$+ \left[\sum_{i=0}^{n-1} \frac{1 + C_i}{2}(\delta_{U_i^{01}} + \delta_{U_i^{11}} - \delta_{L_i^{01}} - \delta_{L_i^{11}}) \right] \quad (14)$$

Let us assume,

$$\alpha_i = \delta_{U_i^{00}} + \delta_{U_i^{10}} - \delta_{L_i^{00}} - \delta_{L_i^{10}}, \quad \beta_i = \delta_{U_i^{01}} + \delta_{U_i^{11}} - \delta_{L_i^{01}} - \delta_{L_i^{11}}$$

Then,

$$\Delta D = \sum_{i=0}^{n-1} \frac{1 - C_i}{2}(\alpha_i) + \sum_{i=0}^{n-1} \frac{1 + C_i}{2}(\beta_i)$$

For convenience, we define $\vec{X}$ and $\vec{Y}$ such that,

$$\Delta D = \vec{X}\vec{W_\alpha} + \vec{Y}\vec{W_\beta} \tag{15}$$

where,

$$\vec{X} = \left\{ \frac{1 - C_0}{2}, \frac{1 - C_1}{2}, ..., \frac{1 - C_{n-1}}{2} \right\}, \quad \vec{Y} = \left\{ \frac{1 + C_0}{2}, \frac{1 + C_1}{2}, ..., \frac{1 + C_{n-1}}{2} \right\}$$

$$\vec{W_\alpha} = \left\{ \alpha_0, \alpha_1, ..., \alpha_{n-1} \right\}, \quad \vec{W_\beta} = \left\{ \beta_0, \beta_1, ..., \beta_{n-1} \right\}$$

In terms of a single weight vector and a single parity vector, the linear additive delay model of an XRRO PUF can be defined as,

$$\Delta D = \vec{Z}\vec{W} \tag{16}$$

where,

$$\vec{Z} = \left\{ \frac{1 - C_0}{2}, \frac{1 - C_1}{2}, ..., \frac{1 - C_{n-1}}{2}, \frac{1 + C_0}{2}, \frac{1 + C_1}{2}, ..., \frac{1 + C_{n-1}}{2} \right\}$$

$$\vec{W} = \left\{ \alpha_0, \alpha_1, ..., \alpha_{n-1}, \beta_0, \beta_1, ..., \beta_{n-1} \right\}$$

The frequency for the upper and lower XRRO selected of the XRRO PUF is given to be $F_{upper} = 2/\Delta D_{upper}$ and $F_{lower} = 2/\Delta D_{lower}$ respectively. If upper XRRO has a greater frequency then the binary response will be 1, else it will be 0. Thus, the response depends on the difference in the total delays for the two consecutive oscillations of both the XRROs(ΔD). This model has been used in Sect. 4 below to simulate an XRRO PUF and to evaluate it against the SVM and LR based attacks. Please note that we have to follow the same procedure as mentioned above for every pair of XRROs and create an instance of SVM/LR model. The collaborative accuracy of all such models provide us the ultimate accuracy of the XRRO PUF instance.

4   Machine Learning Attacks on XOR-Based Reconfigurable PUFs

Now we present our experimental set up and results on the prediction accuracy of modelling attacks on XRRO and XRBR PUFs.

Table 1. SVM attack on XRBR PUF.

Training CRPs	32 bit XRBR PUF	64 bit XRBR PUF	128 bit XRBR PUF
1000	92.40%	91.40%	90.20%
3000	95.76%	94.96%	93.76%
5000	96.32%	95.86%	93.94%
8000	96.60%	96.68%	95.36%
10000	97.55%	96.27%	95.73%

Table 2. SVM attack on XRRO PUF with 8 layers of XRROs.

Training CRPs	31 stage XRRO PUF	63 stage XRRO PUF	127 stage XRRO PUF
10000	87.21%	83.94%	75.21%
40000	91.65%	90.11%	86.97%
70000	94.25%	93.88%	89.69%
100000	95.32%	94.17%	91.38%
120000	96.18%	94.67%	93.16%
150000	96.14%	94.97%	92.81%
200000	96.57%	95.41%	94.00%

Table 3. SVM attack on XRRO PUF with 16 layers of XRROs.

Training CRPs	31 stage XRRO PUF	63 stage XRRO PUF	127 stage XRRO PUF
50000	86.33%	83.18%	78.88%
100000	90.55%	87.12%	81.98%
200000	93.96%	90.88%	87.49%
400000	93.90%	94.37%	90.71%
600000	95.76%	95.24%	92.95%
800000	96.27%	95.52%	93.59%
1000000	96.59%	95.61%	94.31%

SVM Attacks: A SVM classifies data by finding the best hyperplane that separates all data points belonging to one class from those belonging to the other class. The best hyperplane for an SVM is the one with the largest margin between the two classes. The SVM implementation in *scikit-learn* library is used for this work which can be found here [2].

Using the mathematical model discussed in Sect. 3.2, the SVM attack is performed on the XRBR PUF by training the model on the given CRP samples. The feature vector Φ is determined given the challenge vector (C) in the CRP, and the model is trained on that feature vectors and the associated responses. The response of the XRBR PUF(R_C) for the challenge vector C was formulated as $R_C = sgn(\mathbf{p}.\Phi^T)$ where $\mathbf{p}$ was defined as $\{p_0, p_1, ..., p_{n-1}\}$. In SVM formulation, the p_i terms do not appear explicitly as the classifier simply works to find the hyperplane with the largest margin to separate the challenges into two classes based on their responses. Table 1 shows the prediction rates for a 32, 64, and 128 bit XRBR PUF using the SVM method with training sample sizes (CRPs) ranging from 1000 to 10,000. Given 10,000 training CRPs, it is possible to predict the XRBR PUF design with greater than 95% accuracy, even for a large 128 bit XRBR PUF.

Table 4. SVM attack on XRRO PUF with 32 layers of XRROs.

Training CRPs	31 stage XRRO PUF	63 stage XRRO PUF	127 stage XRRO PUF
500000	91.83%	88.23%	84.60%
1000000	94.35%	92.12%	88.93%
1500000	94.35%	93.64%	90.45%
2000000	95.39%	94.23%	92.26%
3000000	96.27%	95.27%	93.61%

Table 5. SVM attack on XRRO PUF with 64 layers of XRROs.

Training CRPs	31 stage XRRO PUF	63 stage XRRO PUF	127 stage XRRO PUF
1000000	88.24%	84.78%	79.41%
1500000	90.27%	87.05%	81.84%
2000000	91.41%	88.50%	84.01%
3000000	92.93%	90.49%	86.98%
5000000	95.02%	92.60%	89.82%
8000000	96.24%	94.239%	92.14%

Table 6. LR attack on XRBR PUF.

Training CRPs	32 bit XRBR PUF	64 bit XRBR PUF	128 bit XRBR PUF
1000	97.10%	96.40%	94.30%
3000	98.80%	98.50%	98.40%
5000	99.22%	98.76%	98.30%
8000	99.12%	98.95%	98.97%
10000	99.53%	99.40%	99.06%

For attacking the XRRO PUF, We have created an instance of SVM model for each pair of XRROs. For each challenge provided, we separate the selection bits of both the multiplexers and the configurable bits to the XRROs. Identifying the pair of XRROs selected by the selection bits (of both multiplexers), we train the corresponding SVM model to the pair of XRROs selected. The training is been done on the configuration bits of the XRROs (i.e., C as going by the notation discussed in Sect. 3.4). The feature vector $\vec{Z}$ is derived from the vector C and the model is trained with the feature vectors and the associated responses. In the SVM formulation, no weight terms α_i or β_i (please ref to Sect. 3.4) appear explicitly as the classifier simply works to find the hyperplane with the largest margin to separate the challenges (Here challenges refers to the configuration signals to the XRROs) into two classes based on their responses. For the experimental purpose, we have chosen 8, 16, 32 and 64 layer XRRO PUF where every XRRO is of 31, 63 and 127 stage long. Table 2, 3, 4, 5 shows the prediction rates for a 31, 63, and 127 stage XRRO PUF having 8, 16, 32 and 64 layers respectively.

LR Attacks: LR method builds a linear model of the system using the correlation between an independent and dependent variable of a known training set. The LR implementation in *scikit-learn* library is used for this work [1].

Table 7. LR attack on XRRO PUF with 8 layers of XRROs.

Training CRPs	31 stage XRRO PUF	63 stage XRRO PUF	127 stage XRRO PUF
10000	90.96%	88.75%	82.65%
40000	97.31%	95.58%	93.48%
70000	98.03%	97.20%	95.29%
100000	98.53%	97.81%	96.99%
120000	98.71%	98.13%	97.17%
150000	98.94%	98.56%	97.42%
200000	99.09%	98.79%	98.30%

Table 8. LR attack on XRRO PUF with 16 layers of XRROs.

Training CRPs	31 stage XRRO PUF	63 stage XRRO PUF	127 stage XRRO PUF
50000	93.29%	90.64%	85.03%
100000	95.18%	93.36%	90.39%
200000	97.21%	95.87%	93.76%
400000	98.56%	97.81%	96.79%
600000	98.89%	98.37%	97.56%
800000	99.10%	98.71%	97.72%
1000000	99.21%	98.85%	98.29%

Table 9. LR attack on XRRO PUF with 32 layers of XRROs.

Training CRPs	31 stage XRRO PUF	63 stage XRRO PUF	127 stage XRRO PUF
500000	95.97%	94.25%	91.45%
1000000	96.94%	96.78%	94.95%
1500000	98.36%	97.61%	96.12%
2000000	98.65%	98.04%	97.00%
3000000	99.11%	98.59%	97.76%

Table 10. LR attack on XRRO PUF with 64 layers of XRROs.

Training CRPs	31 stage XRRO PUF	63 stage XRRO PUF	127 stage XRRO PUF
1000000	93.49%	91.02%	86.29%
1500000	95.64%	92.95%	88.90%
2000000	96.29%	94.22%	90.96%
3000000	97.04%	95.85%	93.34%
5000000	98.21%	96.97%	95.89%
8000000	99.02%	98.06%	97.07%

For attacking the XRBR PUF, The training is done on the CRPs set after transforming the challenge bits as discussed in Sect. 3.2. The model is then trained on the transformed CRPs set. Table 6 shows the prediction rates for a 32, 64, and 128 bit XRBR PUF using the LR method with training sample sizes(CRPs) ranging from 1000 to 10,000. Given 10,000 training CRPs, it is possible to predict the XRBR PUF design with greater than 99% accuracy, even for a large 128 bit XRBR PUF.

Similarly, using the modelling of XRRO PUF discussed in Sect. 3.4, we have performed the LR attack on XRRO PUF. Table 7, 8, 9, 10 shows the prediction rates for a 31, 63, and 127 stage XRRO PUF having 8, 16, 32 and 64 layers respectively. Finally we can conclude from the above mentioned results that LR method provides better prediction accuracy than SVM method in the case of both XRBR and XRRO PUF.

5   Conclusion

In this work, we investigate the security metrics of XRBR and XRRO PUFs which are recently proposed for generating hardware fingerprints in the resource constrained devices for IoT frameworks. Though the PUF architectures demand very low hardware overhead by maintaining substantial uniformity and reliability properties, the strengths of these designs against mathematical modeling was yet unexplored. To the best of our knowledge, this is the first work that tries to make predictive models for the same and scrutinises the vulnerabilities against machine learning attacks. We leverage a common flaw of not incorporating any non-linear elements in the designs and show how that makes both schemes prone to ML attacks. Hence these designs are not any better than a simple RO PUF or BR PUF design. Finally with the experimental validation we have shown that both the designs can be broken using SVM and LR algorithms with the accuracy of approximately upto 99%. Overall, reducing the hardware overhead of such architectures without being prone to ML attacks could be a very challenging research area and can be a potential direction for future work.

References

1. Scikit-learn Logistic Regression. https://scikit-learn.org/stable/modules/generated/sklearn.linear_model.LogisticRegression.html
2. Scikit-learn Support Vector Machine. https://scikit-learn.org/stable/modules/generated/sklearn.svm.SVC.html
3. Becker, G.T., Kumar, R.: Active and passive side-channel attacks on delay based puf designs. Cryptology ePrint Archive (2014)
4. Chen, Q., Csaba, G., Lugli, P., Schlichtmann, U., Rührmair, U.: The bistable ring PUF: a new architecture for strong physical unclonable functions. In: 2011 IEEE International Symposium on Hardware-Oriented Security and Trust, pp. 134–141. IEEE (2011)
5. Chen, Q., Csaba, G., Lugli, P., Schlichtmann, U., Rührmair, U.: Characterization of the bistable ring PUF. In: 2012 Design, Automation & Test in Europe Conference & Exhibition (DATE), pp. 1459–1462. IEEE (2012)
6. Gassend, B., Clarke, D., Van Dijk, M., Devadas, S.: Silicon physical random functions. In: Proceedings of the 9th ACM Conference on Computer and Communications Security, pp. 148–160 (2002)
7. Gu, C., Hanley, N., O'neill, M.: Improved reliability of FPGA-based PUF identification generator design. ACM Trans. Reconfigurable Technol. Syst. (TRETS). **10**(3), 1–23 (2017)
8. Guajardo, J., Kumar, S.S., Schrijen, G.-J., Tuyls, P.: FPGA intrinsic PUFs and their use for IP protection. In: Paillier, P., Verbauwhede, I. (eds.) CHES 2007. LNCS, vol. 4727, pp. 63–80. Springer, Heidelberg (2007). https://doi.org/10.1007/978-3-540-74735-2_5
9. Guajardo, J., Kumar, S.S., Schrijen, G.J., Tuyls, P.: Physical unclonable functions and public-key crypto for FPGA ip protection. In: 2007 International Conference on Field Programmable Logic and Applications, pp. 189–195. IEEE (2007)
10. Holcomb, D.E., Fu, K.: Bitline PUF: building native challenge-response PUF capability into any SRAM. In: Batina, L., Robshaw, M. (eds.) CHES 2014. LNCS, vol. 8731, pp. 510–526. Springer, Heidelberg (2014). https://doi.org/10.1007/978-3-662-44709-3_28
11. Hospodar, G., Maes, R., Verbauwhede, I.: Machine learning attacks on 65nm arbiter PUFs: accurate modeling poses strict bounds on usability. In: 2012 IEEE International Workshop on Information Forensics and Security (WIFS), pp. 37–42. IEEE (2012)
12. Lim, D.: Extracting secret keys from integrated circuits in master thesis. Massachusetts Institute of Technology (2004)
13. Liu, W., et al.: XOR-based low-cost reconfigurable PUFs for IoT security. ACM Trans. Embed. Comput. Syst. (TECS) **18**(3), 1–21 (2019)
14. Lofstrom, K., Daasch, W.R., Taylor, D.: IC identification circuit using device mismatch. In: 2000 IEEE International Solid-State Circuits Conference. Digest of Technical Papers (Cat. No. 00CH37056), pp. 372–373. IEEE (2000)
15. Maes, R., Rozic, V., Verbauwhede, I., Koeberl, P., Van der Sluis, E., van der Leest, V.: Experimental evaluation of physically unclonable functions in 65 nm CMOS. In: 2012 Proceedings of the ESSCIRC (ESSCIRC), pp. 486–489. IEEE (2012)
16. Maiti, A., Schaumont, P.: Improved ring oscillator PUF: an FPGA-friendly secure primitive. J. Cryptology **24**(2), 375–397 (2011)
17. Miskelly, J., Gu, C., Ma, Q., Cui, Y., Liu, W., O'Neill, M.: Modelling attack analysis of configurable ring oscillator (CRO) PUF designs. In: 2018 IEEE 23rd International Conference on Digital Signal Processing (DSP), pp. 1–5. IEEE (2018)

18. Pappu, R., Recht, B., Taylor, J., Gershenfeld, N.: Physical one-way functions. Science **297**(5589), 2026–2030 (2002)
19. Rührmair, U., Sehnke, F., Sölter, J., Dror, G., Devadas, S., Schmidhuber, J.: Modeling attacks on physical unclonable functions. In: Proceedings of the 17th ACM Conference on Computer and Communications Security, pp. 237–249 (2010)
20. Rührmair, U., et al.: PUF modeling attacks on simulated and silicon data. IEEE Trans. Inf. Forensics Secur. **8**(11), 1876–1891 (2013)
21. Sahoo, D.P., Nguyen, P.H., Chakraborty, R.S., Mukhopadhyay, D.: Architectural bias: a novel statistical metric to evaluate arbiter PUF variants. IACR Cryptol. ePrint Arch. **2016**, 57 (2016)
22. Suh, G.E., Devadas, S.: Physical unclonable functions for device authentication and secret key generation. In: 2007 44th ACM/IEEE Design Automation Conference, pp. 9–14. IEEE (2007)
23. Tehranipoor, F., Karimian, N., Yan, W., Chandy, J.A.: Dram-based intrinsic physically unclonable functions for system-level security and authentication. IEEE Trans. Very Large Scale Integr. Syst. **25**(3), 1085–1097 (2016)
24. Xu, X., Rührmair, U., Holcomb, D.E., Burleson, W.: Security evaluation and enhancement of bistable ring PUFs. In: Mangard, S., Schaumont, P. (eds.) RFIDSec 2015. LNCS, vol. 9440, pp. 3–16. Springer, Cham (2015). https://doi.org/10.1007/978-3-319-24837-0_1
25. Zhou, C., Parhi, K.K., Kim, C.H.: Secure and reliable XOR arbiter PUF design: an experimental study based on 1 trillion challenge response pair measurements. In: 2017 54th ACM/EDAC/IEEE Design Automation Conference (DAC), pp. 1–6 (2017). https://doi.org/10.1145/3061639.3062315

HWGN²: Side-Channel Protected NNs Through Secure and Private Function Evaluation

Mohammad Hashemi[1](✉) [iD], Steffi Roy[2], Domenic Forte[2], and Fatemeh Ganji[1]

[1] Worcester Polytechnic Institute, Worcester, MA 01609, USA
{mhashemi,fgangi}@wpi.edu
[2] University of Florida, Gainesville, FL 32611, USA
steffiroy@ufl.edu, dforte@ece.ufl.edu
https://www.ece.ufl.edu/people/faculty/domenic-forte/,
http://vernam.wpi.edu/

Abstract. Recent work has highlighted the risks of intellectual property (IP) piracy of deep learning (DL) models from the side-channel leakage of DL hardware accelerators. In response, fundamental cryptographic approaches, specifically built upon the notion of secure and private function evaluation, could potentially improve the robustness against side-channel leakage. To examine this and weigh the costs and benefits, we introduce hardware garbled NN (HWGN²), a DL hardware accelerator implemented on FPGA. HWGN² also provides NN designers with the flexibility to protect their IP in real-time applications, where hardware resources are heavily constrained, through a hardware-communication cost trade-off. Concretely, we apply garbled circuits, implemented using a MIPS architecture that achieves up to $62.5\times$ fewer logical and $66\times$ less memory utilization than the state-of-the-art approaches at the price of communication overhead. Further, the side-channel resiliency of HWGN² is demonstrated by employing the test vector leakage assessment (TVLA) test against both power and electromagnetic side-channels.

Keywords: Side-channel analysis · Deep learning · Secure function evaluation · Private function evaluation

1 Introduction

An ever-increasing number of applications are demanded from machine learning and, in particular, deep learning (DL). These applications, among other compute-intensive services, have been supported by cloud platforms equipped with hardware acceleration [9]; however, cloud platforms are not the only hosts of DL algorithms and modules. IoT edge devices have embodied modules to perform many tasks, for instance, image classification or speech recognition as required by wearable devices for augmented reality and virtual reality [27]. In addition to those, so-called mobile and wearable devices, low-cost DL chips (e.g., sensors

© The Author(s), under exclusive license to Springer Nature Switzerland AG 2022
L. Batina et al. (Eds.): SPACE 2022, LNCS 13783, pp. 225–248, 2022.
https://doi.org/10.1007/978-3-031-22829-2_13

or actuators) have been employed to support DL-inference in cameras, medical devices, appliances, autonomous surveillance, ground maintenance systems, and even toys. Under DL-inference scenarios, trained neural networks (NNs) are made available to users. To obtain such a trained NN, a large training dataset is used in a time-consuming process to tune NN hyperparameters, which cannot be repeated in a straightforward manner. Therefore, it can be tempting for an adversary to target the DL-inference accelerator and extract those parameters. Besides hyperparameters, the architecture of NNs is another asset to protect as it may (even partially) reveal private information [16,17] or at least help the adversary to reconstruct the NN [1,4]. Since physical access can make it further easier for attackers to reverse-engineer and disclose the assets (i.e., architecture and hyperparameters) corresponding to NNs, usual protections, e.g., blocking binary readback, blocking JTAG access, code obfuscation, etc. could be applied to prevent binary analysis [4]. These, of course, would not stop an attacker from leveraging the information that leaks through side-channels [4,14,52,55].

These attacks have resulted in considerable efforts to devise countermeasures. Intuitively, masking schemes developed to protect cryptographic modules against SCA have been one of the first solutions discussed in the literature [12,13]. These methods come with their own set of challenges, e.g., being limited to a pre-defined level of security associated with the masking order or even to a particular modality. Moreover, evidently, masking cannot stop the attacker from disclosing the architecture of the NN under attack. The natural question to be asked is why fundamental cryptographic concepts that can provide NNs with robustness against SCA have not yet been examined. Concretely, secure function evaluation (SFE), specifically garbled circuits evaluation, has been considered to prevent side-channel leakage cf. [21,33]. Nevertheless, in practice, SFE has not been considered to stop side-channel attacks, perhaps, due to the high overhead initially observed in [21]. Their implementation on a field-programmable gate array (FPGA) is a combination of tamper-resistant hardware with Yao's garbling scheme [53], which comes with an overhead of about factor $10^6\times$ compared to an unprotected AES embedded in an FPGA.

Apart from the leakage properties of SFE and its realization garbled circuits, they have been developed to ensure the security of users' data, when two parties jointly evaluate a known function. Therefore, in a natural way, garbled circuits have been investigated to put forward the notion of privacy-preserving inference-as-a-service [39,40]. In spite of these results, the gap between these studies is evident: design of countermeasures against SCA, software implementation of garbled NNs [20,39,41], and hardware implementations of garbled circuits [44]. To narrow this gap, this paper introduces HWGN^2 (hardware garbled NN) and contributes to the following aims.

– *A secure and private DL-inference hardware accelerator, resilient to SCA.* To protect the NN model (including its architecture and parameters) against SCA, HWGN^2 relies on the principles of private function evaluation (PFE) and SFE, realized through a general purpose processor cf. [44,46]. Interestingly enough, as opposed to the argument in [21,33] suggesting the side-channel resiliency of

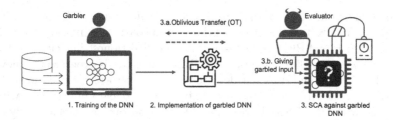

Fig. 1. HWGN^2 framework: The process begins with training the NN as done for a typical DL task. The second step corresponds to the implementation of the garbled NN hardware accelerator along with running the OT protocol. The end-user poses the accelerator and attempts to collect the side-channel traces to extract information on the NN (architecture, hyperparameters, etc.).

garbled circuits, Levi et al. have recently demonstrated a side-channel attack against garbling schemes leveraging the free-XOR optimization [28]. HWGN^2 is not susceptible to this attack since PFE is taken into account to make the function private. It is noteworthy that the privacy of the NN model is understudied even in existing software garbled DL-inference [2,39,41]. Our instruction set-based HWGN^2 is model-agnostic. Moreover, in the most cost-efficient setting with a DL-inference realized by using XNOR operators, our implementation does not require any modification to the NN, in contrast to what has been proposed as software garbled DL-inference [39].

- *Effectiveness and cost-efficiency of SCA protection relying on SFE/PFE.* To evaluate the feasibility of our approach, we identify two implementation scenarios, namely (1) resource- and (2) communication-efficient. In the first category, compared to the unprotected NN, the overhead is up to 0.0011× and 0.018× more logical and memory hardware resources, respectively; however, this relatively low overhead is achieved at the cost of communication between the user and the inference service provider. If communication constitutes a burden on the system, it can be dealt with, even though compared to the unprotected design, the overhead increases to 52.4× and 40.8× more logical and memory hardware resources, respectively. However, even under the communication-efficient scenario, HWGN^2 utilizes up to 62.5× fewer logical and 66× less memory, respectively, compared to the most relevant study [41]. Additionally, the side-channel resiliency of HWGN^2 implementation on the FPGA is assessed by applying T-test leakage detection.

2 Adversary Model

Valuable assets of NNs, as intellectual property (IP), include their NN architectures, hyperparameters, and the parameters critical to achieving reasonable accuracy [4]. On the other hand, these NNs might be used in applications in which their inputs contain sensitive information (e.g., medical or defense records [34]). Hence, the security of inputs given to NNs along with the privacy of the networks themselves must be guaranteed. Note that here the definitions of security and privacy are borrowed from SFE- and private function evaluation- (PFE) related litera-ture [6]. Classically, two threat models have been considered in prior works in the contexts of SFE and PFE: (i) *semi-honest* (so-called Honest-but-curious (HbC)) and (ii) *malicious* (active) adversary. An HbC adversary is expected to follow the protocol execution and does not deviate from the protocol specifications. To be more specific, the HbC adversary may only be able to learn information without interfering with the protocol execution. On the contrary, a malicious adversary may attempt to cheat or deviate from the protocol execution specifications.

In our work, we consider the HbC adversary, whose role is played by Bob (i.e., the evaluator), whereas Alice is the garbler [6,29] (see Fig. 1). Following the definition of the attack model presented in the state-of-the-art (SOTA), e.g., [12,13], the DL model provider (garbler) trains the DL model in an offline fashion, and the evaluator performs the inference. It is important to stress that the hardware implementation encompasses solely the evaluator engine, i.e., nei-ther garbling nor encryption module is implemented on the hardware platform. To evaluate the garbled DL accelerator, the evaluator feeds her garbled inputs prepared in an offline manner. The evaluator can collect power/EM traces from the device either via direct access or remotely, see e.g., [43,56]. For this, the eval-uator follows a chosen-plaintext-type attack model, where she sends her inputs to the device for classification and readily captures multiple traces. These traces will be then used to launch power/EM-based side-channel attacks [8,10,25]. The goal of the garbler is to protect the NN architectures, hyperparameters, and parameters from the HbC evaluator. HWGN^2 fulfills this requirement through SFE/PFE techniques (see Sect. 5).

3   Related Work

3.1   SCA Against NNs

The main goals of SCA targeting DL hardware accelerators can be: (i) extrac-tion of model architectures, and (ii) revealing NN parameters (i.e., weights and biases). For this purpose, Xiang et al. [52] presented a power side-channel attack to extract the model architectures. Using these power consumption models built for different model components, an SVM-based classifier was trained to reveal the model architectures running on the hardware accelerator. This line of research has also been pursued by Batina et al. [4] who introduced an attack scenario based on the EM and timing side-channel to extract the number of layers, the number of neurons in each layer, weights, and activation functions (AF). First, they modeled the timing side-channel of all possible AF (e.g., Relu or Tanh) and extracted the AF used in the NN by comparing the response time of the DL hardware accelerator when it executed the AF and the timing model of each possible AF. This is followed by analyzing EM traces captured when the DL hardware accelerator runs, where the EM patterns determine the number of lay-ers and number of neurons in each layer. By feeding different random inputs to the accelerator and capturing the EM traces, it was possible to launch a Correlation Power Analysis (CPA) to reveal the weights. In another approach,

Table 1. SOTA approaches vs. HWGN² (**P**arameters Secrecy of DL Model. **U**pgrade-able to/supporting malicious security model. **A**rchitecture protection of DL model. Constant-round complexity. **I**ndependence of a secondary server). Inspired by [39].

Approach	P	U	A	C	I
DeepSecure [42]	✓	✓	✗	✓	✓
Chameleon [40]	✓	✗	✗	✗	✗
XONN [39]	✓	✓	✗	✓	✓
BoMaNET [13]	✓	✗	✗	✓	✓
ModuloNET [12]	✓	✗	✗	✓	✓
TinyGarble2 [20]	✓	✓	✗	✓	✓
RedCrypt [41]	✓	✓	✗	✓	✗
HWGN² [This paper]	✓	✓	✓	✓	✓

Breier et al. [7] have presented a reverse engineering attack to extract the DL model weights and biases (parameters) with the help of fault injection on the last hidden layer of the network (see Table 5 in Appendix A).

3.2 Security-Preserving DL Accelerators

To protect NNs against SCA, Liu et al. [32] introduced a shuffling and fake memory-based approach to mitigate reverse engineering attacks that increase the run time of a DL hardware accelerator when the depth of the NN increases. Regarding the similarity between SCA launched against cryptographic implementations and DL accelerators, in a series of work, Dubey et al. have proposed hiding and masking techniques to protect NNs [12–14]. Yet, the differences between these implementations make the adaptation of known side-channel defenses challenging; for instance, integer arithmetic used in neural network computations that is different from modular arithmetic in cryptography, which has been addressed in [12,14]. Despite the impressive achievements presented in these studies, the approaches suffer from the known limitations of masking, i.e., their restriction to a specific side-channel security order. Furthermore, the implementation of masked DL models (i.e., a new circuit should be designed/implemented for different NNs) would be a challenging task. Moreover, masking cannot protect the architecture of DL models.

3.3 Garbled Accelerators

Among proposals put forward to make SFE practical, GarbledCPU [46] and RedCrypt [41] are of great importance to our work since they consider a hardware implementation of garbled circuits, whereas other relevant studies such as [3,20,39,40,42,44] devoted to software-based garbling engine/evaluator (other implementations have been compared in Table 6 in Appendix A). [46] has demonstrated a hardware garbling evaluator implemented on general-purpose sequential processors, where the privacy of NN architectures is also ensured.

While benefiting from the simplicity of programming a processor, their design is specific to Microprocessor without Interlocked Pipelined Stages (MIPS) architecture. This has been addressed by introducing ARM2GC framework, where the circuit to be garbled/evaluated is the synthesized ARM processor circuit that can support pervasiveness and conditional execution [45]. The efficiency in terms of hardware resources and communication cost has been reported as well.

RedCrypt attempts to enable cloud servers to provide high-throughput and power-efficient services to their clients in a real-time manner [41]. For this, FPGA platforms (Virtex UltraSCALE VCU108) have been used as a garbling core to present an efficient GC architecture with precise gate-level control per clock cycle, which ensures minimal idle cycles. This results in a multiple-fold improvement in the throughput of garbling operation compared to the previous hardware garbled circuit accelerator [44,46]. In their scenario, a host CPU is involved in an OT to communicate the evaluator labels/input with the client, which may need high bandwidth. Although RedCrypt [41] has achieved significant improvement in computational efficiency, the DL model implemented on the FPGA cannot be easily diversified. Their proposed hardware DL accelerator suits a specific type of DL model and is built on the assumption that the network architecture is publicly available, which allows an adversary to launch an SCA attack easier [4]. These shortcomings are tackled by $HWGN^2$ that is NN-agnostic and guarantees the privacy of the DL model, i.e., the secrecy of its architecture. A qualitative comparison between SOTA approaches and $HWGN^2$ is provided in Table 1. $HWGN^2$ shares similarities with TinyGarble2 [20], although they are software and hardware accelerators, respectively.

4   Background

4.1   SFE/PFE Protocols

SFE protocols enable a group of participants to compute the correct output of some agreed-upon function f applied to their secure inputs without revealing anything else. One of the commonly-applied SFE protocols is Yao's garbled circuit [53], a two-party computation protocol. To formalize this protocol, we employ the notions and definitions provided in [6] to support modular and simple but effective analyses. In this regard, a garbling algorithm Gb is a randomized algorithm, i.e., involves a degree of randomness. $Gb(f)$ is a triple of functions $(F, e, d) \leftarrow Gb(f)$ that accepts the function $f : \{0,1\}^n \rightarrow \{0,1\}^m$ and the security parameter k. $Gb(f)$ exhibits the following properties. The encoding function e converts an initial input $x \in \{0,1\}^n$ into a garbled input $X = e(x)$, which is given to the function F to generate the garbled output $Y = F(X)$. In this regard, e encodes a list of tokens (so-called labels), i.e., one pair for each bit in $x \in \{0,1\}^n$: $En(e, \cdot)$ uses the bits of $x = x_1 \cdots x_n$ to select from $e = (X_0^1, X_1^1, \cdots, X_n^0, X_n^1)$ and obtain the sub-vector $X = X_1^{x_1}, \cdots, X_n^{x_n}$. By reversing this process, the decoding function d generates the final output $y = d(Y)$, which must be equal to $f(x)$. In other words, f is a combination of probabilistic functions $d \circ F \circ e$. More precisely, the garbling scheme

$G = (Gb, En, De, Ev, ev)$ is composed of five algorithms as shown in Fig. 2, where the strings d, e, f, and F are used by the functions De, En, ev, and Ev (see Sect. 5 for a concrete protocol flow in the case of NNs).

Security of Garbling Schemes: For a given scheme, the security can be roughly defined as the impossibility of acquiring any information beyond the final output y if the party has access to (F, X, d). Formally, this notion is explained by defining the side-information function $\Phi(\cdot)$. Based on the definition of this function, an adversary cannot extract any information besides y and $\Phi(f)$ when the tuple (F, X, d) is accessible. As an example of how the function $\Phi(\cdot)$ is determined, note that for an SFE protocol, where the privacy of the function f is not ensured, $\Phi(f) = f$. Thus, the only thing that leaks is the function itself. On the other hand, when a PFE protocol is run, $\Phi(f)$ is the circuit/function's size, e.g., number of gates.

Oblivious Transfer (OT): This is a two party protocol where party 2 transfers some information to party 1 (so-called evaluator); however, party 2 remains oblivious to what information party 1 actually obtains. A form of OT widely used in various applications is known as "chosen one-out-of-two", denoted by 1-out-of-2 OT. In this case, party 2 has bits X^0 and X^1, and party 1 uses one private input bit s. After running the protocol, party 1 only gets the bit X^s, whereas party 2 does not obtain any information on the value of s, i.e., party 2 does not know which bit has been selected by party 1. This protocol can be extended to support the n-bit case, where party 1 bits $x_1, \cdots, x_n$ are applied to the input of party 2 $X_1^0, X_1^1, \cdots, X_n^0, X_n^1$ to obtain $X_1^{x_1}, \cdots, X_n^{x_n}$. This is possible by sequential repetition of the basic protocol [6]. It has been proven that 1-out-of-2 OT is universal for 2-party SFE, i.e., OT schemes can be the main building block of SFE protocols [24].

4.2   Neural Networks (NNs)

An NN is one of the main categories of machine learning, referring to learning a non-linear function through multiple layers of neurons with the goal of predicting the output corresponding to a given input. To perform such prediction, the input is fed to the first layer of the network (so-called *input layer*), whereas in the next layers (so-called *hidden layers*) the abstraction of the data takes place. For a *multi-layer perceptron* (MLP) that is a fully connected NN, each layer's input (including the input layer) is multiplied by neuron weights, added to the bias, and finally given to a commonly-applied *activation functions* at the output of each layer (excluding the input layer), e.g., Sigmoid, Tanh, and Rectified Linear Unit (ReLu). The activation functions that might be used in DL models include linear, Sigmoid, and softmax.

5   Foundations of HWGN²

Protocol Flow: Here we provide insight into how SFE/PFE schemes can be tailored to the needs of a secure and private DL accelerator. According to the general flow illustrated in Fig. 2, the goal of a garbling protocol G is to evaluate a function f against some inputs x to obtain the output y. The evaluator (i.e., the attacker) is never in possession of the raw NN binaries. Let $f = f_{NN}$ denote the function corresponding to the NN. The attacker aims to obtain the information on f_{NN} by collecting the side-channel traces. To achieve this, here we give an example of SFE protocol G that has OT at its core and follows Yao's garbling principle, i.e., the garbling protocol $G = (Gb, En, De, Ev, ev)$ as shown in Fig. 2. To execute the protocol, the designer of the NN accelerator (garbler) conducts $(F, e, d) \leftarrow Gb(1^k, f)$ on inputs 1^k and f and parses $(X_0^1, X_1^1, \cdots, X_n^0, X_n^1) \leftarrow e$. Afterward, the garbler sends F to the evaluator, i.e., the attacker. In order to perform the function Ev, the attacker and the garbler run the OT, where the former has the selection string x and the latter party has already parsed $(X_0^1, X_1^1, \cdots, X_n^0, X_n^1)$. Hence, the evaluator can obtain $X = X_1^{x_1}, \cdots, X_n^{x_n}$ and consequently, $y \leftarrow De(d, Ev(F, X))$. Note that even with the tuple (F, X, d) in hand, the attacker cannot extract any information besides y and $\Phi(f)$. Moreover, although the NN provider has access to (F, e, d), no information on x leaks. In an inference scenario, x represents the evaluator's input data. Nevertheless, if G is an SFE scheme, $\Phi(f) = f$.

To construct a PFE scheme protecting the architecture, parameters, and hyperparameters of the NN that relies on the scheme G, we first define a polynomial algorithm Π that accepts the security parameter k and the (private) input of the party [6]. The PFE scheme is a pair $\mathcal{F} = (\Pi, ev)$, where ev is as defined for the garbling scheme (see Sect. 6 for more information about Π). The scheme $\mathcal{F}$ enable us to securely compute the *class* of functions $\{ev(f, \cdot) : f \in \{0, 1\}^*\}$, i.e., any function that G can garble. The security of the PFE scheme $\mathcal{F}$ relies on the security of the SFE protocol underlying $\mathcal{F}$ (see Sect. 4.1); however, $\Phi(f)$ is the circuit size, i.e., the function f remains private when executing the SFE protocol. In other words, the NN, its architecture, parameters and hyperparameters are now kept private from the attacker.

Oblivious Inference: Oblivious inference tackles the problem of running the DL model on the user's input without revealing the input or the result to the other party (i.e., garbler in our case). For the latter, another interesting characteristic of SFE/PFE schemes is their ability to adapt to specific scenarios, where the output y should also be protected. This would not be interesting in our case, where the security of the NN against SCA mounted by the evaluator is the objective. Nonetheless, for the sake of completeness, if the decryption of Y should be performed securely, the privacy of inference results can easily be preserved by applying a one-time message authentication code (MAC) to the output and XORing the result with a random input to hide the outcome. These operations can be included in the design of the NN and naturally increase its size and the input fed by the garbler; however, the increase is linear in the number of output bits and considered inexpensive [30].

5.1 Implementation of HWGN²

When defining the PFE scheme $\mathcal{F}$, it is mentioned that $\mathcal{F}$ can securely and privately compute *any* function, which can be garbled by running the garbling

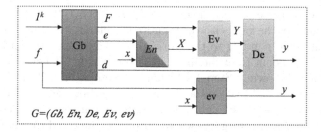

Fig. 2. A generic garbling scheme $G = (Gb, En, De, Ev, ev)$ cf. [6]. Our proposed secure and private DL accelerator is built upon G. For HWGN², the blocks in orange show the operations performed by the NN vendor, whereas the gray ones indicate the evaluator operations. ev denotes the typical, unprotected evaluation of the function f against the input x.

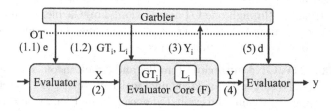

Fig. 3. Flow of HWGN² (L: garbled wire labels, GT: garbled tables, e and d: encryption and decryption labels, X: evaluator's garbled input, Y: garbled output, Y_i, X_i, GT_i, L_i: garbled input, output, tables, wire labels corresponding to i^{th} sub-netlist, respectively, y: evaluator's raw output).

scheme G. Our garbled universal circuit $\mathcal{F}$ depends on the fact that a universal circuit is similar to a universal Turing machine [18], which can be realized by a general purpose processor cf. [44,46]. Note the difference between our goal, i.e., realizing $\mathcal{F}$, and one achieved in [50]: optimizing the emulation of an entire *public* MIPS program. Although we implemented a MIPS-based scheme, the prototypes can be extended to ARM processors. HWGN² garbles the MIPS instruction set with a minimized memory and logical hardware resource utilization (see Sect. 5.1).

Similarities Between HWGN² and TinyGarble2: One of the state-of-the-art GC frameworks is TinyGarble2 [20] offering solely *software* DL inference, without ensuring the privacy of the NN. HWGN² remedies these shortcomings; however, it shares similarities with TinyGarble2, namely regarding the flow of the protocol. The technique presented in TinyGarble2 is based on the division of a large netlist, such as DL models, into i smaller sub-netlists and evaluating them one after another. The size of the sub-netlists could be either one gate or equal to the total number of gates in the f netlist. The fewer gates included in each sub-netlist, the less memory utilization the gates require to be evaluated.

Figure 3 illustrates the flow of HWGN² in the presence of an HbC adversary. First, the garbler chooses input encryption labels (e) (Step 1.1). Afterward, instead of sending the complete set of GTs and L to the evaluator, in each cycle the garbler sends the evaluator a subset GT_i, L_i (Step 1.2), and either e (if the sub-netlist includes the gate with the inputs connected to the f netlist) or X_i (the garbled input corresponding to the sub-netlist). These subsets can be prepared offline and independent from the input of the evaluator. The evaluator also garbles her inputs as shown in Step 2, which is done offline as well. In the next step, the evaluator evaluates the gate and sends the garbler the garbled output Y_i, i.e., garbled output of the ith sub-netlist (Step 3). This process repeats until all i sub-netlists, excluding the gates whose output is connected to the NN outputs, are evaluated. Then in Step 4, the garbler sends the garbled tables and labels related to the gates that are connected to the NN output (so-called NN output layer). After the evaluator evaluates all output layer-related gates, the garbler sends the decryption label (Step 5) along with the concatenated garbled outputs to the evaluator. Finally, the evaluator decrypts the concatenated garbled output Y and achieves his raw output y. Also, instead of sending the complete set of GTs, L, and e through one OT interaction, TinyGarble2 requires one OT interaction per sub-netlist. The trade-off of minimizing the memory utilization using TinyGarble2 is the communication cost.

What Makes HWGN² superior: Parallel and simultaneous evaluation of all input gates might result in the side-channel leakages due to the secret collision; therefore, all input gates must be evaluated one after another without parallelization. However, the rest of the gates (without dependencies) have no information about the secrets, and thus, they can be evaluated simultaneously. Moreover, we have noticed that each gate evaluation (excluding reading/writing its inputs/output from/to the memory) requires one operation code (OP-code) which is an 8-bit part of a MIPS instruction. As we have assigned the reading and writing tasks to the memory handler module, it is possible to combine a set of four gates (non-input gates) and construct one modified MIPS instruction from them. In doing so, in the evaluation phase, all these four OP-codes can be executed using four parallel arithmetic logic units (ALU) on FPGA while this is an impractical task for central processing unit (CPU) due to its limited resources and operating system (OS) limitations. HWGN², contrary to the previous software and hardware accelerators including TinyGarble family [20,44], leverages these parallelization techniques. It also gives the flexibility of tuning the communication costs and hardware resource utilization to the garbler (e.g., NN provider). In the applications where communication cost poses a limitation (such as real-time applications), one can implement DL hardware accelerators by sending the complete set of GTs, L, and e through one OT interaction. This minimizes the communication cost while hardware resources are utilized at the maximum amount. In contrast, in the application with the limitation of hardware resources, one can use the HWGN² that implements DL hardware accelerators with the sub-netlist size of one or a small number of gates. As opposed to TinyGarble2, HWGN² implementation is based on the garbled MIPS architecture, making the circuit private (i.e., no information about the NN architecture leaks) as explained next.

MIPS Evaluator in HWGN². As explained before, in order to ensure the privacy of the NNs, the Boolean function representing the NN (so-called netlist) is converted to a set of reduced instruction set computing (RISC) instruction

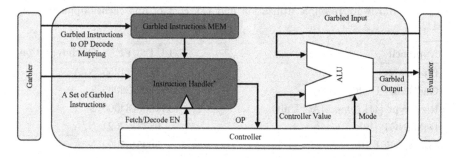

Fig. 4. Garbled MIPS evaluator, able to process any given number of instructions instead of a determined number. The black modules are extended and improved versions of memory and instruction handler in Lite_MIPS architecture [44]: the instruction handler prepares the controller sequence by comparing the garbled MIPS instructions and the OP mapping. The controller runs the process sequence by generating the ALU mode and executing the read and write operations.

set architecture (ISA) and evaluated on a core that executes the MIPS instructions [23]. It might be thought that a subset of instructions required to execute the NN is sufficient to be garbled in order to reduce the overhead; however, this could increase the probability of guessing which instructions are used and, consequently, violates the privacy of the NN.

To implement HWGN^2 on an FPGA, we modify Plasma [38] MIPS execution core emulating a RISC instruction set on the FPGA, to act as the garbled MIPS evaluator. Figure 4 illustrates the architecture of our garbled MIPS evaluator. The garbled evaluator receives three inputs: (i) a set of garbled instructions, (ii) the mapping for the instruction handler to fetch/decode the garbled instructions, and (iii) the evaluator's garbled input. The combination of the first and second ones (i, ii) is the set of garbled tables and labels described before. Our garbled MIPS evaluator can evaluate the garbled MIPS instructions in two modes: (a) by receiving only one instruction and the operation code (OP) mapping and its corresponding instruction each cycle, i.e., the garbled evaluator with the capacity of one instruction per OT interaction, or (b) by receiving the complete set of instructions and their corresponding OP mapping at once. To achieve the resource-efficient implementation (mode i), we have modified the Lite_MIPS instruction handler module in a way that the memory size related to the received garbled instructions (not the OP code mapping) decreases from 128 cells to only one cell. The controller is further enhanced by discarding the unnecessary scheduler, SCD storage memory and its parsing modules and tailoring the core to need of only one instruction conversion per OT. Moreover, we include the erase state in the instruction MEM controller, which sets all memory blocks to 0 after converting each garbled instruction to the OP code. To take advantage of the resource-efficient implementation, an extra step should be taken to divide the netlist into the sub-netlists with the number of gates selected by the user. The sub-netlists are fed to HWGN^2 in the same order provided in the SCD file. This allows the user to make a trade-off between the resource efficiency and performance of the HWGN^2.

Table 2. Hardware resource utilization and OT cost of approaches applied against BM1.

Approach	LUT	FF	OT interaction
Plasma [38]	1773	1255	N/A
GarbledCPU [46]	21229	22035	2
RedCrypt [41] (One MAC Unit)	111000	84000	2
BoMaNET [13]	9833	7624	N/A
ModulaNET [12]	5635	5009	N/A
HWGN^2 (1 instruction per OT interaction)	1775	1278	2346
HWGN^2 Complete set of instructions	94701	52534	2

Specifically, in mode (a), in the first step, the instruction handler module receives one garbled instruction and OP mapping (all possible combinations of garbled MIPS instructions necessary to follow SFE protocol), which are stored in the instructions memory (MEM). In the next step, the instruction handler compares the given garbled instructions with garbled instructions MEM information and converts each garbled instruction to a set of OPs. Finally, the instruction handler sends the OP to the arithmetic-logic unit (ALU), erase instructions MEM, and repeats above-mentioned steps for the next garbled instructions. In mode (b), however, the instruction handler module works similarly to the Lite_MIPS architecture cf. [44]. As both instruction sets and decode mapping are garbled on the garbler side, the evaluator cannot decrypt the garbled instructions. Therefore, the garbler's inputs and the DL model parameters are secure following the SFE and PFE protocols.

6   Evaluation of HWGN^2

6.1   Resource Utilization

To understand the interplay between communication cost, hardware resources utilization, and performance, we have synthesized the garbled evaluator with the capacity of 1 and 2345 (complete set of instructions) garbled MIPS instructions per one OT interaction. We have used Xilinx Vivado 2021 to synthesize our design and generate a bittsream. To ensure the bitstream correctness, we have disabled place-and-route optimization and also utilize the DONT-TOUCH attribute. The garbling framework considered in our implementations is Just-Garble [5], also embedded in TinyGarble2 framework [20], which enjoys garbling optimization techniques such as Free-XOR [26], Row Reduction [36], and Garbling with a Fixed-key Block Cipher [5]. Our implementation is applied against three typical MLPs: the first one, with 784 neurons in its input layer, three hidden layers each with 1024 neurons, and an output layer with 10 neurons that is trained on MNIST (hereafter called **BM1**). The results for applying SOTA approaches against BM1 have been presented in [12,41,46]. The second MLP,

Table 3. Execution time and communication cost comparison between HWGN^2 and the SOTA approaches (for BM1). Results for [46] and HWGN^2 are reported based on FPGA with clock frequency equals to $12.5MHz$. (N/R: not reported, inst.: instructions).

Approach	Time (Sec)	Communication (MB)
GarbledCPU [46]	1.74	N/R
RedCrypt [41]	0.63	5520
HWGN^2 (Complete set of inst. per OT interaction)	0.68	619
TinyGarble2 [20]	9.1	7.16
HWGN^2 (1 inst. per OT interaction)	3.25	12.39

BM2, has 784, 5, 5, and 10 neuron in its input, 2 hidden, and output layers, respectively. The third MLP, **BM3**, consists of 784, 6, 5, 5, and 10 neurons in its input, 3 hidden, and output layers, respectively.

Table 2 shows a comparison between the hardware utilization and OT cost of an unprotected MIPS evaluator core (Plasma [38]), HWGN^2 and the SOTA approaches applied to BM1. To give an insight into how much overhead cost the protection approaches impose, we have implemented Plasma core, an unprotected MIPS evaluator core on an Artix-7 FPGA. Note that we choose this architecture for the sake of a better comparison with the SOTA solutions, e.g., [12]. It is also worth mentioning that since the ultimate goal of our paper is to demonstrate the applicability of garbling techniques for side-channel resiliency, the network mentioned above is chosen to serve as a proof of concept. As the HWGN^2 processes the garbled instructions and inputs with the width of 32-bits, to have a fair comparison, we include the 32-bit MAC unit [41] in the resource utilization reported in Table 2.

In Table 2, BoMaNET and ModulaNET do not use OT to exchange their inputs. RedCrypt uses two OT interactions, one for the evaluator's input and another for the evaluator's output. However, in HWGN^2, in addition to the input and output labels exchange OT requirement, HWGN^2 requires M more OT interactions, where M is the number of sub-netlists. There is an important observation made from Table 2: HWGN^2 with the capacity of one instruction per OT interaction utilizes $0.0011\times$ and $0.018\times$ more logical and memory hardware resources, respectively, compared to an unprotected MIPS evaluator. The reason behind this efficiency is the size of instruction memory which stores only one instruction per OT interaction instead of the complete set of instructions. As mentioned in Sect. 5.1, to minimize resource utilization, one should sacrifice the communication cost, leading to an increased execution time. Hence, we set the size of the sub-netlist to just one gate, and every four gates are converted to a garbled instruction: $M = N_{gate}/4$, where N_{gate} is the number of gates in the netlist. In this setting, HWGN^2 requires $2 + 9380/4 = 2346$ OT interactions, where 9380 is the number of gates included in the BM1 netlist. In real-time applications where the execution time is the bottleneck, the OT interactions must be minimum [41]. Therefore, in Table 2, we also have reported the hardware resource utilization in two cases:

Table 4. Execution time and communication cost of HWGN^2 applied to BM1 accelerator and its XNOR-based implementation.

Architecture	#Instructions	OT Interaction	Execution Time (Sec)	Communication (MB)
BM1	2345	2346	3.25	12.39
XNOR-based BM1	1629	1631	2.31	9.71

(i) when the number of OT interactions is maximum (6th row) and (ii) when the number of OT interactions is minimum (7th row). The results in Table 2 are for the implementation of BM1. As shown in Table 3, HWGN^2 with the maximum performance is 2.5× faster than GarbledCPU [46]. Performance of HWGN^2 is close to the performance of Redcrypt [41], the fastest SOTA approach, while utilizing 62.5× fewer logical and 66× less memory than Redcrypt [41].

Execution Time and Communication Cost Evaluation. To evaluate the cost of HWGN^2 in terms of execution time, we have used a machine with Intel Core i7-7700 CPU @ 3.60 GHz (GHz), 16 Gigabyte (GBs) RAM, and Linux Ubuntu 20 as the garbler and an ARTIX7 FPGA board as the evaluator, which has a clock frequency of 12.5 MHz (MHz). All the garbled instructions, their MEM values, and labels are generated offline and not included in the execution time. To communicate with the FPGA, for the sake of comparison, we have used HostCPU presented in [41]. Note that in a real-world application, where the communication is performed over high latency links, the protocol execution remains fast due to the constant number of rounds in Yao's GC underlying our design cf. [22,31]. Moreover, we have used the EMP-toolkit [51] to establish the OT interaction between the garbler and the HostCPU. Table 3 shows the execution time and communication cost comparison between HWGN^2 and the SOTA approaches employed against BM1. The memory footprint of classical GC approaches is $O(I + N_{gate})$, where I is the number of input wires and N_{gate} is the number of gates in the netlist. In contrast, the memory footprint of HWGN^2 and TinyGarble2 is the same: $O(I + N_{gate,m} + i_m)$ where $N_{gate,m}$ is the number of gates in the largest among sub-netlists included in the design, and i_m is the number of inputs of the sub-netlist, which equals 1 and 2, respectively, in the case of HWGN^2 with the instruction capacity 1 per OT interaction.

To compare the execution time and communication cost of TinyGarbled2 with our approach, we have chosen the semi-honest mode when using their framework. HWGN^2 outperforms the TinyGarble2 implemented on CPU thanks to the parallel implementation made possible by the FPGA. On the other hand, when minimizing the OT interactions by investing more hardware resource utilization, HWGN^2 has a performance close to the RedCrypt with 62.5× fewer logical and 66× less memory utilization.

As an optimization technique, we have implemented the XNOR-based BM1. As the XOR operation is free in the garbling protocol [26], it is possible to decrease the size of the garbled netlists, which results in fewer instructions to be executed. Table 4 shows a comparison between two architectures. Using an

XNOR-based implementation of a DL hardware accelerator decreases the number of instructions, leading to a less OT cost and execution time. The only limitation of this optimization is that the weights of the DL model must be binarized, and such binarization may slightly decrease the DL hardware accelerator output accuracy. Nevertheless, there are methods devised to deal with this, which can be adopted to bring significant benefits to garbled DL accelerators in terms of both OT cost and execution time.

6.2   Side-Channel Evaluation

Side-Channel Measurement Setup. HWGN^2 has been implemented on Artix-7 FPGA device XC7AT100T with package number FTG256. We have captured the power and EM traces (see Appendix C) using Riscure setup, including LeCroy wavePro 725Zi as the setup oscilloscope. We have set our design frequency to 12.5 MHz, the maximum possible clock frequency of Chipwhisperer CW305 target board, and the oscilloscope sampling frequency to 12.5 GHz. For each clock cycle, we have acquired 8100 sample points. Acquiring high-resolution side-channel traces made our design execution time 3.25 s for each classification performed by BM1. For this network, acquiring side-channel traces in the order of millions has high time complexity. Therefore, similar to [12], another MLP architecture, namely, **BM2** is used for traces collection. The changes in MLP architecture hyperparameters allowed us to execute each classification in 31 ms. As HWGN^2 executes each instruction separately in a sequential manner and the nature of the NNs is repetitive, we argue that the smaller MLP architecture can represent a larger one in terms of leakage.

Leakage Evaluation. We have used a common methodology, namely Test Vector Leakage Assessment (TVLA) test, to evaluate HWGN^2 leakage resiliency. Although the TVLA test is subject to two disadvantages – false positive/negative results and limited ability to reveal all points of interests [15,35,47] – it is still the most common methodology used in recent papers to evaluate the resiliency of the approach against side-channel leakage.

In the TVLA test methodology, Welch's t-test is used to check the similarity between two trace groups captured from two populations of inputs. Welch's t-test calculates the t-score as $t = (\mu_1 - \mu_2)/\sqrt{(s_1^2/n_1^2) + (s_2^2/n_2^2)}$, where μ_1 and μ_2 are the means, s_1 and s_2 are the standard deviations, and n_1 and n_2 are the total number of the captured traces for first and second population, respectively. Based on the null-hypothesis, if two populations are chosen from one distribution, their corresponding t-score must be less that ± 4.5. Exceeding t-score magnitude of 4.5 (so-called null-hypothesis) means the design is subject to side-channel leakage with probability greater than 99.99%. In our setup, we choose the non-specific fixed vs. random t-test in a way that our setup, first, captures the power consumption/EM traces from a fixed input computation for all the traces; then, the experiment repeats for a set of randomly generated inputs. Based on the two captured traces, for fixed and random inputs, our setup calculates the t-score based on the aforementioned equation.

Power Side-Channel Leakage Assessment. To illustrate the side-channel protection offered by HWGN^2, we have mounted the TVLA test on power traces of an unprotected MIPS core, Plasma core presented by Opencores projects [38], and HWGN^2, with the capacity of one instruction per OT interaction. Figure 5 (a) and (b) shows the TVLA results of an unprotected MIPS core and HWGN^2, with the capacity of one instruction per OT interaction, respectively. The t-scores are calculated based on 10000 captured traces, 5000 for each fixed and random input population. As one can observe, an unprotected MIPS core t-score has exceeded the ±4.5 threshold with only 10000 traces, while the HWGN^2's t-score remains below the threshold.

To have a design with leakage resiliency, the t-score results must remain below the threshold with the traces populations in the order of millions [11,12,35,47]. Hence, in the next experiment, we have captured a total of 2 million $(2M)$ traces, $1M$ traces for each fixed and random input populations. A low t-score, less than ±4.5, calculated from a trace population in the order of millions confirms the protection strength of HWGN^2. It should be noted that these traces are captured in the low-noise setup (i.e., more optimistic for the attacker) while in the actual scenario, the number of traces to break the garbling scheme should be significantly higher due to more noisy environments.

As a proof of concept that HWGN^2 side-channel resiliency is independent of the function or architecture we also mount the TVLA test on two more implementations: XNOR-based DL hardware accelerator and DL hardware accelerator. Figure 5, (c) and (e), illustrates the t-score of HWGN^2 applied to XNOR-based BM2, with the capacity of complete set of instructions per OT interaction and one instruction per OT, respectively. As can be seen, the t-scores of HWGN^2 stay below the threshold of ±4.5 for different cases of instruction capacity per OT interaction and the function or architecture implemented on an FPGA using HWGN^2. The t-scores in Fig. 5, (d) and (f), indicate that not only HWGN^2 with the capacity of one instruction per OT interaction provides a strong protection against power side-channel attacks but also changes in the number of instruction capacity per OT interaction does not affect this protection (for results of EM leakage detection, see Appendix C).

Can we see the Architecture-Related Patterns? Based on the attack presented by Batina et al. [4], revealing the DL model architecture can enhance the attacker's ability to obtain DL model parameters. They showed that the EM trace captured from an unprotected DL model implementation on Atmel ATmega328P microcontroller, which follows the MIPS architecture same as HWGN^2, with three hidden layers containing 6, 5, and 5 neurons, respectively, has a pattern in which the number of layers and neurons can be revealed. They have used LeCroy WaveRunner 610Zi oscilloscope and RF-U 5-2 near-field EM probe to capture EM traces. To examine if we observe the same patterns as reported in [4], we have implemented the same DL model, **BM3**, and captured 100K EM traces. Figure 6(a) illustrates the captured EM traces from an Atmel ATmega328P microcontroller taken from [4], whereas Fig. 6(b) show the traces collected from our unprotected MIPS evaluator core [38], and Fig. 6(c) presents

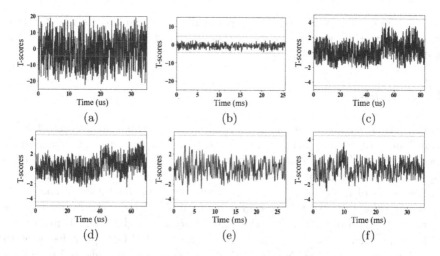

Fig. 5. TVLA test results for implementation of BM2 on (a) an unprotected MIPS core and (b) HWGN^2 with the capacity of one instruction per OT (calculated for 10K traces) (c) HWGN^2 applied to XNOR-based BM2 (capacity whole set of instructions per OT) (d) BM2 with the capacity of complete set of instructions per OT interaction, (e) HWGN^2 applied to XNOR-based BM2 (capacity 1 instruction per OT), and (f) BM2 with the capacity of 1 instruction per OT (calculated for 2M power traces).

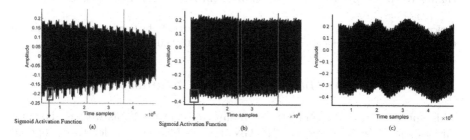

Fig. 6. A randomly chosen EM trace pattern captured from the implementation of BM3 on (a) Atmel ATmega328P microcontroller [4] (b) FPGA with unprotected MIPS evaluator [38] (c) with HWGN^2. Red lines correspond to time-samples, where the unprotected evaluators start the next layer evaluation.

the captured EM traces of HWGN^2 for a randomly chosen EM trace. From Fig. 6, it is observable that there exists a pattern, in which the number of the layers and neurons can be seen, similar to the observation made by Batina et al. [4]: the red lines indicate the borders when MIPS evaluator starts the next hidden layer evaluation and the red squares correspond to the EM peak of Sigmoid AF evaluation. In the case of the HWGN^2, EM traces do not follow a pattern, which could result in revealing the DL model architecture. The reason behind these irregular patterns is that each garbled instruction is encrypted; therefore, in the evaluation phase, the HWGN^2 treats them as two nonidentical instructions, although the generated OP corresponding to them is the same. Note that in addition to this observation, we further conduct t-tests, where no EM leakage is detected (see Appenddix C).

7 Conclusion

In this paper, we have examined the feasibility of garbling to prevent attackers from launching SCA attacks against DL hardware accelerators. We have implemented HWGN^2 as a garbled DL hardware accelerator on an Artix-7 FPGA. By tailoring the concepts known only for software garbled DL accelerator [20] to the needs of a hardware DL accelerator, the implementation of such accelerator is enhanced: HWGN^2 requires up to 62.5× fewer logical and 66× less memory utilization compared to the state-of-art approaches. This is indeed possible at the price of more communication overhead. HWGN^2 provides users the flexibility to protect their NN IP both in real-time applications and in applications where the hardware resources are limited by hardware resource utilization or communication cost. As our leakage evaluation results indicated, for both EM and power side-channels, the t-scores are below the threshold (±4.5), which shows the side-channel leakage resiliency of HWGN^2 with trace population in the order of millions. Another strength of HWGN^2 is the DL model architecture thanks to the SFE/PFE protocol realized through MIPS instructions.

Acknowledgements. This work was supported partially by Semiconductor Research Corporation (SRC) under Task IDs 2991.001 and 2992.001.

Appendix A. Summary of Relevant Studies

This appendix covers recent attacks mounted against NNs as well as the similarities and differences between HWGN^2 and garbled DL accelerators proposed to offer *security of users' data* in Tables 5 and 6.

Appendix B. TinyGarble-Based Implementation of HWGN^2

TinyGarble [44] is a garbling framework that supports Yao's protocol and uses hardware-synthesis tools to generate circuits for secure computation automatically. The main advantage of TinyGarble is the scalability enabled by exploiting a sequential circuit description for garbled circuits and garbling optimization techniques such as Free-XOR [26], Row Reduction [36], and Garbling with a Fixed-key Block Cipher [5]. Figure 7a illustrates the flow of HWGN^2 following TinyGarble [44] approach. At first, garbler chooses input encryption labels (e) (Step 1.1) and constructs the GC of function f by generating garbled tables (GT) of all gates, garbled labels (L) of all wires, and a custom circuit description (SCD) file (Step 1.2), which is the mapping between the GC and function f.

Table 5. Summary of most recent side-channel attacks against DL accelerators.

Paper	Targets	Side-channel modality	Attack scenario	Implementation platform
Xiang et al. [52]	DL Model Architecture	Power	• Modeling the power consumption of different DL hardware accelerator components based on the number of additions and multiplications • Trained a classifier to reveal the DL Model architecture based on the captured power consumption traces	Raspberry Pi
DeepEM [55]	DL Model Architecture	EM	• Presumption of a layer computations • Finding the number of parameters through each layer based on EM traces	Pynq-Z1
CSI NN [4]	DL Model Architecture +Weights +AF	Timing + EM	• Modeling all possible AF timing side-channel • Extracting the AF used in the DL Model Architecture • Distinguishing the EM patterns to find the number of layers and neurons • Launching CPA to reveal the weights	ARM Cortex-M3 + Atmel ATmega328P
Dubey et al. [14]	DL Model Weights	Power	• Capturing the power consumption traces from changing status of pipeline registers • Launching a CPA based attack to reveal weights	SAKURA-X FPGA board
Yoshida et al. [54]	DL Model Weights	Power	• Launching a CPA based attack to reveal weights	Xilinx Spartan3-A

Table 6. Summary of garbled DL accelerators and their features.

Paper	Adversary model	Approach	Contribution	Implementation platform
DeepSecure [42]	HbC	Garbling	• Presentation of pre-processing approach • pre-processing step would reveal some information about the network parameters and structure of data cf. [39]	Intel Core i7 CPUs
Chameleon [40]	HbC	Hybrid	• Performs linear operations using additive secret sharing and nonlinear operations using Yao's Garbled Circuits	8-Core AMD CPU 3.7GHz
Ball et al. [2]	HbC	Hybrid	• Improvement of the BMR scheme [3] to support Non-linear operations	Intel Core i7-4790 CPUs
XONN [39]	HbC	Garbling	• Support Binary NNs • Conversion of Matrix Multiplication to XNOR PopCount	Intel Xeon CPU E5-2650
TinyGarble2 [20]	HbC + Malicious	Garbling	• Provision of protection against malicious adversary • Alleviation garbling memory cost	Intel Xeon CPU E5-2650
GarbledCPU [46]	HbC	Garbling	• Presentation of FPGA accelerator for GC evaluation	Virtex-7 FPGA
RedCrypt [41]	HbC	Garbling	• Minimizing the hardware architecture idle cycles to achieve scalable garbling	Virtex UltraSCALE VCU108

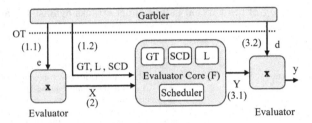

Fig. 7. TinyGarble-based implementation [44] of HWGN^2 (L: wires garbled labels, GT: garbled tables, e: encryption labels, d: decryption labels, x: evaluator's raw input, X: evaluator's garbled input, Y: garbled output, Y_i, X_i, GT_i, L_i: garbled input, output, garbled tables, wire labels corresponding to i^{th} sub-netlist, respectively, y: evaluator's raw output, and SCD: A custom circuit description which allows TinyGarble to evaluate the Boolean circuit).

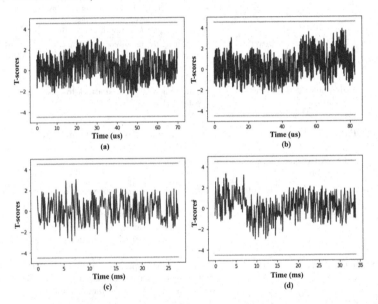

Fig. 8. TVLA test results (a) HWGN^2 applied to XNOR-based BM2 (capacity whole set of instructions per OT) (b) BM2 with the capacity of complete set of instructions per OT interaction, (c) HWGN^2 applied to XNOR-based BM2 (capacity 1 instruction per OT), and (d) BM2 with the capacity of 1 instruction per OT (calculated for $2M$ EM traces).

GT, L, SCD, e are sent through one OT interaction to the evaluator for further garbling protocol process. e is then used by the evaluator to generate garbled input X from the evaluator's input x (Step 2). Afterward in Step 3.1, GT, L, and SCD are used by the evaluator to evaluate the GC based on the given X sequentially using the scheduler module (cf. [44] for more information). In the final step (Step 3.2), output decryption labels (d) are sent to the evaluator to decrypt the evaluator core's garbled output Y and obtain its raw output y. The sequential evaluation supported by TinyGarble provides the GC protocol the scalability of evaluation of larger netlists. However, when one implements the DL hardware accelerator in the garbled format which has a large netlist, memory and logical resource utilization become burdens for DL hardware accelerators [21] (see Sect. 6.1).

Appendix C. TVLA Test Evaluation of EM Side-Channel

One of the first studies that has compared the capabilities of attackers launching power vs. EM SCA is [37], where it is suggested that the EM leakage can provide more information than the power consumption of the same chip cf. [48]. This has been further justified in [48] through the evaluation of the information theoretic and security metrics [49]. Therefore, it might be thought that the EM side-channel could offer some information about the secret, i.e., the weights of the garbled NN. To collect the EM traces, it has been already verified that measurements from the frontside of a chip can offer a high signal-to-noise ratio [19]; hence, we stick to this setting to perform measurements. Our setup described in Sect. 6.2 is equipped with HP EM probe 125 (SN126 0.2 mm). Figure 8 shows the t-scores computed for HWGN^2 applied against BM2. As shown in Fig. 8, the t-scores of EM traces are below the threshold (± 4.5) which is the proof of the EM leakage resiliency of HWGN^2.

References

1. Ateniese, G., Mancini, L.V., Spognardi, A., Villani, A., Vitali, D., Felici, G.: Hacking smart machines with smarter ones: How to extract meaningful data from machine learning classifiers. Int. J. Secur. Netw. **10**(3), 137–150 (2015)
2. Ball, M., Carmer, B., Malkin, T., Rosulek, M., Schimanski, N.: Garbled neural networks are practical. Cryptology ePrint Archive (2019)
3. Ball, M., Malkin, T., Rosulek, M.: Garbling gadgets for boolean and arithmetic circuits. In: Proceedings of the 2016 ACM SIGSAC Conference on Computer and Communications Security, pp. 565–577 (2016)
4. Batina, L., Bhasin, S., Jap, D., Picek, S.: CSI NN: reverse engineering of neural network architectures through electromagnetic side channel. In: 28th USENIX Security Symposium (USENIX Security 2019), pp. 515–532 (2019)
5. Bellare, M., Hoang, V.T., Keelveedhi, S., Rogaway, P.: Efficient garbling from a fixed-key blockcipher. In: 2013 IEEE Symposium on Security and Privacy, pp. 478–492. IEEE (2013)
6. Bellare, M., Hoang, V.T., Rogaway, P.: Foundations of garbled circuits. In: Proceedings of the 2012 ACM Conference on Computer and Communications Security, pp. 784–796 (2012)
7. Breier, J., Jap, D., Hou, X., Bhasin, S., Liu, Y.: SNIFF: reverse engineering of neural networks with fault attacks. IEEE Trans. Reliab. (2021)
8. Brier, E., Clavier, C., Olivier, F.: Correlation power analysis with a leakage model. In: Joye, M., Quisquater, J.-J. (eds.) CHES 2004. LNCS, vol. 3156, pp. 16–29. Springer, Heidelberg (2004). https://doi.org/10.1007/978-3-540-28632-5_2

9. Chakraborti, A., et al.: Cloud computing security: foundations and research directions. Found. Trends® Privacy Secur. **3**(2), 103–213 (2022)

10. Chari, S., Rao, J.R., Rohatgi, P.: Template attacks. In: Kaliski, B.S., Koç, K., Paar, C. (eds.) CHES 2002. LNCS, vol. 2523, pp. 13–28. Springer, Heidelberg (2003). https://doi.org/10.1007/3-540-36400-5_3

11. De Cnudde, T., Ender, M., Moradi, A.: Hardware masking, revisited. IACR Trans. Cryptogr. Hardw. Embed. Syst. 123–148 (2018)

12. Dubey, A., Ahmad, A., Pasha, M.A., Cammarota, R., Aysu, A.: Modulonet: neural networks meet modular arithmetic for efficient hardware masking. IACR Trans. Cryptogr. Hardw. Embed. Syst. 506–556 (2022)

13. Dubey, A., Cammarota, R., Aysu, A.: Bomanet: boolean masking of an entire neural network. In: 2020 IEEE/ACM International Conference on Computer Aided Design (ICCAD), pp. 1–9. IEEE (2020)

14. Dubey, A., Cammarota, R., Aysu, A.: Maskednet: the first hardware inference engine aiming power side-channel protection. In: 2020 IEEE International Symposium on Hardware Oriented Security and Trust (HOST), pp. 197–208. IEEE (2020)

15. Durvaux, F., Standaert, F.-X.: From improved leakage detection to the detection of points of interests in leakage traces. In: Fischlin, M., Coron, J.-S. (eds.) EUROCRYPT 2016. LNCS, vol. 9665, pp. 240–262. Springer, Heidelberg (2016). https://doi.org/10.1007/978-3-662-49890-3_10

16. Fredrikson, M., Lantz, E., Jha, S., Lin, S., Page, D., Ristenpart, T.: Privacy in pharmacogenetics: an {End-to-End} case study of personalized warfarin dosing. In: 23rd USENIX Security Symposium (USENIX Security 2014), pp. 17–32 (2014)

17. Gilad-Bachrach, R., Dowlin, N., Laine, K., Lauter, K., Naehrig, M., Wernsing, J.: Cryptonets: applying neural networks to encrypted data with high throughput and accuracy. In: International Conference on Machine Learning, pp. 201–210. PMLR (2016)

18. Herken, R.: The Universal Turing Machine: A Half-Century Survey. Springer, Heidelberg (1988)

19. Heyszl, J., Merli, D., Heinz, B., De Santis, F., Sigl, G.: Strengths and limitations of high-resolution electromagnetic field measurements for side-channel analysis. In: Mangard, S. (ed.) CARDIS 2012. LNCS, vol. 7771, pp. 248–262. Springer, Heidelberg (2013). https://doi.org/10.1007/978-3-642-37288-9_17

20. Hussain, S., Li, B., Koushanfar, F., Cammarota, R.: TinyGarble2: smart, efficient, and scalable Yao's garble circuit. In: Proceedings of the 2020 WKSP on Privacy-Preserving Machine Learning in Practice, pp. 65–67 (2020)

21. Järvinen, K., Kolesnikov, V., Sadeghi, A.-R., Schneider, T.: Garbled circuits for leakage-resilience: hardware implementation and evaluation of one-time programs. In: Mangard, S., Standaert, F.-X. (eds.) CHES 2010. LNCS, vol. 6225, pp. 383–397. Springer, Heidelberg (2010). https://doi.org/10.1007/978-3-642-15031-9_26

22. Juvekar, C., Vaikuntanathan, V., Chandrakasan, A.: {GAZELLE}: a low latency framework for secure neural network inference. In: 27th USENIX Security Symposium (USENIX Security 2018), pp. 1651–1669 (2018)

23. Kane, G.: MIPS RISC Architecture. Prentice-Hall Inc. (1988)

24. Kilian, J.: Founding crytpography on oblivious transfer. In: Proceedings of the Annual ACM Symposium on Theory of Computing, pp. 20–31 (1988)

25. Kocher, P., Jaffe, J., Jun, B.: Differential power analysis. In: Wiener, M. (ed.) CRYPTO 1999. LNCS, vol. 1666, pp. 388–397. Springer, Heidelberg (1999). https://doi.org/10.1007/3-540-48405-1_25

26. Kolesnikov, V., Schneider, T.: Improved garbled circuit: free XOR gates and applications. In: Aceto, L., Damgård, I., Goldberg, L.A., Halldórsson, M.M., Ingólfsdóttir, A., Walukiewicz, I. (eds.) ICALP 2008. LNCS, vol. 5126, pp. 486–498. Springer, Heidelberg (2008). https://doi.org/10.1007/978-3-540-70583-3_40

27. LeCun, Y.: 1.1 deep learning hardware: past, present, and future. In: 2019 IEEE International Solid-State Circuits Conference-(ISSCC), pp. 12–19. IEEE (2019)

28. Levi, I., Hazay, C.: Garbled-circuits from an SCA perspective: free XOR can be quite expensive. Cryptology ePrint Archive (2022)

29. Lindell, Y.: Fast cut-and-choose-based protocols for malicious and covert adversaries. J. Cryptol. 29(2), 456–490 (2016)

30. Lindell, Y., Pinkas, B.: An efficient protocol for secure two-party computation in the presence of malicious adversaries. In: Naor, M. (ed.) EUROCRYPT 2007. LNCS, vol. 4515, pp. 52–78. Springer, Heidelberg (2007). https://doi.org/10.1007/978-3-540-72540-4_4

31. Lindell, Y., Pinkas, B., Smart, N.P., Yanai, A.: Efficient constant-round multi-party computation combining BMR and SPDZ. J. Cryptol. 32(3), 1026–1069 (2019)

32. Liu, Y., Dachman-Soled, D., Srivastava, A.: Mitigating reverse engineering attacks on deep neural networks. In: 2019 IEEE Computer Society Annual Symposium on VLSI (ISVLSI), pp. 657–662. IEEE (2019)

33. Mantel, H., Scheidel, L., Schneider, T., Weber, A., Weinert, C., Weißmantel, T.: RiCaSi: rigorous cache side channel mitigation via selective circuit compilation. In: Krenn, S., Shulman, H., Vaudenay, S. (eds.) CANS 2020. LNCS, vol. 12579, pp. 505–525. Springer, Cham (2020). https://doi.org/10.1007/978-3-030-65411-5_25

34. Mittal, S., Gupta, H., Srivastava, S.: A survey on hardware security of DNN models and accelerators. J. Syst. Archit. 117, 102163 (2021)

35. Moradi, A., Richter, B., Schneider, T., Standaert, F.X.: Leakage detection with the x2-test. IACR Trans. Cryptogr. Hardw. Embed. Syst. 209–237 (2018)

36. Naor, M., Pinkas, B., Sumner, R.: Privacy preserving auctions and mechanism design. In: Proceedings of the 1st ACM Conference on Electronic Commerce, pp. 129–139 (1999)

37. Peeters, E., Standaert, F.X., Quisquater, J.J.: Power and electromagnetic analysis: improved model, consequences and comparisons. Integration 40(1), 52–60 (2007)

38. Rhoads, S.: Plasma - most MIPS I(TM) opcodes (2001). https://opencores.org/projects/plasma. Accessed 9 Mar 2022

39. Riazi, M.S., Samragh, M., Chen, H., Laine, K., Lauter, K., Koushanfar, F.: {XONN}:{XNOR-based} oblivious deep neural network inference. In: 28th USENIX Security Symposium (USENIX Security 2019), pp. 1501–1518 (2019)

40. Riazi, M.S., Weinert, C., Tkachenko, O., Songhori, E.M., Schneider, T., Koushanfar, F.: Chameleon: a hybrid secure computation framework for machine learning applications. In: Proceedings of the 2018 on Asia Conference on Computer and Communications Security, pp. 707–721 (2018)

41. Rouhani, B.D., Hussain, S.U., Lauter, K., Koushanfar, F.: ReDCrypt: real-time privacy-preserving deep learning inference in clouds using FPGAs. ACM Trans. Reconfigurable Technol. Syst. (TRETS) 11(3), 1–21 (2018)

42. Rouhani, B.D., Riazi, M.S., Koushanfar, F.: Deepsecure: scalable provably-secure deep learning. In: Proceedings of the 55th Annual Design Automation Conference, pp. 1–6 (2018)

43. Schellenberg, F., Gnad, D.R., Moradi, A., Tahoori, M.B.: An inside job: remote power analysis attacks on FPGAs. In: 2018 Design, Automation & Test in Europe Conference & Exhibition (DATE), pp. 1111–1116. IEEE (2018)

44. Songhori, E.M., Hussain, S.U., Sadeghi, A.R., Schneider, T., Koushanfar, F.: Tiny-garble: highly compressed and scalable sequential garbled circuits. In: 2015 IEEE Symposium on Security and Privacy, pp. 411–428. IEEE (2015)

45. Songhori, E.M., Riazi, M.S., Hussain, S.U., Sadeghi, A.R., Koushanfar, F.: ARM2GC: succinct garbled processor for secure computation. In: Proceedings of the 56th Annual Design Automation Conference 2019, pp. 1–6 (2019)

46. Songhori, E.M., Schneider, T., Zeitouni, S., Sadeghi, A.R., Dessouky, G., Koushan-far, F.: GarbledCPU: a MIPS processor for secure computation in hardware. In: 2016 53nd ACM/EDAC/IEEE Design Automation Conference (DAC), pp. 1–6. IEEE (2016)

47. Standaert, F.-X.: How (not) to use Welch's T-test in side-channel security evalu-ations. In: Bilgin, B., Fischer, J.-B. (eds.) CARDIS 2018. LNCS, vol. 11389, pp. 65–79. Springer, Cham (2019). https://doi.org/10.1007/978-3-030-15462-2_5

48. Standaert, F.-X., Archambeau, C.: Using subspace-based template attacks to com-pare and combine power and electromagnetic information leakages. In: Oswald, E., Rohatgi, P. (eds.) CHES 2008. LNCS, vol. 5154, pp. 411–425. Springer, Heidelberg (2008). https://doi.org/10.1007/978-3-540-85053-3_26

49. Standaert, F.-X., Malkin, T.G., Yung, M.: A unified framework for the analysis of side-channel key recovery attacks. In: Joux, A. (ed.) EUROCRYPT 2009. LNCS, vol. 5479, pp. 443–461. Springer, Heidelberg (2009). https://doi.org/10.1007/978-3-642-01001-9_26

50. Wang, X., Gordon, S.D., McIntosh, A., Katz, J.: Secure computation of MIPS machine code. In: Askoxylakis, I., Ioannidis, S., Katsikas, S., Meadows, C. (eds.) ESORICS 2016. LNCS, vol. 9879, pp. 99–117. Springer, Cham (2016). https://doi.org/10.1007/978-3-319-45741-3_6

51. Wang, X., Malozemoff, A.J., Katz, J.: Faster secure two-party computation in the single-execution setting. In: Coron, J.-S., Nielsen, J.B. (eds.) EUROCRYPT 2017. LNCS, vol. 10212, pp. 399–424. Springer, Cham (2017). https://doi.org/10.1007/978-3-319-56617-7_14

52. Xiang, Y., et al.: Open DNN box by power side-channel attack. IEEE Trans. Cir-cuits Syst. II: Express Br. **67**(11), 2717–2721 (2020)

53. Yao, A.C.C.: How to generate and exchange secrets. In: 27th Annual Symposium on Foundations of Computer Science (SFCS 1986), pp. 162–167. IEEE (1986)

54. Yoshida, K., Kubota, T., Okura, S., Shiozaki, M., Fujino, T.: Model reverse-engineering attack using correlation power analysis against systolic array based neural network accelerator. In: 2020 IEEE International Symposium on Circuits and Systems (ISCAS), pp. 1–5. IEEE (2020)

55. Yu, H., Ma, H., Yang, K., Zhao, Y., Jin, Y.: DeepEM: deep neural networks model recovery through EM side-channel information leakage. In: 2020 IEEE Interna-tional Symposium on Hardware Oriented Security and Trust (HOST), pp. 209–218. IEEE (2020)

56. Zhao, M., Suh, G.E.: FPGA-based remote power side-channel attacks. In: 2018 IEEE Symposium on Security and Privacy (SP), pp. 229–244. IEEE (2018)

How Many Cameras Do You Need? Adversarial Attacks and Countermeasures for Robust Perception in Autonomous Vehicles

Tu Anh Ngo(✉)🆔, Reuben Jon Chia, Jonathan Chan,
Nandish Chattopadhyay, and Anupam Chattopadhyay🆔

Nanyang Technological University, 50 Nanyang Avenue, Singapore 639798, Singapore
{anhtu.ngo,anupam}@ntu.edu.sg,
{rchia013,jona0028,nandish001}@e.ntu.edu.sg

Abstract. Deep neural networks have been established by researchers to perform significantly better than prior algorithms in multiple domains, notably in computer vision. Naturally, this resulted in its deployment as a perception module in modern Autonomous Vehicle (AV) and in general for Advanced Driver Assistance Systems (ADAS). ADAS relies heavily on perception module, which harnesses various sensors such as camera, LiDAR, radar, ultrasonic sensor to make navigational decisions. By drawing from the adversarial attacks, which undermine a lot of machine learning applications, recent research shows that the AV perception modules are also vulnerable to adversarial attacks. Suggested countermeasures for these attacks include increasing the number of sensors, which incurs cost overhead and does not present any formal guarantee of protection. Hence, in this paper, we study the robustness and practicality of such a countermeasure. We demonstrate that it is still possible to spoof multiple cameras through adversarial object though, the attack success considerably reduces. Furthermore, the possibility of alternative countermeasures like dimensionality reduction and feature squeezing are investigated. Our study shows that these techniques, when applied together, significantly enhances the robustness of the AV perception system.

Keywords: ADAS · AV · Neural network · Adversarial attack · Adversarial defense

1 Introduction

Recent decades have witnessed a booming in the automotive industry, especially with major technological breakthroughs in autonomous driving. The level of automation in a vehicle has improved significantly, from manual operation to high level of automation. This is achieved mainly with the help of machine learning, which contributes to almost every modules of AV such as perception, localization, planning, prediction, etc. Perception is a fundamental element of

ⓒ The Author(s), under exclusive license to Springer Nature Switzerland AG 2022
L. Batina et al. (Eds.): SPACE 2022, LNCS 13783, pp. 249–263, 2022.
https://doi.org/10.1007/978-3-031-22829-2_14

AVs, involving in most decisions made by other modules. In an AV's perception, sensors like cameras and LiDARs gather information about the surrounding environment such as obstacles, pedestrians and traffic signs. One wrong information from the perception module can lead to consequentially wrong decisions from other modules, which can result in fatal outcomes. Thus, a considerable amount of research on state-of-the-art deep neural networks (DNNs) have been carried out since the introduction of AlexNet [17], winner of the ImageNet Large Scale Visual Recognition Challenge (ILSVRC) 2012.

However, being equipped with state-of-the-art neural networks does not ensure a perception system that is resilient against adversaries. Extensive research is being done to identify various attack vectors in AV's neural networks [6,14,25]. Many such attacks, however, target single perception source like single camera or single LiDAR. On the contrary, many commercial AVs provide multitude of sensors all working in conjunction [6]. With such a multi-sensor setup and a realistic assumption that not all the perception modules are attacked simultaneously, it is concluded in recent studies that multiple sensors present a robust defense against a determined attacker. Cao et al. [6] explored a very interesting way of attacking into both LiDAR and camera, using a 3D printable adversarial object. The authors also believe that using more cameras or LiDARs could improve the robustness of the perception model against this attack.

The growth in usage of multiple sensors can be accredited to the improved availability of public datasets published by major companies, such as [11], nuScenes [5], Argoverse [28], etc. The new public datasets provide a full 360° view of the surroundings, creating many overlapping field-of-views (FoV). With various viewing angles on a single object, it could increase the chance that an object can be detected by the model, like the side of a vehicle as compared to the front. An example of a production-grade AV being used on the road would be the Electric Car company, Tesla. Tesla utilizes a series of modern cameras in the Electric Vehicles for their Autonomous Driving (AD) capabilities [15].

In this paper, we investigate whether increasing the number of cameras helps AV against adversarial object. Furthermore, we look into a few simple countermeasures involving image feature manipulation such as dimensionality reduction and color depth reduction. The rest of the paper is organized as follows: Sect. 3 and 4 details the attack methodology and proposed countermeasures, respectively. Section 5 describes the experiments conducted. In Sect. 6, some limitations of the presented study are discussed, and conclusions are drawn in Sect. 7.

2   Background

2.1   Adversarial Attacks on Image Recognition

Traditional attacks on image recognition systems used strong extra sources of light to physically blind a camera [19,21]. Recently, as deep learning models are becoming more powerful, research trends shifted to attacks on the DNNs of perception system. The pioneering works from Szegedy et al. [27] discovered that state-of-the-art DNNs are susceptible to adversarial attacks. Since then, more researchers investigated adversarial attacks in computer vision domain. In 2017, researchers from Google used adversarial stickers called "Adversarial Patch" [4] with particular properties that can fool machine learning models. These "patches" can be attached to any objects on the street, e.g. road signs, to cause camera perception system to make wrong decisions. In that same year, Eykholt et al. [10] were able to generate robust adversarial perturbations in the forms of only black and white stickers attached on stop signs. This attack achieved high efficacy in both image and video sign classification tasks.

The higher level of automation in self-driving car leads to the use of multiple kinds of sensor. Many AV makers nowadays use both cameras and LiDARs for perception systems, adding more robustness to the object detection performance. Many researchers have studied the vulnerability of LiDAR-based object detectors to 3D adversarial objects. However, there were not a lot of such studies done on the effect of 3D adversarial objects to camera-based object detectors until 2021. Abdelfattah et al. [1] proposed a kind of attack that when they place an adversarial object on top of a car, that car evades being detected by both LiDAR-based detector and camera-based detector. Another work from Cao et al. [6] involves generating a 3D printable adversarial object that can deceive LiDAR-based and camera-based perception models, causing vehicle crashing into it. In most of these prior works, a common countermeasure suggestion is to increase the number of cameras for detection. However, the question remains is whether that suffices as a countermeasure and if yes, how many cameras do we need?

2.2 Motivation

The idea of fooling LiDAR-camera perception model with adversarial 3D object [6] is recent and is a very active area of research. We try to find out whether such kind of adversarial object is still effectively hidden from vehicle's perception system if we use more sources of sensing and manipulate input's features. In our study, we make use of multi-camera setup with overlapping FoVs. One reason to use multiple cameras is that cameras are much more budget-friendly than LiDARs. Furthermore, when an object appears in different camera views, there are distortions in the textures such as color and lighting, which might affect the attack efficacy. Using camera images also allows alternative countermeasures such as feature squeezing and dimension reduction, which we also study in this work.

2.3 Contributions

In this paper, we study the robustness of AV's camera perception model in the event of adversarial attacks. Then, we propose some countermeasures in order to prevent AV's camera perception model from being deceived by 3D adversarial objects. In summary, this work makes the following contributions:

– Studying the vulnerability of multi-camera system to 3D adversarial objects.
– Applying dimensionality reduction [7] and Feature Squeezing [29] to camera images, as potential countermeasures.
– Fusing the above techniques into one unified pipeline for robust countermeasure.

3   Spoofing Multiple Cameras with Overlapping FOV

We use the original attack idea from Cao et al. [6] and extend it to check if it is possible to spoof the perception module from various angles. The corresponding object generation procedure is an optimization process, which is briefly explained in the following subsections for completeness. Interested readers can refer to the detailed methodology in [6]. The goal of this attack is to create an object that is invisible to perception model, which is visualized in Fig. 1.

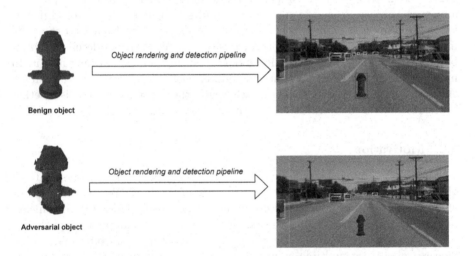

Fig. 1. Attack goal is to create an adversarial object that is invisible to camera model

3.1   Object Detection Output

Popular deep learning-based 2D object detectors can be classified into two categories: two-stage and one-stage detectors. For two-stage detectors, eminent networks are region-based detectors such as RCNN [13] and its more efficient variants, Fast RCNN [12] and Faster RCNN [23]. The two stages of these algorithms can be divided into region proposal and object detection with bounding-box regression. Two-stage detectors have good localization and object recognition performance. However, regarding inference speed, one-stage detectors clearly outperform the two-stage counterparts. Some of the most prominent one-stage detectors include YOLO and SSD. One-stage detectors jointly detect and localize using one unified neural network, without the region proposal stage.

Due to their simplicity, one-stage detectors are suitable to be used in real-time applications. Over the past years, recent improvements have enhanced one-stage detectors' performance, which makes them superior to two-stage ones in terms of speed while preserving respectable accuracy. Some popular open-source autonomous driving platforms employ one-stage detectors in their perception modules, for example, Autoware [16] use YOLOv3 for their camera perception, and Baidu Apollo [3] also utilizes the 3D version of YOLO for the same purpose.

As this attack targets YOLOv3 for camera models, we review a bit on its output here. Given an image, YOLOv3 runs a single CNN to detect objects at three different scale of the original image, aiming to handle small, medium and big objects. At each scale, image is divided into $S \times S$ grid cells. And each cell makes prediction for B different anchor boxes, whereas every box's prediction has $5 + C$ elements, representing:

- 4 values for box center offsets and width/height scales (x, y, w, h).
- 1 value for box confidence/objectness score P_0.
- C values for class scores $P_1, P_2, ..., P_C$.

Therefore, at every scale, the prediction's output has the shape $(S, S, B \times (5 + C))$. For YOLOv3, $B = 3$ because it uses 3 anchor boxes per scale. The attack in [6] adds perturbation to the object's shape so as to minimize the box confidence score P_0 in accordance with it, hence the object's disappearance from the camera object detector.

3.2   Formulation of Attack Objective

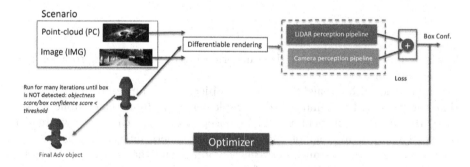

Fig. 2. Attack overview

Figure 2 visualizes the fundamental attack flow. An object is represented by its face-vertex meshes $(v - f)$. Let S denote the benign object and S^a the generated adversarial object. Therefore, the objective of the optimization process is to change the position of the object's vertices to minimize the box confidence to less than a threshold for it to be detected. The objective function is:

$$J = \mathcal{L}_a(S^a, \mathcal{R}^l, \mathcal{R}^c, \mathcal{P}, \mathcal{M}) + \lambda.\mathcal{L}_r(S^a, S)$$

Hence, the optimization problem is:

$$\min_{S^a} J \tag{1}$$

subject to:

$$\Delta(S^a, S) \leq \epsilon \tag{2}$$

in which $\mathcal{R}^l$, $\mathcal{R}^c$ are differentiable rendering functions for LiDAR and camera respectively, $\mathcal{P}$ is the pre-processing approximation function and $\mathcal{M}$ is the Multi-Sensor Fusion algorithm. The total loss J is the weighted sum of the two losses: adversarial loss $\mathcal{L}_a$ for achieving attack goal, or to minimize the bounding box's confidence value mentioned in Sect. 3.1, and realizability loss $\mathcal{L}_r$ for improving surface smoothness, which is useful for 3D-printing.

Equation 1 is a constrained optimization problem, to solve it, Cao et al. [6] uses Projected Gradient Descent (PGD). The optimal value for this problem is achieved by optimizing the shape of the adversarial object S^a, more specifically by changing its vertices' position. The constraint Eq. 2 is to ensure that S^a still has a recognizable shape to human's eye and does not deviate too much from the original object S.

3.3 Robust Adversarial Object Generation

To improve robustness for this attack, it is necessary that the model can be fooled from various angles and distances. Cao et al. [6] apply Expectation over Transformation [2]. Equation 1 becomes

$$\min_{S^a} \mathop{\mathbb{E}}_{t \sim T} J$$

in which T is a set of random 3D transformation to S^a, including rotation and position shifting.

In [6], the authors slightly shift the object's yaw angles to $5°$, $10°$, $15°$. However, we could not find the EoT implementation from their public source code. Hence, we implement the EoT concept from scratch. First, we render the benign object in front of one front-center camera image. Let (x, y, ψ) be a set containing the distance between the object and the vehicle, the object's horizontal distance and the angle of the object's yaw rotation, respectively. In every iteration, we generate five random sets of changes $\{(\Delta x_i, \Delta y_i, \Delta \psi_i) | i \in \mathbb{N}, i \in [1,5]\}$ that are applied to the object's original position, resulting in five positions $\{(x + \Delta x_i, y + \Delta y_i, \psi + \Delta \psi_i) | i \in \mathbb{N}, i \in [1,5]\}$. We select a wider range for yaw rotation changes since we want to produce a robust attack against multiple cameras, specifically $-40° \leq \Delta \psi_i \leq 40°$.

3.4   Spoofing Multiple Cameras

It is quite challenging for an adversary to fool the camera model from various viewing angles. In [20], the author demonstrated that a stop sign cannot consistently fool the camera model if it is viewed from various angles. However, with the use of EoT, the attack robustness is improved significantly. To check the attack efficacy, we randomly select 100 frames from Argoverse dataset. In each frame, we place the object at 3 m / 4 m / 5 m / 6 m in front of the front center camera and 0 m / 1 m to the right, hence a total of 800 (100×4×2) scenarios. We calculate the attack success rate (ASR) over all scenarios. We also experiment with the benign case in which we render the benign fire hydrant at the same positions as in the adversarial case. Then, we evaluate the benign detection rate (BDR) for the fire hydrant. In the following evaluations, a good result is the one with high benign detection rate and low attack success rate.

| (a) front center | (b) front right |

Fig. 3. Multi-cam setup is more robust but not sufficient: in some scenarios adversarial object can fool both cameras

Table 1. Attack evaluation on multi-cam setup

Cam setup	Benign det. rate (%)	Attack success rate (%)
Front center	75.75	78
Front center, Front right	**98.38**	**43.75**

Table 1 shows that using multiple cameras with overlapping FoV is more robust than just relying on one camera. We think it is still not enough to guard the camera model from being fooled. Figure 3 shows a scenario when both front center and front right camera cannot detect the fire hydrant. Therefore, we explore a few additional countermeasures in the next section.

4   Additional Countermeasures

In above section we demonstrate that fusing multiple cameras with overlapping FoVs improve system's robustness, however, there are rooms for improvement. In this section, we discuss a couple of orthogonal countermeasures namely, dimensionality reduction and feature squeezing. We focus on manipulating image feature such as reducing image's dimension or color, since these solutions were shown effective against adversarial examples in the literature. Furthermore, these countermeasures modify input features, which directly improves data bandwidth/storage and more straightforward than modifying the neural network architecture.

4.1   Dimensionality Reduction

This defense is inspired by the effect of the *curse of dimensionality*, which is one of the key causes facilitating the creation of adversarial examples. In [7], dimension reduction is demonstrated effective against adversarial objects, especially in classification problem. This has not been tested in object detection task, specifically when adversarial examples are to affect the bounding box confidence score. Since this can be a potential countermeasure boosting the perception module robustness, we applied the dimensionality reduction flow to camera images and studied its efficacy.

4.2   Feature Squeezing: Color Depth Reduction

There is little research on the effects of color to deep learning models. In [9], color quantization, which reduces color depth, is shown to affect the performance of convolutional neural networks. One hypothesis is color distortions affect the way neural networks perceive the input, due to the shift in image distribution. Indeed, according to [29], a neural network perceives the input space as continuous due to its differentiable manner. However, computers only support discrete representation of data. A digital image is represented by a pixel array, where each pixel is represented by numbers as a color code. Color bit depth is a feature in image representation that might affect the performance of a neural network. Therefore, we consider of color depth reduction as a feasible countermeasure mitigating the effect of adversarial examples. In general, color depth reduction is bracketed within a family of countermeasures termed as feature squeezing [29].

5   Experiments

5.1   Dataset

Due to the lack of real-hardware setup, we make use of readily available datasets. We choose Argo AI's Argoverse 2 dataset [28], which is both open-source and provided by reliable institutions for our experiment. We use the *Sensor Dataset* from Argoverse 2, which consists of 1,000 scenarios from 7 ring cameras, 2 stereo cameras and 2 LiDARs. One notable feature from Argoverse dataset is that each camera has overlapping FoV with it nearby camera. The overlapping areas and the position shift between two neighbor cameras are big enough to make two images disparate, which facilitates object detection from multiple viewing angles. As visualized in Fig. 4, the ring front left camera and the ring front right camera have significant overlapping FoVs with the ring front center camera. We also considered other well-known datasets such as KITTI [11], Waymo Open Dataset [26] and nuScenes [5]. However, there are some disadvantages of camera features in these datasets that do not suit our approach. For example, KITTI provides camera images with very limited position shifts, Waymo Open Dataset and nuScenes do not really provide camera images with overlapping FoV.

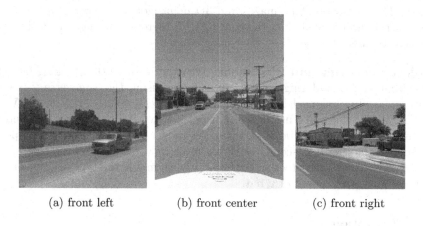

(a) front left   (b) front center   (c) front right

Fig. 4. Views from Argoverse ring front cameras

5.2 Choice of Objects

The first step is to pick a 3D benign object that can be fed into our optimization pipeline. Since we want to evaluate the object detection performance of one particular model, we have to use the objects that appear in the training set on which the model is trained. Here we evaluate our attack on YOLOv3 [22], which is pre-trained on COCO dataset [18]. We prefer to choose objects with not too complex texture and pretty symmetrical shape. There are quite a lot of websites that provide 3D object models, such as https://free3d.com, which has both free and paid 3D objects.

After obtaining a 3D object, we slightly process it using Blender [8], an open-source 3D graphics software.

5.3 Experimental Setup

Perception Models. This paper is inspired by the work from [6], which focuses on white-box attack. The targeted object detection models we choose are Baidu Apollo [3] for LiDAR and YOLOv3 [22] for cameras, the same as in original work [6]. Baidu Apollo is one of the most prominent open-source AV platforms and YOLOv3 is a popular real-time 2D object detector, which is still included in open-source AV platforms such as Autoware.AI [16] and Baidu Apollo [3]. In this study, our focus is on the vulnerability of multi-camera system, hence we use Baidu Apollo v2.5 instead of more recent versions for the sake of better memory usage. This is because the images and 3D point clouds in Argoverse 2 dataset are much more detailed than those in KITTI, therefore, we need to utilize our limited resources better.

Object Rendering and Placement. We experiment with attacking into the ring front center and ring front right cameras using the Argoverse 2 Sensor Dataset, as object can solely be visible to two cameras with overlapping FoVs at a time. We do not make use of scenes from the two stereo cameras, as there is no significant distinction between them. We render the object so that it appears in front of the ring front center and ring front right camera. As the color of an object also affects the detection performance, we mimic the typical color of real fire hydrants, which is mostly red.

5.4 Evaluation

As mentioned in Sect. 3, we selected 100 frames from the Argoverse 2 Sensor Dataset in which there are no objects with the same type as the injected object and rendered it to the aforementioned positions. There are a total of 800 scenarios.

Dimensionality Reduction: One popular method to reduce dimension is Singular Value Decomposition (SVD). From Chart 5, it can be observed that dimensionality reduction does not help much in guarding the model against adversarial attack. With less singular values, the model fails to recognize not only adversarial object, but also the benign one. Keeping just a small number of singular values drastically lowers the detection performance on both adversarial and benign objects. Retaining more singular values is safer for detection performance, however, it is still not useful against adversarial objects.

Color Depth Reduction: We use color quantization technique to reduce a 24-bit image to 8-bit image. The results are consistent for the reduction of various number of colors. From Chart 6, it is obvious that color quantization does indeed resist against adversarial objects, to some extent. Note that if the number of

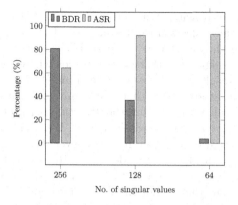

Fig. 5. Dimensionality reduction using SVD

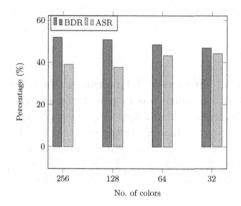

Fig. 6. Color depth reduction

colors is drastically reduced, then the object detection performance also drops accordingly. Hence, a hybrid approach of combining both 24-bit and 8-bit image is adopted (Table 2).

Table 2. Using both color depth reduction and multiple-camera system

	Benign det. rate (%)		Attack success rate (%)	
Color depth	Single-cam	Multi-cam	Single-cam	Multi-cam
24-bit (orig.)	75.75	98.38	78	43.75
8-bit	51.88	84.38	39	17.6
24-bit, 8-bit	78.75	**99**	37.25	**13**

A Unified Countermeasure Pipeline: Due to the low effectiveness of dimension reduction, we only combine color depth reduction and multi-camera setup as one unified countermeasure. One downside of YOLOv3 is that it does not perform well on small objects. In our study, the farther the object's distance to the vehicle is, the higher chance it is not detected by YOLOv3. This is the reason why in the benign case, there are scenarios where the model misses the fire hydrant, which results in a detection rate of merely 75.75%. Regarding color depth reduction, our study shows that it can mitigate the ASR in adversarial case. However, for benign fire hydrant, the detection performance drops dramatically to 51.88% if we only use the 8-bit images. We decide to fuse the original image (24-bit) and the 8-bit one together: whenever there is a detection happens in either image - it is considered a true detection. Regarding the multiple-camera setup, we find it more robust to guard the camera model than the single camera setup. Our results show that combining multiple-camera setup and color depth reduction technique together leads to a much more robust camera perception system, results in 99% benign detection rate and just 13% attack success rate in the adversarial case.

6   Limitations

Physical-World and Simulated Experiment. In this work, we extend the original work [6] and use multi-camera perception system as an attack vector as well as a feasible defense. One major drawback of our study is that we did not try out our concept on a real AV in the physical world due to cost concerns. Furthermore, we did not have the chance to experiment with AV simulators such as LGSVL [24] due to limited time, and due to LG's announcement that they will suspend active development of SVL Simulator from 2022.

Multi-camera Object Projection. In Argoverse 2 Sensor Dataset, like other public datasets, all the calibration parameters and matrices are provided along the data itself. When we render the object with 3D information into 2D images from the dataset, we have to make use of the calibration matrices. We observed that when projecting the object onto side cameras, the final image might not completely reflect the true position of the object. In our belief, it is likely because there are some auxiliary parameters that we did not take into account or there are some misalignment in the cross-camera projection. This flaw does not affect the experiment, at large; nevertheless, it is still worth mentioning as we believe this projection can be improved for the sake of precision.

7   Conclusions

This paper demonstrates our study on two defenses against 3D adversarial object. Even though this attack originally aims to fool both LiDARs and cameras, we focus on defending camera model since a robust camera model leads to a robust perception system in general. Our study shows that feature squeezing methods such as color depth reduction alleviates the attack efficacy, however, it increases the risk of model cannot perform well on other objects. If we also leverage original images, the results are promising. In terms of dimensionality reduction technique, we find it ineffective in our study. Turning to multiple-camera setup, this paper shows that using multiple cameras with overlapping FoVs is more robust compare to the single-camera setup. Furthermore, this setup is also budget-friendly, unlike LiDARs, which are prohibitively expensive. Leveraging color depth reduction and multiple-camera setup at the same time tremendously diminishes attack success rate, from 78% down to only 13%, according to our experiments. Considering the safety of AV perception models, we hope our contributions pave the way for the development of effective and economical defenses.

Acknowledgements. This research was supported by Desay SV Automotive Singapore, as part of NTU-Desay Collaboration project.

References

1. Abdelfattah, M., Yuan, K., Wang, Z.J., Ward, R.: Adversarial attacks on camera-lidar models for 3D car detection (2021). https://doi.org/10.48550/ARXIV.2103.09448, https://arxiv.org/abs/2103.09448
2. Athalye, A., Engstrom, L., Ilyas, A., Kwok, K.: Synthesizing robust adversarial examples. In: International Conference on Machine Learning, pp. 284–293. PMLR (2018)
3. Baidu: Apollo: open source autonomous driving. https://github.com/ApolloAuto/apollo
4. Brown, T.B., Mané, D., Roy, A., Abadi, M., Gilmer, J.: Adversarial patch (2017). https://doi.org/10.48550/ARXIV.1712.09665, https://arxiv.org/abs/1712.09665
5. Caesar, H., et al.: nuScenes: a multimodal dataset for autonomous driving. In: Proceedings of the IEEE/CVF Conference on Computer Vision and Pattern Recognition (CVPR) (June 2020)
6. Cao, Y., et al.: Invisible for both camera and LiDAR: security of multi-sensor fusion based perception in autonomous driving under physical-world attacks. In: 2021 IEEE Symposium on Security and Privacy (SP), pp. 176–194 (2021). https://doi.org/10.1109/SP40001.2021.00076
7. Chattopadhyay, N., Chatterjee, S., Chattopadhyay, A.: Robustness against adversarial attacks using dimensionality. In: Batina, L., Picek, S., Mondal, M. (eds.) SPACE 2021. LNCS, vol. 13162, pp. 226–241. Springer, Cham (2022). https://doi.org/10.1007/978-3-030-95085-9_12
8. Community, B.O.: Blender - a 3D modelling and rendering package. Blender Foundation, Stichting Blender Foundation, Amsterdam (2018). http://www.blender.org
9. De, K., Pedersen, M.: Impact of colour on robustness of deep neural networks. In: 2021 IEEE/CVF International Conference on Computer Vision Workshops (ICCVW), pp. 21–30 (2021). https://doi.org/10.1109/ICCVW54120.2021.00009
10. Eykholt, K., et al.: Robust physical-world attacks on deep learning models (2017). https://doi.org/10.48550/ARXIV.1707.08945, https://arxiv.org/abs/1707.08945
11. Geiger, A., Lenz, P., Stiller, C., Urtasun, R.: Vision meets Robotics: the KITTI dataset. Int. J. Robot. Res. (IJRR) 32(11), 1231–1237 (2013)
12. Girshick, R.: Fast R-CNN. In: 2015 IEEE International Conference on Computer Vision (ICCV), pp. 1440–1448 (2015). https://doi.org/10.1109/ICCV.2015.169

13. Girshick, R., Donahue, J., Darrell, T., Malik, J.: Rich feature hierarchies for accurate object detection and semantic segmentation. In: 2014 IEEE Conference on Computer Vision and Pattern Recognition, pp. 580–587 (2014). https://doi.org/10.1109/CVPR.2014.81

14. Hallyburton, R.S., Liu, Y., Cao, Y., Mao, Z.M., Pajic, M.: Security analysis of camera-lidar fusion against black-box attacks on autonomous vehicles. In: 31st USENIX Security Symposium (USENIX Security 22), pp. 1903–1920. USENIX Association, Boston, MA (2022). https://www.usenix.org/conference/usenixsecurity22/presentation/hallyburton

15. Ingle, S., Phute, M.: Tesla autopilot: semi autonomous driving, an uptick for future autonomy. Int. Res. J. Eng. Technol. **3**(9), 369–372 (2016)

16. Kato, S., et al.: Autoware on board: enabling autonomous vehicles with embedded systems. In: Proceedings of the 9th ACM/IEEE International Conference on Cyber-Physical Systems, ICCPS 2018, pp. 287–296. IEEE Press (2018). https://doi.org/10.1109/ICCPS.2018.00035, https://doi.org.remotexs.ntu.edu.sg/10.1109/ICCPS.2018.00035,

17. Krizhevsky, A., Sutskever, I., Hinton, G.E.: ImageNet classification with deep convolutional neural networks. In: Proceedings of the 25th International Conference on Neural Information Processing Systems - Volume 1, pp. 1097–1105. NIPS 2012, Curran Associates Inc., Red Hook, NY, USA (2012)

18. Lin, T.Y., et al.: Microsoft COCO: common objects in context (2014). https://doi.org/10.48550/ARXIV.1405.0312, https://arxiv.org/abs/1405.0312

19. Liu, J., Yan, C., Xu, W.: Can you trust autonomous vehicles: contactless attacks against sensors of self-driving vehicles. DEF CON (2016). https://doi.org/10.5446/36252 Accessed 22 Mar 2022

20. Lu, J., Sibai, H., Fabry, E., Forsyth, D.A.: No need to worry about adversarial examples in object detection in autonomous vehicles. CoRR abs/1707.03501 (2017). http://arxiv.org/abs/1707.03501

21. Petit, J., Stottelaar, B., Feiri, M., Kargl, F.: Remote attacks on automated vehicles sensors: experiments on camera and lidar. In: Black Hat Europe (2015). https://www.blackhat.com/docs/eu-15/materials/eu-15-Petit-Self-Driving-And-Connected-Cars-Fooling-Sensors-And-Tracking-Drivers-wp1.pdf

22. Redmon, J., Farhadi, A.: YOLOv3: an incremental improvement. CoRR abs/1804.02767 (2018). http://arxiv.org/abs/1804.02767

23. Ren, S., He, K., Girshick, R., Sun, J.: Faster R-CNN: towards real-time object detection with region proposal networks. In: Proceedings of the 28th International Conference on Neural Information Processing Systems - Volume 1, pp. 91–99. NIPS 2015, MIT Press, Cambridge, MA, USA (2015)

24. Rong, G., et al.: LGSVL simulator: a high fidelity simulator for autonomous driving. CoRR abs/2005.03778 (2020). https://arxiv.org/abs/2005.03778

25. Sun, J., Cao, Y., Chen, Q.A., Mao, Z.M.: Towards robust lidar-based perception in autonomous driving: general black-box adversarial sensor attack and countermeasures. In: 29th USENIX Security Symposium (USENIX Security 20). USENIX Association, pp. 877–894 (2020). https://www.usenix.org/conference/usenixsecurity20/presentation/sun

26. Sun, P., et al.: Scalability in perception for autonomous driving: WAYMO open dataset. In: Proceedings of the IEEE/CVF Conference on Computer Vision and Pattern Recognition (CVPR) (2020)

27. Szegedy, C., et al.: Intriguing properties of neural networks (2013). https://doi.org/10.48550/ARXIV.1312.6199, https://arxiv.org/abs/1312.6199

28. Wilson, B., et al.: Argoverse 2: next generation datasets for self-driving perception and forecasting. In: Proceedings of the Neural Information Processing Systems Track on Datasets and Benchmarks (NeurIPS Datasets and Benchmarks 2021) (2021)
29. Xu, W., Evans, D., Qi, Y.: Feature squeezing: detecting adversarial examples in deep neural networks. In: 25th Annual Network and Distributed System Security Symposium, NDSS 2018, San Diego, California, USA, pp. 18–21. The Internet Society (2018). http://wp.internetsociety.org/ndss/wp-content/uploads/sites/25/2018/02/ndss2018_03A-4_Xu_paper.pdf

Network Security, Authentication, and Privacy

SMarT: A SMT Based Privacy Preserving Smart Meter Streaming Methodology

Soumyadyuti Ghosh$^{(\boxtimes)}$, Soumyajit Dey, and Debdeep Mukhopadhyay

Indian Institute of Technology Kharagpur, Kharagpur, India
soumyadyuti.ghosh@iitkgp.ac.in, {soumya,debdeep}@cse.iitkgp.ac.in

Abstract. Smart metering is a mechanism through which fine-grained power consumption profiles of the consumers are collected periodically in a Smart grid. However, a growing concern in this regard is that the leakage of consumers' consumption data may reveal their daily life patterns as the state-of-the-art metering strategies lack adequate security and privacy measures. Since Smart grid communication infrastructure supports low bandwidth, it prohibits the usage of computation-intensive cryptographic solutions. Among different privacy-preserving smart meter streaming methods, data manipulation techniques can easily be implemented in smart meters and do not require installing any storage devices or alternative energy sources. While these proposals are attractive to the privacy-aware smart meter design community, rigorous security evaluations of such schemes highlight their infeasibility by determining individual consumption patterns efficiently, thus compromising their privacy guarantees. Keeping in mind the inadequacies of these schemes, we propose a load signature modification technique, namely *Obfuscate-Load-Signature* that obscures the input power profile utilizing an information-theoretic metric to bound the inherent private information present in the metering stream. Along with providing the coveted privacy guarantees, the privacy preserved output time series profile generated due to our methodology also ensures excellent system utility by providing no aggregation and billing errors over constant tariff. In summary, we highlight how the aggregated metering information can be transformed to obscure individual consumption patterns without affecting the intended semantics of Smart grid operations. Finally, we present a rigorous experimental validation of our proposed methodology using a real-life dataset and suitable Hardware-In-the-Loop testbed.

Keywords: Smart Grid Privacy · Privacy preserving smart meter streaming · Satisfiability Modulo Theory (SMT) · Hardware-In-Loop test-bed

1 Introduction

Smart grids are large scale Cyber Physical Systems (CPS) comprising generation and distribution systems, metered loads, system state sensors and support for multiple real-time protocols. Modern electric grids implement distributed control techniques supported by a bi-directional communication network. The design and implementation principles of this kind of CPS are significantly different from other embedded systems because of the tight coupling of real-valued and dense time system dynamics with software-based discrete automated control. Exponential growth in electricity consumption with limited generation capabilities calls for efficient energy management and load balancing using real-time pricing control and demand response in Smart grids. Such primitives require advanced metering infrastructures which sample and transmit consumer consumption data using smart meters and provide real-time metering signals for enabling different operational primitives like billing, load monitoring, demand response based energy management, etc. [13]. While consumers' fine-grained consumption data is essential for such functionalities, smart meter streams open up serious privacy concerns. Meter reading streams can be analysed to determine consumers' home presence, appliance usage patterns, running time, "ON/OFF" status, etc., leading to severe breaches of customer's social behaviour and daily life routines [4,16]. Simultaneously, assorted non-intrusive load monitoring algorithms [15,32] can disaggregate the power usage profiles over a period to estimate the power consumption readings of the appliances and its corresponding timings, thus compromising the user privacy. The National Institute of Standards and Technology (NIST) highlights these potential privacy concerns that can arise from the collection and use of smart metering data [1]. Also, as shown in [4], on April 28, 2013, no peak power consumption reading for a Naperville resident signifies their home absence on that particular day, leaving them more vulnerable to burglary attacks. Due to such concerns, customers are reluctant to participate in metering and providing their fine-grained measurements to the utility providers (UPs). UPs propose incentives in the form of 1) rewarding schemes by offering incentives to users for their participation, 2) Incentive-based Demand Response schemes to make users reduce their power consumption whenever possible. Such incentive-based demand response schemes mainly rely on trusted third parties (TTP), trusted platform modules (TPM) or cryptographic primitives [14]. These solutions are prohibitive because of computational constraints in metering setups and also their allowance to TTP to track the bidding history of all associated participants, which pose a severe threat to customer privacy. The authors of [29] addressed these privacy issues by providing a TPM-based solution using trusted remote entities to establish trust between customers and UPs. However, apart from the accompanying cost, the demerit of the proposal is the single point of trust which becomes a coveted target for attacks [33]. The above-mentioned problems motivate the search for lightweight privacy preserving schemes which try to hide individual consumption patterns without using the TTP, TPM or traditional cryptography. Various subsequent solutions proposed the injection of random tolerable or zero average noise through components like batteries into the original or aggregated meter readings to obfuscate the input streams. Unfortunately, these schemes are not viable as they trade off aggregation and billing errors for desired privacy. To address this, in [16], the authors propose a low-cost privacy preserving streaming algorithm to modify consumer's smart meter reading profiles by quantifying and bounding the appliances' information leakages, simultaneously keeping low aggregation and billing errors over constant tariff. Here, if we see from the perspective of a naïve observer, the presence of many to many mappings between the input readings and the corresponding privacy preserved output readings in [16] makes it difficult to break the privacy formulation. However, the authors of [12] presented an efficient attacking strategy that helps an adversary to reduce the input search space associated with each privacy preserved output reading drastically, thus violating its privacy claims. Furthermore, they also leverage an interesting invariant property of the privacy transformation to remove the unsatisfactory readings from these input reading choices. In this paper, we mainly focus on the compromised fundamental building blocks of this scheme and offer a more viable solution that can overcome its shortcomings. We target minimizing the inherent private information present in the metering stream and bound it by the desired privacy level irrespective of the adversarial model. As a summary, the major contributions of this work are as follows:

1. We propose a new privacy preserving streaming algorithm, *Obfuscate-Load-Signature*, which obscures appliance's usage patterns to mitigate the attacking methodology of [12] without incurring any aggregation and billing errors over constant tariff. We also provide the necessary privacy analysis of the proposed methodology to highlight its inherent strong privacy guarantees.
2. We perform a rigorous information-theoretic evaluation of our proposed scheme against the proposal of [16] using real-life datasets to justify our privacy claims. Subsequently, we show the real-time feasibility and capability of our proposed privacy preserving scheme to conceal individual consumption patterns by executing it on a Hardware-In-the-Loop test-bed.

Organization. The rest of the paper is organized as follows. Sect. 2 reviews the related works on this topic. We describe our adapted system model and adversarial model in Sect. 3. We discuss the existing privacy preserving streaming model of [16] and its drawbacks in Sect. 4. We follow this by presenting our novel privacy preserving streaming algorithm to eliminate such kind of shortcomings in Sect. 5. We provide evaluations of our scheme in Sect. 6. Finally, Sect. 7 provides concluding remarks and future work directions.

2   Related Work

Over the past couple of decades, various privacy models are proposed for the privacy preservation of the smart metering infrastructure. In this section, we brief these conventional protection methodologies and subsequently highlight their shortcomings as follows

Secure Communication. Many proposed solutions use Diffie-Hellman key exchange and bilinear-mapping to establish secure communication flow between the grid entities [10,19]. Furthermore, [8] used symmetric key and public key cryptography to defend against semi-honest adversaries and malicious attackers. This paper assumes that the keys are already located among all the smart meters and the UPs which makes the solution hard to scale and computationally expensive. Attribute based encryption [17] and multiparty computation based schemes [24, 25] are also being used to mitigate these challenges under the assumption of secured and authenticated communication channels among the grid entities. Solutions based on secure communication between the customers and the utility may provide the overall grid infrastructure better security guarantee, but fails to protect user privacy by leaking original power profiles to the service providers.

Power Profile Reshaping. In an alternative line of work, the overall energy consumption curve is reshaped using storage devices and alternative energy sources (capacitor, batteries, solar cells) to hide the original power consumption profile [28, 39]. Though, these devices are used to maintain an obfuscated load profile by periodically charging and discharging, they require high implementation and maintenance costs. Finally, reduction of the sampling rate of measurements to generate less amount of fine-grained data has also been looked upon as a solution [9]. However it potentially trades off the measurement accuracy. Another possible way to ensure privacy in meter streams can be manipulation of meter data without modifying the original power consumption.

Data Manipulation. Most of the data manipulation based privacy preserving smart metering methodologies highly rely on partially homomorphic encryption [20, 21, 26, 27] and paillier cryptosystem [38] due to their additive features. Furthermore, the infrastructure described in [35] introduces a set of functional entities named *privacy preserving nodes* to collect encrypted customer data by exploiting the homomorphic properties of Shamir's secret sharing scheme [36]. The high computational cost of these aggregation based homomorphic schemes [11] and their inability to support many real-life Smart grid applications [15] leaves major concerns for practical implementation with limited resources. In [6], tolerable noise has been inserted into smart meter reading streams to guarantee the covet privacy. But data injection based privacy schemes can hamper the grid utility by destabilizing grid functionalities such as billing, load forecasting etc. TTP based anonymization solutions can also offer aggregation of fine-grained user level measurements before being sent to the UPs [7, 30]. But due to the questionable trust of the TTPs, these proposals lack feasibility. The data manipulation based privacy preserving scheme proposed in [16] tries to overcome the above mentioned problems by introducing a privacy notion (ϵ, δ^m)-Uncertainty to quantify and bound the information leakage through the input metering stream, where ϵ, δ, m represent three input privacy parameters of the privacy model. However, as shown in [12], the inherent privacy formulation of this scheme can easily be compromised to obtain the original input meter readings with very low guessing entropy. In subsequent sections, we highlight the shortcomings of this scheme to design an alternate methodology that mitigates such issues. However, we first present the adapted system and adversarial models in the next section.

3   System Assumptions

3.1   System Model

The system architecture we have assumed here is that each smart meter reading is generated by summing up the power consumption by individual appliances of each associated household. Now, it is evident that if this stream is sent to the UPs in plaintext, then it can potentially leak critical information such as the "ON/OFF" status of the appliances and the user's home presence. We further assume that these smart meters have sufficient computational capabilities to execute privacy preserving streaming models (as in [16]). These models periodically convert the original power consumption profile of a household to privacy preserved output readings and eventually hide the associated power information of each consumer. The smart meters provide these *privacy preserved reading streams* to nearby Data Concentrator Units (DCUs) as shown in Fig. 1. The DCUs collect these energy usage profiles along with other parameters such as time of day energy data, maximum demand etc., and transmit them to the UPs through the communication channels. The UPs manage services such as billing, electricity usage, load monitoring, demand response etc. using these information. For example, Time-of-Use based (TOU) pricing plans are used as fixed tariffs by the UPs in our assumed system model. In this pricing scheme, electricity tariffs may vary at different times based on peak and off-peak power consumption.

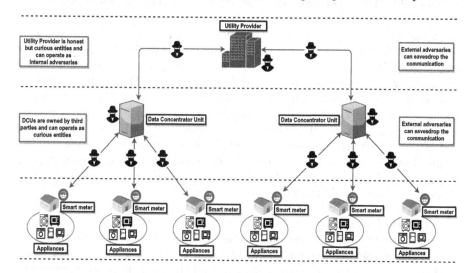

Fig. 1. System Model comprising UP, DCUs, dedicated smart meters and its corresponding appliances. The picture also depicts the attack points that make the system vulnerable.

3.2   Adversarial Model

In our adapted layered Smart grid system model illustrated in Fig. 1, we highlight the vulnerable attack points. Here, the intermediate communication nodes and the DCUs, are generally controlled by commercial enterprises, and their primary role is to help the UPs attain Smart grid functionalities. In the adversarial model, these nodes and UPs are regarded as semi-honest entities. They intend to collect each consumer's consumption data and sell it to another marketing business on a regular basis. They may also preserve all of their consumption data and analyse it to get more information about specific statistics. In addition, as shown in Fig. 1, we assume that external adversaries can also eavesdrop on the communication network or conduct collusion-based attacks amongst several nodes in order to obtain fine-grained raw metering data.

4   Privacy Preserving Streaming Model of [16]

In this subsection, we discuss the privacy preserving streaming model proposed in [16] and subsequently highlight the design drawbacks of this scheme based on the attacking methodology discussed in [12]. We further use these shortcomings to strengthen our privacy preserving metering design philosophy.

4.1   Description of the Privacy Preserving Streaming Model

A smart meter reading stream is basically the power consumption profile of a household that can potentially leak critical information about appliances' "ON/OFF" status and the consumer's home presence. A privacy-preserved streaming algorithm (e.g., in [16]) periodically converts the original power consumption profile to privacy preserved output readings. We denote the vector $R_{in} = \langle R_{in}(1), \cdots, R_{in}(j), \cdots, R_{in}(k) \rangle$ as a k length meter reading stream obtained over a time interval of length $kh\,(k \in \mathbb{N})$. The proposed privacy scheme of [16] introduces a privacy formulation named $(\epsilon,\ \delta^m)$-Uncertainty to quantify and bound each appliance's information leakage by desired privacy levels. Here ϵ, δ, m are the three privacy parameters of the proposed model and are unknown to the adversary. The privacy preserved streaming algorithm of [16] generates a (ϵ, δ^m)-Uncertainty compliant output stream $R_{out} = \langle R_{out}(1), \cdots, R_{out}(j), \cdots, R_{out}(k) \rangle$. This resulting output stream satisfies four properties as summarized below:

- **Individual Reading Boundness:** For each meter reading, this property tries to bound the information leakage through every associated appliance by the input privacy parameter ϵ. This ensures that the information leakages through each output reading of R_{out} for all the appliances are bounded by the input privacy parameter ϵ.
- **m-Consecutive Individual Reading Boundness:** For sequential usage patterns in multiple readings, the information leakage can be higher than individual reading leakages due to their mutual correlations. This property aims to bound the information leakage through each appliance due to m consecutive readings by the privacy parameter δ.

– **m-Consecutive Pairwise Reading Boundness:** Multiple appliances can run sequentially or simultaneously. In such cases, the information leakage can be higher than their original leakages due to their mutual correlation in consecutive readings. This property ensures that these information leakages for all the appliances are bounded by the privacy parameter δ.

– **Closest Safe Reading:** This property ensures lower reading errors between original input readings of R_{in} and its corresponding privacy preserved output readings from R_{out}. Here, each $R_{out}(j)$, $\forall j \in [1, k]$ is the closest reading from $R_{in}(j)$, $\forall j \in [1, k]$, such that the output reading $R_{out}(j)$ satisfies the above three properties of (ϵ, δ^m)-Uncertainty privacy notion.

Furthermore, to minimize the aggregation and billing errors under a fixed tariff, two possible roll over schemes, Cyclic Reading Conversion (CRC) and Dynamic Reading Conversion (DRC) are proposed. Please refer to [16] for more details on these roll over techniques. However, for the current work detailed explanation of these schemes is not necessary.

Observations: From the privacy model presented above, we can deduce that for a naïve observer, as the $R_{out}(j)$ is associated with a large number of possible combinations of the appliances, the number of possible input readings will be similar in size to the candidate reading set. Due to such many-to-one possible mappings between the input readings and the corresponding output readings, it is very difficult for any supervised or unsupervised Non-Intrusive Load Monitoring (NILM) tool to train or guess the precise input stream correctly. On the other hand, with an increasing number of appliances, the size of the candidate set will also increase exponentially. These factors show that the above proposal helps customers maintain privacy, albeit at some incremental cost of the customer's billing cycle over a constant tariff. However, in the next section, we explain the drawbacks of such approaches (as discussed in [12]) in the formulation of privacy preserving metering solutions.

4.2   Drawbacks of Privacy Preserving Streaming Model of [16]

In this section, we highlight the key points that have made the existing privacy preserving scheme of [16] vulnerable to the attacking methodology proposed in [12]. We jot down these loopholes as follows.

– **Bounding Information Leakage from each Meter Reading:** The *Individual Reading Boundness* property tries to hide the information leakage from each input reading by converting each reading to privacy preserved output reading. The leakage through the corresponding output reading is validated against a predefined privacy parameter ϵ. However, this approach comes with a great cost. If any privacy formulation follows this approach, the adversary can easily compute the lower bound of the privacy parameter ϵ. To obtain the lower bound of ϵ, the adversary can find the maximum achieved information leakage among all the output readings. Hence, the initial privacy condition of (ϵ, δ^m)-Uncertainty is easily compromised. This obtained lower bound on ϵ

can later be utilized to find the unsatisfied readings, thus reducing the initial search space for each input reading, from the candidate reading set to this unsatisfied reading set.

- *Reducing Reading Errors by Obtaining Closest Readings:* Many proposed privacy preserving approaches try to keep the reading errors between input readings and their corresponding output readings as minimal as possible while satisfying the required privacy formulation. This property helps to maintain better system utility, such as lower aggregation and billing errors over constant tariffs. However, the *closest safe reading* approach provides very high "Coefficient of determination" values (as shown in Table 1 in Sect. 6) between the input and output reading stream, signifying greater information leakage. This property also helps the adversary to find the closest readings from each output reading that do not satisfy the (ϵ, δ^m)-Uncertainty privacy formulation, thus constructing a possible candidate set of input readings for each output reading [12].

- *Invariant Property of (ϵ, δ^m)-Uncertainty **Privacy Notion:*** As highlighted in [12], the ordering among the (ϵ, δ^m)-Uncertainty compliant output reading pairs are preserved for the corresponding input reading pairs in two possible scenarios[1]. These relation orderings help the adversary to remove more unsatisfactory readings from the possible input candidate reading sets; thus violating the inherent privacy guarantees of (ϵ, δ^m)-Uncertainty privacy formulation.

Keeping these inadequacies in mind, we motivate our proposed formulation and subsequently, in the next section, present a new privacy-preserving smart metering algorithm, *Obfuscate-Load-Signature* to counteract those vulnerabilities.

5   Proposed Privacy Preserving Smart Meter Streaming Algorithm

In this section, we describe our proposed privacy preserving meter streaming methodology that mitigates the above-discussed drawbacks of the existing scheme [16] and also provide the necessary privacy analysis of the proposed scheme.

5.1   Privacy Formulation

We propose an alternative method to generate privacy preserved output streams without inducing any billing or aggregation error over a constant tariff by using a Satisfiability Modulo Theories (SMT) solver. Our approach is based upon a load signature modification technique that obfuscates the original power profile of the meter by inducing noises in the meter readings introduced through the SMT solver. This helps us to create an *undetectability* problem [31] that hides the

---

[1] Please refer to [12] for more details on these conditions.

original input meter readings from the adversary. Simultaneously, from a privacy point of view, we consider that the privacy is protected when the adversary is not able to distinguish among the original load events of the appliances, given an output power profile. If the amount of private information available for learning is measured, then the information leakage can be bounded by the desired level, independent of the attacking mechanism. The information-theoretic metric helps us to quantify this inherent information available for exploitation by measuring the amount of original information present in the noisy data. If the protection method satisfies privacy in information-theoretic sense, then the achieved privacy can be considered acceptable. Hence, it is useful to quantify privacy using information-theoretic metrics. In our work, we consider *coefficient of determination* (denoted as R^2) to quantify the obtained privacy for our proposed scheme. For a simple linear regression of the form $R_{out}(j) = \alpha + \beta R_{in}(j) + \sigma$, the predicted value $\hat{R}_{out}(j) = \alpha + \beta R_{in}(j)$ is affected by some noise σ, where the α and β are defined by the intersection point and the slope factor [22]. We try to analyze the degree to which $R_{out}(j)$ predicts $R_{in}(j)$ using this linear model [18]. Using simple linear regression, it can be shown that the value of R^2 is the same as of the square of the correlation coefficient [22]. For the above described regression and predicted model, we can write the coefficient of determination as follows.

$$R^2 = \frac{[\sum_{j=1}^{k}(R_{in}(j) - \overline{R}_{in})(R_{out}(j) - \overline{R}_{out})]^2}{\sum_{j=1}^{k}(R_{in}(j) - \overline{R}_{in})^2 \sum_{j=1}^{k}(R_{out}(j) - \overline{R}_{out})^2} \tag{1}$$

Here, $\overline{R}_{in}$ and $\overline{R}_{out}$ signify the means of the input reading stream and the corresponding output reading stream respectively. $R^2 = 1$ states that the predictions of the model are fully explained, although $R^2 = 0$ indicates highest privacy protection. With increasing noise, the value of the *coefficient of determination* decreases thus providing higher privacy. Due to the comparatively high computation cost of evaluating R^2 for higher order regression models, we reduce the privacy metric function using the described linear regression model only. Further, the property of zero aggregation error between the input and output power profiles implies that the means of the corresponding profiles are equivalent. This helps us to rewrite Eq. 1 as follows.

$$R^2 = \frac{[\sum_{j=1}^{k}(R_{in}(j)R_{out}(j)) - k\overline{R}_{in}^2]^2}{(\sum_{j=1}^{k}R_{in}(j)^2 - k\overline{R}_{in}^2)(\sum_{j=1}^{k}R_{out}(j)^2 - k\overline{R}_{in}^2)} \tag{2}$$

In the next section, we utilize Eq. 2 to quantify and bound the obtained privacy level from the privacy preserved output stream generated through our proposed algorithm.

5.2   Detailed Description of the Proposed Algorithm

We present the high level strategy of our proposed privacy scheme in Algorithm 1 to generate privacy preserved smart meter output streams that overcomes the three vulnerabilities mentioned in Sect. 4.2. The algorithm takes an

---

Algorithm 1. Obfuscate-Load-Signature()

1: **Inputs:** Pricing signal P, input reading stream R_{in}, privacy parameter τ, metering stream size k;

2: **Output:** Privacy preserved output stream R_{out};

3: **Initialize:** $TotalPrice \leftarrow 0$, $sumInOut \leftarrow 0$, $squareIn \leftarrow 0$, $squareOut \leftarrow 0$, $bounds \leftarrow true$, $privacyMetric \leftarrow 0$;

4: $TotalPrice \leftarrow$ Total billing of input stream R_{in} under the constant tariff P ;

5: $aggregate \leftarrow$ Overall consumption of the input stream R_{in};

6: $maxInput \leftarrow$ Maximum reading in R_{in};

7: $minInput \leftarrow$ Minimum reading in R_{in};

8: $noiseInBounds \leftarrow$ NOISEGENERATOR() ;   ▷ NOISEGENERATOR() provides a random number suitable for cryptographic use

9: **for** $j = 1$; $j <= k$; $j{+}{+}$ **do**

10:     $bounds \leftarrow bounds \wedge ((minInput - noiseInBounds) \leq R_{out}(j)) \wedge (R_{out}(j) \leq (maxInput + noiseInBounds))$;

11: $\phi \leftarrow$ **assert**$((sum(R_{out}) = aggregate) \wedge ((\sum_{j=1}^{k}(R_{out}(j) \times P(j))) = TotalPrice) \wedge bounds)$;

12: **while** (1) **do**

13:     **if** $R_{out} \leftarrow isSatisfiable(\phi)$ **then** $privacyMetric \leftarrow$ COMPUTEPRIVACYLEVEL(R_{in}, R_{out});

14:     **if** $privacyMetric \leq \tau$ **then return** R_{out};

15:     $\phi \leftarrow \phi \wedge \neg R_{out}$;

16: **function** COMPUTEPRIVACYLEVEL (R_{in}, R_{out})

17:     **for** $j = 1$; $j <= k$; $j{+}{+}$ **do**

18:         $sumInOut \leftarrow sumInOut + (R_{in}(j) \times R_{out}(j))$;

19:         $squareIn \leftarrow squareIn + R_{in}(j)^2$;

20:         $squareOut \leftarrow squareOut + R_{out}(j)^2$;

21:     $privacyMetric \leftarrow \dfrac{(sumInOut - k\overline{R}_{in}^2)^2}{(squareIn - k\overline{R}_{in}^2)(squareOut - k\overline{R}_{in}^2)}$;

22:     **return** $privacyMetric$;

---

input stream R_{in}, constant pricing signal P, data window k and the privacy parameter τ as inputs and generates privacy preserved output stream R_{out}. With increasing privacy levels, the aggregation and billing errors due to the privacy algorithm of [16] increase. Contemplating this scenario, we formulate separate SMT clauses to maintain the total aggregation and billing produced through the output stream, same as the corresponding input stream. We evaluate the total billing and power consumption over the data window of the input stream in Lines 4 and 5 respectively of Algorithm 1. Thereafter, we compute the maximum and minimum power consumption of the input stream to restrict the solver's non-deterministic choice space by bounding possible upper and lower values of each reading in the output stream. However, direct assignment of these bounds may leak some information regarding the minimum and maximum values of the input stream as the transformed readings of the output stream never cross the envelop of the actual input stream. Hence, we need to obfuscate these bounds in the resulting output streams such that the adversary can not obtain any information regarding the corresponding input reading streams. In this context, function NOISEGENERATOR() (Line number 8) utilizes /dev/urandom that provides an interface to the OS-specific randomness source. It produces a random data from a constantly reseeded Deterministic Random Number Generator (DRNG) which is cryptographically secure [23]. We use this number as a noise to formulate the bounds for the output readings by subtracting and adding this noise to the minimum and maximum values of the input stream. Such relational constraints for all the readings are collected as SMT clauses in Lines 9-10. The

SMT formula ϕ, thus created using the above clauses (Line 11), is solved to find satisfiable assignments in the while loop of Lines 12-15. For each unique solution, we compute our privacy metric (Lines 17-21), the *coefficient of determination* using Eq. 2 to quantify the achieved privacy level from the output stream w.r.t. the original metering stream. We check its boundness against the desired privacy level τ that can be adapted in run time. Essentially, for each unsuccessful solution, we add the negation of the result as a clause to the solver to get a different answer than before, as shown in Line 15. Successful computation of Algorithm 1 finally provides a privacy preserved output reading stream R_{out} satisfying the required privacy formulation. In the next section, we proceed with the privacy analysis of our proposed scheme.

5.3 Privacy Analysis

Here, we analyse the privacy guarantees of our proposed privacy preserved smart metering scheme based on three unique properties as explained below.

- *Protected Privacy Level:* As discussed in Sect. 4.2, the privacy parameter ϵ of the privacy notion (ϵ, δ^m)-Uncertainty is easily compromised due its unsound formulation. Here, we do not consider the information leakage from each output reading; rather, we focus on altering the whole meter reading stream by bounding the information leakage with the desired privacy level. As a result, the privacy parameter τ can not be compromised by utilizing the attacking methodology of [12].
- *Unpredictability of Output Profiles:* The existing privacy formulation of [16] based on the (ϵ, δ^m)-Uncertainty privacy notion is likely to provide the same privacy preserved output profiles for each input stream in multiple independent runs of the algorithm (due to absence of randomness in the privacy formulation). As a result, the resulting output streams for multiple corresponding input profiles are easily distinguishable. However, in our proposed privacy formulation, the resulting output streams for the same input profile vary due to the solver's non-deterministic choices in each independent run of the algorithm. We provide the empirical evaluation of the same in Sect. 6.3.3. This phenomenon hinders the adversary's capability to utilize the previously discussed shortcomings of (ϵ, δ^m)-Uncertainty privacy notion, such as the *closest reading based approach* and the *invariant property of the scheme.* Hence, strong privacy protection can be guaranteed along with providing higher utility (with respect to aggregation and billing errors) for the Smart grid infrastructure.
- *High Computational Complexity:* Algorithm 1 provides a very high computational complexity against identifying the correct metering stream from the generated privacy preserved output stream. Our load signature modification technique does not guarantee the uniqueness towards determining the satisfiable solutions during privacy transformation. Thus, for a data window of size k, if an attacker tries to construct a rainbow table to find the possible

multiset that could generate an output stream during the execution of privacy preserving streaming algorithm, the table size will have a loose upper bound of 2^{nk} which is significantly large, where n is the number of available appliances and 2^n is the total number of unique power consumption readings. It is to be noted that a rainbow table is a precomputed table that is generally used to crack password hashes. For this context, the adversary constructs this table to identify the original input reading stream given the output stream. We assume that the attacker can find a way to access the table efficiently.

Given the output stream, let us consider M to be a list of multisets that can be used as inputs to generate the same output stream. The attacker will try to find these possible multisets in the rainbow table from the observed stream. Let $M[j]$ be the jth possible input stream that can generate the corresponding output stream during the execution of the privacy preserving algorithm. We consider that, this input sequence contains t number of different values with multiplicity m_i, $\forall i \in [1, t]$. From the concept of permutations of multisets, we know that the number of possible permutations of $M[j]$ is $\dfrac{(\sum_{i=1}^{t} m_i)!}{\prod_{i=1}^{t} m_i!}$. For a simple scenario where every value of the input sequence is different from each other, there exists up to $k!$ permutations for each candidate solution $M[j]$. Therefore, this ensures that even if an attacker seeks to use the rainbow tables to identify the probable input multiset that resulted into the output sequence during privacy transformation, they still cannot perceive the exact ordering of the values in the input reading stream.

6   Experimental Results

In this section, we describe the experimental setup and provide results for evaluation of our proposed privacy preserving scheme *Obfuscate-Load-Signature* as described in Sect. 5.

6.1   Experimental Setup

We analyze our proposed privacy preserving model using the UK dataset provided by Richardson *et. al.* [34]. For the present work, the sanitized dataset is obtained from the UK data archive after following the due process. It is available for academic purposes and has been used for smart meter research purposes in many existing works (like in [16]). This dataset consists of 22 consumers' continuous smart meter energy consumption profile over 2008 and 2009 in East Midlands, UK with a sampling period of one minute. To highlight the efficiency of our scheme, we implement the existing privacy scheme of [16] using a total 25 number of appliances, each with different consumption rates. We choose three distinct combinations of (ϵ, δ, m) i.e. $(0.7, 0.7, 3)$, $(0.6, 0.6, 3)$, $(0.5, 0.5, 2)$ for our experiment to show the impact of different privacy levels with respect to our proposal. We consider the power profiles of the first consumer on 1st, 4th, 5th,

6th, 10th January 2008 from 2:03 AM to 2:17 AM for our experimental purposes (same as [12]). We use these five power profiles to generate different output streams leveraging the privacy algorithm of [16]. For fixed tariffs, Time-of-Use based pricing plans offered by Alectra utilities [5] are used in our methodology.

6.2 Platform

All the experiments were performed on a system with Intel i5 2.20 GHz processor and 4GB RAM, running Ubuntu 18.04 LTS based Operating System.

6.3 Evaluation of "Obfuscate-Load-Signature" Scheme

Here, we evaluate our proposed *Obfuscate-Load-Signature* procedure using the UK dataset mentioned in Sect. 6.1 and our Hardware-In-the-Loop (HIL) simulation test-bed to illustrate its effectiveness and real-time performance.

6.3.1 Evaluation Using the UK Dataset: We consider the previously mentioned five power profiles of the UK dataset to evaluate our proposed privacy preserving streaming method *Obfuscate-Load-Signature* (Algorithm 1). We execute Algorithm 1 with these five power consumption profiles with privacy levels $\tau = 0.5, 0.4$ and 0.3. We can execute the same for any other privacy levels too. We then compare the resulting *coefficient of determination* values of these privacy preserved streams against the output streams computed using the privacy model of [16] under the privacy level of $(0.5, 0.5, 2)$. The privacy scheme of [16] when applied to these five power profiles, guarantees maximum privacy protection under the privacy level of 0.5 (as stated in [12]). Thus, we consider the privacy level of 0.5 and both CRC and DRC roll over schemes in this scenario. Table 1 lists the *coefficient of determination* values for both the privacy schemes under different privacy levels as mentioned. The values obtained from the scheme in [16] are significantly higher than our proposed Algorithm 1 as shown in Table 1. This signifies lesser privacy protection using the methodology of [16] compared to our *Obfuscate-Load-Signature* scheme.

Table 1. "Coefficient of determination" values for both privacy schemes under different privacy levels.

Privacy scheme	Privacy level	Coefficient of determination				
		January 1	January 4	January 5	January 6	January 10
(ϵ, δ^m)-Uncertainty [16]	$\epsilon = 0.5, \delta = 0.5$ (CRC)	0.99967	0.99003	0.59395	0.99982	0.92683
	$\epsilon = 0.5, \delta = 0.5$ (DRC)	0.99929	0.98997	0.54545	0.99988	0.87503
Obfuscate-Load-Signature (Proposed privacy algorithm)	$\tau = 0.5$	0.34819	0.02187	0.0	0.21091	0.00979
	$\tau = 0.4$	0.10453	0.02187	0.0	0.22376	0.00979
	$\tau = 0.3$	0.11722	0.02187	0.0	0.22920	0.00979

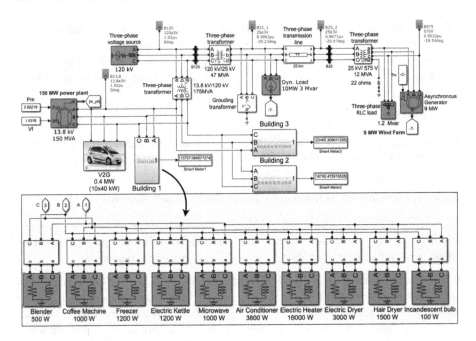

Fig. 2. Our IEEE 5-bus power system model with connected loads.

6.3.2 Evaluation Using Hardware In the Loop (HIL) Test-bed: We evaluate the real-time performance of our privacy scheme by employing a Hardware-In-the-Loop (HIL) simulation test-bed. Our experimental HIL is an OPAL-RT real-time simulator connected with a PC having RT-LAB and Matlab/Simulink software. The host PC based RT-LAB software allows users to edit and modify various power system models, view model data, execute the model and load it into the target simulator i.e. the OPAL-RT.

Power System Modeling Details: For our experiments, we implement a five-bus power system network as shown in Fig. 2. The proposed microgrid power system model comprises three important parts - 1) generation units, 2) a five-bus power system distribution network [2], 3) electrical loads consisting of a Vehicle-to-Grid (V2G) charging system and three building loads. The generation unit consists of a 150 MW power plant and a 9 MW wind farm. The power plant is created using a 13.8 kV synchronous generator which is connected with the 120 kV bus through a 13.8 kV/120 kV transformer. The simplified model of the wind farm produces electrical power using a 9 MW asynchronous generator which is connected to a 25 kV distribution feeder, exporting power to the 120 kV network. The V2G block describes a system where the grid communicates with plug-in electric vehicles to exchange demand response services either by supplying the electricity back to the grid or reducing their charging rate. In Fig. 2, we have multiple electrical vehicles in the base model of V2G system, each having an electrical capacity of 40 KW. Along with that, the grid system consists of three buildings, each having multiple appliances. As shown in our model, these appliances comprise heavy loads like air conditioner (3800 W), electric heater (18000 W), electric dryer (3000 W) etc. along with lighter loads like Incandescent bulb (100 W). The power consumption values have been taken from the standard home appliances power consumption table [3]. We have elaborated this in Fig. 2 for Building 1 that has been used for our experiment.

HIL Test-Bed: Each building is fitted with one smart meter which measures and transmits the aggregated power consumption of building appliance loads in each sampling period. The purpose of this experiment is to generate time stamped sequences of aggregated building load consumption profiles and process them in real-time on a low power single board compute (SBC) platform which is suitable for packaging with privacy enabled future metering systems. The electrical modeling of building loads and real-time power system simulation helps us in that objective rather than always relying on third party metering dataset. Here, we consider one of the building loads in our test-bed. For this building model, we provide a variable load profile signal for switching on/off each of the building appliances. At each such sampling instant, the subsets of loads which will be "ON" are selected by the variable load profile input as shown in Fig. 3 in "User Interface" block. Accordingly, the overall load consumption is aggregated and output as a real-time electrical signal by the OPAL-RT HIL system. These active power measurements are passed to an analog to digital converter (ADC) through a DB37 connector of the OPAL-RT using its analog output I/O ports, thus generating a time stamped stream of aggregated measurement data. This serves as a real-time input to our privacy transformation (i.e. Algorithm 1) executing on a Raspberry pi 4 model B SBC. Given an input reading stream of length k, obtained over some time interval kh (where h is the meter sampling period), we consider our privacy preserving transformation scheme feasible if the execution time required for generating the privacy preserved output stream is bounded by kh.

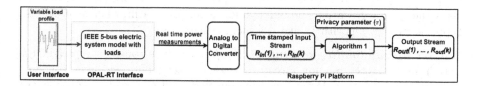

Fig. 3. Overview of HIL setup.

Measurements and Evaluations: For the current smart metering system, the sampling interval and stream size are set as $h = 1\,sec$ and $k = 15$ respectively. Using our setup, we generate a stream of 195 measurements and execute Algorithm 1 in real-time for thirteen consecutive instances with a periodicity of 15 sec for τ values of 0.05 and 0.2. The average execution time of the algorithm in each case was found to be 1.0789 and 1.0498 seconds for $\tau = 0.05$ and 0.2 respectively. This justifies the suitability of our mechanism in a real-time deployment

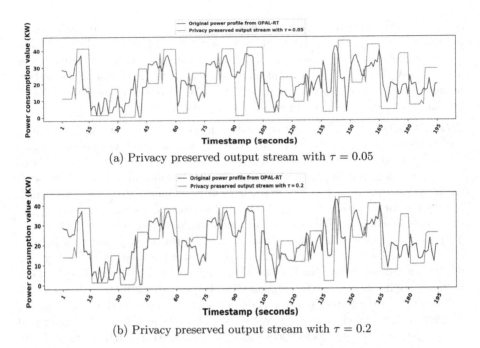

(a) Privacy preserved output stream with $\tau = 0.05$

(b) Privacy preserved output stream with $\tau = 0.2$

Fig. 4. Results of Algorithm 1 in HIL test-bed

setting. Moreover, with this solution, τ can be a tunable parameter which can be set depending on the criticality of building loads. Also, for the same building, τ can be adapted in run time based on privacy critical operational periods.

Figure 4 provides the generated input stream of 195 readings and the corresponding privacy preserved output streams computed in real-time. Figure 4a and Fig. 4b show the output streams generated by Algorithm 1 for privacy levels of $\tau = 0.05$ and $\tau = 0.2$ respectively. The privacy preserved output streams preserve the total aggregation and billing under a constant tariff, whereas previously reported privacy algorithms like [16] incurs such errors.

6.3.3 Unpredictability of Output Profiles: Let us consider an original k-length smart meter reading stream $\langle x_1, x_2, \cdots, x_k \rangle$, obtained over k successive sampling windows. Upon executing our proposed *Obfuscate-Load-Signature* scheme on this input stream, a k-length privacy preserving output stream is generated. We perform L such independent executions of our scheme, such that in the ith execution, the resulting output stream $\langle x_1^i, x_2^i, \cdots, x_k^i \rangle$ is produced. After obtaining these L number of output reading streams, we can construct L length output traces associated with each original input reading x_j, $\forall j \in [1, k]$. For the original meter readings x_j, this output trace can be represented as $\langle x_j^1, x_j^2, \cdots, x_j^L \rangle$. As discussed in Sect. 5, due to the solver's non-deterministic choices, these resulting output traces $\langle x_j^1, x_j^2, \cdots, x_j^L \rangle$ are likely to be unique and significantly different from the original meter reading x_j.

Empirical Evaluation: For this experiment, we consider a $k = 15$ length meter reading stream generated through our HIL test-bed and executes $L = 5000$ independent runs of our proposed *Obfuscate-Load-Signature* scheme on this power profile. Figure 5 illustrates the privacy preserved output traces for the original meter readings $x_1 = 22.122$ KW and $x_{15} = 8.812$ KW, along with the ranges of their privacy preserved traces. As shown in Fig. 5, the original meter readings are significantly distinct from their privacy preserved output traces. Simultaneously, the output traces are also spread over a wide range of possible values. These properties in the output profile hinder the adversary's capability to execute various attacking methodologies. For example, the invariant property present in the existing metering scheme of [16] is absent from our proposed methodology. As a result, the attacking philosophy of [12] will not be applicable against our proposed *Obfuscate-Load-Signature* scheme.

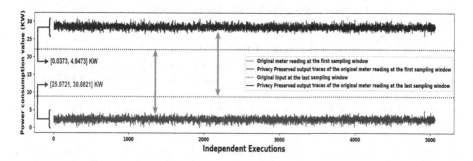

Fig. 5. Privacy preserved output traces of the first (22.122 KW) and last meter (8.812 KW) readings in 5000 independent executions of *Obfuscate-Load-Signature* scheme.

7   Conclusion and Future Work

In this paper, we provide a novel SMT based privacy preserving transformation without aggregation and billing errors over constant tariff, a feature absent in existing schemes. The proposed *Obfuscate-Load-Signature* scheme also eliminates the privacy vulnerabilities present in the existing scheme of [16]. We also highlight its strong privacy guarantees against existing attacking methodologies (such as [12]) on non-cryptographic smart metering schemes. Finally, we demonstrate its usefulness using suitable statistical measures and effectiveness in real-time executions using the HIL test-bed.

The performance of Real Time Pricing (RTP) algorithms are known to be sensitive to disturbances in measurement data [37]. We consider characterizing the impact of such transformations on the performance and stability of RTP algorithms as a possible future work.

Acknowledgement. We would like to thank the projects titled Development of Secured Hardware And Automotive Systems from iHub-NTIHAC Foundation, IIT

Kanpur, Exploring Formal Methods for Smart Grid Privacy and Security (SERB SUPRA), Cyber Security Research in CPS funded by TCG Foundation, India, for partially funding our research.

References

1. Guidelines for Smart Grid Cybersecurity: Vol. 2, Privacy and the Smart Grid.   https://csrc.nist.gov/csrc/media/publications/nistir/7628/rev-1/final/ documents/draft_nistir_7628_r1_vol2.pdf
2. Electric System Model (2021). https://in.mathworks.com/help/physmod/sps/ug/ initializing-a-5-bus-network-with-the-load-flow-tool-of-powergui.html.   Accessed 2021
3. Home Appliances Power Consumption Table (2021). https://www.wholesalesolar. com/solar-information/power-table. Accessed 2021
4. Naperville Smart Meters Keep Track of Household Activities (2021). https:// smartgridawareness.org/2013/10/03/smart-meter-data-reveals/. Accessed 2021
5. Time-of-Use (TOU) Pricing and Schedules (2021). https://www.powerstream.ca/. Accessed 2021
6. Ács, G., Castelluccia, C.: I Have a DREAM! (DiffeRentially privatE smArt Metering). In: Filler, T., Pevný, T., Craver, S., Ker, A. (eds.) IH 2011. LNCS, vol. 6958, pp. 118–132. Springer, Heidelberg (2011). https://doi.org/10.1007/978-3-642-24178-9_9
7. Bohli, J.M., Sorge, C., Ugus, O.: A privacy model for smart metering. In: 2010 IEEE International Conference on Communications Workshops, pp. 1–5. IEEE (2010)
8. Dimitriou, T., Awad, M.K.: Secure and scalable aggregation in the smart grid resilient against malicious entities. Ad Hoc Netw. **50**, 58–67 (2016). https://doi. org/10.1016/j.adhoc.2016.06.014
9. Dong, R., Ratliff, L.J., Cárdenas, A.A., Ohlsson, H., Sastry, S.S.: Quantifying the utility-privacy tradeoff in the internet of things. ACM Trans. Cyber-Phys. Syst. **2**(2) (2018). https://doi.org/10.1145/3185511
10. Erkin, Z., Tsudik, G.: Private computation of spatial and temporal power consumption with smart meters. In: Bao, F., Samarati, P., Zhou, J. (eds.) ACNS 2012. LNCS, vol. 7341, pp. 561–577. Springer, Heidelberg (2012). https://doi.org/ 10.1007/978-3-642-31284-7_33
11. Finster, S., Baumgart, I.: Privacy-aware smart metering: A survey. IEEE Communications Surveys and Tutorials **17**(2), 1088–1101 (2015). https://doi.org/10.1109/ COMST.2015.2425958
12. Ghosh, S., Chatterjee, U., Masburah, R., Dey, S., Mukhopadhyay, D.: Is the whole lesser than its parts? breaking an aggregation based privacy aware metering algorithm. In: 25th Euromicro Conference on Digital System Design, DSD 2022, Spain, 31 August–2 September 2022 (2022)
13. Goel, S., Hong, Y.: Security challenges in smart grid implementation. In: Smart Grid Security. SC, pp. 1–39. Springer, London (2015). https://doi.org/10.1007/ 978-1-4471-6663-4_1
14. Gong, Y., Cai, Y., Guo, Y., Fang, Y.: A privacy-preserving scheme for incentive-based demand response in the smart grid. IEEE Trans. Smart Grid **7**(3), 1304–1313 (2015)
15. Hart, G.W.: Nonintrusive appliance load monitoring. Proc. IEEE **80**(12), 1870–1891 (1992). https://doi.org/10.1109/5.192069

16. Hong, Y., Liu, W.M., Wang, L.: Privacy preserving smart meter streaming against information leakage of appliance status. IEEE Trans. Inf. Forens. Secur. **12**(9), 2227–2241 (2017). https://doi.org/10.1109/TIFS.2017.2704904

17. Hu, C., et al.: A secure and scalable data communication scheme in smart grids. Wirel. Commun. Mob. Comput. (2018). https://doi.org/10.1155/2018/5816765

18. Kalogridis, G., Efthymiou, C., Denic, S.Z., Lewis, T.A., Cepeda, R.: Privacy for smart meters: Towards undetectable appliance load signatures. In: 2010 First IEEE International Conference on Smart Grid Communications, pp. 232–237. IEEE (2010)

19. Kursawe, K., Danezis, G., Kohlweiss, M.: Privacy-friendly aggregation for the smart-grid. In: Fischer-Hübner, S., Hopper, N. (eds.) PETS 2011. LNCS, vol. 6794, pp. 175–191. Springer, Heidelberg (2011). https://doi.org/10.1007/978-3-642-22263-4_10

20. Li, F., Luo, B., Liu, P.: Secure information aggregation for smart grids using homomorphic encryption. In: 2010 First IEEE International Conference on Smart Grid Communications, pp. 327–332. IEEE (2010)

21. Lu, R., Liang, X., Li, X., Lin, X., Shen, X.: Eppa: an efficient and privacy-preserving aggregation scheme for secure smart grid communications. IEEE Trans. Parallel Distrib. Syst. **23**(9), 1621–1631 (2012)

22. Montgomery, D.C., Runger, G.C.: Applied Statistics and Probability for Engineers. Wiley, New York (2010)

23. Müller, S.: Linux random number generator-a new approach (2020)

24. Mustafa, M.A., Cleemput, S., Aly, A., Abidin, A.: An mpc-based protocol for secure and privacy-preserving smart metering. In: 2017 IEEE PES Innovative Smart Grid Technologies Conference Europe, ISGT-Europe 2017, Torino, Italy, 26–29 September 2017, pp. 1–6. IEEE (2017). https://doi.org/10.1109/ISGTEurope.2017.8260202

25. Mustafa, M.A., Cleemput, S., Aly, A., Abidin, A.: A secure and privacy-preserving protocol for smart metering operational data collection. IEEE Trans. Smart Grid **10**(6), 6481–6490 (2019). https://doi.org/10.1109/TSG.2019.2906016

26. Ozgur, U., Tonyali, S., Akkaya, K.: Testbed and simulation-based evaluation of privacy-preserving algorithms for smart grid ami networks. In: 2016 IEEE 41st Conference on Local Computer Networks Workshops (LCN Workshops), pp. 181–186. IEEE (2016)

27. Ozgur, U., Tonyali, S., Akkaya, K., Senel, F.: Comparative evaluation of smart grid ami networks: Performance under privacy. In: 2016 IEEE Symposium on Computers and Communication (ISCC), pp. 1134–1136. IEEE (2016)

28. Pagliari, D.J., Vinco, S., Macii, E., Poncino, M.: Low-overhead power trace obfuscation for smart meter privacy. In: Proceedings of the 56th Annual Design Automation Conference 2019, DAC 2019, Las Vegas, NV, USA, 02–06 June 2019, p. 111. ACM (2019). https://doi.org/10.1145/3316781.3317855

29. Paverd, A., Martin, A., Brown, I.: Security and privacy in smart grid demand response systems. In: Cuellar, J. (ed.) SmartGridSec 2014. LNCS, vol. 8448, pp. 1–15. Springer, Cham (2014). https://doi.org/10.1007/978-3-319-10329-7_1

30. Petrlic, R.: A privacy-preserving concept for smart grids, pp. B1–B14, January 2010

31. Pfitzmann, A., Hansen, M.: A terminology for talking about privacy by data minimization: anonymity, unlinkability, undetectability, unobservability, pseudonymity, and identity management (2010)

32. Piga, D., Cominola, A., Giuliani, M., Castelletti, A., Rizzoli, A.E.: Sparse optimization for automated energy end use disaggregation. IEEE Trans. Contr. Syst. Technol. **24**(3), 1044–1051 (2016). https://doi.org/10.1109/TCST.2015.2476777
33. Rahman, M.S., Basu, A., Kiyomoto, S., Bhuiyan, M.A.: Privacy-friendly secure bidding for smart grid demand-response. Inf. Sci. **379**, 229–240 (2017)
34. Richardson, I., Thomson, M., Infield, D., Clifford, C.: Domestic electricity use: a high-resolution energy demand model, August 2019. https://hdl.handle.net/2134/6997
35. Rottondi, C., Verticale, G., Capone, A.: Privacy-preserving smart metering with multiple data consumers. Comput. Netw. **57**(7), 1699–1713 (2013)
36. Shamir, A.: How to share a secret. Commun. ACM **22**(11), 612–613 (1979). https://doi.org/10.1145/359168.359176
37. Tan, R., Badrinath Krishna, V., Yau, D.K., Kalbarczyk, Z.: Impact of integrity attacks on real-time pricing in smart grids. In: Proceedings of the 2013 ACM SIGSAC Conference on Computer & Communications Security, pp. 439–450 (2013)
38. Tonyali, S., Akkaya, K., Saputro, N., Uluagac, A.S., Nojoumian, M.: Privacy-preserving protocols for secure and reliable data aggregation in IoT-enabled smart metering systems. Futur. Gener. Comput. Syst. **78**, 547–557 (2018)
39. Yang, W., Li, N., Qi, Y., Qardaji, W.H., McLaughlin, S.E., McDaniel, P.D.: Minimizing private data disclosures in the smart grid. In: Yu, T., Danezis, G., Gligor, V.D. (eds.) the ACM Conference on Computer and Communications Security, CCS'12, Raleigh, NC, USA, 16–18 October 2012, pp. 415–427. ACM (2012). https://doi.org/10.1145/2382196.2382242

An Analysis of the Hardware-Friendliness of AMQ Data Structures for Network Security

Arish Sateesan[1(✉)], Jo Vliegen[1], and Nele Mentens[1,2]

[1] imec-COSIC/ES&S, ESAT, KU Leuven, Leuven, Belgium
{arish.sateesan,jo.vliegen,nele.mentens}@kuleuven.be
[2] LIACS, Leiden University, Leiden, The Netherlands

Abstract. Field-programmable gate arrays (FPGA) are increasingly used in network security applications for high-throughput measurement solutions and attack detection systems. One class of algorithms that are heavily used for these purposes, are approximate membership query (AMQ) data structures, which provide a mechanism to check, with a certain false positive rate, if an element is present in the data structure or not. AMQ data structures are used, for example, in distributed denial-of-service (DDoS) attack detection. They are typically designed to work efficiently on general-purpose processors, but when the high throughput of FPGAs is required, hardware-friendly implementations of AMQ modules are indispensable. A hardware-unfriendly AMQ module would considerably slow down the overall system and compromise the security when it is required to operate at line rate in a high-bandwidth network. Hence, choosing a suitable data structure and hardware architecture is of utmost importance. In this work, we propose FPGA architectures for various well-known AMQ data structures and analyze their hardware implementation properties. This work serves as a guideline on FPGA-based AMQ architectures for researchers and practitioners working on high-throughput network security applications on FPGA.

Keywords: Approximate membership query · FPGA · Network security

1 Introduction

As of 2022, every day approximately 5.6 billion Google searches are made, 90 million photos are shared on Instagram, 720,000 h of videos are uploaded to YouTube, 500 million tweets are posted, and a total of 2.5 Quintilian bytes of data are generated [1]. Increasing data rates induce hefty storage and computation costs. This issue becomes even more important in networking applications where data need to be processed at line rate, i.e., the rate at which data are transmitted in the network. The advent of Terabit Ethernet, i.e. Ethernet with speeds above 100 Gigabits per second (Gbps), leads to stringent throughput constraints, which are difficult to meet on resource-limited platforms.

L. Batina et al. (Eds.): SPACE 2022, LNCS 13783, pp. 287–313, 2022.
https://doi.org/10.1007/978-3-031-22829-2_16

Approximate membership query (AMQ) data structures are used for lookups in networking and database applications with strict speed requirements, memory limitations and/or power constraints [34]. As opposed to exact lookup architectures, AMQ algorithms have a small false positive rate. In a typical application, as shown in Fig. 1, AMQ data structures provide an estimate of whether an element (s), also called a key, is present in the data structure (S) not. AMQ data structures can be employed standalone when it is only necessary to know the presence of the key s. When a value needs to be read out as well, AMQ solutions are used in key-value storage mechanisms.

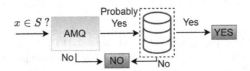

Fig. 1. Role of an AMQ data structure for lookup applications

In distributed denial-of-service (DDoS) attack detection systems, the lookup (AMQ) module checks if the parsed flow identifier or flow ID (f) of the incoming network flow is present in the blacklist or not. This is shown in Fig. 2. The flow is dropped if f is present in the blacklist. If f is not present, a detection module, based on, e.g., pattern matching, probabilistic algorithms or machine learning, examines the flow. Here, false positives of the AMQ lookup structure causes legitimate flows to be labelled as malicious. Therefore, the false positive rate (FPR) of the data structure becomes as important as speed. An example of a DDoS detection system that relies on a setup as shown in Fig. 2, is proposed by Scherrer et al. [33].

Membership queries or dictionary lookups have always been a challenging problem. This is even more so when the number of unique elements to be stored, commonly referred to as the *cardinality*, is very large. AMQ structures perform very well when the data set is static and the cardinality is known upfront. In this paper, our focus is on single and static data sets where the cardinality is already known or predictable. Data structures based on this criterion are the prime requirement for applications such as large flow detection mechanisms, which are used for DDoS detection, where measuring the network flow is stipulated to a specific measurement epoch. In network applications, the flow ID is the key for the lookup and the size of the flow ID is fixed. An IPv4 flow ID is characterised by the 5-tuple ⟨source address, destination address, source port, destination port, protocol⟩ and can be any combination of the 5-tuple. In this paper, the flow ID is taken as a combination of source and destination IP addresses and ports. We ignore the protocol field to keep the size of the flow ID to 96 bits. This means that the key input to the lookup or key-value storage mechanism is 96 bits in the scenario that we consider.

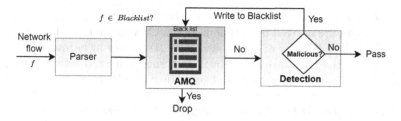

Fig. 2. Role of AMQ data structures for lookups in network attack detection systems

1.1   Challenges in Membership Query Data Structures on Hardware

On software platforms, a dictionary is the easiest solution for storing data as key-value pairs. However, a data structure similar to dictionaries would be very inefficient on hardware. The best available solution without any loss in accuracy for lookup data structures are Content Addressable Memories (CAM), which are too expensive for resource-constrained devices [31]. The operating frequency of a CAM decreases with increasing size, which is a problem when large amounts of data need to be processed at line rate. A large improvement over exact data structures, like CAMs, is offered by probabilistic lookup and key-value storage data structures, i.e., those that can have a small false positive rate in exchange for reduced lookup delay, resources and power consumption. Examples of probabilistic data structures are hash tables (in which false positives can be eliminated through chaining mechanisms), Cuckoo hash tables, and other hash-based techniques. Most AMQ data structures are improved versions of Cuckoo filters, which are derived from Cuckoo hash tables, or Bloom filters.

Even though probabilistic architectures come with many advantages such as lower memory requirements and lower lookup latency, the accuracy and hardware-friendliness are an important concern. When it comes to processing data at line rate on hardware, a number of challenges have to be addressed in order to maximize the accuracy and the lookup speed, and minimize the memory utilization. Data structures such as hash tables employed with linear probing or chaining as collision resistant mechanisms, would be difficult to implement on hardware as the size of the table would keep changing and the feasibility of pipelining is almost naught. Dynamic insertion is another requirement for network security applications, where a full set of flow IDs are not available at the time of construction and new flow IDs need to be added at runtime. Hence, static architectures are not preferred, unless all the required keys or rules which are to be stored are already available such as in regular expression matching.

In this work, we analyze existing probabilistic architectures to find a suitable probabilistic alternative for CAMs on hardware for network security applications. Our approach is to evaluate how suitable the algorithms are to be transformed into a hardware architecture, with a specific focus on achieving a speed-up on FPGA. The efficiency in software of these algorithms does not necessarily give us an idea of which algorithms perform the best in hardware. There are a plethora of such data structures available and analyzing each and every data structure would be too much for this paper. Nevertheless, most of the well-performing data structures are derived from Bloom filters, Cuckoo filters, or hash tables, so we focus on the efficiency of these basic data structures in hardware. Our goal is to evaluate the hardware friendliness in terms of lookup latency, operating frequency, resource consumption, and suitability for pipelining.

2 An Insight into AMQ Data Structures

Starting from hash tables, numerous AMQ data structures have been proposed. The best known AMQ data structures are hash tables, Bloom filters [4] and Cuckoo filters [10]. Most of the prominent AMQ structures are either derived or optimized versions of these structures. Note that hash tables can be turned into exact lookup mechanisms when linear probing or chaining is applied. Besides the classification into Bloom filter based, Cuckoo filter based and hash table based data structures, there can be other ways of classifying, such as fingerprint-based/non-fingerprint based or static/dynamic architectures. Fingerprint-based data structures store either a short digest of the key or the entire key itself whereas non-fingerprint based data structures do not store the key/digest. Static architectures require the whole set of keys to be available at the time of construction, where dynamic architectures can support insertion and deletion of items on-the-fly. The term 'dynamic' may also be used to represent the data structures where resizing of the table at run-time is possible. However, in this paper we do not consider the dynamic resizing of the table at run-time. This is because of the fact that a complete reconstruction or rehashing of the data structure is required for dynamic resizing. This we try to avoid on hardware because it is purely an overhead and does not allow for a fair comparison.

Since we categorize all data structures into three types: hash table based, Bloom filter based and Cuckoo filter based, the remainder of this section elaborates on these three types. Table 1 shows a number of the prominent features of the basic data structures, which are relevant in network security applications. The table gives an average of the features from all three types. It is noted that there might be exceptions to these generalizations.

Table 1. Features of basic AMQ data structures

Data structure	Stores key	Stores fingerprint	Supports deletion	Supports lookups	Supports key-value store	Unlimited insertions
Hash table	✓	✗	✓	✓	✓	✗
Bloom filter	✗	✗	✗	✓	✗	✓
Cuckoo filter	✗	✓	✓	✓	✗	✗

2.1 Hash Table and Its Variants

Hash tables are the simplest and most conventional way to implement a lookup or key-value storage architecture. To add an item x to a hash table with m

locations, a hash function $h(x)$ is used to map the item to the table, where the key, value, or key-value pair are to be stored. A simple representation of the hash table is shown in Fig. 3(a). Before we dive deep into the details, we should clarify the difference between a hash table and a hash map. In a hash table the key is mapped to a location in the table using a hash function and the key is stored in that location. Hash map follows the same process but stores a key-value pair instead of a key. In this paper we use the term 'hash table' invariably for representing both hash table and hash map, and we refer to hash tables without collision resistance mechanisms in the form of linear probing or chaining.

Compared to exact associative array architectures such as CAMs, a hash table requires less memory for storing the same set of elements. However, hash tables are prone to collisions. Occurrences of hash collisions cause two different keys to be mapped to the same location in the table which causes data loss. The load factor α of hash table $\frac{n}{m}$ must be kept to a low value to reduce the collisions, where n and m are the total number of items to be added and the number of buckets in the hash table respectively. A bucket is a hash-indexed location in the table which could store one or more entries. The probability of at least a single collision in a hash table is $\frac{m!}{(m-n)!m^n}$ and the total average number of collisions is $\approx \frac{n^2}{2m}$. This means that there will be an average of $\approx 50\%$ collisions if $n = m$. Hence, α must be lower than 0.5 to keep the collisions to a minimum, which would eventually cause under-utilization of memory. The memory efficiency of a hash table can be configured when the number of elements to be stored is known upfront.

There are many different techniques to minimize the effect of hash collisions, such as chaining, linear/quadratic probing, and double hashing. Chaining is the process where collided items are stored as linked lists, and linear probing searches through the locations in the table sequentially to find an empty slot. Double hashing uses two hash functions where the second hash function is used as an offset to probe for an empty slot in case of a collision. However, techniques such as chaining and linear probing are not really suitable on hardware as the size of the table can increase indefinitely. Also, these techniques worsen the time complexity of hash tables as it may be required to probe over all of the inserted elements in the worst case scenario.

Robin Hood Hashing: Robin hood hashing [6] is a hashing technique to compensate collisions in hash tables. The principle of Robin hood hashing is to keep the keys which are subjected to collisions close to the originally hashed slots, as shown in Fig. 3(b). It uses probe sequence lengths (PSL) to find a slot during insertion. PSL is the number of probes made by an item before it finds a slot, and the PSL has to be stored along with the key. During a collision, probing starts and if a key in the non-empty slot has a lower PSL it is swapped with the key to be inserted. This probing continues until an empty slot is found for the swapped keys.

The most prominent variants of Robin hood hashing are the Quotient filter (QF) [3] and the Counting Quotient Filter (CQF) [26]. QF is practically a linear probing hash table to reduce collisions and QF does not store the whole key but a short fingerprint of the key in a chained manner. Both QF and CQF support deletion and resizing and both exhibit better cache locality. Each fingerprint is divided into quotient and remainder where the remainder is stored in the location indexed by the quotient. The collisions cause the stored remainders to be shifted to the subsequent slots linearly. In, CQF some of the remaining slots are dedicated for counters, which improve the performance of QFs on skewed datasets. Similar to hash tables, linear probing in quotient filters makes it unsuitable for hardware because of the complexity of implementation, dynamic resizing, and unpredictability of the number of cycles required for insertion. Shifting the elements in a linear fashion in memory is also not preferred on hardware as only one location can be read/write in a single cycle. Moreover, the performance declines as the occupancy of the QF becomes high, especially after 60% occupancy.

d-Choice Hashing and d-Left Hashing: Chained hash tables embrace a completely random approach to find a bucket and links the collided keys to the same bucket which could adversely affect the update/query time complexity as the length of the chain in a random bucket becomes longer. d-choice hashing [29] introduced load balancing in the hash table of size m by applying d hash functions and the key is inserted into the bucket which has the lowest load. At the instance of a tie when all the hashed buckets have the same load, a bucket is chosen randomly for insertion. d-left hashing [24] improved the load balancing by using d separate hash tables with each table is associated with a single hash function. In 2-left hashing there are 2 tables of size $m/2$ and the key is hashed to both the tables and the key is inserted to the left table if the hashed bucket in the left table has the lowest load or if there is a tie. Compared to d-choice hashing, the occurrence of ties is less in d-left hashing as the left hash table always has equal or more load compared to the right table. A graphical representation of 2-choice hashing and 2-left hashing is shown in Fig. 3(e) and Fig. 3(f) respectively.

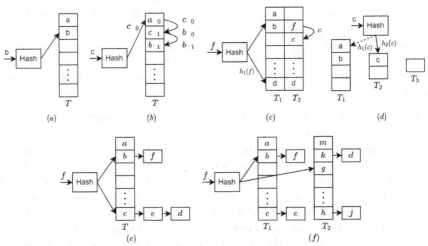

(a) Conventional hashing, (b) Robin hood hashing, (c) Cuckoo hashing, (d) Peacock hashing, (e) 2-choice hashing, (f) 2-left hashing

Fig. 3. Various hashing schemes

Cuckoo Hashing: The issue with most of the hash tables is the worst case query time when enabling collision avoidance techniques. In linear probing and double hashing, the worst case lookup time is $O(log\ n)$, where n is the number of elements inserted. In chained hashing, the worst case lookup time is $O(log\ n/log\ log\ n)$, whereas in two way chaining it is $O(log\ log\ n)$. The best way to eliminate such long lookup times is to use perfect hashing where there are no collisions, but that is more of a hypothetical scenario. A hashing technique that can provide a worst case lookup time of $O(1)$ is Cuckoo hashing [25]. Cuckoo hashing-based data structures provide better collision resistance than hash tables while offering a worst case lookup time of $O(1)$.

A Cuckoo hash table (CHT) uses two tables and two hash functions and each key is stored in only one both tables. A graphical representation of CHT is shown in Fig. 3(c). In case of collisions during insertion, the already existing key in the table is swapped with the incoming key and the swapped key is hashed again and relocates to the hash indexed location if empty. If the relocated index is not empty, this process of kicking out the existing keys continues until it reaches a maximum allocated loop value. If the maximum allocated loop value is reached and insertion fails, the CHT needs to be resized and all the elements should be rehashed with a new hash function. CHT provides a faster query time and better space-occupancy, but the memory requirement is still high as it is required to store the full key in the table. One way to overcome this issue is partial-key Cuckoo hashing, which is the basic principle of Cuckoo filters. A more detailed description of partial-key Cuckoo hashing is given in Sect. 2.3.

Peacock Hashing: Peacock hash table (PHT) is another form of linked/chained hash tables. Peacock hashing [19] is probably the best hardware-friendly solution to chained hash tables. PHT employs multiple hash tables where there is a main table followed by multiple backup tables. The size of subsequent backup tables is scaled down by a scaling factor. All the tables use different hash functions. A graphical representation of PHT is shown in Fig. 3(d). The incoming keys are directed to the larger tables first and if there are collisions, the keys are sent to backup tables. If a predefined probing value is reached and still no empty slot is found, the key is discarded. In order to make the querying faster, a fast filter-preferably a Bloom filter-is associated with each of the backup tables in the on-chip memory and the hash tables are stored in the off-chip memory. Despite being a chained hash table, the number of probes due to collision is limited to the number of tables. The worst case update and query time complexity is $O(log\ log\ m)$, where m is the size of the main table.

2.2 Bloom Filter and Its Variants

A Bloom filter [4] is a space-efficient probabilistic data structure which is commonly employed to perform constant-time membership queries in a set S of n elements, $\{x_1, x_2, ..., x_n\}$, such that $S \subseteq U$ where U is a universal set. Proposed by Howard Bloom in 1970, standard Bloom filters (SBF) became an integral part of most of the applications where conventional membership queries turned out to be impractical given that the amount of data to be handled is large. A

Bloom filter is composed of a single-bit array of m bits and all bits are initialized to 0. A simple representation of a SBF is shown in Fig. 4. A set of k independent hash functions are used to map an input x to k locations.

Compared to hash tables, the use of multiple hash functions in Bloom filters somewhat eliminates the requirement of hash-collision avoidance mechanisms. To insert a new element into the filter, all the bits in the k hash-indexed locations are set to 1. While querying for x, the Bloom filter returns $x \in S$ if all the k hash-indexed locations return 1. If any one of the bits in the k hashed locations are not 1, the filter returns $x \notin S$. Bloom filters are simple, easy to construct, and memory-efficient, but still have some limitations such as no support for deletion. Many different variants of Bloom filters have been proposed to address these limitations [13]. There exist more than 50 variants of Bloom filters and a lot more optimized Bloom filter architectures, but there is always a trade-off between memory, accuracy, and speed among these variants and most of the variants are a workaround to eliminate the limitations of Bloom filters.

Support for Deletion: As Bloom filters cannot support deletion, Counting Bloom filter (CBF) [11] is introduced to enable deletions in a BF, but at the cost of a higher space utilization. A CBF follows the same structure of SBF but each single-bit slot in the BF is replaced by a counter to keep track of insertions. Whenever an item is inserted, the hash-indexed counters are incremented by one and during deletion the corresponding counters are decremented by one. Numerous variants and optimizations to CBF have been proposed in recent times to improve CBF. Deletable Bloom filter (DIBF) [30] tries to address the higher memory requirement of CBF while offering the support for deletion. DIBF divides the bit array of size m into r regions and keeps a bitmap of size r-bits to encode whether or not a region is collision free. Each bit in the bitmap represents the collision status of each region. However the trade-off is a higher FPR as the size of each region is a small fraction of m. Moreover, the deletion becomes impossible when every region has at least one collision and DIBF acts like a normal BF with a worsened FPR. Spectral Bloom filters [8] and Space-code Bloom filters [18] also support deletions by following a similar approach as CBF, but targets multi-sets.

Dynamicity: SBF supports unlimited insertions at the cost of a higher FPR, but does not support dynamic resizing where it resizes the existing filter on the run while retaining the same FPR. Dynamic Bloom filter (DBF) [16] and Scalable Bloom filter (SCBF) [2] propose dynamic resizing of the filter adapting to dynamic datasets. Both dynamic and scalable Bloom filters follow the same data structure which consists of a series of small SBFs appended sequentially and the difference being the sizes of the incremental SBFs. DBF has the same size m for all the SBFs whereas the ith SBF of SCBF has a size equal to $m \times a^{i-1}$, where a is a positive integer. Both approaches are slower and have a lower FPR for the same amount of memory, compared to SBF. SCBF has a lower FPR compared to DBF while DBF is faster than SCBF as it uses homogeneous SBFs while SCBF employs heterogeneous SBFs.

Enhanced FPR: SBF, being a simple data structure which enhances the FPR without a trade-off, is difficult. Retouched Bloom filter (RBF) [9] improves the FPR of the Bloom filter by trading for some false negatives. The removal of false positives in RBF is achieved by clearing the corresponding bits.

Speed Optimizations: The larger size of a Bloom filter compared to the size of the cache line, causes cache misses. This issue along with the poor data locality of Bloom filters is addressed by Blocked Bloom filter (BBF) [27]. A BBF has b small sized standard Bloom filters, each of which has a size less than or equal to the cache line. An SBF block is chosen using a hash function and each item is mapped to that SBF using k hash values. This improves the speed, but at the cost of a higher false positive rate as a small single SBF can be filled quickly. This, in fact, results in a need to increase the size of the filter. The optimization in BBF is to improve the run-time performance on a hardware platform, but not a hardware-oriented design that may leverage the same performance when translated on to hardware. Another technique to enhance the speed is to reduce the hash computations. Through double-hashing Bloom filter, Kirsch et al. [17] have shown that only two independent hash functions are enough to generate all the required hash values in the form of $h_1(x) + i * h_2(x)$ without any increase in the asymptotic FPR, where $h_1(x)$ and $h_2(x)$ are hash values of the item x and i is an arbitrary value.

Some of the optimizations on Bloom filters focus on reducing the latency to a single memory access cycle in the likes of Bloom-1 [28] and Parallel Bloom filter (PBF) [32]. Bloom-1 uses a memory array of size m where each location contains a membership word of 32 or 64 bits and an item is mapped to any one of the membership word using k hash functions. Bloom-1 has a lower false positive rate than SBF because of a smaller of the membership word size and require more hardware resources. PBF on, the other hand, is faster and requires less hash bits compared to SBF. PBF splits the memory block of size m into k sub-blocks of size m/k called a Uni-SBF and each memory block is a single hash function. The FPR of a Uni-SBF is $1 - e^{-kn/m}$ and the FPR of the PBF is $(fpr(Uni\text{-}SBF))^k$ which is equal to the FPR of the SBF. A representation of PBF is shown in Fig. 4. PBF is able to achieve an update and query complexity of $O(1)$ compared to a complexity $O(k)$ of SBF.

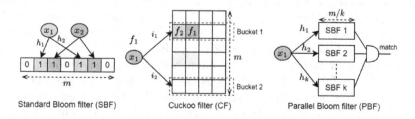

Standard Bloom filter (SBF)   Cuckoo filter (CF)   Parallel Bloom filter (PBF)

Fig. 4. Bloom and Cuckoo filters

2.3   Cuckoo Filter and Its Variants

A cuckoo hash table stores the keys in the hash-indexed buckets which contributes to a larger memory footprint when the key size is large. When it is required to perform processing at line-rate, constraining the lookup architectures within the on-chip memory is of utmost importance. Partial key Cuckoo hashing [21] helps to resolve this issue by storing only a fingerprint of the key. Cuckoo filter (CF) [10] is based on partial key cuckoo hashing which is very much similar to cuckoo hashing but instead of storing a full key, only a fingerprint/short digest of the key is stored. Figure 4 depicts a representation of the Cuckoo filter. It is composed of a memory block having m locations where each location is termed as a bucket which is indexed by hash value. Each bucket is having b entries and b is set to 4 which provides the best space-efficiency. Every item mapped to two buckets. The indices of the bucket B_i for each item x_i are i_1 and i_2, where $i_1 = hash(x_i)$ and $i_2 = i_1 \oplus hash(f)$, where f is the fingerprint of x_i and is generated using another hash function. During an insertion, if either bucket B_1 or B_2 has an empty slot, the item is inserted to that slot. If none of the slots are empty, a bucket and entry is chosen randomly and the existing item is swapped with the incoming item. This process of swapping the item is called kicking. The bucket index of the swapped item f_s is then computed using $i \oplus hash(f_s)$, where i is the existing location of f_s. f_s is then tried to add to the new slot and if that slot is not empty, this process of kicking continues until it finds a new slot or the maximum value of probing is reached. Cuckoo filter can deny an insertion if either the table is full or the maximum loop value of kicking is reached. In such cases resizing and rehashing is required which is not feasible when the processing is at line-rate.

Compared to Bloom filters, Cuckoo filter is faster, more space efficient, and supports deletions. Irrespective of all the advantages, there are some drawbacks which are very critical when implementing on hardware. Other than the complexity of implementation on hardware, the insertion length is indefinite because of kicking as the load factor of the filter increases. The number of kicks could reach the maximum value of the loop, which is set to an arbitrary value of 500 by Fan et al. [10]. Another disadvantage is the insertion limit where no more insertions are possible once the filter is full. Insertion of duplicate items can affect adversely on the false positive rate and will limit the number of unique items that can be entered into the filter. However, denying the insertion of duplicates is not feasible because two different items with the same fingerprint can be mapped to a single bucket due to collisions and denying the insertion would cause removal of the only existing fingerprint during deletion.

Many different variants of Cuckoo filters have been proposed to enhance the performance of Cuckoo filters on various aspects such as space efficiency, FPR, and speed. Nevertheless, there is always a trade-off between these aspects more often than not. Some of the important variants which are worth mentioning are included here.

Enhancing Speed: Morton filter [5] is a compressed version of Cuckoo filter (CF) in which the storage of data is more dense. Morton filter is able to achieve an improved memory access time by efficiently utilizing the cache which also helps to achieve a higher insertion, lookup and deletion throughput on ARM architecture compared to CF. However, reduced support to various fingerprint sizes limits the application range of Morton filter. Vertical CF [12] also reduces the insertion time of the CF by increasing the number of buckets for each item. Vacuum filter [35] is also more space efficient and faster than Bloom and Cuckoo filters while achieving the same false positive rate (FPR) as CF. Vacuum filters follow the same data structure as CF but with better data locality which is achieved by dividing the table into multiple chunks similar to Blocked BF and with two different insertion algorithms based on the number of entries to be stored. This division also helps to keep the table size not a power of two in contrast to Cuckoo filter. This is efficient when the number of elements to be stored is not a power of two. Nevertheless, keeping the size of the filter non-powers of two makes things more difficult on hardware.

Enhancing FPR: Adaptive CF [23] improves the FPR of CF by removing the false positives that already occurred. This halts the repeating occurrence of the same false positives. Length-aware CF [20] is also able to reduce the FPR but with added storage requirements. D-ary CF [36] improves the space utilization with a sacrifice on the insertion, deletion, and query performances. D-ary CF uses d hash functions and can achieve a better FPR for the same amount of memory compared to CF, but a decline in speed makes it unfavourable to be a better replacement of CF.

Dynamicity: Similar to BF, various approaches were proposed to enable dynamic resizing in CF. Dynamic CF (DCF) [7] appends multiple homogeneous CFs together similar to dynamic Bloom filters when it is required to extend the size of the filter. Moreover, it can merge the under-utilized CFs to further optimize the space utilization. While DCF can support dynamic resizing, the lookup performance is worse compared to CF as it is required to access multiple linked CFs. Consistent CF (CCF) [22] is a further improved variant of dynamic CF, where each CCF is composed by attaching multiple index-independent Cuckoo filter (I2CF), where each I2CF can have k buckets and the value of k is a variable depending on the cardinality. The sparse I2CF can also be compressed. Nevertheless, dynamic resizing is applicable only for multi-sets and makes the implementation task more cumbersome on hardware.

Other Filters Which are More Space Efficient than Cuckoo Filters: Xor filter [14] and Binary fuse filter [15] offer smaller memory footprint than Cuckoo filters. The update time of Xor filters and Binary fuse filters is more than Bloom and cuckoo filter, but has a faster query time. However, these filters are immutable, which means that dynamic or in-line updates are not possible, which makes it ill-suitable for streaming applications. In order to update a new set of keys, the filter has to be rebuilt and the full set of keys is required at the time of construction.

To conclude this brief description of these data structures, a summary of the time complexities and FPR of important data structures are shown in Table 2.

We can infer from the table that the best-case update/query complexity of structures derived from hash table and cuckoo filter are $O(1)$, and the worst-case update/query could increase as the table is filling up. In contrast, Bloom filter based data structures have a constant update/query complexities irrespective of the load.

3   Hardware Architectures

3.1   Choosing a Suitable Architecture

The requirements of lookup and key-value stores are not the same for every application. This has to be taken into consideration while choosing the best data structures. Our main focus is on network applications where the cardinality is predictable and the size of the key/flow ID is constant throughout. The most suitable data structures from the existing ones are filtered, based on the above said criteria for hardware evaluation.

Table 2. FPR and time complexities of data structures

Datastructure	False positive rate	Time complexity (Update)		Time complexity (Query)	
		Best case	Worst case	Best case	Worst case
Hash table	NA	$O(1)$	$O(n)$	$O(1)$	$O(n)$
Cuckoo Hashing	NA	$O(1)$	$O(n)$	$O(1)$	$O(1)$
Peacock hashing	NA	$O(1)$	$O(log\ log\ m)$	$O(1)$	$O(log\ log\ m)$
2-choice hashing	NA	$O(1)$	$O(log\ log\ n)$	$O(1)$	$O(log\ log\ n)$
Quotient Filter	$1/2^{r}*$	$O(1)$	$O(log\ m)$	$O(1)$	$O(log\ m)$
Bloom Filter	$(1-e^{-k.n/m})^k$	$O(k)$	$O(k)$	$O(k)$	$O(k)$
Counting Bloom Filter	$(1-e^{-k.n/m})^k$	$O(k)$	$O(k)$	$O(k)$	$O(k)$
Dynamic Bloom Filter	$1-(1-e^{-k(n-c\lfloor n\rfloor/c)/m})^k$	$O(k)$	$O(k)$	$O(k.s)$	$O(k.s)$
Deletable Bloom Filter	$(1-(1-(1/(m-r)))^{k*n})^k$	$O(k)$	$O(k)$	$O(k)$	$O(k)$
Parallel Bloom Filter	$(1-e^{-k.n/m})^k$	$O(1)$	$O(1)$	$O(1)$	$O(1)$
Bloom-1 Filter	Refer [31]	$O(1)$	$O(1)$	$O(1)$	$O(1)$
Retouched Bloom filter	$(1-e^{-k.n/m})^k*(1-z/p_1.m)^k$	$O(k)$	$O(k)$	$O(k)$	$O(k)$
Double-hashing BF	$(1-e^{-k.n/m})^k$	$O(k)$	$O(k)$	$O(k)$	$O(k)$
Cuckoo Filter	$2^{-(C*\alpha-2)}$	$O(1)$	$O(n)$	$O(1)$	$O(1)$
Morton filter	$1-(1-1/2^f)^{\alpha_L.B.S}$	$O(1)$	$O(n)$	$O(1)$	$O(1)$
Vacuum filter	$2b\alpha/2^f$	$O(1)$	NA	$O(1)$	$O(1)$
D-ary CF	$k/2^f$	$O(1)$	$O(n)$	$O(1)$	$O(1)$
Dynamic Cuckoo filter	$2.b.s/2^f$	$O(1)$	$O(n)$	$O(1)$	$O(2.b.s)$
Consistent CF	$s.k.b/2^f$	$O(1)$	$O(N.log\ m)$	$O(1)$	$O(k.b.s.log\ m)$

m = No. of buckets; n = No. of items; f = Fingerprint size; k = No. of hash functions; b = No. of entries in a bucket; s = No. of filters
c = capacity of a single BF; r = No. of regions in the BF; $p_1 = 1 - e^{-kn/m}$; z = No. of bits reset in BF; α_L = logical load factor
α = load factor; C = Bits per item; B = buckets accessed per negative lookup; S = logical slots per bucket; N = max probes allowed;

Lookups: For lookups, where the requirement is only the presence of an item, Hash tables and hash table variants are probably a luxury in terms of memory requirement and implementation complexity. Hash tables are required to store the key which consumes a large amount of memory when the cardinality is large. Moreover, the requirement of collision resistant mechanisms makes it slower where fast lookup is a necessity when considering processing at line-rate. With inherent collision resistant mechanisms, Bloom filters and Cuckoo filters along with their numerous variants offers the best possible accuracy within the lowest memory requirement.

Key-Value Store: For applications where getting the presence of an element is not enough and either the key or value has to be stored and/or returned, Bloom and Cuckoo filters are limited. Bloom filters do not store keys or values and recovering the key from a Bloom filter is impossible. Cuckoo filters store a fingerprint, but the possibility of recovering the key from the fingerprint is also zero. The case is similar to all the data structures which store only a hashed digest. This makes hash tables and its variants more suitable for probabilistic key-value stores. Nevertheless, hash tables must be associated with collision resistant mechanisms. Looking from a hardware perspective, hardware suitability of mechanisms such as chaining and linear probing is low. Probing in the form of Peacock hashing and Cuckoo hashing are more hardware friendly as the size of the table is fixed and are suitable for static data sets.

3.2   Implementation Details

Optimized Hashing. Hashing is one of the most important building block of AMQ data structures as the overall throughput of the system can be affected by the speed of the hash computation. Non-cryptographic hashes with satisfactory avalanche properties are preferred as it is faster and has a low logical depth compared to cryptograhic hashes. Work by Sateesan et al. [31] proposed a fast non-cryptographic hash function Xoodoo-NC, which is derived from the Xoodoo permutation. In this work, Xoodoo-NC is used to generate the required hash bits and these hash bits are then split into required hash values. Xoodoo-NC can generate outputs as multiples of 96-bits. Recent works [28,32] have shown that this method of splitting the hash output to generate Bloom filter hash values has negligible effect on the false positive rate (FPR) of the filter and can achieve multi-fold improvement in latency.

Even though the key size is fixed to 96-bit in our evaluations, a varying key-size will only have a negligible effect on the AMQ algorithms. The FPR is not affected by the size of the input as observed from Table 2 as long as the hash function satisfies the required avalanche properties.

Hash Table. The representation of the hash table (HT) is shown in Fig. 3(a). The implementation of hash table is very straightforward and is implemented using block RAMS (BRAM) as a memory block having depth m and width equal to the size of the key and value. In a naive, straightforward implementation of the hash table, collisions are not addressed, and is implemented as a basic unit for comparisons.

Cuckoo Hash Table. A representation of the Cuckoo hash table (CHT) is shown in Fig. 3(c). Unlike in the figure, the tables T_i and T_2 are implemented as separate BRAM blocks where each memory block is having one entry of each bucket. Such an implementation halves the word-length of one bucket which is equal to $2 * (size\ of\ the\ key + size\ of\ the\ value)$. Since both the memories can be accessed in parallel, the latency to access a bucket is still a single clock cycle.

Peacock Hash Table. To implement Peacock hash table (PHT), the main table and all the backup tables as shown in Fig. 3 are implemented as separate BRAM blocks. The size of the main table is m and scaling factor $r = 2$, which the is most appropriate value of r for hardware. Since our goal is to analyze the performance of only the hash table, no fast lookup mechanisms are employed as presented by Kumar et al. [19]. PHT has $(1 + log_{1/r} m)$ tables and the last table has only one location. The last table is eliminated in the implementation as it is not possible to generate a BRAM block with only 1 location. All memories are accessed in parallel to keep the update/query latency to a bare minimum unlike the original algorithm in which the ith table is accessed only when the results are not found with the $(i-1)^{th}$ table.

Bloom Filter and Parallel Bloom Filter. Standard Bloom filter (SBF) is straightforward and implementation is hassle-free. The data structure as depicted in Fig. 4, is implemented with a BRAM block of depth m and width 1-bit. The number of hash functions k is 8 and these hashes are generated using Xoodoo-NC. SBF with 8 hash functions requires a total of 136 hash bits, and Xoodoo-NC generates an 192-bit output and this output is split into 8 hash values of sizes $log_2 m$ bits each. For parallel Bloom filter (PBF), all the k sub-blocks of size m/k are implemented separately using BRAM. Each sub-block is accessed in parallel, which keeps the memory access latency to a single cycle. Xoodoo-NC is used to generate k hash values for PBF in a similar way as it is for SBF.

Cuckoo Filter. In contrast to Bloom filter, implementing cuckoo filter on hardware requires a bit more effort and engineering. The data structure of CF is shown in Fig. 4. The whole table of CF is implemented as a single BRAM block. The depth of the memory is m and the width of the memory is $b * f$, where f is the size of the fingerprint and b is the number of buckets. The memory is implemented as true dual port RAM with dedicated ports for reading and writing. It requires two clock cycles to read the contents in both the buckets. CF is optimized for the number of memory accesses in such a way that one bucket is read at first in parallel with the computation of the address of the second bucket and the second bucket is read only if no empty slots are found in the first bucket during an update. Similar search is applied during query also, which makes the best case memory accesses to a single cycle both during update and query.

The hardware architecture diagrams of all the implemented data structures except the Bloom filter architectures are presented in Appendix A. The architectures presented in [32] are followed for Bloom filter implementations.

4 Evaluation

The evaluation is performed separately for lookup and key-value store data structures. The analysis is performed in terms of FPR or accuracy, latency, hardware resource usage, speed, insertion throughput, and implementation complexity. Some additional analysis on throughput, memory access cycles and insertion failures are presented in Appendix B.

4.1 Evaluation of Lookup Architectures

For the evaluation, the architectures chosen are Cuckoo filter (CF), standard Bloom filter (SBF), and Parallel Bloom filter (PBF). A total of 16 KB memory is allocated to all the data structures and the size of the tables of each structure is determined based on the allocated memory. The number of bits per item is fixed to 12, the number of items n to be inserted equals 10922. This value of n makes the load factor α of CF to be 0.67 and $m = 4096$. The CF consists of 2 buckets and each bucket is having $b = 4$ entries and the fingerprint size is set to 8-bits. The maximum kick value is set as 500, which is the optimal value employed in the original article [10]. In the evaluation, memory access cycles refers to the sum of memory read and write cycles. The number of hash functions for Bloom filters are $k = 8$ which makes $m = 131{,}072$ for SBF and PBF. Size of a single block of PBF is $m/k = 16384$. The hardware evaluation is performed using synthetic datasets on a Virtex UltraScale+ (xcvu9p-flga2104-2L-e) platform.

False Positive Rate and Space-Occupancy. For a fixed bits/item, the FPR ϵ of CF is better than Bloom filters as shown in Table 3, which means better space-occupancy. CF can have $2*b$ duplicate entries, where b is the number of entries in a bucket. In order to store similar number of duplicates, a CBF would require a 3-bit counter in each location which results in 3 times more memory requirement compared to SBF. However, allowing duplicates will deplete the space and cause higher false positives for CF, which does not happen with SBF.

Latency. The query time complexity of CF is $O(1)$ and of SBF and CBF is $O(k)$. However, PBF outperforms CF in all other aspects, except in terms of number of hash bits and FPR for a fixed number of bits per item. Both the update and query time complexity of PBF is $O(1)$, thanks to the parallel accessing of memory blocks. Memory access cycles to insert an element is constant for Bloom filters irrespective of the load factor. CF consumes more memory access cycles for insertion due to probing/kicking when the filter starts filling up. The analysis given on Table 3 shows that the percentage of memory access cycles due to probing is only around 5.7% more than the actual requirement if the load factor is 75%. However, probing memory accesses increases to 14.2% when load factor is 85% and then a sudden spike to 48.2% when the load factor is 95.5%. The total number of memory access cycles required for PBF is less than that of CF for a load factor up to 85%, and is only less than half than that of CF when the load factor is 95.5%.

Table 3. FPR and latency vs various load factors for lookup data structures

Load factor	False positve rate		Total memory access cycles			Total probe cycles (CF)	% of cycles for probing (CF)
	CF	SBF, PBF	SBF	PBF	CF		
35%	9.8×10^{-7}	5.5×10^{-5}	91,200	11,400	11,480	6	0.05%
50%	1.0×10^{-4}	6.0×10^{-4}	131,200	16,400	16,801	72	0.43%
65%	1.1×10^{-3}	2.7×10^{-3}	170,400	21,300	22,709	500	2.20%
75%	3.4×10^{-3}	6.0×10^{-3}	196,560	24,570	27,699	1,568	5.66%
85%	7.8×10^{-3}	1.1×10^{-2}	222,800	27,850	35,361	5,036	14.24%
95.5%	1.6×10^{-2}	2.0×10^{-2}	250,320	31,290	67,658	32,584	48.16%

Average of 1000 runs; Total memory = 16KB, # of items = 16384 (at $\alpha = 1.0$)
CF-Cuckoo filter, SBF-Standard Bloom filter, PBF-Parallel Bloom filter

Performance on Hardware. The performance results on FPGA are shown in Table 4. The hardware resource requirements and maximum operating frequency of SBF and PBF are better than CF while maintaining the same number of bits per item, but with a lower FPR and more hash bits. CF requires more than 2 times the number of LUTs compared to the Bloom filter counterparts. CF requires 2 cycles for hashing as the second hash computation is dependant on the first. Nevertheless, CF can still achieve a best case query latency of 2 cycles if the memory read of one bucket can be performed in parallel while computing the second hash index. Since the number of probes during insertion can vary up to 500 as α increases, pipelining becomes difficult. PBF has a constant query latency of only 2 cycles (1 cycle for hashing, 1 cycle for memory read) irrespective of the load. Even though SBF is the simplest to implement on hardware, it requires 9 cycles for querying. In terms of throughput, PBF has an edge over CF and delivers the best insertion throughput while BF and CBF has a very low throughput due to its low latency.

Table 4. Performance of Lookup architectures on FPGA

	Cuckoo filter (CF)	Bloom filter (SBF)	Counting Bloomfilter (CBF)	Parallel Bloom filter (PBF)
Load Factor (α)	0.67	–	–	–
FPR (ϵ)	**0.0015**	0.0031	0.3124	0.0031
# of hash bits	**24**	136	136	112
Best case query Latency	**2 cycles**	9 cycles	9 cycles	**2 cycles**
LUT	930	402	412	**336**
FF	267	259	288	259
BRAM	4	4	4.5	4
Max. frequency	435 MHz	476 MHz	435 MHz	**488 MHz**
Insertions/second (Million)	138	28	26	**163**
Implementation complexity	++++	+	++	++

Memory = 16KB, # of items = 10922 (at $\alpha = 0.67$), bits per item = 12

Discussion. Even though CF has some clear advantages over SBF and most of the other variants of Bloom filter (BF), the achievable parallelism in BF helps to generate better results on hardware. PBF helps to achieve an update and query memory access latency of a single clock cycle. While BF has no insertion limit, CF can deny an entry if the number of kicks exceeds the maximum kick value. Incrementing the size of the filter or re-hashing all the elements (when it comes to cuckoo hashing) dynamically is a cumbersome task in hardware, especially for online processing. Duplicate entries have no effect on BF, but drastically worsens the load factor, space occupancy, and FPR of CF. The maximum number of duplicates that CF can accommodate is $2*b$, where b is the number of entries in a bucket. Trying to insert duplicates after $2*b$ times would result in a infinite kicking loop until the max kick length is reached. In network security applications, an attacker can exploit this vulnerability of CF. Deletion support is one of the prominent feature of CF which BF cannot provide. CBF can provide deletion support, but with much higher memory usage. In conlusion, if the choice is for low-latency, lightweight lookup architecture on hardware with the support for pipelining, PBF is the best choice over CF. For a better bits per item with deletion support, where pipelining is not a primary requirement and given that the insertion of duplicates is minimal, CF is the preferred option.

4.2   Evaluation of Key-Value Stores

For the evaluation, Conventional hash table (HT), Cuckoo hash table (CHT), and Peacock hash table (PHT) are compared as discussed in Sect. 3.1. The memory allotted are fixed to 224KB for each data structure. CHT has two tables and each table has a size $m = 8192$ buckets and each bucket has 1 entry each per table. The memory accesses are optimized for CHT similar to the optimizations in CF as discussed in Sect. 4.1. The maximum kick value is set to 500. The size m of the main table in PHT is set as 8192 and the scaling factor $r = 0.5$. The total number of tables t in PHT is 13 with each ith backup table having a size of $m/(\frac{1}{r})^i$ where $1 \leq i \leq t - 1$. HT has a size m of 16384 buckets. The key size is 96-bits and value size is 16-bits. The load factors of CHT is $n/2m$, PHT is $m(1 - r^t)/(1 - r)$, and HT is n/m. In the evaluation, accuracy refers to the ratio of number of correctly queried items from the table and the total number of items inserted to the table.

Loading the Table and Accuracy The accuracy and probing cycles in hash tables increase with increasing load factor α as shown in Table 5. In HT, the probability of failure in inserting an item is high as no collision resistant mechanisms are employed. PHT has an accuracy close to 100% when $\alpha = 0.6$ and the accuracy and number of failed insertions worsens as $\alpha > 0.6$. For CHT, the accuracy is close to 100% even at $\alpha = 0.88$. The accuracy of CHT can be improved by increasing the number of entries in each bucket. Then, the table depth must be reduced accordingly to keep the memory requirement constant.

Table 5. FPR and latency vs various load factors for key-value stores

Load factor	Accuracy			Total memory access cycles			% of cycles for probing	
	HT(%)	PHT(%)	CHT(%)	HT	PHT	CHT	PHT	CHT
35%	84.5	100.0	100.0	11,468	13,635	12,052	18.9	1.9
50%	78.6	100.0	100.0	16,384	21,246	18,751	29.7	7.5
65%	73.6	99.5	100.0	21,300	30,959	29,720	45.3	21.8
75%	70.3	97.4	100.0	24,576	39,928	45,909	62.5	40.3
85%	67.3	93.7	100.0	27,852	51,518	106,891	84.9	70.2
90%	65.9	91.3	99.3	29,492	58,719	328,079	99.1	89.6
95%	64.5	88.9	96.4	31,130	66,185	847,033	112.6	95.8

Average of 1000 runs; Total memory = 16KB, # of items = 16384 (at $\alpha = 1.0$)
HT-Hash table, PHT-Peacock hash table, CHT-Cuckoo hash table

Latency CHT has a worst case query complexity of $O(1)$, whereas the query complexities of other hash tables vary with the chain/probe lengths. CHT has an average update time complexity of $O(1)$, but the probing length increases as α increases. When $\alpha > 0.5$, the number of probes increases drastically for CHT and can go up to a maximum probe length of 500 as set. PHT is very much like a chained hash table, but since the table size is fixed in PHT, the maximum probe length is limited to the total number of tables in PHT. The number of memory access cycles also increases for CHT due to probing as α increases. For example, the increase is $\approx 4417\%$ when the load factor increases from 0.5 to 0.95. The increase in memory access cycles are considerably lower for PHT, which is an increase of $\approx 211\%$ when the load factor increases from 0.5 to 0.95.

Performance on Hardware. The performance results on FPGA are given in Table 6. All the tables in PHT and CHT can be accessed in parallel, which makes

Table 6. Performance of hash table architectures on FPGA

	HT	CHT	PHT
Accuracy at $\alpha = 0.95$	64.5%	96.4%	88.9%
# of hash bits	14	26	91
Best case Query Latency	2 cycle	2 cycle	2 cycle
LUT	606	1745	1399
FF	268	971	267
BRAM	50	50	79
Max. frequency	357 MHz	322 MHz	232 MHz
Insertions/second (Million)($\alpha = 0.75$)	119	68	42
Implementation complexity	+	++++	++

Memory = 224KB, # of items = 15565 (at $\alpha = 0.95$), bits per item = 118
HT-Hash table, PHT-Peacock hash table, CHT-Cuckoo hash table

the query latency of all three architectures equal to 2 clock cycles which include hashing and memory access cycles. It is evident from the table that there is always a trade-off among space occupancy, speed, and accuracy. Conventional hash table is the least accurate, but it is faster and consumes the least amount of resources. The memory footprint is higher for PHT as the memory is split into many smaller blocks which takes a lot more memory than a large single block. This is because of the fact that the targeted FPGA can construct the memory only with either 18Kb/36Kb block RAM (BRAM) modules. Moreover, these blocks, spread around the main logic, cause the routing delay to increase which eventually causes the maximum operating frequency to dip. One remedy is to keep a limited number of tables, but this would cause the accuracy to decline because of the increased number of insertion fails as the probing during collision is limited by the number of blocks. For example, keeping the total number of tables to 4 and each table having equal sizes of 4096 buckets would cause the accuracy to drop to 46% when the load factor is 1.0 compared to 86% of the conventional PHT. In a way, CHT employs the same principle as PHT which probes for an empty slot during a collision, but with a better space occupancy. However, the complexity of the architecture is high for CHT when implementing on hardware. This results in a higher resource consumption in terms of LUTs. Nevertheless, CHT leverages significantly better operating frequency than PHT. In terms of throughput, CHT has better insertion throughput until $\alpha = 0.75$, but the throughput drops drastically for CHT and is only 6 M items/s when $\alpha = 0.95$ whereas PHT still maintains a throughput equal to 30 M items/s at $\alpha = 0.95$.

Partial Key Cuckoo Hashing for Better Performance. Partial key cuckoo hashing is one way to compromise the high resource and memory requirement of CHT and improve the operating frequency if storing/retrieving the key is not required. This can be implemented by storing the value along with the fingerprints in a CF. However, it is required to have an optimal fingerprint size to mitigate the adverse effect on FPR to some extent. The empirical results show that storing values in a CF, using an 8-bit fingerprint, can leverage the similar accuracy as CHT while CF only uses $\approx 21\%$ of the memory that is required by CHT. Moreover, CF can run at a significantly higher operating frequency and insertion throughput compared to CHT. Table 7 shows the results of employing CF as a partial key-value store.

Table 7. Results of partial key cuckoo hashing as partial key-value store

Accuracy ($\alpha = 0.95$)	Total cycles	% of extra cycles for probing	LUT	BRAM	Max frequency	Insertions/second (Million)($\alpha = 0.75$)
100%	62,740	44.47%	1442	11	417 MHz	128

Memory = 48KB, # of items = 15565 (at $\alpha = 1.0$), bits per item = 25, Throughput in Million item/s

Discussion. When choosing the best possible key-value store scheme for hardware, PHT might be having a slight edge over CHT in terms of better probing length at higher load factors and low cardinality. Even though the accuracy is comparatively higher for CHT as observed in Table 5, it comes at a high cost of an extremely large amount of probing cycles when $\alpha > 0.5$. However, as the cardinality increases, implementing peacock hashing becomes hefty as it has to manage a large number of tables, which results in an increased time complexity and much reduced operating frequency. Irrespective of the increased cardinality, query time complexity is always constant with CHT and the operating frequency is also much higher. Hence it can be concluded that PHT is preferable only for a lower cardinality if the criterion is minimal probing cycles whereas CHT can be preferred for any other criteria assuming that the load factor of CHT is kept small. Moreover, if storing/retrieving keys are not required, there is no better alternative than partial key cuckoo hashing to store values.

5   Conclusion

In this paper, various AMQ schemes as well as hash-based probabilistic schemes are analyzed and evaluated based on their hardware-friendliness for network security applications on high-speed networks. A comparison of these schemes is performed in terms of memory efficiency, accuracy, latency, implementation complexity, and throughput. The evaluation results help to identify a suitable data structure for network security applications. Moreover, this analysis also sheds light on the shortcomings of the existing membership query data structures when implemented in hardware, which was unexplored earlier.

Acknowledgement. This work is supported by the ESCALATE project, funded by FWO (G0E0719N) and SNSF (200021L_182005), and by Cybersecurity Research Flanders (VR20192203).

Appendices

A   Hardware Architectures

A.1   Cuckoo Hash Table and Cuckoo Filter

The hardware architecture of Cuckoo filter implementation is shown in Fig. 5. Two hash functions, two copies of Xoodoo-NC, are used for generating the hash values. Due to the low logical depth of Xoodoo-NC, there is negligible effect on the overall computation and latency overhead. Cuckoo filter has two buckets with each bucket having four entries. The first hash function is used to generate the address of the first bucket as well as the fingerprint by hashing the incoming key. The hash output is split to generate the required memory addresses and fingerprint. The second hash function is used to generate the address of the second bucket by hashing the fingerprint. The second hash function is re-used for generating the address of the bucket from the fingerprint during kick operations. A multiplexer determines whether the input to the second hash function is a kicked fingerprint or not. Even though a single hash function is enough to perform all the hashing operations, addition of a second hash function makes pipelining easier and helps to achieve a best case memory access latency of a single clock cycle. The fingerprint is padded with zeroes at the MSB to make a 96-bit input to the hash function. An Finite State Machine (FSM) is employed as the control logic, which controls all the memory read/write operations and the kick operations. The kick logic co-ordinates all the kick operations during the occurrence of a collision. A single dual port BRAM is used as the table and each location in the memory (a bucket) holds four entries.

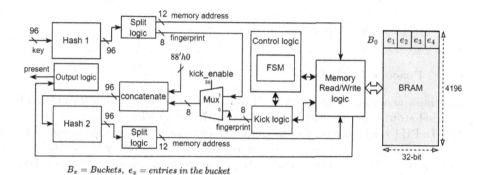

$B_x = Buckets,\ e_x = entries\ in\ the\ bucket$

Fig. 5. Hardware architecture of Cuckoo filter

The hardware architecture of Cuckoo hash table (CHT) is very much similar to Cuckoo filter and is shown in Fig. 6. Cuckoo filter employs partial-key cuckoo hashing where a fingerprint of the key is used to generate the second memory address as discussed in Sect. 2.3, whereas CHT hashes the key to generate both addresses. CHT has two buckets and each bucket contains two entries. Since both hash values can be computed in parallel, two copies of Xoodoo-NC and two separate memory blocks are used to access both the buckets in parallel which limits the read/write latency to a single clock cycle. Each memory block has one entry in each bucket, which also helps to limit the word-length of the memory. The second hash function is re-used to generate the hash values during kick operations and a multiplexer determines whether the input to the second hash function is a kicked key or not. All other operations and logic are similar to the Cuckoo filter architecture.

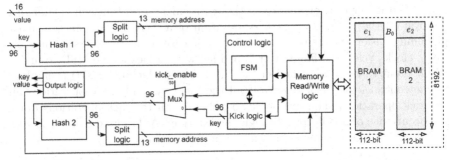

B_x = Buckets, e_x = entries in the bucket

Fig. 6. Hardware architecture of Cuckoo hash table

A.2   Peacock Hash Table

The implementation of Peacock hash table (PHT) is very straightforward and the the hardware architecture is shown in Fig. 7. For an allocated memory size of 224KB, PHT employs a total of thirteen memory blocks as described in Sect. 4.2. In order of minimize the computational as well as latency overhead, a single hash function Xoodoo-NC is used to generate all the required memory addresses. The key is hashed to generate all the required hash bits and a split logic splits the hash output bits to required memory addresses. The probe logic co-ordinates the probing operations during the occurrence of a collision.

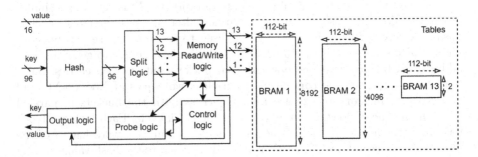

Fig. 7. Hardware architecture of Peacock hash table

B   Additional Analysis

B.1   Memory Access Cycles

The total memory access cycles during the insertion of elements for various data structures is depicted in Fig. 8 and 9. Load factor (α) plays an important role when it comes to number of the memory access cycles of hashing-based data structures such as CHT, PHT, and CF. With increased load factor, the memory access cycles increases for CHT, PHT, and CF because of the kick/probe operations due to collisions. As observed from Fig. 8, there is an exponential increase in the memory access cycles for CHT when $\alpha > 0.75$. Nevertheless, the increase is minimal for PHT because the maximum number of probes is limited by the number of tables. There is a gradual increase in memory access cycles for CF as shown in Fig. 9, but significantly lesser because of the more number of entries per bucket compared to CHT. For Bloom filters, the increase in memory access cycles are constant because of the fact that the number of cycles per insertion is constant throughout irrespective of the load factor.

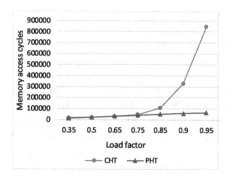

Fig. 8. Memory access cycles for hash tables

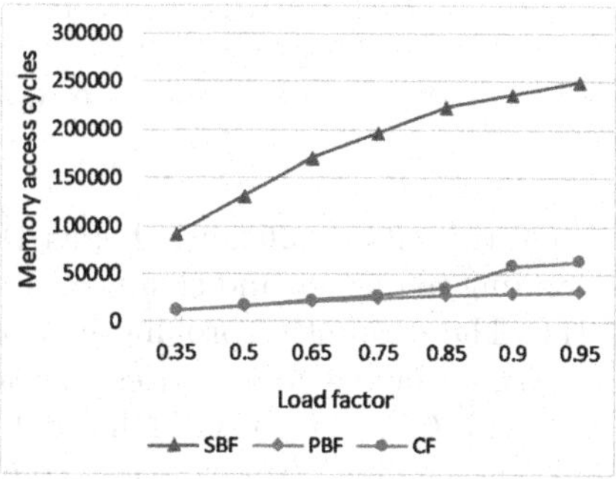

Fig. 9. Memory access cycles of Cuckoo and Bloom filters

B.2   Insertion Throughput

The insertion throughput defines the maximum number of insertions possible per second. The insertion throughput is computed as $\frac{1}{(total\ latency/n))}$, where n is the number of elements inserted and the latency is measured in nanoseconds. The throughput is constant for Bloom filters since the the number of cycles for each insertion is constant. However, the throughput for hashing-based data structures varies with varying load factor because of the extra hash computation and memory access cycles required due to kick/probe operations during a collision. The insertion throughput in terms of million insertions per second of Cuckoo filter (CF), Cuckoo hash table (CHT), and Peacock hash table (PHT) are depicted in Fig. 10.

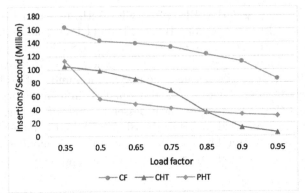

CHT-Cuckoo hash table, PHT-Peacock hash table, CF-Cuckoo filter

Fig. 10. Insertion throughput

CF exhibits significantly higher throughput than CHT, thanks to the higher operating frequency and significantly lesser number of probe cycles compared to CHT. The amount of probing increases drastically for CHT as the load factor increases. Having four entries in each bucket helps to reduce the number of probes for CF, whereas CHT has only two entries in each bucket and this results in a much higher probing cycles compared to CF. Adding 4 entries in a bucket can help to minimize the probing cycles for CHT, but a large memory footprint would still limit the operating frequency. The limited memory footprint of CF contributes to minimal routing delay and hence a higher operating frequency. The throughput of PHT is minimum, even for small load factors, as a result of the lower operating frequency. Yet, the throughput of PHT is almost constant throughout even for higher load factors as the total amount of probing per insertion is limited by the number of tables.

B.3   Insertion Failures

Hash table collisions cause insertion failures while adding elements to the table. Figure 11 shows the insertion failures in hashing-based data structures. It can be seen that insertion failures are very much dependent on the load factor. There are no collision resistant mechanisms such as chaining/probing are employed for the hash table (HT) and it is very much evident from the figure that the collisions are maximum for HT even for lower load factors. When the load factor is 1, the insertion failures for HT is almost 37%. For PHT, the insertion failures start increasing gradually when the load factor is greater than 0.62. For Cuckoo hashing, insertion failures start increasing only after a load factor of 0.87 and the overall failures in CHT is considerably lower than PHT. When the load factor is 1, the insertion failure is around 7% for CHT, whereas it is close to 14% for PHT.

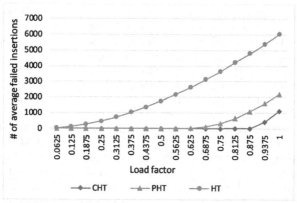

CHT-Cuckoo hash table, PHT-Peacock hash table, HT-Hash table

Fig. 11. Insertion failures in hash tables

References

1. How much data is created every day in 2022? https://earthweb.com/how-much-data-is-created-every-day/. Accessed 25 Jul 2022
2. Almeida, P.S., Baquero, C., Preguiça, N., Hutchison, D.: Scalable bloom filters. Inf. Process. Lett. **101**(6), 255–261 (2007)
3. Bender, M.A., et al.: Don't thrash: how to cache your hash on flash. In: 3rd Workshop on Hot Topics in Storage and File Systems (HotStorage 11) (2011)
4. Bloom, B.H.: Space/time trade-offs in hash coding with allowable errors. Commun. ACM **13**(7), 422–426 (1970)
5. Breslow, A.D., Jayasena, N.S.: Morton filters: faster, space-efficient cuckoo filters via biasing, compression, and decoupled logical sparsity. Proc. VLDB Endowment **11**(9), 1041–1055 (2018)
6. Celis, P., Larson, P.A., Munro, J.I.: Robin hood hashing. In: 26th Annual Symposium on Foundations of Computer Science (SFCS 1985), pp. 281–288. IEEE (1985)
7. Chen, H., Liao, L., Jin, H., Wu, J.: The dynamic cuckoo filter. In: 2017 IEEE 25th International Conference on Network Protocols (ICNP), pp. 1–10. IEEE (2017)
8. Cohen, S., Matias, Y.: Spectral bloom filters. In: Proceedings of the 2003 ACM SIGMOD international conference on Management of data. pp. 241–252 (2003)
9. Donnet, B., Baynat, B., Friedman, T.: Retouched bloom filters: allowing networked applications to trade off selected false positives against false negatives. In: Proceedings of the 2006 ACM CoNEXT Conference, pp. 1–12 (2006)
10. Fan, B., Andersen, D.G., Kaminsky, M., Mitzenmacher, M.D.: Cuckoo filter: practically better than bloom. In: Proceedings of the 10th ACM International on Conference on Emerging Networking Experiments and Technologies, pp. 75–88 (2014)
11. Fan, L., Cao, P., Almeida, J., Broder, A.Z.: Summary cache: a scalable wide-area web cache sharing protocol. IEEE/ACM Trans. Networking **8**(3), 281–293 (2000)
12. Fu, P., Luo, L., Li, S., Guo, D., Cheng, G., Zhou, Y.: The vertical cuckoo filters: a family of insertion-friendly sketches for online applications. In: 2021 IEEE 41st International Conference on Distributed Computing Systems (ICDCS) (2021)

13. Geravand, S., Ahmadi, M.: Bloom filter applications in network security: a state-of-the-art survey. Comput. Netw. **57**(18), 4047–4064 (2013)
14. Graf, T.M., Lemire, D.: Xor filters: faster and smaller than bloom and cuckoo filters. J. Exp. Algorithmics (JEA) **25**, 1–16 (2020)
15. Graf, T.M., Lemire, D.: Binary fuse filters: fast and smaller than XOR filters. J. Exp. Algorithmics (JEA) **27**(1), 1–15 (2022)
16. Guo, D., Wu, J., Chen, H., Yuan, Y., Luo, X.: The dynamic bloom filters. IEEE Trans. Knowl. Data Eng. **22**(1), 120–133 (2009)
17. Kirsch, A., Mitzenmacher, M.: Less hashing, same performance: building a better bloom filter. In: Azar, Y., Erlebach, T. (eds.) ESA 2006. LNCS, vol. 4168, pp. 456–467. Springer, Heidelberg (2006). https://doi.org/10.1007/11841036_42
18. Kumar, A., Xu, J., Wang, J.: Space-code bloom filter for efficient per-flow traffic measurement. IEEE J. Sel. Areas Commun. **24**(12), 2327–2339 (2006)
19. Kumar, S., Turner, J., Crowley, P.: Peacock hashing: deterministic and updatable hashing for high performance networking. In: IEEE INFOCOM 2008-The 27th Conference on Computer Communications, pp. 101–105. IEEE (2008)
20. Kwon, M., Reviriego, P., Pontarelli, S.: A length-aware cuckoo filter for faster IP lookup. In: 2016 IEEE Conference on Computer Communications Workshops (2016)
21. Lim, H., Fan, B., Andersen, D.G., Kaminsky, M.: Silt: A memory-efficient, high-performance key-value store. In: Proceedings of the Twenty-Third ACM Symposium on Operating Systems Principles. pp. 1–13 (2011)
22. Luo, L., Guo, D., Rottenstreich, O., Ma, R.T., Luo, X., Ren, B.: The consistent cuckoo filter. In: IEEE INFOCOM 2019, pp. 712–720. IEEE (2019)
23. Mitzenmacher, M., Pontarelli, S., Reviriego, P.: Adaptive cuckoo filters (2020)
24. Mitzenmacher, M.D., Vocking, B.: The asymptotics of selecting the shortest of two, improved (1999)
25. Pagh, R., Rodler, F.F.: Cuckoo hashing. J. Algorithms **51**(2), 122–144 (2004)
26. Pandey, P., Bender, M.A., Johnson, R., Patro, R.: A general-purpose counting filter: Making every bit count. In: Proceedings of the 2017 ACM International Conference on Management of Data, pp. 775–787 (2017)
27. Putze, F., Sanders, P., Singler, J.: Cache-, hash-and space-efficient bloom filters. In: International Workshop on Experimental and Efficient Algorithms (2007)
28. Qiao, Y., Li, T., Chen, S.: Fast bloom filters and their generalization. IEEE Trans. Parallel Distrib. Syst. **25**(1), 93–103 (2013)
29. Richa, A.W., Mitzenmacher, M., Sitaraman, R.: The power of two random choices: a survey of techniques and results. Comb. Optim. **9**, 255–304 (2001)
30. Rothenberg, C.E., Macapuna, C.A., Verdi, F.L., Magalhaes, M.F.: The deletable bloom filter: a new member of the bloom family. IEEE Commun. Lett. **14**(6), 557–559 (2010)
31. Sateesan, A., Vliegen, J., Daemen, J., Mentens, N.: Novel bloom filter algorithms and architectures for ultra-high-speed network security applications. In: 2020 23rd Euromicro Conference on Digital System Design (DSD), pp. 262–269. IEEE (2020)
32. Sateesan, A., Vliegen, J., Daemen, J., Mentens, N.: Hardware-oriented optimization of bloom filter algorithms and architectures for ultra-high-speed lookups in network applications. Microprocess. Microsyst. **93**, 104619 (2022)
33. Scherrer, S., et al.: Low-rate overuse flow tracer (loft): an efficient and scalable algorithm for detecting overuse flows. In: 2021 40th International Symposium on Reliable Distributed Systems (SRDS). IEEE (2021)
34. Szabo-Wexler, E.: Approximate membership of sets: A survey (2014)

35. Wang, M., Zhou, M.: Vacuum filters: more space-efficient and faster replacement for bloom and cuckoo filters. Proc. VLDB Endowment (2019)
36. Xie, Z., Ding, W., Wang, H., Xiao, Y., Liu, Z.: D-ary cuckoo filter: a space efficient data structure for set membership lookup. In: 2017 IEEE 23rd International Conference on Parallel and Distributed Systems (2017)

RemOD: Operational Drift-Adaptive Intrusion Detection

Vikas Maurya$^{(\boxtimes)}$ ⬥, Nanda Rani ⬥, and Sandeep Kumar Shukla ⬥

Indian Institute of Technology Kanpur, Kanpur 208016, India
{vikasmr,nandarani,sandeeps}@cse.iitk.ac.in

Abstract. The critical infrastructure's (CI) environment is complex and dynamic in nature. The normal behaviour of physical devices changes due to time-dependent operational features and infrastructure component needs. The sensors capturing the changed device behaviour generates measurements in a different operating range due to the time dependent variation in the normal behaviour. Such normal variation in the sensors measurements are called operational drift (OD). The state-of-the-art process-level intrusion detection systems (IDSs) are based on offline training, which leads to repeated false alarms for the ODs. Frequently retraining the offline-based IDS model may be a solution, but it's costly and challenging. To overcome the limitation of offline training, we propose an online learning-based IDS named RemOD. Instead of retraining the entire model, RemOD can adapt the ODs to update itself in online fashion. Updating the RemOD for ODs significantly reduces the false alarms in such dynamic environments. We validate the proposed method on two benchmark datasets: SWaT (dynamic environment) and C-town (stationary environment). On SWaT dataset, RemOD generates 6.88 times lower false alarms than the baseline methods such as PASAD.

Keywords: Critical infrastructure security · Intrusion detection system · Online learning · Operational drift · Security of cyber-physical systems

1 Introduction

Cyber attack on Critical Infrastructures (CIs) compromises the nation's economy, public security, social well-being and even human lives in some cases. The CIs are mostly maintained by Industrial Control System (ICS), which is an integration of supervision and production network. An ICS has many components such as Supervisory Control and Data Acquisition systems (SCADA), Programmable Logic Controllers (PLC), sensors and actuators. These components are inter-connected through the operation technology (OT) network. SCADA is a software application in Cyber Physical System (CPS) that gather sensors and actuators data from remote locations to indirectly control the physical components through local controllers and check their working conditions. There are

ⓒ The Author(s), under exclusive license to Springer Nature Switzerland AG 2022
L. Batina et al. (Eds.): SPACE 2022, LNCS 13783, pp. 314–333, 2022.
https://doi.org/10.1007/978-3-031-22829-2_17

many well-known cyber attacks on CIs is reported worldwide, such as the Iranian nuclear plant in 2009 [1], German steel mill in 2014 [2], Saudi petroleum refinery in 2017 [3], and Ukrainian power grid in 2015-16 [4]. A CI is protected with several layers of network segregation and segmentation by adhering to the firewall filter at each network boundary. However, such protections are still being breached by several intelligent and stealthy attackers. An attacker may breach and bypass layers of security but cannot harm the physical devices or resources until the sensor measurements get manipulated. The malicious activities cause statistical changes in the normal behaviour of the sensor measurements [5]. A process-level intrusion detection system (IDS) is deployed at SCADA to monitor the sensor measurements. It detects attacks which induce statistical changes and raises an attack alarm to protect CI as a last layer security solution.

1.1 The Problem of Intrusion Detection in Presence of Operational Drift

Several process-level IDS have been developed recently, giving the best performance in various measures [6–9]. But existing IDSs are restricted to be trained only in offline settings. These IDSs assume that the timeseries measurements generated by sensors are stationary, i.e., statistical features such as mean, standard deviation etc., remains same throughout the training, testing and implementation. Restriction of offline training is one of the major limitations of state-of-the-art IDSs protecting CIs. According to [10], it is unrealistic to assume that a plant's normal operating range cannot change. Attack is not the only reason behind the statistical changes in the sensors measurements. A CI is normally operated under time dependent variations. It can vary by season (summer and winter), volatility of demand, availability of resources and raw materials, maintenance etc. An operator may modify the operating range of a selected component to meet the requirement [10]. As a result, the statistical feature of the sensor measurements gets changed and form a non-stationary time series. Such statistical changes in the normal measurements are called as operational drift (OD). Traditional IDSs perform well with stationary data streams but unable to adapt ODs, as a result, generates numerous false alarms for non-stationary data streams. Therefore, an online learning based IDS is needed that can adapt to ODs in real-time to reduce the false alarm rate.

The existing IDSs are trained in an offline fashion over a time window of measurements. There are computational limitations for training the model on a long timeseries collected dataset. A few day's training datasets cannot cover entire non-stationary timeseries. An IDS trained on non-stationary timeseries in offline fashion generates continuous false alarm for the ODs and fails to distinguish any attack. Retraining for every ODs can be one solution for existing IDSs. But, it is impractical as the batch training (training the IDS on every ODs with old training datasets) is costly computation. Therefore, the primary motivation of this research is to develop an efficient and accurate IDS which can adapt to the

ODs. To fulfill the gap, we propose RemOD[1] (Remember Operational Drifts) that adapts to ODs in online fashion and reduces the false alarm rate. RemOD saves every suspected operational drift and its statistical information until it gets investigated by the analyst team and get verified whether that is an OD or an attack-induced abnormality. If no attack is involved, then RemOD adapts to the OD and remember the changed normal behaviour.

1.2   The Proposed Approach

The proposed IDS RemOD continuously monitors the timeseries (periodically generated sensor measurements) and facilitates the adaptation to ODs. The adaption capability of RemOD remembers the changed normal behaviors. Initially, RemOD learns a base model in offline fashion. It collects important statistical features of a normal measurements into an optimal feature space. The feature space is used as the memory of RemOD to remember all the normal behaviors of sensor measurements throughout. To test a sensor measurement, we project its statistical feature into the feature space and approximate its density. We implement Multivariate Kernel Density Estimations (MVKDE) to approximate the testing measurement density in feature space, giving an anomaly score for the testing point. If the projected test point falls into a sparse region, then its anomaly score is computed high as compared to the points in the dense region. An attack alarm is raised if the anomaly score crosses a certain threshold.

The RemOD is based on the two thresholds– classifier and maintainer. The classifier threshold is a higher threshold, and the maintainer threshold is a lower threshold. RemOD raises the alarm when the anomaly score exceeds the classifier threshold. The maintainer threshold suspects the ODs. If the anomaly score crosses the maintainer threshold, then its statistical information is saved into a queue for further investigation. Such suspected measurements are named as suspected operational drifts (SODs). Any abnormalities in the sensor-generated measurements are a serious concern for a CI. Even if it is modified by operator, it must be investigated within time. Therefore we maintain a buffer queue to save each SODs until it gets investigated by analysts. Based on the investigation, if it is found that the point in the queue is because of an OD only, then we update the model by adding the statistical feature into the feature space otherwise dropped. An OD causes high anomaly score for the successive measurements that saves repeated entries into the buffer queue. Updating the feature space for a few points in the queue can learn the entire changes.

RemOD is evaluated on two standard datasets, SWaT [11] and C-town datasets [12]. The Secure Water Treatment (SWaT) plant dataset provides testbed sensor measurements which has numerous ODs. The SWaT dataset is suitable for validating an IDS on non-stationary timeseries. The C-town water distribution network dataset provides stationary timeseries data for a nine-month-long duration. The dataset validates an IDS for long testing duration and

---

[1] https://github.com/8biskit/RemOD-Operational-Drift-adaptive-Intrusion-Detection.

stationary distribution. We show the RemOD's result in both online and offline modes. In offline mode, we do not update the model called offline RemOD. Further, we compare performance with the state-of-the-art PASAD method [7]. The experimental results show that RemOD improves upon PASAD for both online and offline modes. Online RemOD improves the average accuracy by 10.69% and 0.47% on the SWaT and C-town datasets, respectively. RemOD is developed for the non-stationary dataset to reduce the false alarms rate and provides more accurate result on the SWaT dataset. The false alarm rate on the SWaT dataset is reduced from 12.5% to 1.8%. Moreover, the offline RemOD's is trained over the same training data as the baseline and performs slightly better.

1.3 Contribution

The key contributions of our work are listed as follows:

- We analyse the challenges of operational drifts for the existing offline training-based IDS as they can fail by generating repeated false alarms in the non-stationary environment.
- We present a novel online learning-based IDS suitable for adapting the operational drifts generated in an non-stationary environment of CI. The adaptive capability of the RemOD significantly reduces the false alarms.
- Similar to the baseline method, we also evaluated RemOD in the offline setting when we do not update it during online testing. Still, its performance is slightly better.
- RemOD is evaluated on two datasets containing diverse attack types and diverse sensor readings of stationary and non-stationary environments.

Organization: In the Sect. 2, we explain the methodology to build RemOD. The characteristic of datasets used for validation is described in the Sect. 3. The Sect. 4 empirically evaluate RemOD and discusses the results. Section 5 presents the limitation of RemOD. The Sect. 6 discusses the related works and research gap. The manuscript is concluded along with possible future work in the Sect. 7.

2 RemOD: Remember Operational Drift

RemOD is an online learning, time-series analysis and density estimation-based IDS, capable of adapting the ODs in the timeseries during online testing. The methodology of RemOD is developed as follows. We first discuss all the preliminaries concepts developed for the RemOD in the Sect. 2.1. Then we discuss the stepwise offline training of RemOD in the Sect. 2.2, presents a base model ready to deploy for online testing. In the Sect. 2.3, we discuss stepwise implementation for online testing and update. The parameters used to implement RemOD are described in the Sect. 2.4. In Sect. 2.5, we discuss the computation cost of RemOD.

2.1 Preliminaries Concepts

This section discusses the essential preliminaries concepts used to develop RemOD.

Multivariate Kernel Density Estimations (MVKDE): MVKDE simulate a kernel density function (KDF) that approximates a random data point in a multidimensional sample space [13,14] (we call it to feature space because it collects statistical features). Suppose $x_1, x_2, ..., x_k$ are the feature vectors in a feature space $\hat{\mathcal{X}}$, then the MVKDE function $\hat{f}$ for a d-variate random vector $x \in \mathcal{R}^d$ is defined as:

$$\hat{f}_{\mathcal{H}}(x/\hat{\mathcal{X}}) = \frac{1}{k} \sum_{i=1}^{k} \mathcal{K}_{\mathcal{H}}(x - x_i) \tag{1}$$

$\mathcal{K}$ is a d-variate kernel function that satisfies the property of being radially symmetric and $\int \mathcal{K}_{\mathcal{H}}(x)dx = 1$. There are many known kernel functions which satisfy the above properties. Among them, the standard Gaussian kernel function (cf. Eq. 2) is a popular choice for MVKDE [13,15,16].

$$\mathcal{K}(x) = (2\pi)^{-d/2}|\mathcal{H}|^{-1/2}exp(-\frac{1}{2}x^T\mathcal{H}^{-1}x) \tag{2}$$

$\mathcal{H}$ is a covariance matrix, which is the symmetric positive definite. There are many choices of $\mathcal{H}$ [13,14] depends on the application. In this paper, we use a scalar covariance matrix $\mathcal{H} = h\mathcal{I}_d$ (cf. Sect. 2.4).

Anomaly Score: MVKDE function $(\hat{f})$ gives a higher score if point x belongs to the dense region. However, RemOD intends to detect the abnormal points which belong to the sparse region of $\hat{\mathcal{X}}$. Therefore, we reverse the MVKDE to define anomaly score $\psi(x)$ (cf. Eq. 3), where $MAX = \mathcal{K}_{\mathcal{H}}(\vec{0})$ is the maximum possible score of the MVKDE function. And, $\vec{0}$ is a zero vector.

$$\psi(x) = MAX - \hat{f}_{\mathcal{H}}(x/\hat{\mathcal{X}}) \tag{3}$$

Thresholds: RemOD model is based on two thresholds: maintainer threshold θ_m and classifier threshold θ_c ($\theta_c > \theta_m$). The θ_m is used for training and updating RemOD. The θ_c is dedicated to raise the alarm when $\psi(x) > \theta_c$.

$$\theta_m = MAX - \mathcal{K}_{\mathcal{H}}(r_1) \tag{4}$$

$$\theta_c = MAX - \mathcal{K}_{\mathcal{H}}(r_2) \tag{5}$$

where $r_1, r_2 \in \mathcal{R}^d$ (cf. Sect. 2.4 for experimental choice) are any points in the radically symmetric kernel space $\mathcal{K}$ at $||r_1||$ and $||r_2||$ distance respectively from $\vec{0}$ vector such that $||r_1|| < ||r_2||$.

2.2   Offline Training

The RemOD is being trained in two phases: offline and online training. In the offline training phase, it is trained entirely over a sub-sequence of measurements collected for some time window. The offline training learns a base model, which further gets updated for every ODs that occurs during online testing. The offline training returns an efficient feature space used during online testing.

Consider a univariate real-valued timeseries $T = m_1, m_2, ..., m_T, m_{T+1}, ...$, where m_t represents measurement at time t. Initial sub-sequences of timeseries T of length T are considered to train the RemOD. Remaining from m_{T+1} onward are streaming measurements used for testing. The offline training phase of the RemOD has the following three steps.

Embedding: Consider a training sequence $T = m_1, m_2, ..., m_T$. A lag parameter L is used to select a L length sub-sequence of T. Therefore, total $K = T-L+1$ sub-sequence are used for training. Each sub-sequences $(T[t - L : t])$ computes feature vector x_t to get embedded into the feature space $\mathcal{X}$.

Each coordinate of x_t represents a statistical feature of sub-sequence $T[t - L : t]$, such as mean, standard deviation, skewness, Kurtosis, percentile, etc. In this paper, we experimented RemOD with two features[2]: mean and standard deviation. Therefore $x_t = [mean(T[t - L : t]), std(T[t - L : t])]$. The collection of every x_t defines a feature space $\mathcal{X} = \{x_t : L \leq t \leq T\}$.

Normalization: Since ICS consist of multiple types of sensors and actuators, each may have a different range of measurements that derives a different scale of feature vectors. Hence, we need to normalize the feature vectors to represent them on the same scale. We use the min-max technique to normalize the sample space $\mathcal{X}$ in the range of [0,1].

Sampling: A sensors generated timeseries are mostly repeated within a normal range. When we take the statistical feature of every L length sub-sequences, most of them are repeated, leads to huge redundancy in $\mathcal{X}$. To remove the redundant feature vectors, we use random sampling without replacement algorithm. The reduced feature space is defined as $\hat{\mathcal{X}}$. Random sampling can miss some important feature vectors of $\mathcal{X}$ in $\hat{\mathcal{X}}$. A feature vector $x \in \mathcal{X}$ is said to be important feature vector if it belongs to the sparse region of $\hat{\mathcal{X}}$. To recover the missed feature vectors, we use the maintainer threshold and check the importance of every removed feature vectors (x_i) in $(\mathcal{X} - \hat{\mathcal{X}})$. If x_i, $\psi(x_i) > \theta_m$ then we include it into $\hat{\mathcal{X}}$.

$$\hat{\mathcal{X}} = \{\hat{\mathcal{X}} \cup \{x_i\} : x_i \in (\mathcal{X} - \hat{\mathcal{X}}), \psi(x_i) > \theta_m\} \tag{6}$$

---

[2] More features overhead the computation cost. We will include the others feature by implementing using self-balancing multi-dimensional tree as future work.

2.3   Online Testing and Updates

In this phase, we test the behaviour of every newly generated measurement and update the model if any ODs are found. We follow the following steps to test a measurement m_t generated at timestamp t.

Algorithm 1: RemOD framework: online test and update

Input : Feature space matrix $\hat{\mathcal{X}}$, Normalizer, Lag parameter L.
Output: Attack Alarm
Data: A testing timeseries $\mathcal{T}$

1 determine θ_m and θ_c;   // thresholds
2 $Q \leftarrow$ An empty queue;
3 **for** $t \leftarrow 1$ **to do**
4      $\tilde{m} \leftarrow \mathcal{T}[t - L : t]$;   // lag vector
5      $x \leftarrow [mean(\tilde{m}), std(\tilde{m})]$;   // feature vector
6      $x \leftarrow nomrmalizer(x)$;
7      $score \leftarrow \hat{f}(x)$;   // anomaly score by eq. 1
8   **if** $score \geq \theta_c$ **then**
9   Generate an attack alarm
10   **end**
11   **if** $score \geq \theta_m$ **then**
12   Q.enque(x,t);   // add the suspected OD in Q
13   **end**
14   updateSample(Q,t);
15 **end**

16 **Function** updateSample(Q,t):
17   x',t'=Q.get();   // get the rear element of Q
18   **if** $t - t' \geq \tau$ **then**
19   Q.deque();   // remove the rear element
20         $score' = \hat{f}(x')$;
21   **if** $score' \geq \theta_m$ *and verified normal* **then**
22             $\hat{\mathcal{X}} \leftarrow append(\hat{\mathcal{X}}, x')$;   // update the feature space
23   **end**
24   **end**
25 **End Function**

Testing a Sub-sequence: To test the measurement m_t RemOD prepare a L length lag vector $\tilde{m}_t$ with the help of preceding measurements; $\tilde{m}_t = m_{t-L+1}, ..., m_{t-1}, m_t$. RemOD computes feature vector $x_t = [mean(\tilde{m}_t), std(\tilde{m}_t)]$ and normalizes them. If the alarm score $\psi(x_t)$ (cf. Eq. 3) crosses the classifier threshold ($\psi(x_t) > \theta_c$), then the attack alarm is raised.

Enqueue: If the anomaly score of a test measurement m_t crosses the maintainer threshold ($\psi(x_t) > \theta_m$), then m_t is considered as SOD, which needs to be investigated further. Therefore we maintain a buffer queue $\mathcal{Q}$. The feature vector x_t and time stamp t of SOD (m_t) is saved in $\mathcal{Q}$ i.e., if $\psi(x_t) > \theta_m$ then $\mathcal{Q}.enque(x_t, t)$. The investigation time of the SODs in $\mathcal{Q}$ can vary in the real environment. In RemOD's experimental setup, we use a sufficiently long time τ and assume that the SODs get verified within τ.

Update the Feature Space: To update the feature space, we get the SOD element $(x_{t'}, t' = \mathcal{Q}.get())$ of $\mathcal{Q}$. If it has been in the queue for more than τ, i.e., $|t - t'| > \tau$, then RemOD dequeues it to verify the SOD. We use the level of the dataset to verify the SOD in our experimental setup. If the measurement at timestamp t' and its previous L measurements (the measurements used for computing the feature vector $x_{t'}$) are marked as normal, then we consider it as OD to update the feature space; otherwise, drop it. Now we update the OD by adding its feature vector $x_{t'}$ into the feature space $\hat{\mathcal{X}}$ when $\psi(x_{t'}) > \theta_m$. Since the OD causes to change every successive measurement which gets added in $\mathcal{Q}$. But the most of them have similar statistical features. Therefore updating only a few x'_t are sufficient to adapt the OD. If a similar statistic is present in $\hat{\mathcal{X}}$, then the anomaly score of x'_t, which was added in the queue because of its high anomaly score is changed to lower anomaly score. Therefore before updating $\hat{\mathcal{X}}$, we check the anomaly score $\psi(x'_t)$. If $\psi(x'_t) < \theta_m$, then there is no need to update.

2.4   Choice of Parameters

There are a total of five parameters that are needed in RemOD: The lag parameter L, the number of nearest points k the bandwidth parameter h, the sampling ratio sr, and radius r (to find thresholds). In [17], the authors suggest a lag parameter L should be long enough to describe the system's dynamics and $L < N/2$. RemOD estimates density on the k nearest neighbours which is chosen to be around 5% of the number of points in feature space after offline training. The kernel smoothing parameter h is the variance ($\sqrt{h}$ is standard deviation) of each co-ordinate of kernel function $\hat{f}$ as our feature space $\hat{\mathcal{X}}$ is normalized between $[0, 1]$. According to the authors in [13,14], the standard deviation of $\sqrt{h} = 0.5$ is wide enough to estimate the entire $\hat{\mathcal{X}}$ very smoothly, i.e. $h < 0.25$. RemOD estimates density on the k nearest points only which shrink the width of estimation. Therefore, Estimating a different Gaussian kernel for each point in the space needs very small h, i.e. $h << 0.25$. The choice of sampling ratio 'sr' is inversely proportional to the initial number of points in the feature space. The base RemOD is trained over a small duration of measurements having similar statistics. Therefore many repeated statistical features are present in $\mathcal{X}$. However, only a few points are needed to describe the feature space. Therefore we choose sr to keep only a few points N in $\hat{\mathcal{X}}$. Parameters $||r_1||$ and $||r_2||$ are the radius of the kernel function $\hat{f}$ computes the thresholds. If a test point's kernel density estimation is more than kernel value at r_1 distance, then it is classified as operation drift by the maintainer threshold θ_m. If a test points kernel density is more than kernel value at r_2 distance point, then the alarm is raised by classifier threshold θ_c. The maintainer threshold aims to remember all the statistics in which the ideal value is zero. But implying r_1 is close to zero vector adds many points and slows down the computation. Therefore some slack must be provided to make it computationally practical. Similarly, the classifier threshold also be at the right place to accurately classify the attack and normal data points. We use $||r_1|| = 0.1$ and $||r_2|| = 0.3$ during our experiments.

2.5   Computation Cost

The offline training phase first collects all the feature vectors in the feature space whose computational complexity is $O(T)$ (T is length of training measurements). Then, the sample is randomly reduced to size $O(N)$. Recovering the lost points needs to check the anomaly score and compare with the θ_m, which has a computational complexity of $O(T \cdot N^2)$. Since the offline training is a one time job, and RemOD is initially trained over a small size data. Therefore training complexity $O(T \cdot N^2)$ is practical.

The pseudo-code of online testing and update is shown in Algorithms 1. Computing the anomaly score $\hat{f}$ is the most costly step. It needs to find k nearest local points from the test point in the feature space of size N. Hence, the time complexity is $O(k \cdot N^2) \approx O(N^2)$ to test one measurement. Since the N is already reduced to very small, therefore the testing computational complexity of $O(N^2)$ is practical to implement. The computation cost can be further improved by implementing using multi-dimensional tree instead on matrix data structure as the future work. The time taken by RemOD in training and testing with the evaluation dataset is given in the Table 3.

3   Validation Datasets

In this section, we use datasets of two different infrastructures to validate the RemOD, one is from the Secure Water Treatment (SWaT) testbed [11], and another is from the C-town network of water distribution plants [12].

3.1   Dataset 1: The Secure Water Treatment (SWaT) Testbed

The SWaT dataset [11] is a real-time water treatment plant testbed dataset provided by the iTrust research center for ICS cyber security. The SWaT plant produces 5 US gallons/hr of filtered water, which is operated by ICS. SWaT testbed was continuously operational for 11 days: 6 days in normal, and the remaining 5 days attack scenarios. The measurements are generated periodically after a second. In the attack phase, there are a total of 36 different attacks launched. A traditional IDS generates high false alarm for SWaT dataset as it has several ODs in the sensor measurements.

3.2 Dataset 2: C-town Network Dataset

The BATADAL dataset [12] is generated by simulating the C-Town water distribution network with the epanetCPA framework [18]. It generates stationary time-series of sensor measurements. The dataset provides three files collected under: normal operation for one year, normal and mixed with 7 different attacks for six months, normal and mixed with 7 different attacks for six months. As our model needs only normal measurements for initial offline training, therefore we use both attack datasets to test all 14 different attacks. The dataset contains the timeseries of 43 sensors/actuators measurements. The measurements are generated periodically after an hour.

4 Experiment and Result

In this section we first discuss the assumptions to perform the experiments in Sect. 4.1 and the evelution matrix in the Sect. 4.2. This section is consists of five experiments used to validate RemOD from various perspective. In the first two experiments Sects. 4.3, and 4.4, we applied RemOD on SWaT (cf. Sect. 3.1), and C-Town dataset (cf. Sect. 3.2). Experiment 4.3 validates RemOD on non stationary timeseries, and the experiment Sect. 4.4 validate on stationary timeseries. In 4.5, we experiment RemOD in offline mode. In Sect. 4.6, shows the comparison of RemOD with baseline method PASAD. In Sect. 4.7, we discuss the computation cost of RemOD in the experiments Sects. 4.3 and 4.4.

4.1 Assumptions

Following two assumption used for experimenting RemOD:

Assumption 1: We assume that the features of SODs present in the buffer queue are verified using the dataset label after a significant time τ. If it is labelled normal, then we consider it as OD otherwise attack.

Assumption 2: Sensors measurement during an attack reach the abnormal state and takes some time to return to the normal even if the attack is disabled. Also, we are preparing the L length lagged vector feature with the help of the previous features. The measurements marked normal just after the attack includes attack measurements which may raise false alarms. Therefore we do not consider false alarms up to $2L$ length just after the attack for evaluation matrix. The same assumption is also applied in the baseline implementation.

4.2 Evaluation Matrix

Along with the visual demonstration results of a few sensors, we present precision and false alarm rate to evaluate RemOD and baseline. Since the true level of the dataset for the sensor measurements is unknown. An attack manipulates the measurements of only a few sensors, not every sensor. Therefore computing the recall for every sensor may not be a suitable parameter. We present a few plots of sensor measurement visual representations cf. Figs. 1, 2, 3, 4,5 for the attack detection capability and the following evaluation matrix for the accuracy of the alarms.

$$precision = \frac{TA}{TA + FA} \times 100 \tag{7}$$

$$false\ alarm\ rate = \frac{FA}{NTM} \times 100 \tag{8}$$

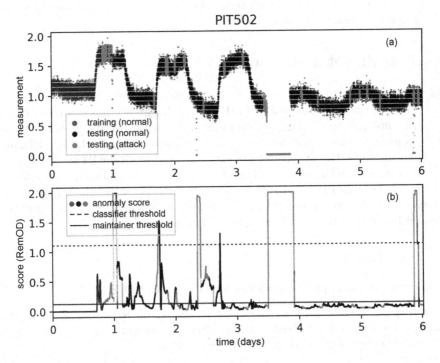

Fig. 1. Application of RemOD on a non-stationary timeseries. The Subfigure (a) represents the sensors (PIT502) generated measurements of SWaT dataset. The initial subseries (green colour) is used for training RemOD in the offline mode and the remaining (black and green) are for testing. The figure shows that statistics of the timeseries is not same during training and testing generates a non-stationary timeseries. During testing, four attack measurements are significantly manipulated. The subfigure (b) represents the corresponding anomaly score generated by RemOD on the entire timeseries. The anomaly score (green scores) during training appearing above the maintainer threshold are the part of training. The changed statistical features of the timeseries cause high anomaly score which are adapted by RemOD and detects the four attack with only a few false alarms. (Color figure online)

where TA (true alarms) is correctly detected alarms, FA (false alarms) is alarms raised for normal measurements, and NTM (normal test measurements) is the number of normal test measurements. Since RemOD is motivated to reduce false alarms and increase true alarm's confidence. Therefore evaluating alarms in terms of their precision and false alarm rate provides better evaluation matrix. An ideal IDS should have high alarm precision to raise a confident alarm.

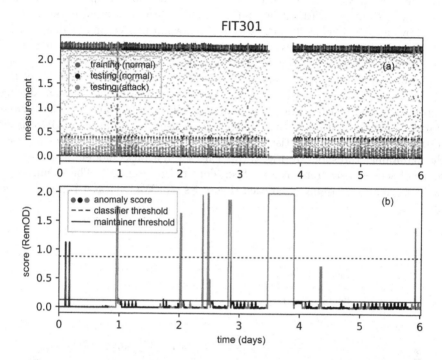

Fig. 2. Application of RemOD on a stationary timeseries. The Subfigure (a) represents the sensors (FIT301) generated measurements of SWaT dataset. The initial subseries (green colour) is used for training RemOD in the offline mode and the remaining (black and green) are for testing. The figure shows that statistics of the timeseries are the same during training and testing generates a stationary timeseries. Visually, only one attack is appearing manipulated and other are hidden in between the normal measurements range. The subfigure (b) represents the corresponding anomaly score generated by RemOD on the entire timeseries. The anomaly score (green scores) during training appearing above the classifier threshold are the part of training. The figure shows that the anomaly score of the normal measurements are remain below the maintainer that do not needs to update the model. There are seven attack mostly hidden within the normal margin are detected without any false alarms. (Color figure online)

4.3 Exp.1: Evaluation on SWaT Dataset

In this experiment, we run RemOD on every process variable of a SWaT dataset. We demonstrate two sensor variables which are PIT502 and FIT301 in the Fig. 1 and 2. Figure 1(a) represent a non-stationary timeseries that includes multiple ODs, while Fig. 2(a) shows a stationary timeseries. As shown in Figs. 1(a), 2(a), initial measurements of green colour are used for offline training, and the remaining are used for testing. As the Fig. 1(a) belongs to the non-stationary time-series causes anomaly score crosses the maintainer threshold many times initially. Even it raises two false alarms, shown in Fig. 1(b). When the model adapt to every ODs and becomes stationary after a while. Then no more adaptation is needed and it keeps working without any false alarms. In Fig. 1, there are four attacks are showing a significant deviation from the normal measurements detected by RemOD. We efficiently detect the attacks because of the adaptive nature of the RemOD otherwise it would be mixed with the false alarms and could not be distinguished. Another scenario (cf. Fig. 2) is a stationary timeseries of the SWaT dataset. As the statistical distribution of the timeseries is the same during the training and testing. The base model has all the information of the normal statistics present during testing. Therefore no need to update RemOD during testing as no significant statistical is changed in measurements causes to cross the maintainer threshold. In Fig. 2, there are seven attacks hidden in the normal range of sensor measurement have been detected by RemOD. The summary of the performance of RemOD on each timeseries on SWaT dataset is given in the Table 1.

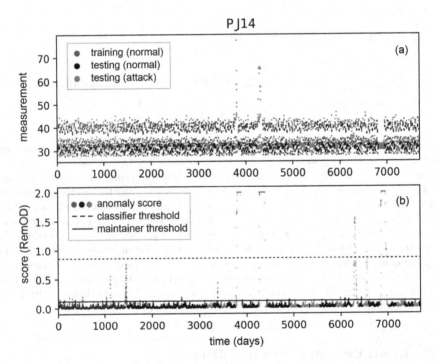

Fig. 3. Application of RemOD on the 'PJ14' sensor of C-Town network. RemOD detects five attacks and not raising any false alarm. Anomaly score on a few normal measurements are above the maintainer threshold gets adapted with time.

4.4   Exp.2: Evaluation on C-town Dataset

In this experiment, we applied RemOD to every process variable of the C-Town dataset. The experiment is performed similarly to the experiment Sect. 4.3. C-Town dataset contains stationary timeseries sensor measurements. Figure 3 shows that the RemOD can detect 4 attacks reflected in the sensor PJ14. There are a few measurements initially slightly differing from the training measurements cross the maintainer threshold, which RemOD adapts. The performance summary on the C-town dataset is given in the Table 1.

4.5   Exp.3: Offline RemOD

In this experiment, we evaluate RemOD on both SWaT and C-town datasets when there is no online update is performed. We train the model only once during offline training using the training measurements (green measurements) and apply the model on the testing measurements without any further updates. RemOD's better attack detection capability (cf. Figs. 5) slightly improve the result even in offline mode. The average alarm's accuracy of offline RemOD on the both dataset is given in the Table 1.

Table 1. RemOD and PASAD performance comparison on SWaT and C-Town dataset

Method	Precision (%)		False alarm rate (%)	
	SWaT	C-Town	SWaT	C-Town
RemOD Online	**96.3**	99.9	**1.8**	0.1
RemOD Offline	86.8	99.8	11.3	0.1
PASAD	**85.6**	99.4	**12.5**	0.6

Table 2. Choice of parameters for experiments by RemOD

Experiment	L	h	k	τ	sr
C-town	75	0.08	10	1 week	0.3
Exp.3	200	0.08	10	NA	0.3

4.6   Exp.4: Comparison with PASAD

We compare RemOD with the state-of-the-art method PASAD [7] as the baseline. We applied PASAD on each process-variables of SWaT and C-Town datasets by following the guidelines provided in the paper [7]. We used the same training and testing sequences on both models (RemOD and PASAD) for a fair comparison. We show two visual demonstrations of non-stationary and stationary distribution in Fig. 4 and 5. In the non-stationary distribution, measurements

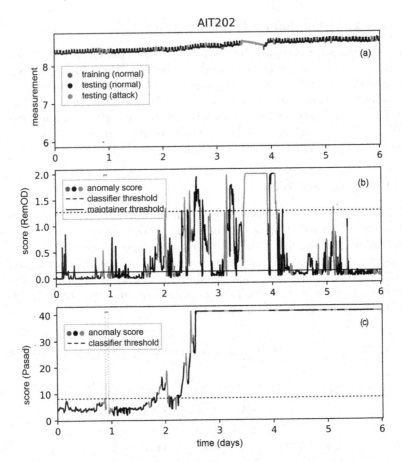

Fig. 4. Comparison of RemOD with PASAD on a non-stationary timeseries sensor-variable 'AIT202' of SWaT dataset. A scenario when the statistics of the measurements are continuously changing. RemOD keep adapting the changes to down the anomaly score. When all the statistics are adapted it do not raise false alarms anymore. While PASAD could not adapt the changes continuously raising false alarms.

of AIT202 (cf. Fig. 4) is continuously increasing, which is normal for this sensor. Since the baseline method is restricted to offline, it could not adapt to the changes and continue raising false alarms. On average of every sensors of the SWaT dataset PASAD raise 12.5% false alarms. Another hand, RemOD's adaptive capability make it possible to adapt to the change. After a while, RemOD adapts all the ODs and minimize the false alarm rate. In this way, RemOD reduces the average false alarms to 1.8%, which is 6.88 times lower than the baseline method. However, the offline RemOD raises equivalent but slightly lower false alarms than the baseline.

In Fig. 5, we are demonstrating another sensor measurements of the SWaT dataset which shows the detection capability of RemOD. RemOD can detect six

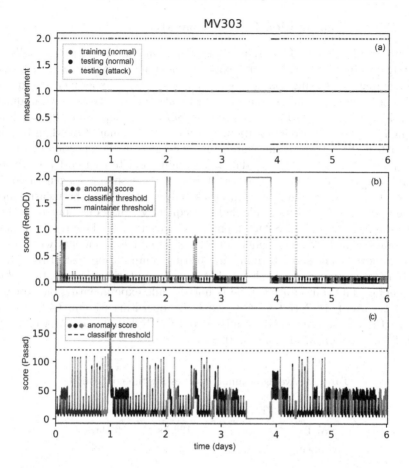

Fig. 5. Comparison of RemOD with PASAD on sensor-variable 'MV303' of SWaT dataset. A stationary timeseries when PASAD fails to detect may attacks. Even Pasad's anomaly score is close to zero for the attack manipulates the measurements to continuously generating only one value. While RemOD detects the five attacks in the same scenario.

attacks in MV303, while the baseline method fails to detect most of them. In such a way, RemOD has more capability to detect an attack, resulting higher precision shown in the Table 1. The strong attack detection capability and its adaptive nature leads to improve the alarm's accuracy by 10.69% for the SWaT dataset. The false alarm rate on the C-town dataset is already small because of stationary distribution. Still, RemOD (both online and offline) is raising lower number of false alarms as compared to the baseline. The average accuracy on the C-Town dataset is equivalent (slightly improved by 0.47%) to the baseline as it has stationary distribution. When we don't update RemOD during online testing, then its (offline RemOD's) performance is closer but slightly better than the baseline.

4.7   Exp.5: Computation Cost of RemOD

An important concern of the RemOD is that it should be computationally efficient to produce the test result before the next measurement gets generated.
The training and testing computation cost for the three experiments is given in
the Table 3. As the model is trained by just collecting the dataset, it can quickly
train the base model within a few seconds. Since the adaptation process during
testing is applied for a long duration, therefore it takes more time than training.
Still, it tests SWaT sensor measurements generated in the duration of six days
within 122.5 s. For the C-town dataset, training and testing cost are within a
second. The average time to compute the sensor measurements generated during the time period of nine months took only 0.84 s. Since the measurements
of the C-town dataset gets available less frequently (takes one hour to generate
a measurement) than the SWaT (generates at every sec). This results in lesser
computation on C-town as model processes fewer measurements with smaller
lag parameters. The small training and testing computation cost of RemOD on
the both validation datasets shows that it is computationally realistic to build
and deploy. The computation time is noted while experimenting on processor:
'Intel(R) Core(TM) i7-4770 CPU @ 3.40 GHz', operating system: '64-bit Ubuntu
16.04 LTS', RAM size: 16 GB, implemented in 'Python 3.6.5 :: Anaconda, Inc'
with libraries: numpy, random, math etc.

Table 3. Average training and testing time of RemOD

Experiment	Training cost	Testing cost	Duration
SWaT	26.54 s	122.5 s	6 Days
C-town	0.23 s	0.84 s	9 Months

5   Limitation

Complete automation of adapting to the OD is a challenging task for an IDS.
An adaptive-intelligent attacker can compromise fully automated adaptive IDS
by the data poisoning attack. In targeted attacks, attackers can manipulate the
sensor measurements during the OD to poison the training data. When RemOD
adapts to such poisoning data, it remembers the attack measurements as normal
and misclassifies them as normal during further testing. Therefore, RemOD is a
semiautomatic IDS, which gets updated only for the manually verified normal
measurements to avoid the data poisoning attack. It may add some delay if the
attack is not verified within the stipulated time. The data poisoning attack is a
challenge for most of the available IDS. They also assume the training dataset
to be poisoning free.

6   Related Work

Over the past few years, several machine learning-based process level IDS has been proposed for anomaly-based intrusion detection. In [19], the authors use k-means clustering method with the algorithms discussed in [20] and named it y-mean clustering method for network intrusion detection. In [21], authors used one-class SVM with kernel PCA to detect attacks in the Gas Pipeline testbed and water treatment plant [22]. Authors of [23] improved the SVM method by using PCA and the genetic algorithm. In [24], the authors proposed hierarchical monitoring with distributed and parallel PCA. Many authors have also proposed deep learning based IDS [25–28]. In [25], authors implement RNN models for fault detection in Tennessee Eastman Process chemical plant [29]. Abokifa et al. [26] employ PCA with an artificial neural network. Authors of [27] use an unsupervised generative deep learning model. In [30], authors applied ensemble method by combining multiple anomaly detection method such as statistical fences, FFNN model and PCA. Li et al. [28] proposed a Generative Adversarial Networks (GANs) based unsupervised anomaly detection method, which is validated using the SWaT dataset. [11]. There are a few univariate solutions are found most effective [6,7,9]. In [9], authors proposed an auto regression-based model to detect abnormal sensors measurements. Aoudi et al. [7] demonstrate singular spectrum analysis (SSA) based noise effective and computationally efficient univariate IDS. Authors of [6] leverage SSA with the ellipsoid decision boundary to improve [7] and introduced a new micro stealthy attacks(MSSA). They presented improved IDS to make more accurate for detecting MSSA.

All of the above discussed methods are offline training based and assume stationary distribution of the senors measurements during training, testing, and implementation. These state-of-the-art methods fail to detect operational drifts in the normal behaviour and raise numerous false alarms. In [10], authors depicted the need for an IDS to adapt ODs for real-time implementation in order to reduce the false alarms. To the best of our knowledge, there is no research available to adapt the ODs in IDS. Therefore we propose RemOD– a univariate, process level, and online learning based IDS. An adaptive IDS can provide a more layer of security to CI and reduce disruption in CI function, as continuous false alarm may disrupt CI functionality for some time. RemOD quickly detect the abnormal structural changes and adapt the ODs to reduce the false alarms. We consider state-of-the-art method PASAD as baseline to compare performance. The comparison is present in Sect. 4.6 and result is found in support of RemOD. Result shows that RemOD is highly accurate and generates few false alarms comparatively.

7   Conclusion

It is an unrealistic assumption to consider a stationary environment always in CI. This paper presents the cases when the statistics of the normal measurements can change because of genuine reasons during testing. The traditional

IDSs are offline learning-based, fail in the non-stationary environment. To overcome this limitation of offline IDS, we propose RemOD. RemOD is fully automatic for intrusion detection and semi-automatic for OD adaptation. We validate RemOD on two benchmark datasets that show RemOD is accurate in detecting attacks and adapting the ODs to reduce the false alarms significantly. The proposed method RemOD is a semi-supervised that assumes the training measurements belong to the normal class. The future direction of the research is to develop robust online learning-based unsupervised IDS. A robust model can ignore the noise and poisoned data (attack mixed within the normal measurements). Along with robustification, we would like to extend RemOD to improve performance by implementing additional statistical features and a self-balancing multi-dimensional tree.

Acknowledgement. We thank to the C3iHub (Technology Innovation Hub on Cyber Security and Cyber Security for Cyber-Physical Systems) at IIT Kanpur for partially funding this research project.

References

1. Falliere, N., Murchu, L.O., Chien, E.: W32. stuxnet dossier. White paper. Symantec Corp. Secu. Resp. **5**(6), 29 (2011)
2. Lee, R.M., Assante, M.J., Conway, T.: German steel mill cyber attack. Ind. Control Syst. **30**, 62 (2014)
3. Johnson, B., Caban, D., Krotofil, M., Scali, D., Brubaker, N., Glyer, C.: Attackers deploy new ICS attack framework "triton" and cause operational disruption to critical infrastructure. Threat Research Blog (2017)
4. Defense Use Case. Analysis of the cyber attack on the Ukrainian power grid. Electricity Information Sharing and Analysis Center (E-ISAC) (2016)
5. Cardenas, A., et al.: Attacks against process control systems: risk assessment, detection, and response. In: ACM Symposium on Information, Computer and Communications Security, pp. 355–366. ACM (2011)
6. Maurya, V., Agarwal, R., Kumar, S., Shukla, S.K.: Epasad: ellipsoid decision boundary based process-aware stealthy attack detector. arXiv preprint arXiv:2204.04154 (2022)
7. Wissam Aoudi, Mikel Iturbe, and Magnus Almgren. Truth will out: Departure-based process-level detection of stealthy attacks on control systems. In Conference on Computer and Communications Security, pages 817–831. ACM, 2018
8. Chen, Y., Poskitt, C.M., Sun, J.: Learning from mutants: using code mutation to learn and monitor invariants of a cyber-physical system. In: 2018 IEEE Symposium on Security and Privacy (SP), pp. 648–660. IEEE (2018)
9. Hadžiosmanović, D., Sommer, R., Zambon, E., Hartel, P.H.: Through the eye of the plc: semantic security monitoring for industrial processes. In: Annual Computer Security Applications Conference, pp. 126–135. ACM (2014)
10. Gauthama Raman, M.R., Ahmed, C.M., Mathur, A.: Machine learning for intrusion detection in industrial control systems: challenges and lessons from experimental evaluation. Cybersecurity **4**(1), 1–12 (2021)
11. Mathur, A.P., Tippenhauer, N.O.: Swat: a water treatment testbed for research and training on ics security. In: 2016 International Workshop on Cyber-physical Systems for Smart Water Networks (CySWater), pp. 31–36. IEEE (2016)

12. Taormina, R., et al.: Battle of the attack detection algorithms: disclosing cyber attacks on water distribution networks. J. Water Resour. Plann. Manage. **144**(8), 04018048 (2018)
13. Wand, M.P., Jones, M.C.: Kernel smoothing. Chapman and Hall/CRC (1994)
14. Silverman, B.W.: Density Estimation for Statistics and Data Analysis. Routledge (2018)
15. Ramlau-Hansen, H.: The choice of a kernel function in the graduation of counting process intensities. Scand. Actuar. J. **1983**(3), 165–182 (1983)
16. Otneim, H., Tjøstheim, D.: The locally gaussian density estimator for multivariate data. Stat. Comput. **27**(6), 1595–1616 (2017)
17. Golyandina, N., Zhigljavsky, A.: Singular Spectrum Analysis for time series. Springer, Heidelberg (2013). https://doi.org/10.1007/978-3-642-34913-3
18. Taormina, R., Galelli, S., Tippenhauer, N.O., Salomons, E., Ostfeld, A.: Characterizing cyber-physical attacks on water distribution systems. J. Water Resour. Plann. Manage. **143**(5), 04017009 (2017)
19. Guan, Y., Ghorbani, A.A., Belacel, N.: Y-means: a clustering method for intrusion detection. In: CCECE 2003-Canadian Conference on Electrical and Computer Engineering. Toward a Caring and Humane Technology (Cat. No. 03CH37436), vol. 2, pp. 1083–1086. IEEE (2003)
20. Hansen, P., Mladenović, N.: J-means: a new local search heuristic for minimum sum of squares clustering. Pattern Recogn. **34**(2), 405–413 (2001)
21. Nader, P., Honeine, P., Beauseroy, P.: l_p-norms in one-class classification for intrusion detection in scada systems. IEEE Trans. Industr. Inf. **10**(4), 2308–2317 (2014)
22. Lichman, M., et al.: UCI machine learning repository (2013)
23. Gao, X., Hou, J.: An improved SVM integrated GS-PCA fault diagnosis approach of tennessee eastman process. Neurocomputing **174**, 906–911 (2016)
24. Zhu, J., Ge, Z., Song, Z.: Distributed parallel PCA for modeling and monitoring of large-scale plant-wide processes with big data. IEEE Trans. Industr. Inf. **13**(4), 1877–1885 (2017)
25. Filonov, P., Kitashov, F., Lavrentyev, A.: RNN-based early cyber-attack detection for the tennessee eastman process. arXiv preprint arXiv:1709.02232 (2017)
26. Abokifa, A.A., Haddad, K., Lo, C.S., Biswas, P.: Detection of cyber physical attacks on water distribution systems via principal component analysis and artificial neural networks. In: World Environmental and Water Resources Congress 2017, pp. 676–691 (2017)
27. Chandy, S.E., Rasekh, A., Barker, Z.A., Ehsan Shafiee, M.: Cyberattack detection using deep generative models with variational inference. J. Water Resour. Plann. Manag. **145**(2), 04018093 (2018)
28. Li, D., Chen, D., Jin, B., Shi, L., Goh, J., Ng, S.-K.: MAD-GAN: multivariate anomaly detection for time series data with generative adversarial networks. In: Tetko, I.V., Kůrková, V., Karpov, P., Theis, F. (eds.) ICANN 2019. LNCS, vol. 11730, pp. 703–716. Springer, Cham (2019). https://doi.org/10.1007/978-3-030-30490-4_56
29. Downs, J.J., Vogel, E.F.: A plant-wide industrial process control problem. Comput. Chem. Eng. **17**(3), 245–255 (1993)
30. Abokifa, A.A., Haddad, K., Lo,, C., Biswas, P.: Real-time identification of cyber-physical attacks on water distribution systems via machine learning-based anomaly detection techniques. J. Water Resour. Plann. Manage. **145**(1), 04018089 (2018)

A Short Note on a Paper Titled: A Delaunay Quadrangle-Based Fingerprint Authentication System with Template Protection Using Topology Code for Local Registration and Security Enhancement

SrinivasaRao SubramanyaRao$^{(\boxtimes)}$ (iD)

Cybersecurity Researcher and Consultant, Canberra, Australia
`srinivasa.subramanya.anu@gmail.com`

Abstract. In this short note, we show that a Delaunay Quadrangle based Fingerprint authentication system proposed in a 2014 IEEE-TIFS paper has issues in it. Specifically, the authors of the proposed system use a so called *Topology Code* to compare quadrangles in the context of Fingerprint authentication. We show that there are shortcomings in this proposal. As the original proposal along with its deficiencies has been utilized and built upon in further research, there is a need to further correct the record and motivate changes to the original proposal as well as the papers that built upon the original proposal.

Keywords: Authentication · Biometric security · Delaunay triangulation · Delaunay Quadrangle · Topology code

1 Introduction

In the July 2014 edition of the IEEE Transactions on Information Forensics and Security, a paper titled *A Delaunay Quadrangle-Based Fingerprint Authentication System With Template Protection Using Topology Code for Local Registration and Security Enhancement* [1] was published. Hereafter we refer to this paper as the Delaunay Quadrangle paper or DQ for short. In this article, we focus on a major issue in the DQ paper. While we refer the readers to the DQ paper for complete details about Delaunay Quadrangulations, we provide a very brief background here to motivate the discussion of this issue.

A well known technique from Computational Geometry [6] commonly used by researchers in fingerprint biometrics is Delaunay Triangulation. For example, the authors in [7] studied the utility of Delaunay Triangulation in fingerprint identification. An overview of Triangulation in Fingerprint Biometrics is provided in [8]. The authors of the DQ paper intended to generalize this idea beyond trianglulation. They use a 4-sided polygon (quadrilateral) instead of a 3-sided polygon (triangle). Whilst motivating the use of quadrangles for fingerprint biometrics, the authors of the DQ paper write.

L. Batina et al. (Eds.): SPACE 2022, LNCS 13783, pp. 334–341, 2022.
https://doi.org/10.1007/978-3-031-22829-2_18

We propose a Delaunay quadrangle based fingerprint authentication system to deal with nonlinear distortion-induced local structural change that the Delaunay triangle-based structure suffers. Fixed-length and alignment-free feature vectors extracted from Delaunay quadrangles are less sensitive to nonlinear distortion and more discriminative than those from Delaunay triangles and can be applied to existing template protection directly. Furthermore, we propose to construct a unique topology code from each Delaunay quadrangle. Not only can this unique topology code help to carry out accurate local registration under distortion, but it also enhances the security of template data . . . .

It is this so called topology code referred to by the authors of the DQ paper that will be the focus of this article. In the next section, we show that there is a flaw in the usage of this topology code and that it is not appropriate to use the topology code to compare quadrangles.

While we do not provide an alternative to the utility of topology code in this paper, we highlight the need for further work to correct the DQ paper and as well as other literature that builds upon the DQ paper.

2   Topology Code for Delaunay Quadrangles

The topology code is a mathematical property used by the authors of the DQ paper to compare quadrangles. The authors of the DQ paper write

A unique topology code is derived from each Delaunay quadrangle.

They also write that the topology code should satisfy the following two properties:

(1) it should uniquely describe the different shape of each Delaunay quadrangle; (2) it should reflect the impact of different starting point selections. The second property of such a descriptor is highly critical in helping us to decide the starting point of a Delaunay quadrangle in local registration

To explain what the topology code is, instead of paraphrasing the authors of the DQ paper, we repeat the example provided by the authors in the DQ paper (Fig. 1). The example consists of a pair of quadrangles which the authors denote as $Q(ABCD)$ and $Q(A'B'C'D')$. The authors focus on finding the starting vertex for comparing the two quadrangles in Fig. 1. The authors consider the absolute value of the four angles in the quadrangles and write.

. . . using absolute geometric measurement in deciding a starting point under distortion is inaccurate. Naturally the quantization operation is expected to solve this issue because it can make angle values insensitive to small-scale differences . . .

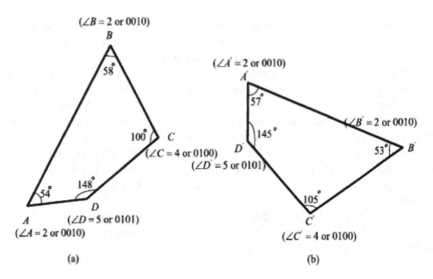

Fig. 1. Delaunay quadrangles (sourced from the DQ paper)

The 4 angles in each of the quadrangles above are first *quantized* with a quantization step size of $\pi/6$. For instance, an angle of 20° is quantized as 1 and an angle of 40° is quantized as 2. Thus in Fig. 1, $\angle A$ is quantized to 2 and so is $\angle B$. To show how the Topology code is calculated, we again quote the authors of the DQ paper below:

The angles, $\angle A$, $\angle B$, $\angle C$ and $\angle D$, of Q(ABCD) are quantized into '2', '2', '4' and '5', respectively. We observe that, by changing the starting point from A to D and counting the quantized angle values sequentially in clock-wise direction, four different code strings, 2-2-4-5, 2-4-5-2, 4-5-2-2 and 5-2-2-4, can be generated. Similarly, four code strings, 2-2-4-5, 2-4-5-2, 4-5-2-2 and 5-2-2-4, can also be produced for Q(A'B'C'D'). We shall now seek a descriptor from each Delaunay quadrangle that owns two properties: (1) it should uniquely describe the different shape of each Delaunay quadrangle; (2) it should reflect the impact of different starting point selections. The second property of such a descriptor is highly critical in helping us to decide the starting point of a Delaunay quadrangle in local registration. In order to make each quadrangle correspond to a unique descriptor, we use an equation from [2] as follows:

$$TC = p_1\Gamma^3 + p_2 \times \Gamma^2 + p_3 \times \Gamma^1 + p_4 \times \Gamma^0 \tag{1}$$

where $\{p_i\}_{i=1}^4$ *are the quantized angle values of the Delaunay quadrangle and $\Gamma = max(p_1, p_2, p_3, p_4) + 1$. Using Eq. (1), we calculate a value for each of the four code strings and choose the smallest value to be the descriptor of the Delaunay quadrangle under consideration. The descriptor obtained by Eq. (1) is unique and the proof of the uniqueness of this descriptor can be found in [2]. Since the descriptor TC describes the shape feature of the Delaunay quadrangle, we call it topology code in this paper. According to the topology code TC generation rule, each Delaunay quadrangle can be indexed by a unique value. For example, it follows from Eq. (1) that the resulting values of the four code strings, 2-2-4-5, 2-4-5-2, 4-5-2-2 and 5-2-2-4, from Q(ABCD) are 533,*

608, 1058 and 1168, respectively. Hence, the smallest value 533, which corresponds to the starting point of A, is chosen as the topology code of Q(ABCD). Similarly, the topology code of Q(A'B'C'D') is also calculated to be 533, which is corresponding to the starting point A'. The starting points A of Q(ABCD) and A' of Q(A'B'C'D') are just the correct corresponding points that we want to find. By this means, accurate local registration is achieved and the mistake that point B' is considered as the starting point of Q(A'B'C'D') by using the absolute geometrical measurement can be avoided.

There are multiple problems with the above approach in the DQ paper.

In Fig. 1(a), say if we change $\angle A$ from $54°$ to $59°$ and $\angle C$ from $100°$ to $95°$, and adopt the above approach provided in the DQ paper to obtain the code strings, the resulting values of the code strings are 2-2-4-5, 2-4-5-2, 4-5-2-2 and 5-2-2-4. The TC will be associated with the code string 2-2-4-5 beginning with A. Now, if in Fig. 1(b), if we change $\angle A'$ to $61°$, $\angle B'$ to $58°$, $\angle C'$ to $93°$ and $\angle D'$ to $148°$, and adopt the above approach again to obtain the code strings, the values of the code strings will be 3-2-4-5, 2-4-5-3, 4-5-3-2 and 5-3-2-4. The smallest topology code in this case will be associated with the code string 2-4-5-3 corresponding to the starting vertex of B'. However, as per the description above provided by the authors of the DQ paper, this is exactly the result that was not wanted.

The reason for the above problem is this: As the authors in the DQ paper write, Eq. (1) was adapted from a paper titled *Matching Perspective Views of a Polyhedron Using Circuits* [2], authored by Gu, Yang and Huang and published in the May 1987 edition of the IEEE Transactions on Pattern Analysis and Machine Intelligence (PAMI). Hereafter, we refer to this paper as the PAMI paper. The PAMI paper provides with a method of comparing two polygons and while there is nothing wrong with the PAMI paper, there is a problem in the adaptation and usage of Eq. (1) in the DQ paper. To see this problem, we first illustrate the usage of this equation in the PAMI paper. This is best done by quoting the authors of the PAMI paper:

Because of the scaling and shape distortions between the two line drawings caused by perspective changes, the absolute geometrical measurements of a circuit in a drawing such as its area and perimeter, line lengths, and the angle values between two adjacent lines can hardly be used to identify the corresponding circuit in the other drawing.

Our motivation here is to seek a descriptor of the circuit shape which is more invariant. RLCC code proposed by us is a boundary shape code, which describes the main shape features of a circuit but is invariant to scaling, rotation and to some extent perspective distortions. RLCC code is the abbreviation for "run length code of convex and concave angle strings around a circuit," the circuit being traced in a counterclockwise direction for one cycle.

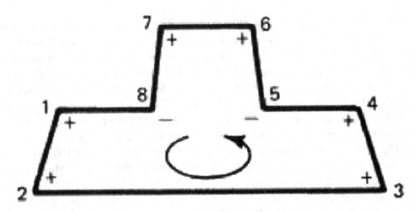

Fig. 2. Illustrating RLCC code (image sourced from the PAMI paper)

For example, in Fig. 2, *starting from vertex 1, we can get a circuit 1 2 3 4 5 6 7 8 and the angle string is "+ + + + - + + -," where " +" stands for a convex angle and "−" stands for a concave angle, so that the RLCC code of the circuit is 4121. In this code word the first digit "4" means the first string is a convex angle string with length 4, the second digit "1" means the second string is a concave angle string with length 1, and so on. In order to make a circuit correspond to an RLCC code uniquely, two stipulations are made: 1) We always start a code with a convex string. 2) If there are several separate convex angle strings around a circuit, then we pick the starting convex string in such a way that the code value (defined below) is maximized.*

Definition: Let $a_1 a_2 .. a_i .. a_N$ be an RLCC code of a circuit, the corresponding code value (CV) is

$$CV = \sum_{i=1}^{N} a_i B^{n-i} \qquad (2)$$

where N is the length of the code word which equals to the number of separate (convex and concave) angle strings around a circuit for a cycle, a_i is the value of the digit in the code located at the ith position, B is the base value, and

$$B = max\{a_i\}_{i=1...N} + 1 \qquad (3)$$

Further, after proving theorems related to uniqueness, the authors of the PAMI paper write

Assume that for a circuit there are m separate convex angle strings. Among the m codes we select the code with the largest code value as the normalized RLCC code (NRLCC code) of the circuit.

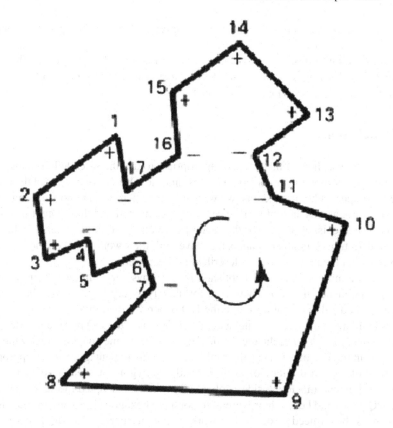

Fig. 3. Illustrating RLCC code (image sourced from the PAMI paper)

As an example, for the circuit of Fig. 3, there are four separate convex strings 13 14 15, 1 2 3, 5, and 8 9 10. Using each of these strings as the first string for encoding, there will be four corresponding codes: 3 1 1 2 3 2 3 2, 1 2 3 2 3 2 3 1, 3 2 3 2 3 1 1 2, and 3 2 3 1 1 2 3 2. For calculating these code values, the base value B = max{a_i}$_{i=1...N}$ + 1 = 3 + 1 = 4, therefore the code values of the four codes, according to (1), are 44022, 28397, 61142, 52592, respectively. So the NRLCC code of the circuit of Fig. 5 is 3 2 3 2 3 1 1 2. The starting point for the encoding is at vertex 8 in the circuit.

There is a small typo in the above content reproduced from the PAMI paper. The corresponding codes for the convex strings '1 2 3' and '5' have been swapped.

Now Eq. (1) referred to above in the DQ paper is the same as that of Eq. (2) referred to above in the PAMI paper. From the above reproduced content from the PAMI paper, we can see that the number of terms in Eq. (2) is the same as the number of separate angle strings and this can vary depending on the shape of the object. However, Eq. (1) in the DQ paper always has a fixed set of terms equal to the number of sides in the polygon under consideration. Equation (1) in the DQ paper is about the size of the angles in a Quadrangle, whereas the corresponding equation in the PAMI paper is about the shape of any polygon under consideration in terms of convex and concave angles. Thus, it is inaccurate and not appropriate to use the *Topology code* in the DQ paper to compare two 4-sided polygons.

From the above considerations, it can be noted that the NRLCC code for the Quadrangles in Fig. 1 is always 4 as per the PAMI paper. This is different from the topology code for these polygons as per the DQ paper.

3   Conclusion

In this article, we showed that it is not appropriate to use the so called Topology code to compare Quadrilaterals in the context of Biometrics. When we contacted the authors of the DQ paper with our concerns, we were informed that they are not working on this topic anymore, as this area of work is apparently saturated and thus cannot provide us with any comments. However for the sake of correctness of the DQ paper (which has been cited 75 times) and other papers that have built their work based on the DQ paper, it is worth documenting the issues described in this paper.

In the literature, a paper [3] published in 2016 has very similar content as in the DQ paper published in 2014. There is unfortunately a very large overlap between the two papers and [3] does not even cite the DQ paper. Further, in another paper, [4] the authors build upon the idea of using a 4-sided polygon in the DQ paper and extend it to a 5-sided one. They too use the idea of the Topology code and adapted exactly the same method as in the DQ paper. Thus their method to compare pentagons is not appropriate as well. Building on the idea of using a 4 sided polygon, the authors of yet another paper in [5] extend this to a 6 sided polygon, but they too adapted the same method as in the DQ paper and hence their method to compare hexagons is not appropriate too.

There is thus a need to do further work to suitably correct the DQ paper and the subsequent papers that depend and build on the DQ paper.

Acknowledgements. Many thanks to the anonymous reviewers of SPACE 2022 for their valuable feedback.

References

1. Yang, W., Hu, J., Wang, S.: A Delaunay Quadrangle-Based Fingerprint Authentication System With Template Protection Using Topology Code for Local Registration and Security Enhancement. IEEE Trans. Inf. Forensics Secur. (2014). https://doi.org/10.1109/TIFS.2014.2328095
2. Gu, W.K., Yang, J.Y., Huang, T.S.: Matching perspective views of a polyhedron using circuits. IEEE Trans. Pattern Anal. Mach. Intell. (PAMI) (1987). https://doi.org/10.1109/TPAMI.1987.4767921
3. Abirami, C., Baritha Begum, M.: Biometric cryptosystem based on delaunay quadrangle structure for fingerprint template protection and person identification. Middle-East J. Sci. Res. 24(S2), 53–57 (2016). https://doi.org/10.5829/idosi.mejsr.2016.24.S2.116
4. Suganya, A., Sagayee, M.A.: A delaunay pentangle-based fingerprint authentication system for preserving privacy using topology code. In: IJREAT International Journal of Research in Engineering & Advanced Technology, vol. 2, no. 6, December–January 2015. http://www.ijreat.org/Papers%202014/Issue12/IJREATV2I6019.pdf

5. Kumari, S., Moghe, A.A.: Delaunay Hexangle based finger print matching scheme for authentication. In: International Journal of Advanced Research in Computer Science and Software Engineering, vol. 6, no. 5, May 2016
6. Devadoss, S.L., O'Rourke, J.: Discrete and Computational Geometry. Princeton University Press (2011)
7. Bebis, G., Deaconu, T., Georgiopoulos, M.: Fingerprint identification using delaunay triangulation. In: International Conference on Information Intelligence and Systems, October-November 1999. https://doi.org/10.1109/ICIIS.1999.810315
8. Maltoni, D., Maio, D., Jain, A.K., Prabhakar, S.: Handbook of Fingerprint Recognition, 2nd edn. Springer, London (2009). https://doi.org/10.1007/978-1-84882-254-2

Author Index

Printed in the United States
by Baker & Taylor Publisher Services